W9-BOZ-170

DePaul

M-0186

$2425#

8513.80

Exploring Religion

EXPLORING RELIGION

Roger Schmidt

San Bernardino Valley College

Wadsworth, Inc. Belmont, California

ISBN 0-87872-244-0

Exploring Religion was prepared for publication by the following people:
Copy Editor: Amy Ullrich
Interior and Cover Designer: Trisha Hanlon
Cover photograph by: Patricia Hollander Gross, Stock, Boston
Photo Researcher: John Pini
Production Coordinator: Robine Storm van Leeuwen

Wadsworth, Inc.

© 1980 by Wadsworth, Inc., Belmont, California 94002. All rights reserved. No part of this book may be reproduced, stored in a retrieval system, or transcribed, in any form or by any means, electronic, mechanical, photocopying, recording, or otherwise, without the prior written permission of the publisher, Wadsworth, Inc., Belmont, California.

Library of Congress Cataloging in Publication Data

Schmidt, Roger, 1931-
   Exploring religion.

   Bibliography: p.
   Includes index.
   1. Religion. I. Title.
BL48.S372   200   80-10978
ISBN 0-87872-244-0

Printed in the United States of America
                7   8   9 - 85

I must confess, that, personally I have learned many things I never knew before . . . just by writing.

St. Augustine
De Trinitate

for Ann, Leigh, and Jeffrey

Contents

Preface

We shall not cease from exploration
And the end of all our exploring
Will be to arrive where we started
And know the place for the first time.

T.S. Eliot
Four Quartets*

Imagine, for a moment, that the study of religion is analogous to a journey around the earth. For such a long journey you will need at least two kinds of maps: a general map that traces the broad outlines and a set of detailed maps that locates particular places.

Like a trip around the world, the study of religion is enhanced by two types of maps. The general map provides the broad outlines or the plan and purpose of the study. The detailed maps allow you to move from the universal and abstract character of religion to the richness of detail in individual religious phenomena and personalities. The purpose of this introductory section is to provide you with a general map of the entire text.

*T.S. Eliot, Four Quartets (New York: Harcourt, Brace & World, 1971), p. 59.

The perspective of this text is that religion is a seeking and responding to what humans experience as holy or ultimate. In one sense religion points to personal experiences of ultimacy that are vital, expansive, liberating, and transforming. In a second sense religion is a seeking and responding to holiness through acts of devotion (worship, prayer, meditation, sacrifice), through reflection (stories, beliefs, doctrines), and through communion and fellowship with those who share common concerns, experiences, and traditions. The purpose of this text is to introduce students to religion through an examination of dimensions of religious expression that are general features of all religious traditions.

The study of religion can be introduced in several ways. The two most widely employed formats introduce the subject either through a survey of the origins and historical development of different religious traditions, including the major world religions, or through a study of biblical literature. In recent years an alternative model for a first course in religion has emerged that introduces the subject through a study of the primary forms of religious expression—religious acts, communities, experience, language, rites, and symbols. This approach allows teachers and students to draw on a wide range of religious phenomena and to move freely in time and space.

The principal dimensions of religious expression can be organized under four very broad and often overlapping categories: the conceptual, the ritualistic, the social, and the personal. The conceptual dimension includes things primarily spoken or thought, from such story-forms as myths and parables to more formalized beliefs, like creeds and doctrines. Moral imperatives and ethical reflection are another aspect of the conceptual dimension, for all religious belief systems provide ultimate values and guides for the conduct of life. The ritual dimension includes devotional acts, such as prayer, sacrament, and sacrifice, that are points of contact with a holy or divine being, as well as procedures or techniques, like meditation and yoga, that lead the seeker to a higher state of consciousness. The personal dimension includes experiences in which humans believe their lives have been touched and transformed by a direct, personal experience of ultimacy. Finally, the social dimension relates to the ways holy communities are organized, including the patterns of interpersonal relationships in religious groups, their basis of association, and types of governance.

The text is divided into four parts. Part I asks, What is religion?, examines the problem of defining religion, introduces the reader to the study of religion as a discipline, and discusses ways of understanding the holy. The central part of the text focuses on the four primary dimensions of religious expression. Part II examines the conceptual and ritual dimensions. The study of the conceptual dimension includes a consideration of the symbolic or meaning-giving process, an analysis of the main features of religious language, and a discussion of different types of sacred stories. Part II concludes with an analysis and description of sacred rites. Part III concentrates on the personal and social dimensions, including patterns and types of religious experience and holy communities.

Part IV returns to the conceptual dimension by shifting from a discussion of religious language to a consideration of belief and disbelief, such as belief in God and loss of faith. The final chapter readdresses the question that was raised at the outset of our study: What is religion? This time, however, the question is addressed by examining different senses and contexts in which humans might be said to be nonreligious and by introducing humanism as an alternative to religious belief systems. With the conclusion of part IV, the journey is completed; readers who have not tired of their study will be in a position to judge its value and whether it has ended or merely begun.

Although in this text the conceptual, ritual, personal, and social dimensions of religious expression are arbitrarily separated for the purposes of description and analysis, in practice they often overlap. A sacred rite, for example, is a drama of word and gesture that is both conceptual and ceremonial. It is also a way in which the sacred is made present; therefore a rite can be a source of personal transformation. Finally, a sacred rite is a social phenomenon—an act of communion performed by a believing community. Throughout the book all these dimensions are interwoven.

Exploring Religion is designed primarily as a text for introductory courses that analyze and describe the forms of religious expression that religious traditions have in common. As a primary text for such a course, it can be used effectively with supplementary resources. It can, for example, be used in conjunction with a reader that includes a collection of essays on myth, ritual, and holy communities. If *Exploring Religion* is used as a resource that provides students with a basic analysis and description of a variety of religious phenomena, then it can be supplemented with fictional or biographical resources. Several works, such as Graham Greene's *The End of the Affair,* Hermann Hesse's *Siddhartha,* Archibald MacLeish's *J.B.,* Carlos Castaneda's *The Teachings of Don Juan,* and John Niehardt's *Black Elk Speaks,* can facilitate a discussion of many of the forms religion takes. Other works, including James Joyce's *A Portrait of the Artist as a Young Man,* Elie Wiesel's *Night,* Joseph Conrad's *Heart of Darkness,* Colin Turnbull's anthropological field study, *The Mountain People,* and Albert Camus's *The Stranger* and *The Plague,* contain powerful images of the loss of faith.

Since *Exploring Religion* covers ground that is normally part of the philosophy of religion, it can also be used as a text in philosophy of religion classes. It includes, for example, discussions of religious language and its relationship to aesthetic and scientific ways of seeing and speaking, of symbols and the symbolic process, and of the questions, Why do we suffer and die? Does God exist? and What is our destiny?

As part of the back matter, *Exploring Religion* provides a glossary to aid the student in understanding difficult terms or terms used in a specific way; a bibliography, which is broken down by chapter; and—specifically for the instructor—a media guide, broken down by part, which lists relevant films and slides.

In putting the finishing touches on the manuscript, I became aware how much books are joint efforts. Without the aid of a great many people, such endeavors would not be possible. Primary assistance and encouragement has come from my wife, Ann, whose background in literature and ear for the English language have been invaluable. She also graciously typed the manuscript. In a very real sense, this book is our joint production. I am also indebted to John Kase, who took time from his graduate studies at the University of California at Santa Barbara to read the text critically. His background in Buddhist studies was particularly helpful. My appreciation is also extended to Professor Frank Attardo of Fresno City College, Dr. C. Milo Connick of Whittier College, Professor Charles O. Ellenbaum of the College of DuPage, Professor Makota Harada of Northern Essex Community College, Dr. Robert Michaelsen of the University of California at Santa Barbara, Dr. Lynn Ross-Bryant of the University of Southern California, Dr. Ninian Smart of the University of California at Santa Barbara, and Dr. Jerome A. Stone of Kendall College, whose reviews of the manuscript helped enormously; and to Robert Gormley, Katharine Gregg, Robine Storm van Leeuwen, and Amy Ullrich of Duxbury Press for their encouragement and editing. Deserving a special note of gratitude are those who have guided me in the study of things religious, including my mentors, Gordon C. Atkins, Harold S. Confer, Douglas G. Eadie, Edwin S. Gaustad, and my colleagues and students at San Bernardino Valley College.

Roger Schmidt

Acknowledgments

The author gratefully acknowledges permission to reprint copyrighted material:

From "Little Gidding" in *Four Quartets* by T.S. Eliot; copyright 1943 by T.S. Eliot; renewed 1971 by Esme Valerie Eliot. Reprinted by permission of Harcourt Brace Jovanovich, Inc. and by Faber and Faber Ltd., Publishers.

From "Birches" and "The Most of It" from *The Poetry of Robert Frost* edited by Edward Connery Lathem. Copyright 1916, © 1969 by Holt, Rinehart and Winston. Copyright 1942, 1944 by Robert Frost. Copyright © 1970 by Lesley Frost Ballantine. Reprinted by permission of Holt, Rinehart and Winston, Publishers.

Reprinted by permission G.P. Putnam's Sons from *Waiting for God* by Simone Weil, translated by Emma Craufurd. Copyright 1951 by G.P. Putnam's Sons.

Excerpts (appearing on pp. 31, 32, 202, 216, 229, 243 of this volume) from *To a Dancing God* by Sam Keen. Copyright © 1970 by Sam Keen. Reprinted by permission of Harper & Row, Publishers, Inc.

From "Nature's Questioning" from *Collected Poems* of Thomas Hardy. New York: Macmillan, 1953. Reprinted by permission.

From *The Wisdom of Laotse* translated and edited by Lin Yutang. Copyright 1948 by Random House, Inc. Reprinted by permission.

From Victor W. Turner, *The Ritual Process.* Copyright © 1969 by Victor W. Turner. Reprinted, with permission, from *The Ritual Process* (New York: Aldine Publishing Co.).

From Clifford Geertz, "Religion as a Cultural System" in Michael Banton, ed., *Anthropological Approaches to the Study of Religion.* London: Tavistock Publications Ltd, 1966. Reprinted by permission.

Excerpted from *An Introduction to Haiku* by Harold G. Henderson. Copyright © 1958 by Harold G. Henderson. Reprinted by permission of Doubleday & Company, Inc.

From "Tell All the Truth." Reprinted by permission of the publishers and the Trustees of Amherst College from *The Poems of Emily Dickinson,* edited by Thomas H. Johnson, Cambridge, Mass.: The Belknap Press of Harvard University Press, Copyright © 1951, 1955 by the President and Fellows of Harvard College.

From *The Gates of the Forest* by Elie Wiesel. Translated by Frances Frenaye. Copyright © 1966 by Holt, Rinehart and Winston. Reprinted by permission of Holt, Rinehart and Winston, Publishers.

From *Natural Symbols* by Mary Douglas. © 1970, 1973 by Mary Douglas. Reprinted by permission of Pantheon Books, a Division of Random House, Inc.

From *Sing and Pray and Shout Hurray,* compiled by Roger Ortmayer. Copyright © 1974 by Friendship Press. Used by permission.

From *A Religious History of the American People* by Sydney Ahlstrom. New Haven, Conn.: Yale University Press, 1972. Reprinted by permission.

Reprinted with permission of Macmillan Publishing Co., Inc. and A.P. Watt Ltd. from "Sailing to Byzantium" in *Collected Poems* by William Butler Yeats. Copyright 1928 by Macmillan Publishing Co., Inc., renewed 1956 by Georgie Yeats.

Excerpt from "Decisions for Christ" © 1976 by Newsweek, Inc. All rights reserved. Reprinted by permission.

From "Theory of Truth." Copyright 1938 by Robinson Jeffers. Reprinted from *The Selected Poetry of Robinson Jeffers,* by Robinson Jeffers, by permission of Random House, Inc.

From *Four Sacred Plays* by Dorothy L. Sayers. London: Victor Gollancz Ltd, 1948. Reprinted by permission.

From *The Letters of Emily Dickinson,* edited by Thomas H. Johnson, The Belknap Press of Harvard University Press, 1958; and from *Poems of Emily Dickinson,* edited by Thomas H. Johnson, The Belknap Press of Harvard University Press, 1955. Reprinted by permission.

From *Conversation at Midnight* by Edna St Vincent Millay. New York: Harper & Row, Publishers, Inc., 1937. Copyright 1937, 1964 by Edna St Vincent Millay and Norma Millay Ellis. Reprinted by permission.

From *Collected Poems* by Conrad Aiken. New York: Oxford University Press, 1953. Reprinted by permission.

Photo by Ellis Herwig, Stock, Boston

PART I
INTRODUCING
RELIGION

The Preface has given you a general outline or map of the text; you are now ready to begin a serious exploration of religion. At the outset of any study, however, you need to have a feel for what to look for, a familiarity with the kinds of questions appropriate to the subject matter, and an understanding of how the study is to be conducted. To better prepare you for your journey, part I introduces the subject and study of religion. Chapter one begins with the question, What is religion? and attempts to shed light on the question by examining problems related to defining religion.

Chapter two continues the introduction by distinguishing between two different approaches to the subject—the academic and the theological—and looks at the kinds of questions that are characteristic of each. Chapter three provides a capsule view of the historical development of religion. It begins with a consideration of magic and its relationship to religion, raises questions about the origin and evolution of religion, and concludes with a typology that classifies the various religions on the basis of whether they are local, national, or universal. This typology also helps to explain how differences in societal structures affect the forms of religious expression.

Chapter four plunges into the deepest and most profound part of the journey—an exploration of what is implied by such terms as God, Tao, nirvana—what this text refers to as the holy. Since the distinction between what is religious and nonreligious focuses on what humans regard as ultimately real or holy, an analysis of such terms as ultimate, sacred, or holy is an important point of departure for studying the different dimensions of religious expression in subsequent chapters.

Chapter One
What Is Religion?

An act can be evaluated from different points of view. . . . The religious man evaluates in regard to total value, ultimate meaning.

Gerardus van der Leeuw
Sacred and Profane Beauty: The Holy in Art[1]

As the dawn signals the beginning of a new day, men and women, scattered throughout the four directions, act out rites of consecration and lift their voices in songs and prayers. From the minaret comes the call to prayer. Devout Muslims, their bodies purified by water, recite from the Koran, "Praise belongs to God, the Lord of all Being." In a medieval abbey church, its interior still cloaked in shadows, Christian monks share in the sacrifice of the Mass and the singing of the Sanctus, "Holy, Holy, Holy, Lord God of hosts." An American convert to Nichiren Shōshū of America recites "Namu-Myōhō-Renge-Kyō" in order to obtain material and spiritual well-being. A Bushman from South Africa exhorts his God to help in the hunt, ". . . help us. We are dying of hunger."[2]

The rhythm of the sacred day begins with a sense of renewal. Each day is holy, and all of life is sanctified through acts of worship. Black Elk, a Lakota Sioux, spoke of the sense of such acts of devotion: "My day, I have made it holy";[3] and the Hebrew Psalmist celebrated God's creation with a song of praise: "This is the day which the Lord has made; let us rejoice and be glad in it."[4]

Religion has played a role in the life of human beings from the very earliest of times and is as universal to human societies as language. People in every society, whether primitive or modern, have some conception of a superempirical or nonordinary reality, such as gods, spirits, or impersonal forces, that they believe influences or governs human existence. The mere presence of religion in every society does not prove that it is an essential feature of human societies or that humans are inherently religious. In fact, in modern times, the survival of religion has become more problematic than ever before. A scientific world view has challenged religious conceptions and has made them harder to sustain and defend.

Modern societies have become increasingly secular—that is, traditional religious symbols and rites are gradually being edged out of public life. A secular order that appears to have no need of sacred things threatens to make traditional religion obsolete. While many countries, like the United States, seem to have drifted toward **secularism*** unintentionally, others have consciously attempted to construct religionless societies. Although short-lived, the abolition of the worship of God and the substitution of a Cult of Reason during France's Reign of Terror (1793–1794) was one such attempt. Twentieth-century **Marxism** or communism has made a more systematic and sustained effort to replace religion with a world view or ideology that defines what is real without reference to the supernatural. Whether religion will gradually disappear in communist countries is an unanswered question; however, even in those communist countries that are aggressively inhospitable to traditional religion, formal worship still survives. Somehow, in spite of the challenge of modernity, religion continues to be a vital part of the human story. Its tenacious survival suggests that religion either is deeply rooted in human nature or is an extremely obdurate case of cultural lag.

This chapter provides an initial sense of what religion is by considering what it is about human beings that makes religion a phenomenon present in all human societies and by examining different ways of defining religion. After arriving at a workable definition of religion, the chapter turns to questions related to the truth of religious beliefs. It concludes with a statement of the perspective employed in this text.

*Boldfaced terms throughout this text are defined in the glossary.

What is the meaning of human life, or of organic life altogether? To answer this question at all implies a religion.

Albert Einstein
The World as I See It[5]

Are Humans Inherently Religious?

Since religion is so characteristically human, scholars in a number of fields have argued that it is appropriate to think of human beings as religious animals. The ubiquity of religious experience suggests that human beings have a kind of inner capacity, even an inherent desire, for experiencing the world as sacred. In *Religion without Revelation* Julian Huxley, a biologist, maintained that humans have an inherent or innate capacity for an experience of holiness. "Not only does the normal man have this capacity for experiencing the sense of the sacred, but he demands its satisfaction," Huxley asserted.[6]

Like Julian Huxley, Abraham H. Maslow, a psychologist, argued for the naturalness and desirability of religious or what he labeled "peak" experiences. Maslow maintained that transcendent or peak experiences are widespread in contemporary society, even though many such spiritual experiences occur outside the framework of traditional religion. In fact, for Maslow such experiences were so widespread and natural that he came to view "non-peakers" not as people unable to have such moments, but rather

ubiquity- everpresent

Lascaux Cave Painting, Dordogne, France. Humans create a world of meaning through art and religion.

Photo: The Bettman Archive, Inc.

as people who are either afraid of them or who suppress them.[7] Maslow believed that the core elements of the peak experience are common to both religious experiences and those creative, self-expanding experiences that occur in art, love, and therapy. Transcendent experiences draw us outside ourselves and fill us with joy and a sense of communion with our world.

Do you believe that humans are inherently religious? Is religion essential to group life, like the motor is to an automobile, or is it dispensable, like a hood ornament? Do you agree with Huxley and Maslow that religious experience is an important dimension of human nature? Certainly many people long for an experience of holiness. Whether such a longing is innate, as Huxley suggests, or merely a response to oppressive socioeconomic conditions, as a Marxist would have it, something in most of us desires to address the universe and to receive an answer. As Robert Frost says in his poem, "The Most of It":

> He thought he kept the universe alone;
> For all the voice in answer he could wake
> Was but the mocking echo of his own
> From some tree-hidden cliff across the lake.
> Some morning from the boulder-broken beach
> He would cry out on life, that what it wants
> Is not its own love back in copy speech,
> But counter-love, original response.[8]

Speculation on whether humans are inherently religious raises the question of our essential nature. Do we have an essential nature? Is it rationality that separates us from other living things? Are we the rational animal, as Aristotle believed, or is our uniqueness more the happy result of an inventive nature housed in a physical structure that allows us to fashion tools and make things? Are we primarily toolmakers and builders? If human beings are inherently religious, perhaps we might fruitfully think of ourselves as religious beings. If so, can a person or a people be nonreligious? Certainly there have been and will continue to be people who do not believe themselves to be religious.

Isolating the manner in which we are essentially different from other animals is difficult, if not impossible. Research during the past two decades indicates that human beings are not the only rational and tool-making animals. Chimpanzees make tools and are being taught English. The intelligence of the dolphin is so remarkable that some scholars refuse to draw a sharp line separating them from human beings and insist that dolphins and perhaps other animals are also human. The issue is further complicated by the possibility, even the probability, that beings living on another planet may have human qualities (intelligence or creativity) that are manifested in tool making, use of language systems, and religious behavior.

Difficulties are inherent in suggesting an answer to the question of our essential nature; however, some persuasive reasons exist for thinking of man as a meaning-giving animal. Even if we are not alone in this characteristic, we do have a basic drive toward understanding our situation. The experience of pain and pleasure is common to humans and other animals, but it is distinctively human to reflect on the reason for the pain and to be aware that pleasure is fleeting. Humans die, as do all animals, but only humans know that they must die, and only humans are aware of puzzling discrepancies in the justice of this world. The gap that humans perceive between what should be and what is presses them toward resolutions of such discrepancies through what Max Weber regarded as "systems of meaning" or what Clifford Geertz, an anthropologist, calls "systems of significance."[9] Religious worlds of meaning are, in part, systems for resolving, or at least holding in creative relief, the ambiguities of human existence.

In *The Sacred Canopy* Peter Berger, a sociologist of religion, characterizes the human being as a "world-building animal." Humans have a biological nature, but they also create a "second nature"—that is, they create culture, a complex of meanings and social relationships. A child is created through a biological process and reared in a cultural context; thus humans have a history as well as a biological development.[10] Human beings construct tools, develop language, formulate a world view, and practice religion; they create society with its network of meaning.

People live in a world of meanings as well as in a physical world. As Jesus observed, we do not live by bread alone. Bread and meaning, the physical and the spiritual, are two parts of the human equation. Neither can be ignored without disastrous results. Humans find meaning and even societal survival through the secondary worlds they have created such as art, ideology, values, and social structures. Religion especially can be seen as a meaning-giving activity. Certainly the religions of the world are some of the principal systems of significance for resolving ambiguities and getting a handle on life as a whole.

Even if human beings are not inherently religious, they do produce worlds of meaning, including religious ones. Of course, from one religious perspective religion is more of a divine revelation than a human creation. Without making a judgment as to whether religion is revealed or given by God, we can appropriately see religion as an expression of our need to structure and fashion a meaningful world in response to clues found in human experience. Religion is not the only way to give meaning to life, but it does represent an ambitious attempt to give the universe significance.[11] In this respect, the fundamental religious posture, whether it embraces or flees

ultimate – utmost, extreme

from the physical world, is at its core affirmative. Religion affirms that the cosmos has meaning; human life is ultimately significant.

The true meaning of a term is to be found by observing what a man does with it, not what he says about it.

P.W. Bridgman
The Logic of Modern Physics [12]

Problems in Defining Religion

A good way to begin a study is to start with a definition that sets some boundaries and helps focus on the salient features of the study. How, then, should religion be defined? Can the term be applied to a certain set of things? Can we formulate a defensible definition that separates the religious from the nonreligious? Religion is not a term that can be precisely delineated. It is a collective term that is applied to such a wide range of phenomena and conflicting beliefs that it may well be impossible, except arbitrarily, to provide a single principle by which it can be defined.

ambiguity – uncertainess

The ambiguity of the term is, in part, a reflection of the dynamic and inexpressible quality of religious experience itself. Religion addresses fundamental aspects of human existence, such as suffering and death, love and ecstasy. Such experiences are intense and personal. No definitions can exhaust their depth because they are mysterious and indefinable. Religion, like poetry, participates in the sphere of impassioned speech and the indefinable mystery of life; it seeks to set before us a view of life that is grounded in the ultimate structure of reality.

Despite the difficulties of definition, a study cannot begin without some initial conception of what is to be studied. Many definitions of religion are instructive and serviceable; however no definition is completely adequate. In one context, religion is synonymous with belief in God. In another, religion is simply, as theologian Michael Novak suggests, "the telling of a story with one's life."[13] Alternative ways of thinking about religion are useful because we must be able to approach it from many different perspectives in order to develop a whole picture.

Perhaps a good definition to begin with is one that associates religion with a belief in God or gods. E.B. Tylor, an anthropologist, defined religion as a "belief in Spiritual Beings."[14] Tylor's definition states what most Westerners regard as the essential feature of religion. It is a defensible definition. For example, the major religious traditions of the West (Judaism, Christianity, and Islam) share a monotheistic faith, and most, if not all, primitive societies give assent to the presence of powerful spirits or gods. Tylor's definition is analytical—that is, it allows us to place some beliefs outside of the class of religion. Marxism, for example, would be an ideology or a philosophy rather than a religion because it explicitly rejects a belief in the supernatural.

Such a definition, however, raises some problems. Belief in God or gods has not been central, if acknowledged at all, in at least four Asian traditions (Buddhism, Confucianism, Jainism, and Taoism). Although some forms of Mahayana Buddhism are exceptions to this generalization, should the logic of Tylor's definition be followed, these major Asian traditions would not, for the most part, be counted as religions. Is Tylor's definition too narrow a focus? Can we formulate a definition of religion that includes such dissimilar perspectives as **theism,** the belief in a God who is personally involved in the life of his creation, and nontheistic belief systems that do not think of the ultimate as a personal being?

Students beginning a study of religion may be tempted to define religion in terms of their own experience or religious tradition. First, they have a limited reservoir of information; understanding and comparisons are difficult. Thus they are likely to begin the study of religion within the context, regardless of how sketchy, of a particular religion or tradition. Second, if the students' faith is vital, they are apt to perceive it as uniquely and absolutely true.

Before exploring further the question of definition, why not formulate your own definition of religion? Would you be satisfied with Tylor's definition? One student offered a more parochial definition when she observed that religion was believing in God, reading the Bible, and attending church. Another student, a young Black Muslim, could see religion only as submission to the one true God, Allah.

In developing your definition, keep in mind the following considerations: Avoid a definition that is narrowly exclusive. Remember, if religion must affirm God, soul, and personal immortality, then some forms of Buddhism are certainly outside the sphere of religion. Buddhism is generally nontheistic, and many Buddhists believe that the question of the existence of an all-powerful and all-knowing God is not only unanswerable but irrelevant to the issues confronting human existence.

A definition that is too inclusive is also a problem. Consider Michael Novak's suggestion that religion is telling a story with one's life. What are the implications of such a perspective? Everyone has a story to tell. Are all of us, in some sense or in some degree, religious? Using Novak's point of departure, can a person, movement, or society be nonreligious?

Take care that your definition is not blatantly biased or egocentric. Is religion only the acceptance of Christ Jesus? Does religion exist where Christ is confessed, and is religion absent where he is denied or unknown? Advocates of Nichiren Shōshū, a Buddhist sect active in the United States as well as in the land of its birth, Japan, sometimes declare that Nichiren is true Buddhism, that their faith is true religion, while others are implicitly false. Such an approach answers the question, What is religion? by equating it with an individual's personal faith.

You should also avoid definitions with a disapproving bias. Sometimes religion is regarded as a security blanket—a support to which insecure people cling in order to cope with life. Religion is also seen as an opiate—a way of substituting fantasies for unpleasant realities. Religious expressions, in this view, are nothing more than infantile responses to concrete problems that demand human solutions. Such biases, whether disapproving or approving, may reveal more about the people expressing the views than they do about religion.

If you have written a definition of religion, why not compare it with other definitions? If your study of religion is shared with other students, use the opportunity to initiate a dialogue on the subject. How do your friends define religion? If possible, question a religious leader about his or her understanding of religion. The interaction of people and ideas is important. Books are powerful sources for stimulating religious sensitivities and understandings, but religion is much more than books. Knowledge of religion, like knowledge of God, requires direct experience. As the Hindu sage, Shri Ramakrishna, said, "He who tries to give an idea of God by mere book learning is like the man who tries to give an idea of the city of Benares by means of a map or a picture."[15]

Definitions of religion are plentiful; nearly everyone has an opinion as to what it is. An examination of two types of definition, the functional and the substantive, can help clarify what religion is.

Functional Definitions of Religion

Functional definitions focus on the role that religion plays in serving human needs. They are predicated on the following kinds of inquiry: For what purpose is religion practiced? What function does religion perform for the individual and for society? What is there in human experience that triggers a religious response?

Functional definitions are human centered. The wellspring of religion is to be found in human needs; thus functionalists stress the ways in which religion serves our emotional, intellectual, and social needs. For example, religion has performed an important social function, which has prompted some functionalists to see religion primarily as a force for the integration and preservation of society. They see religion as providing a system of commonly held beliefs and ritual practices that are a stabilizing force, especially in primitive societies. In binding people together, religion reaffirms group values and protects group life.

From the functional perspective, the problematic nature of human existence has produced religion—that is, religion is a response to such enduring aspects of human existence as death, suffering, and the need to construct a human community. In a functional sense, religion is a prodigious effort to give life significance—to construct a kindred cosmos. J. Milton Yinger, a sociologist of religion, formulated a definition of religion that stresses its meaning-giving function:

> *Religion can be defined as a system of beliefs and practices by means of which a group of people struggles with these ultimate problems of human life. It is the refusal to capitulate to death, to give up in the face of frustration, to allow hostility to tear apart one's human associations.*[16]

Functionalists agree that religion ministers to human needs. They disagree, however, on whether religion is indispensable. Some feel that some problems can never be solved; since religion is an attempt to explain those problems, it will always endure. According to Yinger, religion endures because "it is an attempt to explain what cannot be otherwise explained; to achieve power, all other powers having failed us; to establish poise and serenity in the face of evil and suffering that others have failed to eliminate."[17] Human beings are thus incurably religious because the persistent function of religion cannot be adequately performed in other ways.

Other functionalists argue that religion is only one way, and an inferior one at that, to meet basic needs. Negatively perceived, religion can be viewed as an illusory and ineffectual means of alleviating genuine human suffering. Sigmund Freud and Karl Marx are only two of several shapers of modern thought who judged religion harshly. Karl Marx wrote: "Religion is the sigh of the oppressed creature, the heart of a heartless world, and the soul of soulless conditions. It is the opium of the people."[18] From a Marxist perspective, a Marxist revolution seeks to alleviate the real causes of oppression, whereas religion is content to comfort the alienated with promises of otherworldly rewards; as people are liberated from social and economic inequalities, the need for religion should gradually disappear. We should note that some functionalists would include Marxism as a religion since, in spite of its atheism, it is a system of significance that provides, like the traditional religions, a view of the ultimate nature of things.

Substantive Definitions of Religion

Substantive definitions attempt to delineate the essential nature of religion. Such definitions are not primarily concerned with how people act or even for what purpose they act the way they do. Functional approaches define religion in terms of what it does, while substantive definitions define it in terms of what it is. Substantive definitions seek the essence of religion.

The thought of a Protestant theologian, Paul Tillich, can serve as a transition from a functional to a substantive approach. In an attempt to communicate something of the depth of religion, Tillich wrote: "Religion, in the largest and most basic sense of the word, is ultimate concern. And ultimate concern is manifest in all creative functions of the human spirit."[19] The definition, isolated from the context of Tillich's work, fits within the functionalist perspective. Religion is the human-centered quest for ultimacy; it serves a meaning-giving function.

In Tillich's definition, if people seek what is ultimate—that is, something valued for itself and by which other things are judged—they are religious. Consequently, people who are not associated with any religious tradition and who do not consider themselves to be religious are nevertheless religious because of their commitment to seeking what is **ultimate.** In a broad application of Tillich's view, scientists dedicated to a search for truth are, by virtue of their quest, religious, and the hoped-for achievement of a classless society is the aspect of ultimacy in a Marxist's utopia. Mao Tse-tung would be considered a deeply religious man in spite of his militant atheism, as would a miser who values money for itself rather than any of its uses. Should we conclude, as the functionalist might but as Tillich would not, that all people who have concerns are religious?

Tillich's definition, by itself, is functional, but his interpretation of ultimacy fits more clearly a substantive or essentialist perspective. For Tillich, concern is only one dimension of the religious equation. The object of our concern, the ultimate itself, is also an essential component. In Tillich's theology the ultimate is the creative ground of existence; it is both **holy** and **eternal.** His sense of an ultimate that is also eternal allows some discrimination in judging the religiosity of commitment. For instance, a dedication like the miser's would not, for Tillich, qualify as an ultimate concern because such a commitment is more instrumental than ultimate and cannot lead to an awareness of the eternal.

Essentialists like Mircea Eliade and Paul Tillich would agree with the functionalists that religion serves to give life meaning and to bind humans together. Humans fashion religious worlds of meaning, but they do so, essentialists would argue, in response to what they experience as holy. To define religion in terms of human needs is, in Eliade's judgment, to ignore "the one unique and irreducible element in it—the element of the sacred."[20] Tillich came to a similar conclusion: "The universal religious basis is the experience of the holy within the finite."[21] If religion is centered in our experience of a sacred reality, as essentialists or substantivists insist, then questions about the sacred, as the focus of the religious consciousness, are at least as important as the question of how religion serves human needs.

Perhaps by now you are overwhelmed. The definition of religion may have seemed such a simple matter. You may even share with Dr. Samuel Johnson the feeling that "sometimes things may be made darker by definition."[22] Obviously, religion cannot be defined once and for all by a single formulation. In fact, a definition may sometimes narrow our vision and close us off from the larger possibilities of our subject, especially if the subjects to be defined are rich in meaning. However, thinking critically about the problem of definition can be valuable. It can, for instance, help provide a broader sense of what religion is. A working definition must try to do justice to the complexity of the subject and be reasonably defensible, and yet must not wall out the unexpected and mysterious.

For the purposes of this text, religion is defined as seeking and responding to what is experienced as holy or ultimate. It is a substantive definition that avoids the narrowness of Tylor's definition of religion and is flexible enough to embrace theistic and nontheistic senses of ultimacy. It acknowledges the significance-giving character of religion, but insists that ultimate meaning distinguishes religion from other meaning-giving enterprises, such as science and history. All that is religious is, as the functionalist insists, meaning-giving, but only ultimate or sacred meaning-giving is religious.

The Truth of Religion

For most people it is a difficult task to do justice to the viewpoint of others when the spiritual issues of life are at stake.

W. Brede Kristensen
The Meaning of Religion[23]

If religion is part of the world-building process, then rituals, creeds, holy books, and even conceptions of the ultimate are humanly conditioned. The observation that religious images are **anthropomorphic** is not new. In the sixth century B.C., the Greek philosopher Xenophanes of Colophon observed: "If oxen or lions had hands which enabled them to draw and paint pictures as men do, they would portray their gods as having bodies like their own: horses would draw them as horses, and oxen as oxen."[24] Although he believed human beings created the gods in their own image, Xenophanes still believed in a supreme God. He did, however, suggest that "no man has existed, nor will exist, who has plain knowledge about the gods."[25]

The nineteenth-century German philosopher Ludwig Feuerbach made a more radical critique of the truth-claims of religion. Feuerbach argued that the essence or reality behind the facade of religion is man rather than God. Counter to those monotheistic religions that affirm that God is the creator of all things, Feuerbach insisted that the idea of God is a human creation. For Feuerbach, human beings created God out of the most valued human qualities—power, knowledge, love. Thus the latent and real content of religion is the worship of human beings. Religion, wrote Feuerbach, "not indeed on the surface, but fundamentally, not in intention or according to its own supposition, but in its heart, in its essence, believes in nothing else than the truth and divinity of human nature."[26] Feuerbach's radical unmasking of religion was accompanied by a plea to supplant its traditional forms with a religion that has humans at its center.

Even though religion is, at least in part, a human creation, its images or projections need not be entirely illusory or subjective. From the perspective of religious belief, religious images result from an experience of a sacred reality. In this view the essential structure of reality, its ultimate meaningfulness, exists in its own right. For Christians, God is encountered and not merely fabricated. Nirvana is, for Buddhists, an enlightening and liberating experience and not simply a psychological state. Seen in this light, religious experience is an experience of reality as ultimate or sacred, and the forms that religion has taken—that is, the different religious traditions—are, at least in part, responses to personal experiences of a sacred reality. As Peter Berger observed: "Put simply, this would imply that man projects ultimate meanings into reality because reality is, indeed, ultimately meaningful, and because his [man's] own being (the empirical ground of these projections) contains and intends these same ultimate meanings."[27]

Is religion true or is it, as Feuerbach argued, illusory? This is an enormously complex question that must begin with the prior question, What is truth? Is truth an objective quality of things in our world, or is it more properly thought of as a property of a sentence? Can a person be said to be true? Jesus, for instance, made such a claim in the Gospel of John when he proclaimed, "I am the way, the truth, and the life."[28] The Vedas, the religious literature of classical India, mention "doing the truth," and the "great-souled one" of modern Hinduism, Mohandas Gandhi, taught the practice of a way of life predicated on a nonviolent truth-force. How is the truth to be known? Is all knowledge derived from the senses? What of the claims that some truths are revelations from God? Are there, as many Eastern traditions teach, truths open to the eye of intuition but inaccessible to logical or scientific methods? In what sense, if any, are the truths of faith verifiable?

The question of truth is further complicated by the existence of many diverse religious traditions peopled by a multitude of different-minded adherents. The question, Is religion true? becomes, What religion is true? Contradictory truth-claims are voiced not only by different faiths but also by **denominational** and **sectarian** divisions within a single tradition.

What is your response to these questions? Is religion a genuine response to what is experienced as holy, or is it a human invention? Is there one true faith by which other traditions can be judged false? Be careful of falling into an either-or analysis: Either religion is a human response, or it is a human invention. Either a religion is true, or it is false. Perhaps religion is both a response to holiness and a human invention.

The comparison of religions is only possible, in some measure, through the miraculous virtue of sympathy . . . the study of different religions does not lead to a real knowledge of them unless we transport ourselves for a time by faith to the very center of whichever one we are studying.

Simone Weil
Waiting for God[29]

A Phenomenological Perspective

This book describes and analyzes the structure and variety of religious phenomena from a **phenomenological** perspective. While phenomenology is a term with complex philosophical and psychological meanings, it is used here to stand for a method that is descriptive, analytical, and **empathetic.** As a descriptive method, phenomenology records the data of religious expression without judging its value or truth. Consequently, the text does not intend to proclaim the truth of religion or the exclusive truth of a religion but rather observes religious phenomena and describes them as accurately as possible.

As an analytical method, phenomenology examines the forms religion takes—beliefs, rituals, stories—in order to isolate their basic patterns. For example, through a comparative study the general features of holy rites can be identified, and they can be classified according to types. Of course, religion is particular rather than general; personal faith is rooted in specific experiences and a particular religious tradition. Consequently, the question, What is religion? must always begin with the religious experience and symbol system of a specific person or people. However, a comparative and phenomenological study of many religious traditions can make some tentative and guarded generalizations about the nature of religion and the various dimensions of religious expression.

While phenomenologists suspend judgment about the truth of faith, they do insist that an understanding of religion is impossible without empathy for the absolute nature of religious conceptions. Believers are committed to the truth of their faith. Aborigines do not perceive their faith as primitive. Nor are there any professing idol worshippers; worship of an idol, something that has no power and to which devotion is misguided, can only be something that an outsider does. Idolatry is the religion of the outsider. The insider, the devotee, by contrast, knows and lives the truth.

The phenomenologist seeks to understand the believer's faith, but the distance between a living faith and a faith that is described or interpreted makes a study of religion difficult. Talking about religious experiences is different from undergoing them. Geertz pointed out that "worship and

Easter Island Figures. Outsiders often regard these monumental and mysterious figures as idols, but for Easter Islanders they appear to have been sacred images.

Photo: Editorial Photocolor Archives

analysis are simply impossible to carry out together, for the one involves being thoroughly involved, caught up, absorbed in one's experience, in what one is living through, while the other involves standing back and, with a certain detachment, looking at it."[30] Because a method that only describes and analyzes religious phenomena is not sufficient to allow us to enter the world of the believer, the inner world of intentions and meaning can be partially opened by an empathetic attempt to see the world from the vantage point of the person of faith. From a phenomenological perspective, empathy, the capacity to see and experience the world through the eyes of another, is necessary as a way of entering the world as perceived by the believer.

Concluding Remarks

As indicated, religion is a system of significance that provides humans with a way of getting a handle on what is ultimately real. As a world view it provides a symbolic universe that enables people, individually and collectively, to get a feel for who they are and to whom or what they belong. Geertz has characterized the heart of the religious perspective as the view that the "values one holds are grounded in the inherent structure of reality, that between the way one ought to live and the way things really are there is an unbreakable inner connection."[31]

We live in an unprecedented world community that is increasingly aware of other faiths. Their accessibility provides us with unparalleled opportunities for a more knowledgeable awareness of other faiths. The issue of the truths of religion or the truth of a particular religion is not easily resolved. This text does not attempt such a resolution, nor does it claim to possess a truth superior to what has passed for religious wisdom. Reality can be understood in more than one way. No systems of significance—philosophies or religious traditions—can entirely resolve the discrepancies or puzzles of human existence.

This text defines religion as a seeking and responding to what is experienced as holy. Its substantive perspective demands that religion be studied in itself or on its own terms as well as through the social and psychological functions it serves. Religion and religious experience should not be explained exclusively in terms of other elements of human existence. Although membership in a Buddhist monastic community, for example, may provide a sense of security, the act of joining is also intended to culminate in a religious experience called nirvana. The question of what is believed and practiced is at least as important as the question of how religion serves human needs.

One should begin a study of religion with the assumption that each religious tradition has something of value to offer; in addition, one should be open to the possibility that truth is not confined to one religious tradition. Paul Tillich contended that all religion possesses revealing and saving powers.[32] Similarly, Swami Vivekananda, writing from within a modern Hindu tradition, claimed to have experienced truth through various paths. "I accept all the religions of the past and I worship God with every one of them. Can God's book be finished? Must it not be a continuing revelation?"[33] Such an approach does not resolve the philosophical difficulties in respect to the competing truth-claims of different religious traditions, but it does serve as a vantage point from which each religion can be taken seriously.

Notes

1. Gerardus van der Leeuw, *Sacred and Profane Beauty: The Holy in Art* (London, Weidenfeld and Nicholson, 1963), p. 5.

2. Mircea Eliade, *From Primitives to Zen* (New York: Harper & Row, 1967), p. 268.

3. John G. Niehardt, *Black Elk Speaks: Being the Life Story of a Holy Man of the Oglala Sioux* (New York: Pocket Books, 1972), p. 39.

4. Psalms 118:24.

5. Albert Einstein, *The World as I See It,* trans. by Alan Harris (New York: Philosophical Library, 1949), p. 1.

6. Julian S. Huxley, *Religion without Revelation* (New York: Harper & Brothers, 1957), p. 110.

7. Abraham H. Maslow, *Religious Values and Peak Experiences* (Columbus: Ohio State University Press, 1964), pp. 19–29.

8. Robert Frost, *Complete Poems of Robert Frost* (New York: Holt, Rinehart and Winston, 1964), p. 451.

9. Clifford Geertz, *Islam Observed: Religious Development in Morocco and Indonesia* (New Haven, Conn.: Yale University Press, 1968), p. 95.

10. Peter L. Berger, *The Sacred Canopy: Elements of a Sociological Theory of Religion* (Garden City, N.Y.: Doubleday, 1969), pp. 4–8.

11. Berger, *Sacred Canopy,* p. 28.

12. P.W. Bridgman, *The Logic of Modern Physics* (New York: Macmillan, 1961), p. 7.

13. Michael Novak, *Ascent of the Mountain, Flight of the Dove* (New York: Harper & Row, 1971), p. 11.

14. Edward B. Tylor, *Primitive Culture* (New York: Gordon Press, 1974), vol. I, p. 383.

15. In Nancy Wilson Ross, *Three Ways of Asian Wisdom* (New York: Simon and Schuster, 1966), p. 11.

16. J. Milton Yinger, *Religion, Society and the Individual* (New York: Macmillan, 1957), p. 9.

17. Ibid., p. 10.

18. Karl Marx, *Early Writings,* trans. and ed. by T.B. Bottomore (London: Watts, 1963), pp. 43–44.

19. Paul Tillich, *Theology of Culture* (New York: Oxford University Press, 1959), pp. 7–8.

20. Mircea Eliade, *Patterns in Comparative Religion* (New York: World, 1963), p. xiii.

21. Paul Tillich, "The Significance of the History of Religions for the Systematic Theologian," in Joseph M. Kitagawa, ed., *The History of Religions,* vol. I (Chicago: University of Chicago Press, 1967), pp. 247–48.

22. George Birkbeck Hill, ed., *Boswell's Life of Johnson* (New York: Bigelow, Brown, & Co.), vol. III, p. 278.

23. W. Brede Kristensen, *The Meaning of Religion* (The Hague: Martinus Nijhoff, 1960), p. 15.

24. In Philip Wheelwright, *The Presocratics* (New York: Odyssey Press, 1966), p. 33.

25. Ibid.

26. Ludwig Feuerbach, *The Essence of Christianity* (New York: Harper Torchbooks, 1957), p. xxxvi.

27. Berger, *The Sacred Canopy,* p. 180.

28. John 14:6.

29. Simone Weil, *Waiting for God,* trans. by Emma Craufurd (New York: Harper & Row, 1973), first published by G.P. Putnam's Sons in 1951, pp. 183–84.

30. Geertz, *Islam Observed,* p. 108.

31. Ibid., p. 97.

32. Tillich, "The Significance of the History of Religions," p. 242.

33. In Ross, *Asian Wisdom,* p. 9.

Chapter Two
The Study of Religion

Philosophy begins in wonder. And, at the end, when philosophic thought has done its best, the wonder remains. There have been added, however, some grasp of the immensity of things, some purification of emotion by understanding.

Alfred North Whitehead
Modes of Thought[1]

Proteus, a god of the sea, possessed the power to transform himself into innumerable forms. He could, at will, assume the appearance of an animal or a plant. Supplicants who desired advice from the wise old god had first to catch him. When seized, he would take different forms in an effort to free himself. Proteus granted the requests of those who held fast and were not deceived by his disguises. Religion is protean; it takes many forms. There are many different religions and a bewildering array of religious phenomena. Nearly everything known to humans—sun or moon, rock or stick, snake or bull, spirit or god—has been perceived by someone as holy. The study of religion is a confusing and often unsettling study; but for those who, like the seekers of Proteus, persevere, it can be deeply rewarding.

A story from the Zen Buddhist tradition might serve as a point of departure and as a reminder that serious study can begin only on the premise that something can be learned. Nan-in, a modern Zen master, had a visitor who came to learn about Zen. The visitor did not listen but talked only about his own ideas. In the course of the conversation, Nan-in served tea. He poured tea into his visitor's cup until it was full, and then he poured some more. The visitor watched the overflow and finally said, " 'It is overfull. No more will go in!' Nan-in responded, 'Like this cup you are full of your own opinions and speculations. How can I show you Zen unless you first empty your cup?' "[2]

Study without thought is useless. Thought without learning is dangerous.

Confucius
The Analects[3]

The Study of Religion: Two Approaches

Critical studies of religion take place in two principal contexts: the academic and the theological. While both are reflective enterprises, they do represent different orientations. Theologians work within the circle of a community of faith. For example, in the Christian tradition the theologian is a committed spokesman for the Christian faith. In the Jewish tradition the rabbi's theological task is to be a vital part of the ongoing interpretation of the Torah and to communicate something of its vitality and relevance. Theology is critical, reflective, and systematic, but theologians are also defenders of their faith.

Like theologians, academicians bring to their studies a set of suppositions and values; the academic orientation insists that ideological or theological considerations must not interfere with observation and interpretation of historical, sociological, or psychological data. Academicians are more interested in providing description and analysis than in making judgments as to the truth or falsity of religious belief. Their purpose is to understand and inform, whereas religious or theological education seeks to liberate and transform. Metaphorically speaking, academic studies address the head and only indirectly the heart. Of course, one need not be religious in order to make a scholarly study of religion. In fact, some academicians have argued that a religious commitment negates the open inquiry that academic studies require, since the believer accepts as true the very assertions that a critical study is obliged to test.

Since the terms *academic* and *theological* have specialized meanings, understanding how they are used in this context is important. For example, the literal meaning of **theology** is "a study of God," and the term is usually associated with the intellectual traditions of the major monotheistic faiths: Judaism, Christianity, and Islam. In these traditions the theologian's primary

Jacob Binder, The Talmudist. *The study of Torah, God's instructions, is a sacred duty in the Jewish tradition.*

Photo courtesy Museum of Fine Arts, Boston

work is the explication of God's revelation as manifested in sacred scripture and in the history of doctrine. A broader usage of the term *theology* is intended here. By extension, theology is an interpretation and intellectual defense of any religious belief system, not just those of monotheistic faiths. Theology focuses on ultimate existence. The aim of theologians, whether Buddhist or Christian, is to interpret the received tradition of which they are a part in the light of their own experience. The theologian is thus engaged in systematically formulating, in language that is relevant and intelligible today, the reasons for belief.

Although the theological context is reflective and critical, it has a committed and experiential character that is usually absent from academic studies. Theologians interpret their inherited traditions with a concern for the relationship of reflection to the religious life. They address the heart as well as the head. Theological education seeks not just knowledge but deliverance or enlightenment. For example, when a prospective student presents himself at the gates of a Buddhist monastery and asks to be admitted, he expects instruction in a Buddhist way of being. Since nirvana is the primary focus of Buddhist theology, his education or discipline will be aimed at achieving nirvana.

Although both kinds of study can occur outside of traditional patterns, theological education is normally associated with a parochial structure, and academic studies usually occur in a collegiate environment.

Within the academic environment is a cluster of disciplines whose methods and techniques may be employed in a study of religion. Thus no single method is peculiar to an academic study of religion; it can be studied through such diverse disciplines as anthropology, history, philosophy, psychology, and sociology. In this respect, religion is neither a subject nor a discipline with its own distinctive methodology; it is more appropriately conceived, according to Professor Walter Capps, as "a *subject field* within which a variety of disciplines are employed and an enormous range of subjects are treated."[4]

The following examples can illustrate how religious phenomena are studied by several academic disciplines. The inner character of religious experience lends itself to psychological studies; hence, the psychology of religion focuses on the ways individual needs are met through religion. The sociology of religion addresses itself to the role religion plays in society. Anthropologists seek an understanding of the religious life of all peoples. Still another orientation is that of the philosophy of religion, with its concern for an analysis of the truth-claims and logical consistency of religious belief.

This text is primarily an academic rather than a theological study and is not intended to give religious instruction. Rather, it seeks to provide the reader with knowledge about religion through a description of religious phenomena and a comparative study of religious beliefs, rites, symbols, stories, and communities. It makes no judgment as to the truth or relative value of one religious world of meaning as opposed to another. In an academic study, detachment, the suspension of one's own faith in the interest of balanced judgment, is necessary. An academic study of religion is, like all academic studies, a critical one; thus, faith cannot be shielded from unsettling questions. Disbelief as well as belief must be examined and alternative perspectives must be heard.

Questions about Religion and "Religious" Questions

Because knowledge about religion is not identical with being religious, there is a value in distinguishing between questions that are primarily helpful in seeking knowledge about religion and questions that address ultimate concerns. "Religious" questions address the meaning of life itself; they are the kinds of questions that help us locate ourselves religiously. Who am I? Why am I here? Where am I going? and In whom or what shall I trust? are some of the perennial questions that have prompted religious responses because they help us focus on that aspect of ultimacy in our personal story.

In contrast, questions about religion are primarily useful in increasing our knowledge and understanding of the story of religion. If, for instance, we are to be knowledgeable about religion, we must ask historical questions about the origin and development of specific religious traditions. Religious questions force us to examine our own spiritual condition, our autobiography, whereas questions about religion encourage an intellectual inquiry into a broad range of religious phenomena.

Methods

The distinction made in the previous paragraph applies to methodology as well. A method is a way or procedure through which a given end may be obtained. A method useful in a scholarly study of religion should not be confused with the ways in which a person's life is religiously transformed. Some steps or procedures are designed to serve as vehicles to religious experience or self-knowledge. The discipline of Zen, with its practice of meditation, is a rigorous method that may culminate in a religious experience. Prayer is believed to be an avenue through which communion between the sacred and the human takes place. Still other devotees advocate the efficacy of yoga—with its disciplined control of body and mind—as a means to transformation. In contrast, academic methodologies are not primarily intended to lead to religious experiences. They are methods or procedures for acquiring knowledge about religion and for arriving at defensible conclusions.

Every age in the history of philosophy has its own preoccupation. Its problems are peculiar to it. . . . The "technique," or treatment, of a problem begins with its first expression as a question. . . . In our questions lie our principles of analysis, *and our answers may express whatever those principles are able to yield.*

Susanne K. Langer
Philosophy in a New Key[5]

Academic Studies: Three Important Questions

The results of an inquiry depend on the fruitfulness of the questions that it raises. Every age has its own way of seeing things and peculiar set of questions that it asks. For example, prehistoric societies could not have asked, What is religion? Although there is evidence of religion in archaic societies, they did not have a word for what we call religion. Even advanced civilizations like Egypt had no linguistic equivalent; nor did they give their own religion a name; thus we simply identify their faith as the religion of ancient Egypt.[6] The question, What is religion? can only occur when religion is separated from other aspects of life.

Academic questions are primarily intended to add to a body of knowledge, while theological or religious questions force us to think about the ultimate grounds of existence. Both kinds of questions deserve attention.

We will follow a discussion of academic questions with a treatment of more theological questions. In the academic study of religion, three lines of inquiry have proven particularly valuable: the questions of what happened, of function, and of interpretation.

What Happened?

The historical question of what happened precedes either explanations of how something occurred or interpretations of the significance of events. In its primary sense, the question calls for a description, a historical reconstruction, of what occurred at a specific time and place. A history of a religious tradition starts at the time and place of its beginnings and traces its meanderings, conflicts, and modifications throughout its historical life. Since the early 1800s historians have engaged in an unprecedented effort to reconstruct the historical developments of a host of different religious traditions. Of course, the monotheistic traditions had already placed great emphasis on their history, but they saw history as the story of God's revelation and mighty acts of salvation. Modern historians have been more concerned with a historical and cultural matrix in which humans are the principal actors.

Ascertaining what happened is usually accompanied by attempting to explain how things happened; thus, historians are interested not only in recovering the details of Muhammad's flight from Mecca to Medina, but also in providing an explanation of why such a flight was necessary. In the nineteenth century anthropologists, historians, and theologians were excited by the possibilities of discovering the origins of various religious traditions. For example, some European scholars turned their attention to a search for the Jesus of history who, though presumably obscured by centuries of theological interpretation and liturgical practice, was, they believed, available to moderns through historical research. Description and explanation are important ongoing tasks in religious studies.

What Is Its Function?

A second important focus of academic studies of religion is the question of the purposes or functions that religion serves. This question shifts the focus from a description of the content of a religious act to a concern for the function such an act serves. An interpretation of the role of **prayer** in human experience is an instructive example of a functional approach. From the standpoint of faith, prayer is a way of addressing or communicating with God; the believer also assumes that there is a God who hears the prayers. In a functional approach the question of the truth of what is believed can be suspended in order to examine the behavior from the perspective of what human needs prayer serves. Prayers of contrition can help remove guilt feelings. They can also be an effective introspective device leading to self-discovery. Public and private prayer may serve as a vehicle for behavioral changes; thus prayer can have psychological and even sociological consequences irrespective of the existence or nonexistence of the God to whom such prayers are addressed.

The question of religion's function or purpose has been quite fruitful for contemporary students of religion, particularly for such behavioral scientists as anthropologists, psychologists, and sociologists. The question of function leads to an examination of the role religion plays in the life of both the individual and the community. Religion serves several functions: it is part of our attempt to understand the world, it provides ways of expressing our feelings, it serves social and personal needs, and it is one of the principal instruments through which human life is given meaning.

Religion has an intellectual function. Sometimes religion is understood as a body of prescientific explanations for how things came to be as they are; thus, for example, the story of the Tower of Babel in the Hebrew Bible accounts for the genesis of different languages, just as the story of Prometheus provides an account of how human beings came to have the use of fire. Since, in modern times, scientific explanations have tended to replace religious ones, we can see more clearly that the intellectual function of religion is primarily one of understanding our position in the universe rather than of providing factually descriptive explanations for things in the natural world. As anthropologist Clifford Geertz suggests, religious belief systems are a response to the dissatisfaction humans derive from looking at the world exclusively through the eyes of common sense.[7] The religious imagination breaks through the screen of common sense by perceiving a deep and abiding order in the cosmos and by providing a way of understanding who we are and what we can become.

Religion serves an emotional function. It is one way humans affirm life in spite of its tenuousness. Religion is a source of hope and courage in the face of fear, uncertainty, suffering, and death. In times of frustration, it can provide solace. In times of danger and deprivation, humans perform the acts and utter the words that they hope will protect them from danger or result in bountiful harvests. Religion is both a conviction and a feeling that humans are not alone and helpless, that power is available to them. Magic and ceremony, spells and prayer are part of the human effort to have access to this power.

Religion serves several social functions. It has traditionally preserved and integrated tribe or society. Commonly held beliefs, rituals, and social structures are powerful forces of stability and role clarification. The social character of religion and, in particular, holy rites provides a structure in which the crises of personal and group life can be resolved. In binding together, religion serves as a form of social control. As a source of stability and order, religious institutions are sometimes reactive and repressive, but they can also be instruments of reform and change for society as a whole. In its social role, religion celebrates, integrates, and sustains the community.

Religion has a personal function. It serves individual as well as communal needs—the human desire for protection from material deprivation, for recognition of personal worth, and for self-expression. People need guidance and strength for achieving goals, love and consolation for overcoming loneliness and despair. In varied ways, religious traditions minister to such needs; religious communities sustain and support, thus providing security and recognition. Because humans lack power, they lift their voice to God, who is the source of their strength. In all traditions, humans experience themselves as lost and cry out in anguish for restoration. All faiths point to paths that lead to authentic or transformed life. Religion meets human needs, and nowhere is this ability more evident than in the capacity of religion to invest life with meaning.

How Is It to Be Interpreted?

Academic studies of religion are also concerned with the problem of interpretation or meaning. The question, What does it mean? has many ramifications. One group of scholars is primarily concerned with correctly translating and interpreting religious texts to reconstruct the meaning of such texts as understood by their authors or compilers. A close corollary to the interpretation of sacred texts is the attempt to understand religious faith from the standpoint of the believer. The question has also led to an emphasis on analyzing religious myths and rituals as keys that not only provide us access to ancient and alien religious worlds of meaning but also provide us with clues or insights relevant to our own time and condition.

In religious studies, the task of interpretation is known as **hermeneutics.** Initially, hermeneutics was narrowly associated with the interpretation of a text or document, but it is now regularly employed to stand for the entire range of interpretation. The world of humans is an interpreted world; each question that is asked and each answer that is given is part of the interpretive circle. Whatever is "known" has been filtered through the perceptual and conceptual field of an interpreter; thus there are no uninterpreted facts. Historians, philosophers, theologians, and even natural and behavioral scientists share the same boat: namely, the knower and the known are tied together in the hermeneutical circle; the experimenter is part of the experiment.

One dimension of hermeneutics is the **exegesis** of sacred literature— that is, the attempt to draw out or critically explicate ancient texts. Exegesis is not a simple task; interpretation is more than an adequately translated text. Care must be taken to reconstruct the meaning of the sacred text in the context in which it was written. Familiarity with the religious worlds of meaning of those who wrote or compiled religious texts is essential.

Because sacred literature is normative or authoritative in many religious traditions, exegesis is important to both the academic and theological approaches. If, from a theological perspective, the Koran is believed to be Allah's revelation, then understanding the text as Muhammad and other Muslims have understood it is of primary importance. Likewise, if the Bible is the word of God, the chief task of Christian scholarship is the interpretation of scripture.

Hermeneutics is not confined to interpreting sacred texts. It also entails an attempt to understand religious phenomena and beliefs empathetically. Because an outsider usually experiences the believer's faith as foreign and implausible, the transition is difficult. For example, outsiders who believe drugs have no place in authentic religious experience may quickly reject the Native American Church because peyote occupies an important place in its ritual. The suspension of judgment as to the truth of the viewpoints and practices of others allows the outsider to enter, at least initially, the world of the insider.

From still another perspective, hermeneutics is neither limited to an exegesis of sacred literature nor simply the sympathetic reconstruction of the meaning of religious phenomena from the standpoint of the participants. The question of interpretation also entails some consideration of the meaning of religious phenomena for the investigator. As philosophy professor J. Christopher Biffle argues, the objective observer can also be a passionate observer without sacrifice of clarity.[8] The passionate observer seeks to enter the world of the believer phenomenologically and to gain in the process access to worlds that have the power to stimulate and even transform understanding. One of the most compelling reasons for studying religion is that it can help throw light on the meaning of human existence. Thus we now turn from those questions that are academically useful to those ultimate concerns that have prompted religious worlds of meaning and that in their asking may lead to a deeper understanding of our own worlds of meaning.

Why do I wish to know whence I come and whither I go, whence comes and whither goes everything that environs me, and what is the meaning of it all? For I do not wish to die utterly, and I wish to know whether I am to die or not definitely. If I do not die, what is my destiny?

Miguel de Unamuno
The Tragic Sense of Life[9]

Theological Questions: Ultimate Concerns

In a series of cartoons that revolved around the perennial questions of human existence, one character, in a sensitive but slightly affected way, was engrossed in asking the questions: Who am I? Why am I here? and

Where am I going? "That," he assures his friend, "is philosophy." To which the practical and earthbound friend replies, "Sounds more like amnesia."

Sometimes such perennial or religious questions can almost swallow us up or so disorient our compass that we can become lost for a time and need to be reminded of more mundane things; yet such inquiries, if they lead to self-knowledge, can be helpful, enriching, and practical. In any case, such questions are inescapable; existence presses them upon us. Each life is like a candle that burns brightly for a time but that must inevitably flicker and be extinguished. To suffer and die, as philosopher Karl Jaspers observed, is at once a universal feature of human existence and yet relentlessly personal: "I must die, I must suffer, I am subject to chance, I involve myself inexorably in guilt. We call these fundamental situations of our existence ultimate situations."[10] Ultimate situations force us to raise questions about the ultimate meaning of human existence. They press ultimate concerns upon us, and we find ourselves asking, Who am I? Why am I here? Where am I going?

Exploring the more theological or religious questions is relevant to an academic study. Attention to the perennial questions—Who am I? Why

Paul Gauguin, Whence do we come? What are we? Where are we going? *The artist poses through visual images the questions that concern us ultimately.*

Photo courtesy Museum of Fine Arts, Boston

am I here? Where am I going?—serves two important purposes: First, familiarity with some of the responses to the ultimate questions can open doors to a broader understanding of religious worlds of meaning. Second, religion is personal, and a study of religion requires some sensitivity to its experiential character. Questions that lead to ultimacy can unlock the personal dimension of faith and develop an empathetic understanding of systems of significance other than our own.

Who Am I?

If religion is telling a story with our lives, then each biography has a spiritual quality. The introspective task is, then, to search our experience for hints of ultimacy. Since most people are not visited by angels or other extraordinary reminders of the holy, we must look to the ordinary for what Peter Berger calls "signals of transcendence."[11] In his *To a Dancing God,* Sam Keen puts the question this way: "Is there anything on the native ground of my own experience—my biography, my history—which testifies to the reality of the holy?"[12] Because the sacred is, for many, a symbol for something esoteric and problematic, Keen rephrases the question: "Is there anything in

my experience which gives it unity, density, dignity, meaning and value—which makes graceful freedom possible?"[13] Are there any hints, any signals of the holy in your experience, no matter how mundane or commonplace, no matter how antagonistic you might be to such signals?

The question, Who am I? is a good point of departure for looking for hints of transcendence. It arises in personal existence, in the autobiographical and leads to the larger question, What are human beings? Autobiographies are first of all stories of individuals; they are particular and concrete. We are neither statistic nor principle, but flesh and spirit. Each of us stands out in our uniqueness, in our separateness. Jewish theologian Martin Buber believed that each person "is a new thing in the world and is called upon to fulfill his particularity in this world."[14]

Our aloneness, our uniqueness is, however, tempered by an experience of a common humanity. Autobiographies are stories of individuals, but in each story there is a universal quality, a fraternity with our fellow creatures. As Sam Keen puts it, "in the depths of each man's biography lies the story of all men."[15]

Art, because it often profoundly touches the chords of shared experience, can be particularly effective in shifting the question, Who am I? to its inclusive and communal dimension without losing touch with the individual and personal. In *The Secret of Father Brown,* G.K. Chesterton's priest-detective places himself, as much as possible, in the soul of the murderer he seeks to entrap. This is only possible if, in every person, all forms of human character are at least potentially present. Actors, more than other artists, are masters of assuming the character of others. Dutch theologian Gerardus van der Leeuw made the following connection between drama and compassion: "To find all men in yourself, that is the secret. And that is not only the secret of drama, but also the secret of forgiveness and love."[16]

Autobiographies are at once particular and universal, distinctive yet common. They have several levels of meaning and are part of other stories. In what stories is your autobiography entwined? What, for example, is your relationship to America's story? Are you deeply rooted in a particular community, or do you feel more like Moses, "a stranger in a strange land"? Is your biography female or male? How does the color of your skin influence your story? Is a sacred story a significant part of your personal history? Is it even possible to live without a story? What stories do you find meaningful: atheist, Buddhist, Christian, Jewish, humanist, Muslim, Marxist, scientific?

The story of Malcolm X took form within the context of a great many traditions. His identity, his spirituality was inseparable from the larger story in which he lived. Malcolm Little was a black American. He was raised in an America that was "for whites only." He turned to crime and violence as a way of life and was convicted on a charge of burglary. In prison Malcolm began to study the Nation of Islam, a Black Muslim movement under the leadership of Elijah Muhammad. At some point in his odyssey, Malcolm Little was transformed into Malcolm X, servant of Allah. Stripped of his cultural heritage through an educational system that devalued black contributions and brutalized by the ghetto, Malcolm X came, in a courageous act of spiritual preservation, to the simple dialectic: black is beautiful and good; white is ugly and evil.

But Malcolm's torturous quest was not to end in a gospel of racism. As a committed Muslim he made a pilgrimage to Mecca, the holy city. There, he discovered in profound ways that the story in which he lived was not exclusively that of a black American male; it reached back in time and was enlarged by the stories of Islam and Africa. Black was beautiful because of the inherent richness of the African heritage. In Mecca he came to realize in a very moving way that the God of Islam is Lord of all peoples and all nations. Malcolm's pilgrimage, his obligation to God, carried him to the depths of his own story where he discovered not only a fraternity of blackness but a common humanity:

> *Since I learned the* truth *in Mecca, my dearest friends have come to include all kinds—some Christians, Jews, Buddhists, Hindus, agnostics, and even atheists! I have friends who are called capitalists, Socialists, and Communists! Some of my friends are moderates, conservatives, extremists—some are even Uncle Toms! My friends today are black, brown, red, yellow, and white!*[17]

What story are you telling with your life? Is there anything in your story that hints at holiness or suggests an ultimate concern? Where is holiness to be found? Can Malcolm's story, with its crossing over from hatred to love, be a signal of transcendence?

Who am I? is a fruitful starting point for theological reflection. The question leads, as we have seen, inward to the telling of personal stories, yet presses beyond the autobiographical to the question, What are human beings? Are we condemned to inventing meaning for human existence without hope of immortality, or are we children of the infinite, on a pilgrimage, like Dante, through shadows of despair to the celestial city? Are we merely upright and clever animals, or are our faces an image of the sacred? Our individual stories with their hints of ultimacy lead us to ask Why am I here? and Where am I going?

Why Am I Here?

Like the query, Who am I? the question, Why am I here? is both personal and universal. It can be answered autobiographically: Who are my parents? What chain of events brought me to this moment in time and to this location in space? What significance do I attach to being here? Amidst the confusions and vagaries of life, can I discern a purpose or design? What am I to do with my life? In what sense, if any, am I free?

Why am I here? raises the question of the purpose of human existence—a consideration of our position in the cosmos. The magnitude of the universe, an infinity in which the sun and the planets are but very small points, exhausts our powers of conception. The earth, this planet on which we live, is from the vantage point of space all but lost among the stars. The visible world, the seventeenth-century French philosopher Blaise Pascal noted, is only an imperceptible atom in nature. The universe, he wrote, "is an infinite space, the centre of which is everywhere, the circumference nowhere."[18]

When we try to contemplate the fullness of nature, we are humbled by the breathtaking view that emerges from either the telescope or the microscope. Just as the question of our place in the cosmos leads to the outer reaches of space, so also it takes us inward to the atom, the smallest unit of reality. The atom is equally astonishing—the world in miniature, a microcosm of the whole. What then are humans? Are they nothing in comparison to the universe—ants on an inconsequential planet? By what stretch of the imagination can there be something in the incomprehensible vastness of this universe that cares for, or even takes notice of, human existence? Yet, in monotheistic traditions the faithful believe that there is a God who at once creates the universe and is solicitous of the well-being of each individual. The Psalmist's words reflect this faith:

> When I look at thy heavens, the
>   work of thy fingers,
> the moon and the stars which thou
>   hast established;
> what is man that thou are mindful of
>   him,
> and the son of man that thou dost
>   care for him?
> Yet thou hast made him little less
>   than God,
> and dost crown him with glory
>   and honor.[19]

If the question, Why am I here? is pressed to its logical conclusion, we must ask whether the universe is inherently purposive, a conscious creation, or whether it is the result of a blind, unconscious collision of forces. Why in the ultimate sense am I here? Why is there life at all?

Can consciousness have evolved from matter, or is matter the work of conscious design? When did consciousness emerge? Did it evolve from a simple protein molecule and, if so, what fortuitous combination of atoms produced a single protein molecule? Perhaps consciousness has always been and everything has subsequently unfolded from thought as Robert Frost suggested:

> There was never naught,
> There was always thought.[20]

If thought created the cosmos, then what kind of being is it? Thomas Hardy asked:

> Has some Vast Imbecility
> Mighty to build and blend
> But Impotent to tend
> Framed us in jest and left us now to hazardry?[21]

Or is there a God whose love beckons us to center our lives in him?

Where do you stand on this question? Do you believe the universe is inherently meaningless and that humans, who alone among the animals covet a meaningful existence, must invent it? Or do you believe in Holy Being? If you do believe in Holy Being, what do you mean by such an affirmation? Is it a personal being or a process? Can it be both a personal being and a process? Is it a Being utterly beyond the world or is sacredness in every part of it?

Where Am I Going?

If the question, Why am I here? gravitates to the origins and purposes of human existence, then the question, Where am I going? leads in the direction of destinies and ends. The question can begin with a series of autobiographical concerns. What are my immediate and long-range goals? For what can I hope?

The question of where we are going, of our future, leads us to reflect on death as that which negates the future and sweeps away past and present. The world, as we know it, is transitory. Human existence is a movement toward death. A generation is born, a generation dies. We are in a cosmic play and must dance a dance of death as well as a dance of life. For each of us, death is not a question of if, but of when. And since we must die, what is our destiny?

The interruptions and pauses of life force us to consider our destinies. As Dr. Samuel Johnson wrote in one of his essays, at "points of time where one course of action ends and another begins"—such as a loss of a friend, an end of a marriage, a change of employment, or the movement from childhood to adulthood—"we are forced to say of something, *this is the last."* In such moments we are poignantly aware that to every life the last hour must come. Johnson wrote: "This secret horrour of the last is inseparable from a thinking being whose life is limited and to whom death is dreadful." [22]

Concluding Remarks

The study of religion is approached primarily from two orientations, the academic and the theological. The questions that academicians ask of religion are intended to increase knowledge and understanding of religious phenomena, while theological questions lead in the direction of the ultimate and the autobiographical. The distinction between the two contexts is, of course, relative rather than absolute. Questions of what happened, of function, and of interpretation are extremely important to communities of faith, and religious questions or what Karl Jaspers called "ultimate concerns" may be asked, as they are here, in an academic context.

Ultimate situations, suffering and death, press ultimate concerns upon us: Who am I? Why am I here? Where am I going? Although the answers sometimes seem, almost in the moment of clarity of vision, to dissolve, they give us a feel for the depth of human existence. Religious systems of significance seek to provide a context in which death, suffering, and other disparities between what should be and what is are integrated into a larger picture of reality.

The autobiographical character of theological reflection asks us to consider our personal stories for evidence of ultimacy. Martin Buber tells a story in which the Rabbi of Kotzk was asked, "Where is the dwelling of God?" The Rabbi responded, "God dwells wherever man lets him in." [23] In another of Buber's favorite stories, Rabbi Pinhas, when confronted with the misery of the needy, was grief stricken. After a time, he responded, "Let us draw God into the world and all need will be quenched." Buber draws this lesson from the stories of the Rabbi of Kotzk and Rabbi Pinhas:

> *God's grace consists precisely in this, that he wants to let himself be won by man, that he places himself, so to speak, into man's hands. God wants to come into his world, but he wants to come to it through man. This is the mystery of our existence, the superhuman chance of mankind.*[24]

If the holy comes into the world wherever humans let it in, then perhaps our lives are, after all, fertile grounds for experiences of the sacred.

Notes

1. Alfred North Whitehead, *Modes of Thought* (New York: Capricorn Books, 1958), p. 232.

2. Paul Reps, *Zen Flesh, Zen Bones: A Collection of Zen and Pre-Zen Writings* (Garden City, N.Y.: Doubleday), p. 5.

3. Confucius, *The Analects,* trans. by W.E. Soothill (New York: Paragon Book Reprint Corp., 1968), p. 165.

4. Walter H. Capps, "On Religious Studies, in Lieu of an Overview," *Journal of the American Academy of Religion* 42 (Dec. 1974): 727.

5. Susanne K. Langer, *Philosophy in a New Key* (New York: Mentor Books, 1964), pp. 15-16.

6. Wilfred Cantwell Smith, *The Meaning and End of Religion* (New York: New American Library, 1964). See chapter two.

7. Clifford Geertz, *Islam Observed: Religious Development in Morocco and Indonesia* (New Haven, Conn.: Yale University Press, 1968), p. 95.

8. J. Christopher Biffle, "The Passionless Observer," *The Nation* (June 4, 1977), pp. 693-94.

9. Miguel de Unamuno, *The Tragic Sense of Life* (New York: Dover Books, 1954), p. 33.

10. Karl Jaspers, *Way to Wisdom* (New Haven, Conn.: Yale University Press, 1951), p. 20.

11. Peter L. Berger, *A Rumor of Angels* (Garden City, N.Y.: Doubleday, 1969), p. 65 ff.

12. Sam Keen, *To a Dancing God* (New York: Harper & Row, 1970), p. 99.

13. Ibid.

14. Martin Buber, *The Way of Man* (New York: Citadel Press, 1970), p. 16.

15. Keen, *To a Dancing God,* pp. 102-03.

16. Gerardus van der Leeuw, *Sacred and Profane Beauty: The Holy in Art* (London: Weidenfeld and Nicholson, 1963), p. 102.

17. *The Autobiography of Malcolm X* (New York: Grove Press, 1965), p. 381.

18. Blaise Pascal, *Pensees,* trans. by W.F. Trotter (New York: Random House, 1941), p. 22.

19. Psalms 8:3-5.

20. Robert Frost, *In the Clearing* (New York: Holt, Rinehart and Winston, 1970), p. 35.

21. Thomas Hardy, *Selected Poems of Thomas Hardy,* ed. by John Crowe Ransom (New York: Macmillan, 1961), p. 4.

22. *Samuel Johnson Selected Prose and Poetry,* ed. by Bertrand H. Bronson (New York: Rinehart, 1952), pp. 194-95.

23. Buber, *The Way of Man,* pp. 40-41.

24. Ibid., p. 40.

Chapter Three
Religion and Magic

There are innumerable definitions of God, because his manifestations are innumerable. They overwhelm me with wonder and awe and for a moment stun me. But I worship God as Truth only. I have not yet found Him, but I am seeking after Him.[1]

Mohandas K. Gandhi
An Autobiography

Return for a moment to the metaphor of the study of religion as an extended journey. Your itinerary is now mapped out. You know where you are going, and the definition of religion as seeking and responding to what is holy has provided you with a clue to what you are looking for. You have also acquired a set of questions, some primarily academic and some primarily theological, that can be directed to the forms of religious expression with which you come in contact. Of course, you must determine how and in what context they are appropriate. One of the thrilling aspects of the trip is that you will come in contact with those things that are very old and those things that are relatively new as well as both exotic and familiar cultures. In order to provide a feel for things old and new, exotic and familiar, and to acquire additional conceptual handles for understanding religion, this chapter examines the relationship of religion to **magic,** reflects on the origin and evolution of religion, and distinguishes between primitive and modern communities of faith.

What Is Magic?

Whatever purpose magical practice may serve its direct motivation is the desire to symbolize great conceptions. . . . its central aim is to symbolize a Presence, to aid in the formulation of a religious universe.

Susanne K. Langer
Philosophy in a New Key[2]

Religion is so closely linked, at least historically, to magic that an introduction to one requires a consideration of the other. In fact, magic and religion have been so entwined that some scholars argue that a sharp division between the two is artificial and arbitrary; therefore they speak of magico-religious conceptions and practices rather than those that are exclusively one or the other. In part, this approach is a corrective to the judgment that magic is bad and illusory and religion is good and true.

Magic as a Belief System

We can begin our study with the proposition that magic is closely related to religion and science. For example, magic, like religion and science, shares the view that the universe is filled with power. Although each of these human activities is fascinated by power, they have somewhat different conceptions of and approaches to this power. In science, power is referred to as energy and regarded as a natural and ordinary part of the world, whereas in magic and religion, power is nonordinary and superempirical. Seen in this light, both magic and religion are a seeking for and responding to a holy power that transcends the natural and the empirical. Magical and religious power can be conceived of as an impersonal silent force, like an energy field, that can be transmitted from things to people and from people to things, or it can be anthropomorphized as a personal being, such as God or Satan.

The magical belief system shares with the scientific perspective the view that the power of the universe can be manipulated and controlled. Scientists seek to understand and control energy through empirical and experimental methods. Magicians also believe that methods are available that allow those who correctly apply them to control the superempirical power of the universe. In this sense, magic, like science, is both an organizing model of reality and a method for controlling reality. In contrast to the methods of science, those of magic are more hidden than open, more traditional—that is, handed down from master to apprentice—than experimental.

While religion, magic, and science are fascinated with power, the mysterious, nonordinary power that religionists seek communion with or consciousness of is not a power that can be controlled or manipulated. Magicians believe that correct practice brings the desired results; thus magical power is automatically available through the proper performance of a magical act or formula. The power that religionists seek and respond to is not commanded but supplicated through prayer, not coerced but invited to be present in sacred rites, not manipulated and controlled but submitted to and communed with. Of course, in practice it is very difficult to determine the point at which prayer ceases to be an act of communion and becomes coercive, or when meditation ceases to be a method aimed at a liberating form of consciousness and becomes a formula that the devotee believes is guaranteed to work. In short, magic and religion have been and continue to be so closely related that knowing precisely where one ends and the other begins is difficult.

Now that we are familiar with some similarities and differences among magic, science, and religion, we can focus our attention on understanding magic more fully. In the magical world view, cosmic power is governed by basic principles or laws. Nothing is accidental—that is, whatever takes place is caused by or acts according to the laws of the cosmos. Fundamental to this perspective is the conviction that phenomena that often appear to be only marginally related are, in fact, causally linked. Heavenly bodies, for instance, might seem to have little relationship to human behavior; however, astrologers believe that their configurations directly influence human behavior and disposition.

The magical conception of cause and effect can be better understood by a familiarity with its underlying principles. The belief that like produces like is one of three such principles. In this conception of causal relationships, an image of something—for example, a painting of a buffalo—is believed to be mysteriously linked to the thing it depicts. The power that animates the buffalo is also believed to be present in its image; thus whoever has power over the image has power over the buffalo. A second "law" of magic is the principle of contiguity, which maintains that what was once part of a person or thing continues to be a vital part of it. For example, fragments of a person's hair or fingernails continue to be linked to that person in a direct way and can be used by a witch to do harm. A third principle of magic is that of antipathy, which assumes that one force can be repelled by an opposite force. Some Christians, for example, believe that the pronouncement of a holy name, Jesus Christ, can exorcise a demon—an evil and alien will—from the body of someone possessed by it.

In addition to the conception that the universe is governed by a regulative force, the magical belief system argues that knowledge of such a force can be employed to enhance human control. In this view, magic is at once a body of knowledge and a method (the magical arts) for employing such knowledge. Magical knowledge is directly applicable to the practical and concrete; thus the power of the universe can be controlled through the methods and techniques that are part of the magician's craft and can be applied to such immediate and concrete concerns as success in hunting, agricultural ventures, love making, and protection against evil forces. Rather than merely contemplating knowledge, the magician attempts to bend the force of the universe to his or her will through spoken formulas (curses, incantations, and enchantments), reading signs (divination), the manipulation of objects (fetishes and compounds), and the imitation of sounds, gestures, and movements. For example, a rainmaker, acting on the presumption that like produces like, may imitate the sound of thunder in order to produce rain. Similarly, a hunter, before he goes out to hunt, may wear something associated with his prey and imitate the animal in dance and song in order to transfer the power possessed in the ceremonial context to that of the hunt.

If, as the magician believes, there is a superempirical power that can be used to extend human control over the conditions of existence, why are most people so ignorant of it? The answer that magicians, such as Paracelsus (1493–1541), give to this question is that magic is hidden wisdom that is imperfectly known because of man's lack of belief and imagination.[3] Knowledge of magic is therefore occult—that is, hidden. Those who seek such knowledge must have, if they are to pierce the veil of the occult, a forceful imagination and (usually) a teacher who is expert in such matters.

Occult learning is a traditional body of wisdom that is handed down from practitioner to apprentice. The occult arts are usually not easily acquired. Sometimes magicians pass their skills to protégés who have demonstrated singleness of purpose by surviving rigorous ordeals and who have had personal contact with the nonordinary through visions and trances. In some cases, the parents' magic is a hereditary right of their children. Regardless of the circumstances associated with acquiring magical power, the magician's knowledge is more private and secretive than public and open. In fact, the efficacy of magic is proportional to its distribution; thus magic that is known to all members of a community is of little value. The value of magic is determined socioeconomically; if it is in great supply and widely distributed, it is in little demand.[4]

Types of Magic

A typology is helpful in understanding magic. One typology of magic uses the classification of high and low. High magic is sophisticated, complex, intellectually demanding, and more capable of universal generalization. Low magic is less sophisticated and more parochial.[5] A second typology distinguishes between magic that is used to enhance the well-being of a believing community and that used for malevolent and antisocial purposes.

High and Low Magic

As noted, high magic is sophisticated and intellectually demanding. It is a belief system that provides an understanding of our place in the larger cosmos. In fact, from the point of view of high magic, knowledge of human beings is the key to an understanding of the universe. This homocentric, or human-centered, perspective assumes that humans are a microcosm, a small but equally complex reflection of the macrocosm. Paracelsus wrote, "The human spirit is so great a thing that no man can express it; eternal and unchangeable as God Himself is the mind of man; and could we rightly comprehend the mind of man, nothing would be impossible to us upon the earth."[6]

Astrology, alchemistry, necromancy, and numerology are some of the specialized forms that high magic takes. From the perspective of astrology, the temperaments, sexual drives, and destinies of individuals are causally linked to the sun, moon, planets, and stars; therefore study of the juxtaposition of the heavenly bodies and expertise in reading the twelve signs of the zodiac provide insights into personality patterns and evidence for foretelling the future of an individual's proposed ventures in such concrete activities as marriage, travel, vocation, and investments. Thus successful investment in the stock market is less dependent on a knowledge of the Dow-Jones averages than it is on a daily consultation of the horoscope. The practice of alchemistry assumes that knowledge and mastery of chemical elements can produce a process whereby base metals may be changed into precious ones and that potent elixirs can be concocted that either reverse the aging process (a restoration of youth) or that prolong life indefinitely. Necromancy is the art of making contact with those who have died; necromancers believe that they have the power to summon and consult the spirit of those who have "passed over." As a complex world view, numerology argues that each thing in the universe has a numerical value; thus reality has a mathematical structure. In most cultures certain numbers are believed to be either more potent or more significant than others. In tribal cultures, four is often a magico-religious number and is associated with the four winds, directions, and seasons.

In contrast to the complex high magic, low magic is more direct and intellectually less demanding. The purposes of low magic are practical and immediate; it is concerned with control of the weather, assurance of a good harvest, success in love making, and protection from witchcraft. As a concrete art, magic employs an assortment of techniques and procedures in the assumption that a properly performed magical act (spells, formulas, rites) automatically brings the desired result. Like high magic, low magic assumes that things act on one another at a distance because they are invisibly united. One form of low magic, called imitative or homeopathic magic, assumes that

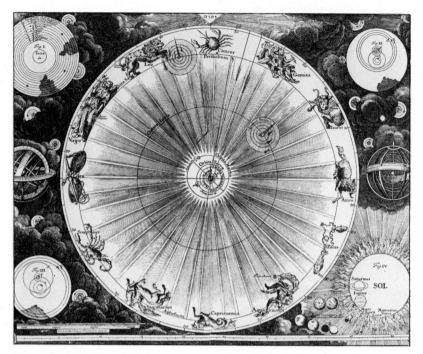

Signs of the Zodiac. The zodiac wheel is based on the movement of heavenly bodies. This eighteenth-century concept of the cosmos depicts in Fig. I (upper left) the earth-centered Ptolemaic understanding of the cosmos and in Fig. IV (lower right) the sun-centered Copernican system. In the center of the photograph are the zodiac signs.

Photo: The Bettman Archive, Inc.

like produces like; thus, a doll-image or photograph of a person may be used by the magician to do harm to the person. Still another example of imitative magic is an attempt to produce rain clouds by blowing smoke toward the sky. Contagious magic is another form of low magic. Contagious magic is based on the principle of contiguity—namely, things that were once connected continue to act on each other; thus whatever was once part of something can subsequently be used to act upon it or its kind. Among the Azande of the Congo, powerful magicians are believed to be capable of catching a person's words in a box and thereby gaining power over him or her. Still another example of contagious magic is the belief that a name is so inseparable from the individual that knowing a person's name gives power over him or her.

A magician's work is generally enhanced by a host of assistants or allies that are believed to contain power, although the most powerful magicians may be able to exercise their will independent of a set of physical objects. Most practitioners, particularly those who practice low magic, usually employ **fetishes** or power objects. A fetish is an object with magical powers that can be used by magicians to achieve their ends. Fetishes are often worn to protect from illness or to insure safe journeys or success in hunting.

Beneficial and Malevolent Magic

Magical power can be used for good or evil. Benevolent or protective magic is used to insure the success and legitimate well-being of a community and to protect against the malevolent use of magical power. The use of magic for malevolent purposes or evil-doing is commonly referred to as **witchcraft** or sorcery. Among tribal peoples the witch is an "upside down person" who uses magical power for illegitimate and antisocial ends. Witches or sorcerers are those who are so twisted by jealousy, greed, and ambition that they use their power to harm others. In the Christian tradition, witches have been associated with demons or the Devil; thus witches are sometimes believed to have made a pact with the Devil in which they exchange their souls for magical power. Sometimes scholars distinguish between witches and sorcerers on the basis of whether their antisocial and malevolent behavior is acquired (the sorcerer) or innate (the witch).

Where magic is believed to be a potent reality, misfortune, disease, and death are closely associated with the doing of evil. In such a community, the question of the cause of disease is not so much one of what but more a question of who. Even accidental deaths or injuries may be viewed as intentional; thus the injured party is believed to have been possessed by an alien spirit or brought to grief by a witch. Here, magical power is the antidote that mitigates or neutralizes the evil-doing of witches; thus where there are witches there are also those who specialize in protective magic. Just as incantations, formulas, fetishes, and rites are tools of harm, so too can they be used to heal and protect. Spells can be broken and spirit possession exorcised by ceremonies that drive out demons. Sweat baths, sand paintings, and bloodletting are some of the remedies tribal doctors have used in exorcising undesirable spirits. In the Christian tradition, the sign of the cross, Saint Christopher medals, the Bible, and formulas like "Matthew, Mark, Luke, and John, Bless the bed that I lie on" have, on occasion, been employed as a form of protective magic.

Magic and Religion in the Twentieth Century

Although some see ours as a scientific age that should have rendered magical and religious ways of seeking for and responding to the holy superfluous, neither magic nor religion has died out. In fact, both appear to be experiencing a revival. A renewed interest in the superempirical is evident in the changing temper of college campuses. During the 1950s such subjects as angels, demons, survival after death, astrology, and witchcraft were seldom addressed in an academic context. These topics were regarded as curious but misguided products of the imagination that modern philosophies and the scientific way of seeing had exorcised from academe. Today the situation is quite different. Students, often impatient with their professors' reluctance or diffidence, are eager to discuss a wide range of magico-religious phenomena, from witchcraft and gifts of the Holy Spirit to the existence of extraterrestrial beings. The books they read and the films they see often proclaim the message that we are not alone.

Perhaps, like the Roman deity Janus, every age has two faces. One face of the twentieth century is that of industrial and agricultural productivity, scientific and technological accomplishment, optimism, and self-confidence. In less than a century, people have revolutionized their modes of travel and communication from the horse-drawn buggy to nuclear-powered spaceships and radio-beamed satellites. Humans have walked on the moon and looked at the earth from a vantage point in space. Our mobility is so accelerated that two hundred years ago the trip from Los Angeles to San Francisco took as long as it now does to get from the earth to the moon. The earth is temporally smaller, and we know, in a way never known before, that the fortunes of all nations and peoples are inseparable.

A second face of the twentieth century is one of crisis, dislocation, and violence. It is a time of estrangement and uprootedness in which many are so alienated from themselves and others that they have all but shed their humanity. Our century has been the occasion for two unparalleled world wars, continuous global strife between the Soviet and Western spheres of influence, and the struggle of the peoples of the Third World for political and socioeconomic independence. The optimism and confidence in the future with which the century began has been replaced by a suspicion that if the bomb doesn't destroy civilization with a bang, then the world will gradually, through the pollution of the earth, end in a whimper.

In a world in which many have perceived that the scientific and technological way of doing things has contributed as much to creating contemporary problems as to resolving them, the hope that science and technology have the answers and solutions for nearly everything has been shaken. Some have responded to their feelings of helplessness by turning to magic and religion. Magic, in particular, counters feelings of helplessness with the proposition that humans can master their world through occult power. As Malinowski argued, "Magic appears in those phases of human action where knowledge fails man."[7] In the light of Malinowski's analysis, we should not be surprised that the decline of confidence in science and technology has been accompanied by a contemporary revival of magic and witchcraft.

As indicated, magic and science are closely related. Both seek knowledge in order to manipulate and control the power in the universe. The magical world view insists that it is possible, through knowledge of the nature and uses of occult power, to employ such power for one's advantage, while science, in part, seeks to transform nature's power into forms of energy that can be used to extend human mastery over our natural and social worlds. The power to control is rightfully valued. The harnessing of energy has made modern civilization and its material well-being possible. Without the "magic" of science, we would have no leisure, and, without leisure, culture is necessarily anemic. Conversely, the power to control can so corrupt, blind, and intoxicate that we can become consumed by it. When this happens, we become so possessed by our possessions, whether they be material, magical, or intellectual treasures, that we may forget how to live. While religion shares with magic and science a keen awareness of power, sacred power is neither tamable nor controllable; thus religion seeks to place human existence in an ultimate context and is concerned more with how to live than with how to manipulate and control sacred power.

Issues Concerning the Origin and Evolution of Magic and Religion

By seeking the beginning of things, a man becomes a crab. The historian looks backward: in the end he also believes backward.
Friedrich Nietzsche
Twilight of the Idols [8]

Scholars in the late nineteenth and early twentieth centuries were intrigued with the origin and evolution of magic and religion. The stimulus for this concern is in part traceable to the enormous impact of Charles Darwin's ideas on evolution. If living organisms develop from the simple to the complex, is it not possible that the same principle applies to culture? Karl Marx, for example, was so profoundly influenced by Darwin's work that he dedicated his *Das Kapital* to Darwin. Marx's interpretation of history as a dialectical and progressive movement culminating in communism is indebted to Darwin as well as to the German philosopher, Georg Hegel. Even before Darwin's publication of his *On the Origin of Species by Means of Natural Selection* in 1859, philosopher Auguste Comte (1798–1857) believed that history could be divided into three evolutionary stages. The first two stages, the ages of superstition and metaphysics, which Comte compared to childhood and adolescence, were, he believed, in the process of being displaced by a scientific or positive age in which existence could be understood and lived without reference to the superempirical.

In such an intellectual milieu, a milieu that translated evolution in the natural sphere into a conviction that history is a story of human progress, some scholars were, not surprisingly, concerned with the origins and development of magic and religion. Did magic precede religion? Did low magic precede high magic? Is the history of religion evolutionary? Is monotheism a later development than polytheism? Are the earlier forms of religion inferior to those that appear later? Although the quest for origins has been abandoned as misleading and unanswerable by most contemporary scholars, some of the answers, even though discredited, are intriguing enough to merit attention. We shall take a brief look at the ideas of E.B. Tylor and Sigmund Freud on the origin of religion and the theories of Sir James Frazer and Bronislaw Malinowski on the evolution of religion.

Speculation Regarding the Origin of Religion: Tylor and Freud

How did religion begin? Was it born of a need to explain? Was it a response to fear? Did it grow out of a need for security? Was it prompted by an experience of holiness or by a misunderstanding of natural forces? In *Primitive Culture,* which appeared in 1871, Edward Burnett Tylor, an anthropologist, located the origin of religion in the primitive's attempt to understand and rationalize such puzzling aspects of human experience as death, dreams, and hallucinations. For primitives death must have been particularly mystifying since the dead continued to live in their dreams and memories. When is a person dead? Is it when the vital signs of the brain cease or when a person is no longer remembered? For moderns as well as for primitives, those who have died seem to come by their own volition into our dreams or even to impinge upon our waking consciousness so that we have an uncanny sense of their presence. Like death, dreams can be intense enough to blur the distinction between waking and sleeping. Tylor hypothesized that the primitive inferred from such experiences the existence of a self that does not die as the material self does. Gradually, according to Tylor, the idea of an *anima,* a nonmaterial and eternal soul, emerged. Such ideas stemmed in Tylor's view, from a prescientific misunderstanding of dreams and death.

Scholars also argued that religion began as a response to the tenuousness of human life. Sigmund Freud, for example, saw religion as growing out of humankind's helplessness. In his view the gods emerged from the human need to temper the terrors of nature and to reconcile people to suffering and death. According to Freud, "Man's self-regard, seriously menaced, calls for consolation; life and the universe must be robbed of their terrors."[9] Religion humanizes nature. The sun and other elements of nature become powerful gods who, in turn, respond to prayers and sacrifices.

For Freud, religion and the gods have their prototype in the child-parent relationship, particularly in the relationship between father and son.

The child, like early man, exists in a state of helplessness. One's parents are at once protectors and disciplinarians to be loved and feared. Religion transforms nature into gods that are given the character of parents. Seen in this light, the father God of Israel is a projection of the father-son relationship into the cosmos—the earthly father becomes the Heavenly Father. The social and religious significance of filial relationships and obligations is especially evident in those religious communities that practice **ancestral devotion.** In ancestral cults, the honor and obedience owed to parents continues beyond the grave and takes on the form of reverence for ancestral spirits.

Freud saw religion as an illusion—a mistaken conception of reality and a misplaced wish-fulfillment. Sun, moon, parents, and ancestors are not gods. Nature and the parent-child relationships are better understood, controlled, or resolved through science than through religious rites and symbols. Even though religion is rooted in the need to temper nature's harshness, it is still an illusion. Freud stated that "men cannot remain children forever; they must in the end go out into "hostile life'. We may call this 'education to reality'."[10] Religion can, Freud believed, be surpassed through the human capacity for rationality, in spite of the power of the instinctual and the emotional.

Both explanations of religion's origin examined thus far are primarily critical. Religion originates in human fear and helplessness or spins its theological webs from misunderstandings of such natural phenomena as dreams and death. More sympathetic approaches see religion as proceeding from something fundamental and enduring; one such approach finds the origin of religion in an experience of holiness. In this view, humans are confronted by a sacred power—a feeling of the presence of a sacred reality that exists outside of one's subjectivity. As William James wrote, "It is as if there were in the human consciousness a *sense of reality, a feeling of objective presence, a perception* of what we may call *'something there'.*"[11]

No conclusive answer to the question of the origin of religion is possible. The archeological record is confusing and irreparably incomplete. The question of origin was enthusiastically embraced by late-nineteenth-century scholars seeking not only the beginnings of religion but a key to its evolution. The question stimulated research and prompted valuable speculation. However, the question for the most part no longer dominates contemporary scholarship. Recent speculation has, however, proffered the interesting argument that the visions, voices, and ecstatic experiences we often associate with the religious consciousness reflect the right hemisphere of the brain's affective way of appropriating the world. In this view, religion has its origin in the dominance, among primitives and premodern peoples, of the right side of the brain, while the decline of such ecstatic experiences as hearing the voice of God is indicative of the dominance, in modern culture, of the left hemisphere of the brain, with its more rational way of organizing reality.[12]

Whether religion originated in fear of the unknown and a sense of helplessness in face of a hostile and indifferent environment, was initially a product of right-brain dominance, or was a response to a sacred presence cannot be determined. No method exists for isolating a single dimension of human experience as the source of religion. The question also invites a dangerous and simplistic reductionism. If religion began in fear, is that the end of the story? The demand for justice may have begun merely with a cry for revenge, but it has been ennobled by such concepts as justice tempered by mercy and equality before the law. Religion is, like law, something more than its origins.

Speculation Regarding the Evolution of Magic and Religion: Frazer and Malinowski

In his multi-volumed *Golden Bough,* the Scottish anthropologist Sir James Frazer offered an evolutionary perspective of the relationship of magic, religion, and science. In Frazer's view, magic preceded religion. Magic, he argued, was the earliest attempt to know how the universe works and to use this knowledge to control it. Seen in this light, magic is closely related to science; where the magician attempts to harness power by formulas and spells, the scientist seeks to do so by a clearer understanding of causal relationships. Religion stemmed from the breakdown of magic; therefore when spells, rites, and formulas failed to produce the desired results, primitive peoples sought to achieve their ends by cajoling and supplicating the gods.

From Frazer's perspective the evolution from a magical to a religious stage entailed a shift from confidence in mastery of a power that could be tamed through magic to a feeling of dependence on a supernatural power. If the gods could not be controlled, they could at least be won over through prayer and sacrifice. In this view, the formula of religion is one of petition and sacrifice: "Dear God, if you will grant me what I desire, then I will give you a gift in return." Frazer's view assumed that magic and religion are based on a mistaken understanding of the universe; thus in the course of our cultural evolution, religion and religious explanations should decrease as scientific explanations increase. We should note that anthropologists no longer accept Frazer's theory of stages.

Still another evolutionary approach viewed religion as progressing from an initial stage in which the world was believed to be filled with magico-religious power (**mana**) or in which everything was potentially animated by a spirit **(animism)** to those religions in which the animating spirits had assumed the form of independent gods and goddesses **(polytheism)**. In this perspective, the movement from polytheism to monotheism was facilitated by a **henotheistic** stage in which a people's fortunes became so entwined with one god that the other gods were very nearly eclipsed. Finally, the argument concluded, at the highest and most progressive stage, **monotheism** appeared. Like Frazer's theory of stages, this evolutionary scheme that placed monotheism at its apex is now thoroughly discredited by modern anthropological studies.

Scholars are no longer concerned with making inferences as to how concepts of ultimacy have evolved in a kind of logical progression from animism to monotheism. Rather, contemporary thinking has shifted to developmental models that concentrate on changes in social structures. For example, anthropologist Bronislaw Malinowski offered a corrective to evolutionary schemes like Frazer's. Malinowski's work in the Trobriand Islands led him to the view that tribal peoples experience and know their world through magic, technology, and religion. The more unpredictable, uncontrollable, and dangerous a situation, the more likely magic would be employed. In activities where Trobriander technology was adequate and little was likely to go wrong, magic was not used. In those activities where the outcome was more problematic or dangerous, such as fishing for sharks, love making, war, or the planting of yams, the Trobrianders supplemented their skills with magic. Thus magic is employed when the limits of our pragmatic and technological skills have been reached. For Malinowski, "the function of magic is to ritualize man's optimism, to enhance his faith in the victory of hope over fear. Magic expresses the greater value for man of confidence over doubt, of steadfastness over vacillation; of optimism over pessimism."[13] Seen from Malinowski's perspective, magic and technology are primarily concerned with how to control; thus they differ functionally from religion (including the religions of tribal peoples), which is concerned with the fundamental issues of human existence.

While the question of the origin of religion has been abandoned because of the absence of data, the view that religion has evolved from the simple to the complex has been either set aside or reformulated because the evidence does not sustain the kind of evolutionary interpretations that earlier scholars claimed for it. Modern scholarship has rejected the argument that magic preceded religion because the evidence indicates that magic, religion, and technology existed together from the earliest times. In addition, the assumption of some evolutionists that later religious developments are progressive and superior while earlier forms are backward and inferior has been critically reexamined. The belief systems of primitives may be less scientific than ours, but they are not less religious.

The field studies now available on the life of primitive peoples indicate that tribal conceptions of the sacred cannot be adequately understood by such terms as animism, mana, or **totemism.** Tribal religion ranges from animism to polytheism to monotheism. In fact, such a range of perspectives may be found within a single tribal community. For the tribal mind the world is charged with power. All of life is viewed as holy.

For example, in his book *Nuer Religion,* E.E. Evans-Pritchard made the point that the Nuers, a cattle-herding people from the Sudan, conceived of God both as a single Spirit who is seen in many diverse things and as a spirit who is regarded separately and differently; thus God is *Kwoth,* the Spirit that sustains and animates all and yet is also *Kuth*—that is, discrete and independent spirits. In a sense the sacred is both a unity (a tribal **monism** or monotheism) and a multiplicity (a tribal polytheism or animism) rather than exclusively one or the other. This monistic-pluralism has prompted some scholars to refer to the tribal way of thinking about the holy as a diffused monotheism.

Believers may have thought of their religion as a goal but never as an intermediate link. No believer considers himself a primitive. . . . The concepts "primitive" and "highly developed" forms of religion are therefore fatal for historical research. Religious ideas and sacred rites are degraded to a series of relative values, whereas in reality they have functioned as absolute values.

W. Brede Kristensen
The Meaning of Religion[14]

Three Developmental Classifications of Religion

Although nineteenth-century evolutionary perspectives have fallen into disfavor, the archeological, ethnological, and historical evidence support at least a modified theory of the evolution of religion. Scholars have developed several classifications that can serve as conceptual handles for understanding the development of religion; they also avoid the pitfalls of earlier evolutionary schemes. Three classifications are discussed, including one that merely distinguishes between primitive and modern societies and religions, a more complex classification associated with sociologist of religion Robert Bellah, and a classification of religions according to whether they are local, national, or universal.

The Distinction between Primitive and Modern Societies and Religions

The first and broadest developmental typology contrasts the simplicity of primitive religions and societies with the complex character of modern ones. The relatively undifferentiated character of primitive social systems is reflected in their religious life. In primitive societies, religion and politics are not separated from each other as they are in modern societies, where political roles and functions are separated from religious ones. Primitive societies have few separate religious organizations, such as priestly or monastic orders, which have as their primary function the nurture and preservation of the religious life. The absence of those institutional structures and hierarchies that moderns often assume are features of all religions sometimes makes it difficult for us to separate the religious from the nonreligious in tribal life, or even to see that tribal peoples are at all religious. The Apache leader Geronimo, sensitive to his people's lack of religious institutions, protested in his autobiography that the Apaches also had a religious life: "We had no churches, no religious organization, no sabbath day, no holidays, and yet we worshipped. Sometimes the whole tribe would assemble to sing and pray, sometimes a smaller number perhaps only two or three."[15]

Bellah's Developmental Classification

A second classification, formulated by Robert Bellah, offers a wider range of distinctions for understanding the development of religion. In the evolution of religion, Bellah argues, change does not necessarily imply progress. A modern prophet like Martin Luther King, Jr. is not more religious than Amos of Tekoa, a Hebrew prophet of the eighth century B.C., merely because he speaks God's word at a later point in time, just as the paintings of a modern genius like Pablo Picasso are not necessarily superior to those of Rembrandt. Similarly, the religious life of primitive people is neither more nor less religious than that of moderns. It is, however, quite different, because very real differences exist between primitive and modern societies. Bellah believes that religion has developed primarily in the direction of increased differentiation and complexity of organization rather than towards greater spirituality. For example, world religions like Buddhism, Islam, and Christianity differ from primitive religions in size, level of complexity, elaborateness of structures, and differentiation of functions, as well as in their conceptions of ultimacy.[16]

Bellah's classification links different types of society to five distinct configurations of religious expression, which he identifies as primitive, archaic, historic, early modern, and modern religions. Major changes in religious belief systems, patterns of relationships, and worship are paralleled by shifts from one type of socioeconomic system to another.

Primitive religions are rooted in preliterate societies and range from the relatively unstratified societies of hunters and gatherers, such as the

Bushmen and pygmies of Africa and the Shoshones of the western United States, to the more complex societies of settled tribal communities sustained by the domestication of animals and primitive agriculture, such as the Yoruba and Ibo of Nigeria, the Zuni of New Mexico, and the Hopi of Arizona. Archaic religions emerged in the agricultural societies and empires of ancient Egypt, Sumer, China, India, and Central and South America. The historic religions, like the archaic religions, blossomed in preindustrial agricultural societies but differed from the archaic in that their sacred words and stories were written as well as spoken. The premodern forms of Buddhism, Confucianism, Roman Catholic and Eastern Orthodox Christianity, Jainism, Judaism, Islam, Sikhism, and Zoroastrianism are examples of historic religions. In Bellah's analysis the early modern and modern forms refer not only to the appearance of new religions but to the changes in the liturgies, belief systems, and organizations of already existing communities of faith that have resulted from their interaction with modern ways of thinking and doing. Because they have been touched by modern industrial societies, all living religions—whether they are primitive or historic—are faced with problems of accommodating and rejecting modern values and social systems.

For Bellah, the shift from a historic to an early modern religious consciousness that reflects a shift from a feudal to an industrial society is most evident in the emergence of classical Protestantism out of the fabric of medieval Christendom. Classical Protestantism is the paradigm of early modern religion because it embodies, even helps to fashion, several of the themes of modern culture. Its opposition to the authority of religious institutions and hierarchies, which took the form of rejection of papal authority and of the infallibility of church dogma and repudiation of any spiritual elitism implied in the distinction between priests and the people by emphasizing a "priesthood of all believers," was indicative of the struggle in the whole of society for freedom and equality. Still another modern theme, that of individualism, is evident in the Protestant emphasis on personal religious experience, a salvation directly available to the man or woman of faith, rather than a salvation mediated through the sacraments of the church.

As noted, in Bellah's typology each major change in the way social systems are structured—for example, the shift from a hunting and gathering society to an agricultural society—is accompanied by changes in religion. The level of organizational complexity, social stratification, and division of labor in a society is reflected in its religious structure and symbol system. The unity and simplicity of tribal life, in which kinship is the primary determinant of social relationships, is paralleled by a world view that envisions a single cosmos. In tribal belief systems, the human being and nature are one; as Black Elk put it, "The two-legged and the four-legged lived together like relatives."[17] In contrast, the hierarchies and divisions characteristic of feudal and preindustrial societies (ruler-ruled, lord-serf) are reflected in religious hierarchies (clergy-laity) and highly structured lines of authority. The stratified nature of such societies is paralleled in the historic religions by a dualistic understanding of the cosmos, exemplified in such dualisms as those of body and soul, this world and the next, the visible and the invisible, man and God. According to Bellah, the ideal of the religious life in the historic religions is separation from the world; thus the end of religious action is to seek salvation or enlightenment in another realm of reality or consciousness.[18] The direction of early modern and modern religious belief systems, Bellah argues, is away from the dualisms and hierarchies of the historic religions. This is evident not only in the demand for self-determination and equality in the secular and political spheres but also in the capacity of the historic religions to accept religious pluralism and in their efforts to democratize their structures and modes of governance.

The Local-National-Universal Classification

Because the history of religion is one of change, in which modern forms differ from earlier ones, a typology like Bellah's is valuable for gaining an overview of the historical development of religion. A less complex classification that still provides a criterion for discriminating between the forms that religion has taken is presented here. It classifies religions according to whether they are local, national, or universal on the basis of whether religions are primarily bound together biologically, culturally, or ideologically. Because local religions and societies are tied together by the natural tie of kinship, membership in such a society and participation in much of its religious life is a condition of birth. Although they have affinities of a racial and national character, national religions extend beyond tribal boundaries and are united primarily by shared customs and a common language. In contrast to the biological and cultural associations characteristic of local and national religions, universal religions unite people with diverse racial and cultural backgrounds on the basis of a common set of beliefs and devotional practices.

This typology is not only helpful in understanding the evolution of religion but also valuable for developing a feel for different forms of living religions. While many religious traditions have disappeared, local religions and primitive societies continue to follow their traditional ways, just as such national religions as Shinto and such universal religions as Buddhism and Islam are living faiths. Of course, all living traditions have been changed by their contact with modernity.

Local Religions

Local religions are variously referred to as tribal, folk, primitive, cosmic, or primal; the standard practice is to refer to them as primitive. The term *primitive* is not intended to suggest that the religious life of tribal peoples is inferior; primitive refers to the absence of a written language in such societies. Primitive peoples do not have holy books or sacred scriptures, but must keep their sense of the sacred alive through the spoken and remembered word and by acting it out in sacred dramas. Throughout this text, local religion will usually be referred to as tribal or primitive rather than cosmic, local, or primal. We should note at the outset that local religions are more numerous than are either national or universal religions. For example, 1,000 tribal religions are estimated to exist in Africa alone. In addition, each American Indian tribe has a distinctive religious life, as do the primitive communities of Australia, Melanesia, and Polynesia. Although many tribal religions continue to survive, some, like that of the Anasazi, the cliff-dwelling Pueblo people of the Four Corners area in the United States, have disappeared, and others, like those of the Celts and Norse, survive only through assimilation of some of their motifs into the dominant Western culture.

Primitive peoples support themselves in various ways. The simplest primitive societies are comprised of those who, like the pygmies of Africa and the aboriginals of Australia, are hunters and gatherers. The pygmies live today, as their ancestors lived before them, relatively untouched by the revolution in agriculture and the domestication of animals developed by other sub-Saharan African peoples some 6,000 years ago. Other tribal peoples are nomadic herders or live in settled communities supported by an archaic agricultural technology. Primitive societies and religions are usually small and limited in geographical extension, although some hunting societies have a geographically large range. Hunting and gathering groups may be associations of no more than a few families—more a band than a great tribe. However, where forage for large domestic herds is plentiful or agriculture makes fixed village life possible, the tribal community may be much larger. For instance, the Yoruba and Ibo of Nigeria number approximately 10 million people each. Of course, in the past 200 years many of the Yoruba and Ibo have turned from their tribal tradition to convert to Christianity or Islam.

The social and religious life of primitives is united by the bonds of kinship—that is, by real or assumed biological relationships. Family, clan, and tribe provide its natural ties. Folk religions are local rather than world religions because they are tied to a specific land or a specific people. Their sacred stories and ritual ways are so rooted in sacred places and kinship patterns that they can neither be nationalized nor universalized. Although tribal societies have voluntary religious organizations and secret societies, religious affiliation is primarily a matter of birth or marriage; thus to be born into a tribe is to participate in its religious life. Because tribal life is relatively self-contained and takes place within a circle of kinship relationships, tribal religions do not seek converts. Apaches do not seek converts among the Navaho, nor do Ashantis who follow their tribal faith ask a Yoruba whether he or she has been saved.

The point has already been made that religion is not separated from other aspects of life in tribal societies. That religion is not compartmentalized from social and economic life is supported by one scholar's observation that primitive peoples do not have a word in their diverse languages that is translated by the word *religion,* nor do they give names or labels to their particular ritual ways.[19] All aspects of tribal existence have religious significance. Tribal life is tradition bound and looks backward to the ancient ones for guidance. Ancestral ways are familiar and reassuring. What is new is often disruptive and frightening; nevertheless tribal cultures do change either internally, through the influence of visions and dreams that serve as a force for modifying and redirecting tribal beliefs and practices, or externally, through contact with other societies. Local religions and preliterate societies have sometimes been weakened or obliterated by contact with national and universal religions and industrial societies. Throughout the text much more will be said about the religious symbol systems of tribal peoples.

National Religions

National religions are associated with a particular racial-national group united by a common language and culture. They usually extend over a greater geographic area and involve larger numbers of people than do tribal religions. Although national religions are not limited by kinship, they are still so closely identified with the fortunes of a particular people or nationality that their symbols and practices are not readily transferable to other lands and peoples. Many national religions, including those of ancient Egypt, Babylon, Greece, and Sumer, have long since ceased to move people to dance and pray. Among modern faiths, Shinto has been almost entirely limited to Japan, and Confucianism has been all but inseparable from the Chinese experience. Likewise, Hinduism, a name for an incredible variety of India's indigenous religious life, is so much an Indian way of life that it has had only limited success in being exported.

National religions appeared when the agricultural revolution made possible permanent settlements supporting greater numbers of people. The earliest national religions, like those of Egypt and Sumer, were part of ancient empires based on complex agricultural systems utilizing irrigation water available from some of the world's great rivers. Often, national religions grew from the soil of agricultural and commercial empires and

Frieze, Kom Ombo Temple, Egypt. This frieze portrays the pharaoh, the divine king, and the jackal-headed god, Anubis, with the symbol of life (ankh) in his left hand.

Photo by Klaus D. Francke, Peter Arnold, Inc.

ceased to be when the empire of which they were an integral part disintegrated. Although the religions of such empires as those of the Mayas, Aztecs, and Incas have not survived, the adaptability of national religion is evident in such traditions as Confucianism, Hinduism, and Shinto, which have survived shifts in modern times from feudal to industrialized societies.

National religions are more complex and specialized than tribal religions. The shaman, a tribal specialist in sacred things, is a healer, storyteller, priest, and magician imbued with sacred power. In more complex societies, politics, religion, and medicine gradually became the specialized provinces of kings, priests, and healers. Social and religious hierarchies, which separated master from slave, lord from peasant, priest from laity and buttressed vertical lines of authority, replaced the social and religious distinctions of tribal existence that were based on sex, age, and function rather than on class or caste.

The diffused monotheism of tribal religion gave way in national religions to a pantheon of gods, although the national religions are not without monistic themes that unite their many gods. Many of the gods had separate cults and shrines attended by priests whose specialized knowledge qualified them to perform the necessary sacrificial rites and to serve as intermediaries through whom contact with the gods was facilitated.

Polytheistic traditions tend to be less exclusive, their gods and priests more tolerant of rivals, than has been the case for monotheistic religions.

Characteristic of many, but not all, national religions is the divine king. For example, the myths of ancient Egypt affirmed that the pharaoh's office was introduced at the time of creation. In Egypt, politics and religion were bound together in the person of the pharaoh, who was god, priest, and ruler. The Egyptian state was a theocracy in which all that was Egypt belonged, in principle, to the divine king. The goddess Isis and Re, the life-giving sun deity, were the divine powers behind the throne. By virtue of sitting on the throne, the king became the son of Re, a deified being who united the invisible and the visible and who sustained the cosmic order. The importance of the mikado in the Shinto tradition and that of the emperor in ancient and classical China who ruled by a "Mandate of Heaven" are variations on the theme of the divine king. The shift in modern times away from monarchies to republics and democracies and from feudalism to capitalist and socialist economies has weakened the influence and strength of national faiths that, like Shinto and Confucianism, have been closely allied to the old hierarchies.

Universal Religions

Universal or world religions are not narrowly associated with a particular people, land, or nation. They are convert oriented, and, because their membership is based on spiritual or ideological commitment rather than national or biological association, their symbols and belief systems may take hold anywhere. Christianity, Buddhism, and Islam are the purest examples of the universal type. Christians have responded to Christ's words, "Go therefore and make disciples of all nations," by seeking to do just that. Missionaries from Saint Paul onward have proclaimed the Gospel throughout the world, and in 1979 its adherents were estimated to include 950 million people. The influence of Christianity on Western civilization is incalculable. It is a dominant and dynamic faith in much of sub-Saharan Africa, and its presence in Asia, although more limited, is not inconsequential.

Like Christianity, Buddhism has been able to extend its message and practice far beyond India, the land of Buddha's birth. Dedicated monks have spread the message and practice of the Enlightened One in every direction. Tibet, Sri Lanka, Burma, Thailand, Cambodia, Vietnam, China, Korea, and Japan are either predominantly Buddhist countries or have been profoundly influenced by Buddhism. The Buddhist presence in the United States has been spearheaded by Asian Americans, although two Buddhist denominations, Zen and Nichiren Shōshū of America, have attracted many non-Asians.

Muhammad's message, submission to Allah, and his charismatic leadership overcame Arab tribal loyalties and conflicts and succeeded in establishing a universal religious community. Within 100 years of Muhammad's death in A.D. 632, the Muslim faith became the dominant force in Syria, Iraq, Palestine, Egypt, Iran, North Africa, and Turkey. The push of Islam from Arabia northward to Persia and westward to Africa was matched by its successes in central and southeast Asia. It has been estimated that of the world's more than 4 billion people, 700 million are Muslims.

Mixed Types

Some traditions are difficult to classify according to the local-national-universal typology. Judaism is a case in point. The Jewish religious experience has been tribal, national, and universal. The early legacy of Judaism is a story of transition from the tribal faith of Abraham, Isaac, and Jacob, including Yahweh's deliverance of the Israelites from bondage in Egypt, to the establishment of a Jewish nation in the land of Canaan. The Jewish tradition has been so closely identified with ethnic purity or tribal relationships (a people chosen of God) and a Jewish nation (a promised land) that incorporation into the House of Israel has been primarily associated with being born of Jewish parents. Although Judaism has many features of a national faith, it is not without some characteristics of a universal one. First, because historically the Jews have been repeatedly forced out of their Holy Land, they have become a people who are widely distributed throughout the world; thus the Jewish faith is practiced in many lands. Second, although Judaism is not presently a convert-oriented faith, it has sought converts at times in its past and remains open to them today. Third, since the destruction of the Temple of Jerusalem in A.D. 70, Jews have become almost exclusively a people of a holy scripture rather than a people of a holy place; thus the Jewish experience has been made more easily transferable to other places and cultures. Because of these ambiguities, Judaism is more appropriately classified as a mixed national-universal type.

Concluding Remarks

A study of the primary forces of religious expression requires some reflection on the nature of magic and its close relationship to religion. Both magic and religion are fascinated by power. Magicians believe that the power of the universe can be controlled through the magical arts, whereas religionists are more concerned with how to live than how to control. The distinction between religion as meaningful living and magic as self-enhancing mastery over the world is a difficult one to maintain since, in practice, the quests for meaningful living and for self-enhancing power often overlap.

In raising the question of the origin of religion, the point was made that the question of the origin of magic and religion should be set aside as unanswerable and misleading. Also rejected was the argument implicit in some evolutionary perspectives that contemporary forms of religious expression are superior to earlier forms, or that religion is an evolutionary stage that can be laid aside or rendered obsolete as science helps us mediate our fears and dependencies. Little evidence can be found to indicate that magic preceded religion; both existed together from very early times. In primitive cultures, magic is very nearly inseparable from religion, and magic continues to play a part in modern forms of religious expression.

In addition to examining what magic is and reflecting on the origin and evolution of religion, this chapter introduced three ways of understanding and classifying changes in the forms that religion has taken. For instance, the lack of differentiation in primitive societies is reflected in primitive religions, just as the complexity of modern societies is reflected in modern religions. The distinction between local, national, and universal religions can be particularly helpful in understanding some of the interdependencies of social and religious structures.

Notes

1. Mohandas K. Gandhi, *An Autobiography: The Story of My Experiments with Truth,* trans. by Mahadev Desai (Boston: Beacon Press, 1962), pp. xiii-xiv.

2. Susanne K. Langer, *Philosophy in a New Key* (New York: Mentor Books, 1964), p. 52.

3. Lewis Spence, *An Encyclopaedia of Occultism* (New York: University Books, 1960), p. 261.

4. John Middleton, ed., *Magic, Witchcraft and Curing* (Austin: University of Texas Press, 1967), pp. 16–17.

5. Jeffrey B. Russell, *Witchcraft in the Middle Ages* (Ithaca, N.Y.: Cornell University Press, 1972), pp. 1–26.

6. Spence, *Encyclopaedia of Occultism,* p. 261.

7. Bronislaw Malinowski, *A Scientific Theory of Culture and Other Essays* (Chapel Hill: University of North Carolina Press, 1944), p. 198.

8. Friedrich Nietzsche, *Twilight of the Gods* in Oscar Levy, ed., *The Complete Works of Friedrich Nietzsche,* vol. XVI, trans. by Anthony Ludovici (New York: Russell & Russell, 1964), p. 4.

9. Sigmund Freud, *The Future of an Illusion* (Garden City, N.Y.: Doubleday, Anchor Books, 1964), p. 22.

10. Ibid., p. 81.

11. William James, *The Varieties of Religious Experience* (New York: New American Library, 1958), p. 61.

12. Julian Jaynes, *The Origin of Consciousness in the Breakdown of the Bicameral Mind* (Boston: Houghton Mifflin, 1976).

13. In Joseph Needham, ed., *Science, Magic and Reality* (New York: Macmillan, 1925), p. 83.

14. W. Brede Kristensen, *The Meaning of Religion* (The Hague: Martinus Nijhoff, 1966), p. 14.

15. *Geronimo: His Own Story,* ed. by S.M. Barrett (New York: Ballentine Books, 1971), p. 77.

16. Robert Bellah, *Beyond Belief* (New York: Harper & Row, 1970), pp. 20–50.

17. John G. Niehardt, *Black Elk Speaks: Being the Life Story of a Holy Man of the Oglala Sioux* (New York: Pocket Books, 1972), p. 39.

18. Bellah, *Beyond Belief,* p. 22.

19. See Wilfred Cantwell Smith, *The Meaning and End of Religion* (New York: New American Library, 1964).

Chapter Four
The Holy

We have seen the highest circle of spiraling powers. We have named this circle God. We might have given it any other name we wished: Abyss, Mystery, Absolute Darkness, Absolute Light, Matter, Spirit, Ultimate Hope, Ultimate Despair, Silence. But we have named it God because only this name, for primordial reasons, can stir our hearts profoundly.

Nikos Kazantzakis
The Saviours of God [1]

Since we have defined religion as seeking and responding to what people experience as holy, we must understand what the holy means. The concept is a difficult one to define or to describe. This is so for several reasons: First, it is a complex term with rich overtones of meaning. Like other complex words, such as beauty and justice, it stands for a cluster of ideas. Second, although the holy is known in human experience, it is interpreted and understood through the contextual filter of the individual and the culture of which he or she is a part. In one milieu the holy is a Great Spirit encountered in living things and in the rhythmic movement of nature. In another context the sacred is "the Holy One of Israel," the living God who spoke to Moses from a burning bush. In yet another historical frame, the holy is the Tao, which does nothing and yet through which all things are done. In short, the faces of the holy are so numerous and culturally conditioned that its essential nature is difficult to isolate.

A third and even more insurmountable difficulty stems from the hiddenness of the holy. Because the holy is a symbol for the eternal and

Prayer at the Wailing Wall, Israel. A devout Jew, with his head covered to acknowledge God, worships at the Wailing Wall, a sacred place in the Jewish tradition.

Photo: Photoworld Div. of F.P.G.

unlimited, it is, at least in some measure, hidden; thus no words, no definitions can encompass or exhaust its meaning. Whether the holy is encountered as God or is intuitively experienced as an inward state of being, it is not experienced as a sensible object. "No man has seen God at any time" is a theme in the Bible, and "Who ever has seen Indra?" is a query in the Hindu holy book, the Rigveda. The holy bursts the boundaries of human understanding because it is unlike ourselves or things in ordinary experience. The unfathomableness of the holy is expressed in a saying of the Ila of Africa: "God has nowhere or nowhen, that he comes to an end."[2]

The paradox of the holy is that it is both known and hidden. The holy is revealed or known in human experience, but it is not definable in human categories. It is something that transcends the boundaries of ordinary speech. The holy touches and transforms human lives, yet words are always powerless to exhaust its depth. Humans can know more than they can express; nowhere is this more true than in an experience of holiness. Black Elk, the Lakota Sioux holy man, in describing his life-transforming vision, echoed something of the difficulty of speaking about the sacred: "And while I stood there I saw more than I can tell and I understood more than I saw; for I was seeing in a sacred manner the shapes of all things in the spirit and the shape of all shapes as they must live together like one being."[3]

If the holy transcends human categories, then all talk about it is necessarily metaphorical, and all definitions must be regarded as provisional. Religious language is thus more like a mirror through which we catch a glimpse of the sacred. However, things can be said that help us understand the meaning of the holy; the holy is indefinable, but it is not unintelligible. The meanings of terms are known by how they are used. The holy is such a term; thus a cluster of ideas in both common and scholarly usage provides some sense of what is intended by the holy or the sacred.

Familiarity with words that are used for the holy can be helpful. The holy or the sacred is called by a great many names. In some religious traditions the focus is on a personal deity addressed variously as Allah, God, Lord Krishna, Shiva, Yahweh, He Who Dwells Above, Mother Kali, and by a host of other names. In other religious traditions holiness is more of a process than a holy being, more an experience than a relationship. In Buddhism, for example, the word that points to ultimacy is nirvana, a liberated way of being that Buddhists believe illuminates the whole universe. In Confucianism the ultimate focus is *jen,* sometimes translated "humaneness." The holy has been addressed intimately and affectionately as Grandfather or Grandmother or as our Father or our Mother. More abstractly and impersonally, it has been referred to as the Good by Plato, as Brahman in the Hindu tradition, as the "ground of being" by Paul Tillich, and as the One by Plotinus.

In the Bhagavad Gita, a sacred book in the Hindu tradition, the names of the holy are said to be so numerous that they are like "god, Infinite, with the faces in all directions."[4] Prominent in Islamic devotional practices is the repeated pronouncement of the Ninety-nine Names of God as the worshipper runs a rosary (a string of beads) through his fingers. The divine names are spoken, one for each bead, but a hundredth Name remains hidden and reminds the devotee of the mystery and inexhaustible depth of the holy.

Knowing some of the names by which the holy is called can be helpful because some of them are familiar to us; however it can also be misleading because we may tend to treat the holy as a synonym for the familiar. A broad understanding of what is meant by the holy is important; because the holy is that which distinguishes the religious from the non-religious. One fruitful way of thinking about the holy is to think of it as ultimate and nonordinary.

The name of this infinite and inexhaustible depth and ground of all being is God. That depth is what the word God means. And if that word has not much meaning for you, translate it, and speak of the depths of your life, of the source of your being, of your ultimate concern, of what you take seriously without any reservation.

Paul Tillich
The Shaking of the Foundations[5]

The Holy as Ultimate: The Theological Approach of Tillich

As noted in chapter one, Paul Tillich defined religion as ultimate concern; we can now attempt to understand more clearly his conception of ultimacy. For Tillich, to say that the holy is ultimate means that it is absolute, eternal, infinite, and unconditioned being. To borrow from Saint Anselm's (1033–1109) understanding of God, nothing greater than ultimate being either exists or can be conceived. In short, the holy is incomparable. Holy Being is not simply a being among beings. It is the ultimate basis of reality, of all things; thus Holy Being is not something that exists in the same way that other beings or things do. It is not a quality of things like brown or softness, neither is it a class or genus. Holy Being, to use Tillich's image, is the eternal and enduring ground of being that makes the existence of all things possible.

Tillich wrote that personal life is integrated in ultimate being.[6] Alienation and inauthentic existence are conditions that stem either from being ignorant of or separated from the holy. According to Mircea Eliade, "Sacredness is above all *real*. The more religious a man *is* the more real he is, and the more he gets away from the unreality of a meaningless life."[7] The holy is therefore the ultimate source of meaning. This is so because the sacred, wrote John E. Smith, "is the standard for judging the profane since the holy provides us with a vision of what life should be, and thus reveals the extent to which mundane existence falls short of its ideal."[8]

The ultimate is unconditioned and absolute—that is, it is a primary and final value. All of life is to be judged by reference to the ultimate. The unconditioned and absolute is that which demands and deserves unqualified commitment. A number of gods, concerns, or commitments entreat us to court them. The pressing question is, To what am I committed? A commitment to the ultimate is one that is without reservation, one that holds nothing back.

An ultimate value is primary, absolute, and unconditioned, in contrast to values that are secondary, relative, and instrumental. Why not make a list of personal concerns. Can you rank them? Which concerns on your list are secondary? Good health, for example, is usually valued more than a college diploma. Is there something more fundamental than good health? Where do you rank yourself, your family, your country? Which concerns are instrumental—that is, things not desired for themselves but chiefly for their uses? Money, for instance, is a legitimate concern, but it is almost never a final value. Is happiness on your list? What standards do you use for judging the concerns you have? Are you able to locate something that is ultimate for you? Is there anything, for example, for which you would be willing to sacrifice your life? Is God a good symbol for ultimate concern?

There is no religion in which it [the nonordinary, nonrational quality of the holy] does not live as the real innermost core, and without it no religion would be worthy of the name.

Rudolf Otto
The Idea of the Holy[9]

The Holy as Nonordinary: The Theological Approach of Otto

The holy is ultimate and nonordinary. In the sense used here, ultimacy points to a rational dimension of holiness. The ultimate is thus that aspect of the holy that can be more readily conceptualized. For instance, the ultimate as unconditioned and uncreated serves to provide an explanation for the world as conditioned and created. The holy as a final value makes ethical judgments something more than individual or group preferences; thus the holy is associated with the good. As a concept, ultimacy is primarily a theological interpretation of an experience of holiness.

The holy, however, is not exclusively ethical or rational. It is something more than the good and the true. The holy is felt as well as believed in. The heart as well as the mind is engaged; thus the holy has a nonrational quality that elicits a wide range of feelings. Fear, dread, fascination, ecstasy, joy, and love are human responses to the incomparable power and mystery of the sacred.

The Incomparable Mystery
of the Holy

Rudolf Otto, in *The Idea of the Holy,* used the term *numinous* to stand for the nonrational quality of the holy or for what is referred to here as the nonordinary. In Otto's analysis the **numinous** is something more, a "wholly other" that is radically different from the ordinary and familiar.[10] The mystery of the holy is experienced as a nonordinary presence that falls outside the limits of the ordinary and thus fills the mind with wonder and astonishment. A vivid sense of an incomparable presence is described by American philosopher and psychologist William James in *The Varieties of Religious Experience:*

> *I remember the night and almost the very spot on the hilltop where my soul opened out, as it were, into the Infinite, and there was a rushing together of two worlds, the inner and the outer. It was deep calling unto deep . . . . The ordinary sense of things around me faded. For the moment nothing but an ineffable joy and exultation remained . . . . The darkness held a presence that was all the more felt because it was not seen. I could not any more have doubted that He was there than that I was. Indeed, I felt myself to be, if possible, the less real of the two.[11]*

The mystery of the nonordinary is more than a sense of a holy presence. The depth, the mystery of being, is hidden beyond the power of human conception. Some mysteries are, like certain aspects of the moon, not yet known; but they are, in principle, knowable. The inexhaustible ground of holy being, however, is an essential mystery that more research will not dispel. The impenetrable mystery is like a darkness, "a cloud of unknowing" that cannot be pierced. A fourteenth-century Christian monk wrote:

> *No matter what you do, this darkness and this cloud is between you and your God and because of it you can neither see Him clearly with your reason . . . nor can you feel Him with your affection in the sweetness of love . . . . For if you are ever to feel Him or to see Him, it will necessarily be within this cloud and within this darkness.[12]*

St. Paul expressed something of the hiddenness of God when he contrasted man's imperfect condition, with its fragmentary knowledge, to the coming of perfection: "For now we see in a mirror dimly, but then face to face. Now I know in part; then I shall understand fully, even as I have been fully understood."[13] The ineffable mystery, the hiddenness of the holy, is attested to by Eastern as well as Western religious traditions. Perhaps no expression is more memorable than the initial lines of the Chinese classic, the *Tao Te Ching:*

The Tao that can be told of
Is not the Absolute Tao;
The Names that can be given
Are not absolute Names.[14]

The Incomparable Power of the Holy

In addition to mystery, the nonordinary has a second dimension: its majestic power. The holy is awesome, overpowering, wonderful. The holy, Otto argues, is encountered as something that is active and vital. Holy Being is dynamic; it actively empowers, wills, brings into being, and makes itself manifest. The wholly other is thus not entirely obscured, for it draws near and is known in human experience.

The majestic power of the holy is like the energy of a consuming fire. In the Christian tradition, the symbolic image of the coming of the Holy Spirit on the day of Pentecost is fire. The Holy Spirit, the book of Acts reports, came upon Christ's disciples "like the rush of a mighty wind . . . there appeared to them tongues as of fire," and they began to speak in other languages.[15] The Jewish tradition, too, vividly communicates this sense of a powerful living God. The children of Israel make a covenant with a God who demands obedience. During the Exodus, the Lord goes before the Israelites by day as a cloud and by night as a pillar of fire.

Holy power moves humans to go and to do. This dynamic and personal quality of the divine power inspired Blaise Pascal to contrast the abstract, impersonal ultimate of the philosophers that "is simply the author of geometrical truths and of the elements" with the biblical God to whom humans respond in the depths of their souls.[16]

The mystery and majesty of the nonordinary, when it breaks into the sphere of the commonplace, is often both attractive and frightening. The conjunction of attraction and repulsion, adoration and fear is illustrated by Arjuna's vision in the Bhagavad Gita. Arjuna was a young Indian prince who, prior to leading his army in battle, engaged his charioteer in conversation concerning the implications of war and the deeper meaning of human existence. Arjuna was initially unaware that his charioteer, Krishna, was a divine incarnation, an avatar. During the conversation, Arjuna recognized the divine presence in Krishna. When he did so, he asked to see the form of God as Supreme Spirit. Krishna replied "thou canst not see Me" by your own eye; thus "I give thee a supernatural eye" in order that you might "behold My mystic power as God."[17] Arjuna was overwhelmed at the wonder of what he saw, but at the same time the awesome power of God so frightened him that his hair stood upright. Arjuna then did what countless humans have done; he bowed before the God. The majesty of God is clearly evident in the following excerpt from Arjuna's vision:

> *I see Thee, infinite in form on all sides;*
> *No end nor middle nor yet beginning of Thee*
> *Do I see, O All-God, All-formed!*

> *With diadem, club, and disc,*
> *A mass of radiance, glowing on all sides,*
> *I see Thee, hard to look at, on every side*
> *With the glory of flaming fire and sun, immeasurable.*

> . . .

> *Without beginning, middle, or end, of infinite power,*
> *Of infinite arms, whose eyes are the moon and sun,*
> *I see Thee, whose face is flaming fire,*
> *Burning this whole universe with Thy radiance.*[18]

The conjunction of attraction and repulsion in Arjuna's experience illustrates what Otto referred to as the fascinating quality of holiness.[19] The holy can inspire trust, love, and bliss, but it can also make a person tremble with fear. It is wondrous, amazing beyond the powers of description, but its overpowering majesty can also be so terrifying that it forces humans to their knees like Arjuna, "stammering, greatly affrighted, bowing down."[20] Humans shudder as well as rejoice before the awesome power of the sacred. The radiant, compassionate aspect of God is countered by his power, which makes the worlds tremble and which can make us shake with fear and cry out for mercy.

Fear of God and love of God are common to religion. A holy power that attracts and repels is found in most tribal religions and is by no means absent from modern religious tradition. In the Jewish canon, the Lord is the shepherd who restores the soul. He is the Lord who is to be loved and served. "Hear O Israel: The Lord our God is one Lord. And you shall love your God with all your heart, and with all your soul and all of your might."[21] But fear before God, as well as love, is also the proper posture of humans:

> *Let all the earth fear the Lord*
> *let all the inhabitants of the world*
> *stand in awe of him!*
> *For he spoke and it came to be;*
> *he commanded and it stood forth.*[22]

In Hinduism, Vishnu, the god who protects and preserves, is a creative and life-giving power. Vishnu's power is balanced by the rhythmic cosmic dance of Shiva, the auspicious one, whose dance destroys as well as gives birth. The right hand of the divine implores while the left hand of god consumes and destroys.

Many Asian traditions have calmer images of the holy; the power of the nonordinary engenders more a feeling of harmony than of fear. The Tao is, for instance, the movement of the universe, the mother of everything. The Tao is calm, effortless, empty, yet its active power is everywhere. The nonordinary in Zen Buddhism is not the wholly other but is as near to us as ourselves. The ultimate dimension of human existence, nirvana, is experienced in ordinary, everyday activities. The holy is ultimate and mysterious, but it is not so much objective and external as it is subjective and inward. The holy is not a being encountered outside ourselves but is experienced and perfected within the individual in ordinary, everyday activities. An appropriate image for the Zen experience of holiness is a monk sitting in silent meditation, gazing inward, serene and undisturbed, projecting enlightened wisdom in daily activities.

The believer may not experience each quality of the holy mentioned here; one may experience fear before the sacred, while another feels love. The scripture "God is love" is balanced by the scripture concerning wisdom: "Behold, the fear of the Lord, that is wisdom." The human family has different experiences, different understandings of holiness. The active, willing, transcendent otherness of the Judeo-Christian tradition is contrasted by the nonstriving, harmonious, and natural process of the Tao and the interior character of nirvana. To assume that all the qualities associated with the holy as ultimate and nonordinary are dominant themes in each religious tradition is unnecessary and even misleading. Much of Otto's analysis of the nonordinary character of holiness, for example, does not fit nontheistic religious traditions. Nor should we assume that the qualities discussed are exhaustive, for the sacred is intrinsically inexhaustible and unlimited.

God is free to manifest himself under any form—even that of stone or wood. Leaving out for a moment the word "God," this may be translated: the sacred may be seen under any sort of form, even the most alien. In fact what is paradoxical, what is beyond our understanding, is not that the sacred can be manifested in stones or in trees, but that it can be manifested at all, that it can thus become limited and relative.

Mircea Eliade
Patterns in Comparative Religion[23]

Manifestations of the Sacred: The Phenomenological Approaches of Eliade and Kristensen

Phenomenologists like W. Brede Kristensen and Mircea Eliade would object to this book's characterization of the holy as that which is ultimate and nonordinary, an approach that is indebted to Tillich's concept of ultimacy and Otto's idea of the holy. They criticize the approaches of Tillich and Otto and the synthesis of their ideas presented here as too abstract and theological. Both phenomenologists agree that the holy or sacred is the essential element of religion. They argue, however, that an understanding of the sacred should begin with the way in which it has been present and manifest in human experience rather than with abstract and theological interpretations. Kristensen finds that attempts to define or delineate the holy ignore the way people actually experience or think of it in favor of an abstraction. Rather, the concrete and particular character of a believer's experience must be allowed to express itself—a goal that definition may frustrate.[24]

While the understanding of the holy as ultimate and nonordinary is valuable and defensible, from the phenomenological perspectives of Eliade and Kristensen it does represent a theological interpretation of experience rather than a concrete religious experience. Eliade and Kristensen emphasize that the sacred is present or manifest in particular beings and things and in specific times and places; thus a phenomenological study of those things or moments humans have experienced as sacred may illuminate what is meant by the holy in ways that theological formulations may exclude.

In *Patterns in Comparative Religion,* Eliade eschewed any more of a distinction than "the sacred and religious life are the opposite of the profane and secular life."[25] Eliade's phenomenological approach is confined to a comparative study of how the sacred has been understood or experienced and leaves open the question of what the holy is in itself; thus Eliade's concept of the sacred can accommodate both theistic and nontheistic conceptions of ultimacy. His sacred/profane dichotomy is open-ended and expansive; it concentrates on the forms or modes through which the sacred has been manifested and understood. Each culture, each individual has a particular way of expressing the holy. Locating the sacred in the heavens is a frequent mode of religious expression, but it is, in Eliade's approach, inappropriate to conclude that sky imagery is essential. Inwardness, interior religious experience, is also an important image. What is sacred in one context may be profane in another. A holy icon, a painted image of a sacred person, may be revered and kissed because a worshipper can see the holy through it. A different person might find himself unmoved by the painting and scandalized by what he regards as idolatry. The Black Hills are sacred to the Sioux, but their power to disclose the holy is muted for those unaccustomed to seeing the divine in nature.

Eliade's work does, however, provide some sense of what is implied by the terms *sacred* and *profane.* While the profane is ordinary, the sacred is nonordinary. Profane things are not valued in themselves, but for their uses. An ordinary cup is of value because it can be used for drinking. Its worth is relative to its utility; a broken cup is a useless thing. By contrast, something that manifests the sacred is valued for itself and is marked off as something holy. A Catholic church is, for example, more than simply a meeting place where people gather to be instructed. It is a sacred space because it is a place where the Divine is mysteriously present in the host on the altar. The chalice, with its contents of wine transformed into the precious blood of Christ, is more than something useful, for it points to the larger reality in which it plays a part.

Sacred things are treated reverently, even fearfully, for they are the loci through which the divine power is mediated. Sacrilege of holy things, abuse of marked-off or **tabooed** things, is a serious offense and fraught with danger. The ark of the covenant, for instance, was regarded by the Israelites during the conquest of Canaan as a dangerous yet life-sustaining power. It was to be touched only by sanctified persons. In the days of King David, the ark, a wooden chest containing God's commandments, was carried with the Israelites as a witness to God's nearness to his chosen people. On one occasion, the oxen drawing the cart stumbled and Uzzah tried to steady the ark with his hand, apparently to protect it from damage. But "the anger of the Lord was kindled against Uzzah; and God smote him there because he put forth his hand to the ark; and he died there beside the ark of God."[26]

Sacred things, or what Eliade calls **hierophanies,** are those in which the holy is manifest. Hierophanies are like windows through which the believer apprehends the holy. For example, twilight is a hierophany in Carlos Castaneda's *The Teachings of Don Juan.* According to Don Juan, the Yaqui man of knowledge, "The twilight is the crack between the worlds."[27] Humans have seen the sacred through many cracks, many windows. Because moderns live in a desacralized cosmos, a world in which it is difficult to find anything that is regarded as sacred, we are sometimes surprised to learn that nearly everything has at one time or another been regarded as a hierophany through which the holy has been manifested or made present. In tribal religion, for instance, sacred power was felt to permeate existence; thus animals and plants, heaven and earth, man and the elements have been hierophanies. Eliade observed that probably all important plants and animals have at some time had a place in religion. [28]

Time as a Hierophany

Sacred time is fulfilled time—a time when the sacred is unveiled or disclosed. For instance, the God of the monotheistic faiths (e.g., Judaism, Christianity, and Islam) primarily reveals himself in history. Because they stress the work of God in time, monotheistic faiths celebrate moments of divine revelation in their rites and beliefs. Sabbath and Passover are sacred times in the Jewish faith. Jews believe that God revealed himself to Moses and called him to lead the Israelites out of bondage in Egypt; Passover is an annual commemoration of God's mighty act of liberation. In weekly Sabbath observances worshippers draw near to God in a moment of divine self-disclosure. Sabbath is, as Jewish philosopher and theologian Abraham Heschel characterized it, a sanctuary of the eternal in time.[29] Christians believe the fullness of God's disclosure took place during the time and in the person of Christ. The calendar, liturgy, and theology of Christianity focuses on Christmas and Easter as the moments in which God's plan of salvation was culminated. In Islam, Allah's fullest self-disclosure took place in the time of Muhammad who, because of the authoritative nature of the revelation he received, is believed to be the "seal of the prophets." Muslim rituals and obligations thus are reiterations of Allah's revelation to Muhammad.

Space as a Hierophany

In the faith of ancient Egypt, the temple at Heliopolis was believed to be located on the spot where the sun god emerged from the water of chaos and made a mound of dry land; thus the temple stood on the hill at the center of creation. The shape of the pyramids, the royal tombs, were stylized forms of the primeval hill. The Yoruba of Nigeria believe that Ile-Ifé is a sacred city because it is located on the spot where their gods, Ol-orun, the owner of the skies, and Orisha Nla, Great God, brought the earth and the Yoruba into being.

A sacred place is concrete; it is located spatially rather than in the fulfilled time that is fixed in the mind through acts of remembrance. The land of tribal peoples is often a hierophany. *Wirikuta* is the sacred land of the Huichol Indians of Mexico, the sacred place where their ancestors came into being. For the Taos Indians of New Mexico, Blue Lake is the place where the sacred is manifested. There is no more sensitive and profound expression of the sacredness of the land than that expressed in a speech by Chief Seattle of the Duwamish tribe on the occasion of the surrender of his homeland to the United States in the Medicine Creek Treaty of 1854:

> *"Every part of this soil is sacred in the estimation of my people. Every hillside, every valley, every plain and grove, has been hallowed by some sad or happy event in days long vanished."*[30]

Although monotheistic religions look to God's revelation in time, they are not without sacred places. Mecca, Jerusalem, and, to a lesser extent, Rome are holy cities. Following Muhammad's example, Muslims are obligated to make a pilgrimage at least once in their lives, to Mecca. The pilgrims worship at the Ka'ba, a holy building, which has set in one of its corners a black stone believed to be a vehicle of Allah's blessings. Devotion to Allah takes the form of kissing the stone and circling the building. Before its destruction in the first century A.D., the Temple of Jerusalem was a holy place, a sanctuary in space, for Jews, and contemporary Jews continue to worship at its remnant, the Wailing Wall. While destruction of the temple shifted Jewish worship from its focus on temple sacrifice to focus on a holy book, Jews are still a people linked to their holy land. Because of the miraculous powers associated with them, the shrine at Lourdes in France and Our Lady of Guadaloupe Church in Mexico are sacred places for Roman Catholic Christians.

Other Hierophanies

In addition to hierophanies of time and place, there are sacred objects or things. Power objects, such as crystals, feathers, and necklaces, are part of the sorcerer's and healer's craft. Some things associated with sacred persons are precious. Without making a judgment as to their authenticity, such items include relics of saints, Buddha's tooth housed in a Buddhist temple in Sri Lanka, Christ's crown of thorns preserved in the reliquary at Notre Dame Cathedral in Paris, and his burial shroud at the Turin Cathedral in Italy. Sacred words are primarily chanted or prayed, like "Om," "Hara-Hara," and "Hail Mary"; some are contained in sacred books like the Bible, the Vedas, and the Book of Mormon, which are primarily studied, recited, and proclaimed. In sacred rites the divine is believed to be present. Sacred

Sixteenth-Century Italian Reliquary. The glorification of hierophanies, of sacred things and persons, is very common. Relics associated with saints and martyrs have been highly prized. Venerated objects are preserved in reliquaries such as this one from Italy.

Photo courtesy Museum of Fine Arts, Boston

persons (e.g., cult-religion founders, prophets, priests, sages, and shamans) are vehicles of sacred power or have had profound experiences that serve as models of ultimate human existence.

Is there something precious to you in your experience that you regard as a hierophany? Remember that sacred things are set apart from profane things. The Bible is, for instance, often treated quite differently from other books. It is frequently kept in a special place; in some cases no other book can be placed on top of it. There are Christians who always have a Bible with them and who feel uncomfortable without it. Muslims have a similar reverence for the Koran. Do you wear a medal, carry a rosary, recite a chant or prayer, or have a sacred image that serves as a point of contact with the sacred?

Concluding Remarks

The holy is ultimate and nonordinary. As ultimate, the holy is unconditional and absolute. It is the ground of being, or, in the words of the *Tao Te Ching,* it is "the mother of all things." As unconditional and absolute, the holy is not a thing among things but the source and basis of all things. Ultimacy is the highest conception that we are capable of—a conception that both makes us aware of our finitude and gives our lives significance. As Dag Hammarskjöld wrote, "How insignificant is everything else, how small are we—and how happy in that which alone is great."[31] The holy is an ultimate value by which all life is judged. All that is conditioned and relative stands in relationship to it.

As nonordinary, the holy is an impenetrable mystery and majestic power. The numinous or affective quality of the holy has moved some people to dance and sing and others to meditate quietly and passively. As nonordinary, the holy attracts and repels. Its fascinating majesty and even its awesome destructiveness have the power to transfix or to compel. It can be experienced as an unspeakable bliss or as a terrifying power that is approached in fear and dread.

Paradoxically, the sacred is a nonordinary power that is, nevertheless, known in human experience. It is a mysterious yet manifest presence. The holy is thus near and present in concrete hierophanies of time and place, beings and things, yet at the same time the holy is infinitely removed and nonordinary. It is subjective and inward, yet objective, external, and transcendent. Martin Buber wrote, "God is the 'wholly Other'; but He is also the wholly Same, the wholly Present. Of course He is the *Mysterium Tremendum* that appears and overthrows; but He is also the mystery of the self-evident, nearer to me than my I!"[32]

Notes

1. Nikos Kazantzakis, *The Saviours of God,* trans. by Kimon Friar (New York: Simon and Schuster, 1960), p. 101.

2. In John Mbiti, *African Religions and Philosophy* (New York: Praeger, 1969), p. 31.

3. John G. Niehardt, *Black Elk Speaks: Being the Life Story of a Holy Man of the Oglala Sioux* (New York: Pocket Books, 1972), p. 39.

4. *The Bhagavad Gita,* trans. by Franklin Edgerton (New York: Harper Torchbooks, 1964), p. 56.

5. Paul Tillich. *The Shaking of the Foundations* (New York: Scribner's, 1948), p. 57.

6. Paul Tillich, *Dynamics of Faith* (New York: Harper Torchbooks, 1957), p. 106.

7. Mircea Eliade, *Patterns in Comparative Religion,* trans. by Rosemary Sheed (New York: World, 1963), p. 459.

8. John E. Smith, *Experience and God* (London: Oxford University Press, 1968), p. 60.

9. Rudolf Otto, *The Idea of the Holy,* trans. by John W. Harvey (New York: Oxford University Press, 1958) p. 6.

10. Ibid., pp. 12–19.

11. William James, *The Varieties of Religious Experience* (New York: New American Library, 1958), p. 67.

12. *The Cloud of Unknowing,* trans. by Ira Progoff (New York: Julian Press, 1961), p. 62.

13. 1 Corinthians 13:12.

14. *The Wisdom of Laotse,* trans. and ed. by Lin Yutang (New York: Random House, 1948), p. 41.

15. Acts 2:24.

16. Blaise Pascal, *Pensees,* trans. by W.F. Trotter (New York: Random House, 1941), p. 182.

17. *The Bhagavad Gita,* p. 55.

18. Ibid., pp. 56–57.

19. Otto, *The Idea of the Holy,* chapter 6.

20. *The Bhagavad Gita,* pp. 57–60.

21. Deuteronomy 6:4–5.

22. Psalms 33:8–9.

23. Eliade, *Patterns in Comparative Religion,* pp. 29–30.

24. W. Brede Kristensen, *The Meaning of Religion* (The Hague: Martinus Nijhoff, 1960), pp. 16–18.

25. Eliade, *Patterns in Comparative Religion,* p. 1

26. 2 Samuel 6:6–8.

27. Carlos Castaneda, *The Teachings of Don Juan* (Berkeley: University of California Press, 1968), p. 91.

28. Eliade, *Patterns in Comparative Religion,* p. 12

29. Abraham Heschel, *The Sabbath* (New York: Farrar, Straus and Young, 1951), pp. 10–19.

30. In Vine Deloria, Jr., *God Is Red* (New York: Dell, 1973), p. 176.

31. Dag Hammarskjöld, *Markings,* trans. by Leif Sjoberg and W.H. Auden (New York: Knopf, 1964), p.161.

32. Martin Buber, *I and Thou* (New York: Scribner's, 1958), p. 79.

Photo by Ernst Haas, Magnum Photos

PART II
THE CONCEPTUAL
AND RITUAL
DIMENSIONS OF
RELIGION

The definition of religion as a seeking for and responding to what humans experience and conceive of as holy is a useful orientation for a study of religious phenomena. You are now ready to explore the conceptual, ritual, personal, and social dimensions of religious expression. Since saying and doing are the two primary forms of all human expression, religious language and action, including sacred rites, are a good place to begin a study of the forms of religious expression. Part II introduces the conceptual and ritual dimensions through a discussion of religious symbols, language, and rites. Religious language and action differ from other ways of saying and doing in that they are forms of human expression through which humans employ words and gestures to symbolize the ultimate and nonordinary.

Because an understanding of the symbolic or meaning-giving character of human expression is important to a study of the dimensions of religious expression, part II begins with a discussion of the symbolic process and a distinction between symbols that function signally, representationally, and presentationally. Chapter six compares and contrasts three different ways of seeing—the scientific, the aesthetic, and the religious—and identifies the salient features of religious language. Chapter seven concludes the discussion of religious language with the argument that when religious language has the holy as its subject, it should be regarded as story or metaphor rather than as factually descriptive discourse. Chapter seven also includes a discussion of such explicit forms of sacred stories as myth and parable.

Religious expression includes acts that are performed as well as words that are spoken or written. Since ritual is a primary mode of religious action, an analysis of the general features and purposes of holy rites is the subject of chapter eight. The discussion of the ritual dimension concludes in chapter nine with the proposition that just as religious language is a metaphorical discourse that relates humans to the ultimate, sacred rites are best understood as a drama or play through which the participants can experience transformed existence. Chapter nine also analyzes the ritual process and describes different types of sacred rites.

Chapter Five
The Symbolic Process

So, for limited purposes only, let me define religion as a set of symbolic forms and acts that relate man to the ultimate conditions of his existence.

Robert Bellah
Beyond Belief [1]

If religion is, as Robert Bellah suggests, a symbol system that relates human beings to the ultimate conditions of their existence, we can appropriately begin a study of religious expression with an analysis of the symbolic or meaning-giving process. The human world is an interpreted world—a universe of meanings. This is not intended to deny the reality of the world; but "facts" are mute without the human equation—that is, the process of interpretation. In *Breakfast of Champions,* Kurt Vonnegut, Jr. vividly illustrates the role of the symbolic or meaning-giving process:

> *I wrote on the tabletop, scrawled the symbols for the inter-relationship between matter and energy as it was understood in my day: $E=Mc^2$. It was a flawed equation, as far as I was concerned. There should be an "A" in there somewhere for* Awareness *—without which the "E" and the "M" and the "C," which was a mathematical constant, could not exist.* [2]

An uninterpreted world is either a contradiction, like a squared circle, or a silence void of human awareness. To be human is to live in a world of meanings and to play a part in the hermeneutical or interpretive task. Religious discourse and religious actions are significant parts of the effort to make sense out of the human situation. Because symbols are the vehicles of meaning, analysis of them is important to an understanding of religious expression.

Symbols

A word is a symbol, because it stands for its meaning. The sign + is a symbol because it stands for the operation of addition. A lily, in religious art, is a symbol, because it stands for purity. . . . The flag in battle is a symbol, because it stands for the ideals and the honour of the mother country. In theology, the Creed is a symbol, because it stands for a truth which its words cannot completely express.

Mary Anita Ewer
A Survey of Mystical Symbolism[3]

A symbol is something that stands for or points to something else. The symbolic or meaning-giving process is a primary and fundamental activity like eating and drinking. It is such a pervasive and constant activity that it even goes on in our sleep in the form of dreams. A large measure of human behavior involves a symbolic process through which gestures, objects, and words are employed to stand for or conceptualize something other than themselves. For example, the raised arm with the index finger extended is such a common feature of American sports that all but the most culturally isolated know that it signifies "We're number one!" Words are symbolic; thus the word *cup* is not a vessel used for drinking, but is rather a symbol representing the object. The term *holy* stands for that which is ultimate and nonordinary. In the Christian sacrament of Holy Communion, consecrated bread and wine are symbols for Christ's presence.

Words are the vital keys of the symbolic process, the primary vehicles of human communication. In fact, the power to think is rooted in the formation of words; all conceptualization is a form of implicit or explicit speech. Words that are used religiously function normally but must also draw us from our rootedness in the ordinary toward the unconditional. Religious discourse is a way of speaking about the unspeakable—of representing in words that which lies beyond the power of language. The test of all religious symbols is whether they point beyond themselves to the sacred.

The symbolic process is therefore one of perceiving and employing meanings where something represents or is a sign of something else. It is grounded in the complex interaction of experience and the symbols used to stand for the experience. The ways in which a symbol can mean or stand for something else are potentially unlimited. While some symbols are quite familiar, others are unfamiliar or known only by specialists. Most symbols are ambiguous or multivalent—that is, capable of standing for a variety of things—while others have only one meaning. The primary basis for distinguishing between different kinds of symbols is in the relationship of the symbol to the thing symbolized. Symbols are related to the things they signify in three principal ways: they may function signally, representationally, or presentationally.

Symbols as Signs

In scholarly and ordinary language, the term *sign* is employed in different ways. In this context a sign is a condition that is regularly or even causally correlated in experience with something else. Dark clouds, for instance, so regularly remind us of rain that they can be called a natural sign. Ordinarily, signs are not words but rather things, conditions, or events. A sign is not entirely separate from the thing it points to; thus a sign is either causally connected or so regularly symptomatic that its presence, like the presence of dark clouds, signifies something.

The reading of signs is an important part of the symbolic process. The skilled diagnostician is expert in recognizing the presence of a material or mechanical condition as an indicator of a second condition. For the plumber, backed-up water in both a bathtub and a toilet indicates a clogged pipe rather than simply a clogged drain. Likewise, physicians are aided in making diagnoses through the observation of their patients' symptoms.

Are there religious signs—that is, conditions, events, or things in ordinary experience that regularly point to the holy? Signs have a prominent place in the Christian tradition. Christian signs are conceived of as conditions that reveal God's power or indirect presence through his work. In one view, **miracles,** defined as wondrous and mighty acts of God, are vivid signs of God's power that create faith. For example, in the gospel of John, Jesus' transformation of water into wine during the marriage at Cana was understood by his disciples as a sign of God's presence in him. In this sense, a miracle signifies divine power just as a book presupposes an author.

Religious signs are not universal, unlike the regular correlation of dark and cloudy skies with rain. Even within religious communities there is precious little unanimity as to what conditions or activities signal holiness. In the synoptic Gospels, for example, miracles are frequently misunderstood and do not always produce faith. In fact, Jesus condemned those who demanded to see miraculous signs of his authority. Signs, he suggested, do not convince, for if such people "do not hear Moses and the prophets, neither will they be convinced if someone should rise from the dead."[4] For many moderns, it appears that ours is the generation to which, as Jesus said, no signs are given; we live, some say, in a time where the signals of holiness have been nearly extinguished.

In marked contrast to those who see no signs of holiness are those who claim signs are everywhere, if we would but see them. The popularity of Hal Lindsey's *The Late Great Planet Earth* indicates that a sizable number of contemporary Christians are eagerly waiting the return of their Lord. In expectation of Christ's Second Coming, end-of-time– and judgment-day–oriented Christians watch closely the signs that are thought to be indicators of the temporal nearness of their Lord's advent. They believe, in accord with the thirteenth chapter of the Gospel of Mark, that wars, famines, earthquakes, persecution of the righteous, falling stars, and a darkening of the sun and moon are signs that foreshadow the end of Satan's dominion over this corrupt and wicked age.

In addition to miracles and signs of the last days, other phenomena are regarded by some Christians as religious signs: what the New Testament calls **"gifts of the Holy Spirit."** Pentecost is the day on which Christ's disciples received the gift of the Holy Spirit—that is, the spirit of God working in the human heart; Pentecostal or charismatic Christians claim to have been baptized by the Spirit and to have received spiritual gifts. These gifts include such overt powers as healing, prophecy, performance of miracles, and speaking in tongues (glossolalia), as well as more subtle powers, such as wisdom, knowledge, and faith. For Pentecostals, a manifestation of such gifts signals the presence of the Holy Spirit.

Signals of the spirit are not confined to Christendom; **spirit possession** is widespread among tribal faiths. The Western Dinka of the Sudan, for example, honor a divinity, Flesh, who is at once a consuming fire and a source of truth and peace. When Flesh manifests itself in a ritual context, the Dinkas' legs quiver and shake uncontrollably as they are engulfed in trancelike states. While such effervescent outbreaks of the spirit are prized by the Dinka, similar signs or manifestations of spirit possession are often feared by other tribal peoples.

What is a religious sign for one person is often mere foolishness for another; thus religious signs are ambiguous. While Christians imbued with an apocalyptic vision see the signs of the times as indicative of the imminent return of Christ; others, both Christian and non-Christian, consider such a vision as but a mistaken and pitiful cry of those who can deal with the horrors of our age in no other way. Among the Dinka, signs of the presence of divinity are valued, but outsiders may make fun of or fear their trancelike ecstasies.

Representational Symbols

A second type of symbolization is representational or conventional. Signs are closely connected to what they symbolize; in contrast, representational symbols tie together things that are distinct from one another as, for example, an experience and its interpretation, or a symbol and the thing that it symbolizes. Words primarily function representationally—that is, words are separate from the things that they point to and do not participate in or have the qualities of the things they symbolize. For example, the word *fire* signifies heat and flames, but the word itself is not hot. The term *long* is not a long word, nor do the terms *soft* and *rough* have the qualities that they point to or stand for. In addition to words, there are nonlinguistic representational symbols: a flag represents a state or nation; a red traffic light is regularly associated with a command to stop. Of course, not everything is symbolic. A donkey is simply a donkey, but in the context of a political rally it can symbolize the Democratic party.

The connection between representational symbols and the things they symbolize is a matter of customary practice or arbitrary stipulation; thus the meaning of representational symbols is related to their usage. To paraphrase Ludwig Wittgenstein, symbols are dead by themselves, but in their usage they are given life, given meaning.[5] Meanings are dynamic and interchangeable; one meaning can be substituted for another arbitrarily or by shifts in conventional usage. For example, during the war in Vietnam, the forming of the fingers in a V-shape was employed in the peace movement to represent peace; during World War II the same gesture customarily symbolized military victory.

Representational symbols, more than any other form of symbolization, are the primary vehicles of the symbolic process. Representational symbols are indispensable conceptual tools for comparing and analyzing data and formulating arguments. They also represent our feelings, our experiences, our relationships to the world. The ideas that representational symbols convey are instruments through which the conflicts and contradictions of experience are made somewhat coherent and orderly; they help us communicate to others what is going on in our common world.[6] Symbols are like bridges; they not only connect experience to the meaning of experience but also provide passageways through which we can conceptually explore different worlds of meaning. Understanding the symbols of other times and places can provide access to worlds of meaning far beyond our spatio-temporal boundaries.

Conventional religious symbols differ from religious signs in that their connection to holiness is a matter of regular practice or custom rather than a symptomatic or intrinsic connection. A representational religious symbol points beyond itself to the holy it represents and makes communication about sacred subjects possible. For example, the Roman Catholic tabernacle illustrated here includes several important Christian symbols. From very early times, Christian iconography has employed the first and last letters of the Greek alphabet, the *A* and *Ω*, to point to the eternal Christ; the symbols are based on the passage in Revelation in which Christ is identified as the Alpha and Omega, the beginning and the end. At the center of the tabernacle is the cross, the primary symbol of Christianity, bearing the letters IHS, the first three letters of Jesus' name in Greek. The IHS is superimposed on a circle, which symbolizes eternal life and the perfection of God. The doves are at once symbols of the Holy Spirit and of peace; their beaks are dipped into the chalice that is a reminder of the Last Supper and Holy Communion. Together, the circle, the IHS, and the doves represent the essential unity of the trinitarian God as Father, Son, and Holy Spirit.[7]

   Although words that function representationally are the primary conceptual units of religious expression, conventional nonlinguistic religious symbols are also used. In the Buddhist tradition, for example, an eight-spoked wheel symbolizes the Wheel of Dharma (doctrine). The eight spokes

Roman Catholic Tabernacle. Religious symbols are precious cups of meaning that remind believers of important ideas and events. This tabernacle includes several important Christian symbols.

Photo by John Pini

represent the Buddha's teaching of the Noble Eightfold Path. In India a trident (a staff with three prongs) carried by an Indian holy man identifies a devotee of the god Shiva. The Jew covers his head with a hat or skullcap as a reminder of God the Almighty. In these examples the connection between the symbol and the symbolized is rooted in the conventions of their respective religious communities; their power to communicate to people unaware of their meaning is negligible.

One more example can help to clarify the difference between signs and representational symbols. In the book of Genesis, a rainbow is made by God to stand as a sign of a covenant between God and the generations following Noah and his family. Within the story the rainbow signifies for both God and man that "the waters shall no more become a flood to destroy all flesh."[8] In Noah's story the rainbow is used representationally rather than signally for the following reasons: The relationship of the rainbow and the covenant, unlike most signs, is neither natural nor mechanical. Neither is the rainbow a symptom of a covenant, like aching joints can be a sign of arthritis. The connection between the two is intentional. The rainbow did not produce the covenant. It has no association with the covenant unless the rainbow is given such a significance by God, and future rainbows serve only as symbolic reminders of the covenant rather than as signs that causally renew it.

Presentational Symbols

In a third type of symbol, the signification is neither symptomatic, as in signs, nor exclusively representative, as in conventional symbols. A presentational symbol, or what some scholars call an image, is a form of symbolism that participates in or is similar to, but not identical with, the thing symbolized as, for example, a curve painted on a road resembles the curve ahead. Maps are presentational images that on a reduced scale resemble the reality they stand for. In religious studies *icon* and *sacrament* are terms roughly synonymous with what is intended by a presentational symbol or image. Since maps or photographs are similar but not identical with the things they signify, they are sometimes called iconic symbols. However, **icon** also has a more restricted religious meaning and, like **sacrament,** refers to something through which the sacred is present.

A presentational religious symbol—that is, a sacred image or sacrament—is something through which the holy is manifested or made present. Put another way, the holy, rather than being merely represented as in conventional symbolism, participates or is present through the sacrament or sacred image. For instance, members of the Hare Krishna movement believe that in chanting the divine name the devotee directly associates with God. The words of the *Mahamantra,* the great or ultimate chant, are: "Hare Krsna, Hare Krsna, Krsna, Krsna, Hare Hare, Hare Rama, Rama Rama, Hare

Hare.'' The chant is more than a symbolic reminder of Hare Krishna because the divine is believed to be present in the **mantra.** Similarly, in some Hindu and Buddhist practices the chanting of ''Om'' is believed to be efficacious in itself because the sound participates in the sacred energy.

Because images are believed to participate in or evoke the presence of the thing symbolized, they cannot be easily changed or substituted without a loss of meaning. In contrast, conventional symbols are more easily interchanged with synonyms or arbitrarily assigned new meanings. Words, for example, have regularly employed meanings, but they can effectively be given new definitions through a contextual stipulation. The arbitrary or stipulative capacity of words is humorously illustrated by a conversation between Lewis Carroll's Humpty Dumpty and Alice:

> Humpty Dumpty: *There's glory for you.*
> Alice: *I don't know what you mean by glory.*
> Humpty Dumpty: *Of course you don't—till I tell you. I meant, "There's a nice knock-down argument for you."*
> Alice: *But "glory" doesn't mean a "nice knock-down argument."*
> Humpty Dumpty: *When I use a word, it means just what I choose it to mean—neither more nor less.*[9]

Conventional symbols are, of course, not used quite as arbitrarily as Humpty Dumpty suggests, but they are open to different usage because their relationship to the things they represent is a matter of practice. Images are not as interchangeable or arbitrary. For example, the significance of such natural symbols as water and sky is not entirely a matter of conscious choice. Water suggests cleansing, both physical and spiritual; it is an image found in the religious and dream life of almost every culture. Likewise, the height and infinite space of the sky is a natural symbol for the ultimate.

Presentational symbols play an important role in both religion and depth psychology. According to depth psychologists, all human beings possess innate tendencies to form images. Dreams, in particular, harbor such recurring images. Thus the presentational symbols manifested in dreams arise out of a complex interaction of unconscious and conscious elements within personal experience and the surfacing of archetypal or universally shared images that are part of each person's unconscious collective heritage. Rollo May, a humanistic or existential psychotherapist, cited the following dream fragment in his book, *Symbolism in Religion and Literature:*

> *I was sitting at the mouth of a cave, with one foot in and one out. The cave inside was dark, almost black. The floor in the center of the cave was a swampy bog, but it was firm on each side. I felt anxiety and a strong need to get out.*[10]

According to May's analysis, the cave is a womb and vagina symbol that threatens annihilation;[11] it is a dream symbol that does more than represent. It is presentational in that the cave, as an opening, provides a vital and qualitative clue as to its import and is similar to the thing symbolized.

An element in the *Isoma* rite of the Ndembu of northeast Zambia illustrates what is meant by a sacred image. The *Isoma* is performed to remove an ancestral curse or affliction that has nullified a couple's fertility. According to anthropologist Victor Turner, the Ndembu believe that when their ancestors are forgotten or affronted they become troublesome to the living; thus the failure to procreate is viewed as a willful misfortune caused by a spirit of one of the couple's deceased kin. In an initial stage of the ritual, a tribal doctor opens a giant rat's underground home, which the animal has burrowed out and sealed off. The burrow, with its blocked hole, is an image that resembles and embodies the afflicted wife's spiritual or invisible malady, while the opening of the hole, a symbolic opening of the womb, is an important step in providing a remedy. The giant rat is also an image that makes present the spirit who is responsible for the wife's affliction and is addressed accordingly: "Giant rat, if you are the one who kills children, now give the woman back her fertility, may she raise children well."[12]

Presentational symbols resemble, participate in, or make present their signification but are not identical with it. The giant rat is not identical with what it symbolizes; it is a symbolic image rather than an example of the Ndembu's failure to distinguish between a symbol and its import. And yet the image and what it points to are not entirely separable; thus the giant rat is a presentational symbol that makes the immaterial visible, present, and intelligible. The Ndembu's embodiment or envisagement of the transcendent draws the invisible near and is symptomatic of much religious expression.

A symbol is an image or sacrament when the holy is believed to be present through it. It ceases to be an image and becomes a representational symbol when the spirit or sacred presence is no longer visible through it. As sacraments, images are luminous passageways or cracks between the worlds through which the holy is present. If the image is transparent enough, it becomes a mirror through which the divine is seen. An image is always something more than words and gestures; it is a presence. Jesus' proclamation, "I am the way, the truth, and the life,"[13] is an image in the sense that his being is inseparable from his message. Christ is present in the message. It is through images and sacraments, Thomas Merton wrote, "that man enters affectively and consciously into contact with his own deepest self, with other men, and with God."[14]

Religious traditions are a storehouse of sacramentals or **yantras**— that is, instruments through which the holy breaks into the ordinary; thus sacred sounds and words (mantras, scriptures), sacred pictures (icons,

mandalas), sacred gestures and postures (**mudras,** asanas), and sacred objects (sacramentals, fetishes), are believed to evoke or manifest a holy presence in a proper ritual context. For example, innumerable sacred sounds or mantras, including chants, curses, shouts, and songs, are believed to evoke a nonordinary presence. Divine names, as in the *Mahamantra,* are images for those who believe that holy power is evoked by the name. Similarly, some Christians believe that demons can be exorcised by calling upon Christ's name. In the Bhagavata Purāna, even the calling of the sacred name in ways that are not intentionally religious can bring divine grace; thus the saying of the Lord's name forgives sin no matter why or how it is uttered.[15]

Pictorial images (paintings and sculpture) have also played an important role in a number of religious traditions. The circle, an image of wholeness, is a frequent motif. In Buddhism and Hinduism, a sacred image called a mandala is sometimes employed in meditation. The circular form of the mandala is believed to be a microcosm of the structure of the universe that can awaken consciousness to an awareness of and participation in cosmic reality. Icons, from the Greek *eikon,* image, are revered in the Greek or Eastern Orthodox Christian church. Icons are pictures, usually painted on wood, that represent the venerated figures of Christ, the Blessed Virgin Mary, or a saint. The icon is more than a vehicle for edification or instruction. Unlike ordinary paintings, an icon is afforded such marks of veneration as kisses and genuflexions because, in Eastern Christendom, the icon is sacramental; thus if it is luminous enough the divine can be seen in and through it. The icon can be, like the seven sacraments of the Roman Çatholic faith, a channel or instrument of divine grace.

In an Ndembu ritual context, almost every gesture employed, every song or prayer, every unit of space and time, by convention stands for something other than itself. It is more than it seems, and often a great deal more. The Ndembu are aware of the expressive or symbolic function of ritual elements.

Victor W. Turner
The Ritual Process[16]

The Symbolism of Religious Rites

Because the belief that presentational symbols are so fused to the things they symbolize that they can actually be a vehicle of a sacred presence is so crucial to an understanding of religious symbolism, we should distinguish between rites thought of as representational and those that are believed to be presentational. Where rituals are understood representationally, the holy is not believed to be present in the rite, and the ritual elements (gestures, words, objects) serve only as symbols of inward changes or as reminders and commemorations of the exemplary and normative acts performed by a people's venerated or sacred predecessors. In contrast, the presentational view of ritual maintains that in some holy rites the thing symbolized is not simply pointed to, as in representational acts, but is actually present to the worshippers through the symbol. Image and icon are terms often used to stand for presentational symbolism, but because in practice they have been more narrowly associated with the signification of words and paintings, they are not entirely suited to stand for the symbolic import of rites. Sacrament is a preferable designation for those rites in which the sacred is believed to be present. Icons and images are something to look at or through, whereas sacraments are something done or performed.

Baptism as a Presentational Symbol

The distinction between ritual as a sacramental presence and as a symbolic representation is illustrated by two quite different conceptions of Christian baptism. While most Christian groups practice baptism, they are deeply divided over its timing (infant or adult baptism), its form (sprinkled with or immersed in water), its efficacy (what it does, if anything), and its nature (sacrament, ordinance, or memorial). As a sacrament, baptism, like the other Christian sacraments, is an act of God, and the Christian sacraments are an objective and material expression of God's presence— vehicles through which his work of redemption or salvation is exercised. In the sacraments, spiritual reality is embodied in a material form in a manner analogous to God's incarnation or enfleshment in Christ. Baptism is thus a visible and dramatic performance through which God's grace is conveyed in the material element of water and in the repetition of the triple formula, "I baptize you in the name of the Father, the Son, and the Holy Spirit."

Viewed as a sacrament, baptism, like the *Isoma* rite of the Ndembu, does something. It is believed to work in several ways: Through the ritual, the initiate's sins are washed away and the process of growing in Christian living is initiated. Baptism changes the celebrant's status in respect to God and the Christian community; thus through the ritual, God's redeeming grace is mediated, and the initiate is incorporated into the church. Some believe that the rite makes inclusion in God's eternal kingdom possible. Baptism is also said to resemble Christ's burial and resurrection. As Christ was buried, so also is the initiate symbolically buried in the water. As Christ arose, so also the Christian arises, through baptism, to a new life; thus in the sacrament, the Christian participates in or becomes one with Christ.

Baptism as a Representational Symbol

In contrast to the sacramental view of baptism is the conviction, shared by some Protestants, that baptism is an outward symbol representing an inward change rather than a vehicle through which God's grace and presence is mediated. As a presentational symbol or sacrament, baptism is believed to bring about the incorporation of the initiate into the body of Christ. Protestants who reject this focusing of the divine presence in the material and visible elements of the ceremony insist that the water and triple baptismal formula are symbolic of an inward change and do nothing, in themselves, to change the communicant's relationship to God.

Protestants who reject the sacramental understanding of baptism believe that God is primarily present through the preaching and hearing of his word as revealed in the Bible. For them the revealed word, rather than the embodied rite, is the chief instrument of salvation. Words are addressed to minds and hearts; thus salvation is accomplished by a conscious response to Christ rather than through ritual acts. Not surprisingly, then, the focus of most Protestant services is on the reading of the Scripture and the preaching of the word.

The argument that religious rites are only symbolic representations is exemplified in an emphatic rejection of infant baptism by some Protestant bodies. They do not view the baptismal rite as an objective vehicle of salvation; its meaning is the primary justification for its performance. The decisive moment comes at the point of making a decision for Christ. This a baby cannot do, and thus, the argument goes, baptism must be deferred until the person is aware of what the rite signifies. The emphasis on conscious commitment indicates that baptism is not valuable for what it does; its meaning counts the most. In one approach it is primarily a memorial service following the example of Christ's baptism. Baptism strengthens, through reflection, the initiate's resolve to live the Christian life. It also stands as a symbolic representation of an inward change. Where baptism is considered a representational symbol, its importance is diminished, and in some cases the rite is dispensable.

In other Christian bodies, such as the Roman Catholic, the Eastern Orthodox, the Episcopal, and the Lutheran, infant baptism is practiced. In these churches baptism is a sacrament that works as well as signifies. They believe that the infant, though unaware of the meaning of the rite, becomes incorporated into the invisible body of Christ and into the Church as the visible body of Christ; thus in spite of the absence of understanding, something happens to the infant in baptism that is subsequently deepened and brought into consciousness through the child's spiritual growth.

Presentational Symbols: Linguistic Confusion, Magic, Idolatry, or Sacrament?

From one religious perspective, images or sacraments border either on idolatry, the treating of a symbol as the holy it represents rather than as a yantra or instrument through which the holy is manifested, or magic, the

Baptism as Sacrament. Through water and the baptismal formula, a Catholic priest incorporates an infant into the Church, which represents the body of Christ.

Photo by Eve Arnold, Magnum Photos

belief that ritual acts are sufficient in themselves to control sacred power and bring about the desired results. The association of pictorial and sculpted figures, for example, with idolatry undergirds the biblical injunction to neither make nor worship images or likenesses; thus Judaism, Islam, and much of Protestant Christianity have been primarily traditions of holy words (Torah, Koran, and Bible) and have been inhospitable to or uncomfortable with representational art. As noted earlier, in the magical world view, curses and incantations are believed to be effective because they are vehicles of sacred power. Sorcerers believe that they can manipulate this power through a command of charms or spells.

In addition to reservations about the sacramental perspective from within religious traditions, modern scholars and philosophers have argued that the belief in presentational symbols stems from a failure to distinguish between symbols and the things they point to or stand for. They view the presentational or sacramental perspective as a legacy of a tribal wonder that experiences the world as filled with spirits. The disenchantment or desacralization of the modern world is, in part, a function of perceiving that the symbolism of rites and words are representational—a matter of convention rather than a sacred presence.

The argument that the sacramental viewpoint reflects a linguistic confusion has influenced the modern religious consciousness. Icons, images, and sacraments—in short, those things that were formerly believed to mediate holiness—are shunted aside by many moderns as magical, idolatrous, or linguistic confusions; they favor a direct personal relationship between the individual and ultimate existence. Some Protestant Christians, for example, reject the view that God's grace can be mediated through the ritual process and insist that the separation of the divine and the human can be bridged only through personal faith.

The problem, however, with **iconoclasm**—the opposition to icons or images—and the antisacramental point of view is that in warring against idolatry and magic, these critical stances also tend to force the holy out of the ordinary altogether. The insistence that religious symbols are representational rather than presentational and the substitution of personal encounters for mediated salvation have tended to secularize and desacralize the world. When this happens, holy things, places, persons, or rites—situations in which humans find themselves on holy ground—tend to be obscured or to disappear altogether. To say that there are no images or sacraments is, in a sense, to say that there are no openings, no places where the holy can enter the world. The holy is eclipsed when its symbols are powerless.

The Symbolic Context and Religious Expression

The meaning of a word is its use in the language.

Ludwig Wittgenstein
Philosophical Investigations [17]

In a study of religious expression, we must understand the character of symbols because they are the irreducible units of the symbolic or meaning-giving process. This understanding, however, is just an initial step. We need to consider the relationship of the symbolic context to religious expression. Speech, body movement, and natural and created things are vehicles of meaning, but what makes a gesture, a word, or a thing religious? Susanne K. Langer, a philosopher, makes the point that probably no human expressions are exclusively or universally religious. She writes, "Religion is a gradual envisagement of the essential pattern of human life, and to this insight almost any object, act, or event may contribute. . . . Sacred objects are not intrinsically precious, but derive their value from their religious use."[18]

Words, for example, can be employed for very different purposes. Ordinarily, father and son are terms representing a parent/child relationship. In the Christian sacrament of baptism, the same two words are incorporated in the baptismal formula, "I baptize thee, in the name of the Father, Son, and Holy Spirit," and they are made to point to a filial relationship in the

Godhead. The reverse is also true—that is, words or expressions with the most obvious religious connotations can be used in a nonreligious sense. Jesus Christ may be an epithet, a swear word, or the name by which the holy is known. In a magico-religious context, incantations and curses may be powerful formulas, but in a nonbelieving context they may appear empty and ludicrous.

Basically the same kind of analysis applies to acts. Their meaning is contextual; thus the same physical movement can in one situation be a holy act and, in another context, lack religious significance. Acts are expressive independent of words, but their meaningfulness arises only in a symbolic context. The placing of the right hand over the heart during a recitation of the Pledge of Allegiance stands for a posture of patriotic respect; a similar gesture in a physician's office may signal a physical problem. In the Christian faith, the movement of the right hand from forehead to chest and then from shoulder to shoulder is known as the sign of the cross. In Catholic, Anglican, and Eastern Orthodox practice, the gesture sanctifies facets of daily life, just as prayer at meal times is believed to hallow eating. In contrast, some Protestant Christians who regularly pray before eating condemn the sign of the cross as a magical practice, which the devotee mistakenly assumes will bring good fortune and protection. For non-Christians the same gesture may suggest entirely different meanings. The meaning of an act is thus influenced by the circumstances in which it is performed.

Like words and gestures, natural and created things serve as symbolic devices and are an important part of religious expression. Like all symbols, their significance is contextual. Colors, for example, can have religious connotations. In the West, light colors are usually associated with positive, pleasant things and dark colors with sad, undesirable things. Christians associate white with the purity of the Virgin, who is believed to have conceived the Christ child without sin; in Christian liturgy, white is the color that accompanies the celebration of Christ's birth and symbolizes, during Easter, his innocent suffering. For Westerners, black has signified death, misfortune, grief, and evil. In contrast, the Chinese symbolize grief and death with white as well as black and oppose both colors with red, the Chinese symbol of joy. In India the blackness of the female goddess, Kali, is not so much a symbol of her destructiveness as an indication of the divine energy that is formless and colorless; thus blackness or darkness symbolizes the dissolving of distinctions. Among some African peoples, black is associated with grim things and white with purity, good health, and fortune; however for the Konso of Ethiopia black symbolizes health and white is inauspicious.[19]

If things are religious in a symbolic context, how are such ordinary acts as eating, drinking, dancing, laughing, sitting, and washing transformed into holy acts? What constitutes a religious use of language and enables natural things like water or sky and created things like a mandala or a cross to signify or manifest holiness?

Religious expression is here understood as discourse and behavior concerned with the relationship of human experience to the ultimate and nonordinary; thus things are religious by virtue of their association with the holy. Religious language (the spoken and written word), religious acts (what one does), and religious things (sacred objects), are expressions of aspects of human experience in which sacredness is present. In this sense all religious expressions are double-intentional—that is, they are said or performed in the context of the finite world but, as Christian theologian Langdon Gilkey argued, intended to point beyond the ordinary "to the dimension of sacrality, of infinity, ultimacy and unconditionedness, to a holy that is manifest in and through the finite medium."[20]

Concluding Remarks

Since symbols are the vehicles of meaning for all human expression, including religious expression, an understanding of the symbolic process is important to the study of religion. Symbols are related to the things they symbolize signally, representationally, and presentationally. Signs are symbols in which a condition is a symptom of something else (e.g., dark clouds signal the possibility of rain). There is much disagreement as to what constitutes a religious sign. In some cultures, for example, a trance may be evidence of spirit possession; in another context a trance may be regarded as symptomatic of a form of schizophrenia. Like humorist Woody Allen, many moderns desire a sign, some assurance of the reality of holy being. "What if everything is an illusion and nothing exists?" Allen asks rhetorically and answers, in a splendid juxtaposition of an ultimate with an instrumental concern, "In that case I definitely overpaid for my carpet. If only God would give some clear sign! Like making a large deposit in my name in a Swiss bank."[21]

Representational symbols, unlike signs, are related to what they symbolize by practice or convention rather than by the regular association of one set of conditions with another. Much religious expression is representational. In Christian iconography, for example, the peacock has been used to symbolize paradise. Since the connection between them is not natural or necessary, the association of the peacock with paradise is a conventional one. In fact, this convention, for the most part, is no longer part of contemporary Christian symbolism.

In contrast to conventional symbols, presentational symbols participate in or make present the thing they symbolize. Presentational religious symbols are vehicles through which the holy is made present or manifest.

When religious symbols (words, gestures, things) function representationally, they are employed as a way of pointing beyond themselves to the holy. When they function presentationally or sacramentally, they serve as a way through which the sacred is made present. The same symbol may be representational in one context and presentational in another. In one Christian context baptism is a representational rite that is performed because of Christ's example and to signify an inward change. In a sacramental context, however, the same elements and words are believed to facilitate spiritual birth and manifest a sacred presence. Anything can serve as a symbol of holiness because, as Christian theologian John Macquarrie observed, holiness is present in everything. Macquarrie reminds us that "the test of a symbol is its adequacy in lighting up Being."[22]

Notes

1. Robert Bellah, *Beyond Belief* (New York: Harper & Row, 1970), p. 21.

2. Kurt Vonnegut, Jr., *Breakfast of Champions* (New York: Dell, 1973), p. 241.

3. In Philip Wheelwright, *The Burning Fountain* (Bloomington: Indiana University Press, 1959), p. 19.

4. Luke 16:31.

5. Ludwig Wittgenstein, *Philosophical Investigations* (New York: Macmillan, 1953), p. 20e.

6. See Langdon Gilkey, *Naming the Whirlwind: The Renewal of God-Language* (Indianapolis, Ind.: Bobbs-Merrill, 1969), p. 269.

7. For understanding Christian symbols, consult George Ferguson, *Signs and Symbols in Christian Art* (New York: Oxford University Press, 1971).

8. Genesis 9:15.

9. Lewis Carroll, *Through the Looking Glass* (New York: Avenel Books), pp. 123–24.

10. Rollo May, *Symbolism in Religion and Literature* (New York: George Braziller, 1960), p. 14.

11. Ibid.

12. Victor Turner, *The Ritual Process* (Chicago: Aldine, 1969), pp. 20–22.

13. John 14:6

14. In Joseph Campbell, *Myths to Live By* (New York: Viking Press, 1972), p. 257.

15. In William de Bary, *Sources of Indian Tradition* (New York: Columbia University Press, 1958), p. 338.

16. Turner, *The Ritual Process,* p. 15.

17. Wittgenstein, *Philosophical Investigations,* p. 20e (43).

18. Susanne K. Langer, *Philosophy in a New Key* (New York: Mentor Books, 1964), p. 136.

19. Raymond Firth, *Symbols: Public and Private* (Ithaca, N.Y.: Cornell University Press, 1973), p. 68.

20. Gilkey, *Naming the Whirlwind,* p. 291.

21. Woody Allen, *Without Feathers* (New York: Random House, 1975), p. 6.

22. John Macquarrie, *Principles of Christian Theology,* 2nd ed. (New York: Scribner's, 1977), pp. 142–43.

Chapter Six
Three Ways of Seeing and Speaking

> *. . . to speak of "the religious perspective" is, by implication, to speak of one perspective among others. A perspective is a mode of seeing . . . a particular manner of construing the world, as when we speak of an historical perspective, a scientific perspective, an aesthetic perspective, a common-sense perspective, or even the bizarre perspective embodied in dreams and in hallucinations.*
>
> Clifford Geertz
> *"Religion as a Cultural System"*[1]

An understanding of symbols clears the deck for a consideration of ways in which humans know and speak about their world. We need to place discussion of religious expression in a context that allows comparisons to other modes of expression, including art and science. The way people know or see their world is closely related to the way they speak about it. The rational-empirical method of science, for example, calls for descriptive and matter-of-fact language, while the revelatory and intuitive character of religious belief is clothed in more indirect and paradoxical language.

Before examining the scientific, aesthetic, and religious ways of seeing and speaking, we need to say something about a philosophical approach to religion. Philosophy of religion is the branch of philosophy that critically examines religious ways of knowing, speaking, and believing. Philosophers of religion are particularly interested in a rational scrutiny of those religious beliefs that make assertions about what is real **(metaphysics)** and what can be known **(epistemology).** Since this chapter is concerned with seeing, speaking, and knowing, we begin with distinctions that philosophers have made between the words *know* and *believe.*

For the eighteenth-century German philosopher Immanuel Kant, knowledge is that which cannot be reasonably doubted or supposed false; thus to say that ''I know'' something to be the case indicates that I am aware of its truth both subjectively and objectively. Even if there may be reasonable grounds for belief, what is believed cannot be objectively demonstrated to be true. If the terms *knowledge* and *belief* are understood in this fashion, all talk about the holy, because it points to something **transempirical,** is a form of belief rather than of knowledge. Since scientific statements can be verified on objectively sufficient grounds, it is philosophically more appropriate to speak of scientific knowledge and religious belief.

Because speaking of aesthetic perception might imply that there is a unique aesthetic way of knowing, the term *seeing* is used here as a substitute for knowing, believing, and perceiving. Seeing can be understood as direct perception or, in a more extended sense, as a way of apprehending, organizing, or understanding what is experienced. In the latter sense, ways of seeing are perspectives or models that are not so much true or false as they are useful or useless as tools for organizing and understanding human experience. This conception of ways of seeing as a model or perspective for organizing and interpreting experience can be applied to the scientific, aesthetic, and religious ways of appropriating the world without prejudice as to whether what is seen is knowledge or belief.[2]

. . . religion, when it is being examined within the framework of science, is dealt with as part of the natural world, subject to the laws of cause and effect and the rules of logic.

J. Milton Yinger
Sociology Looks at Religion [3]

The Scientific Way of Seeing and Speaking

The scientific way of seeing and speaking has profoundly influenced and shaped the modern consciousness. The spectacular success of the sciences has provided a body of knowledge with unparalleled technological application. Applied science has been instrumental in harnessing new sources of power and in providing much of the material well-being of modern societies.

The scientific revolution has had enormous impact on religion; humans seek control and mastery of their environment through scientific knowledge. Sir Francis Bacon's aphorism that knowledge is power might be modified to read that scientific knowledge is the most marvelous of all power—the power to predict and control. The theoretical, predictive, and technological achievements of science have fostered the judgment that the only legitimate way of validating observations about matters of fact is through science. Contemporaries want their beliefs, like their medicines, to be laboratory tested, and they are acutely aware that scientific explanations and methods offer alternatives to traditional beliefs and practices. In such a milieu the value of religious activities can appear problematic and inconsequential when compared to the products that result from science.

The Rational-Empirical Method of Science

Science is an umbrella term for the natural sciences (physics, chemistry, geology, astronomy, biology), the behavioral sciences (anthropology, psychology, sociology), and the social sciences (economics, cultural geography, history, politics). It encompasses all those disciplines and subject fields, including the academic study of religion, that employ a rational-empirical method in pursuit of knowledge. The **empirical** character of science requires that its conclusions be supported and tested by controlled observation. Scientific observation requires careful and precise notice of things and the collection of data for critical analysis. Science is rational as well as empirical in that scientists analyze empirical data in order to work out the logical or formal relationships implicit in their concepts and theories.

While all the sciences work within a rational-empirical rather than intuitive or revelatory framework, their techniques for sorting out what is accepted or rejected varies according to the discipline. For example, where possible, scientists are experimental—that is, they manipulate conditions in order to have control over the variables that might affect their experiments. Ideally, experiments can be repeated by other research scientists with like results. Some sciences, however, are more theoretical than experimental. In astronomy, for example, the phenomena to be observed or, in some cases, inferred are not experimentally controllable. When an experimental design is impossible, other techniques may be employed, such as detailed observation and description, field studies, surveys of self-responding subjects, and analysis of data in order to isolate variables of agreement and disagreement.

Although in this text history is classified with the social sciences, we should note that its nonexperimental and nonpredictive character has prompted some scholars to argue that history is one of the humanities rather than a science. History is treated here as a scientific activity because it rests on empirical evidence (the data and artifacts of history) and explains the relationship of one set of events to another through natural rather than supernatural explanations. Because historical studies have contributed so much of what humans know about religion, the distinction between historical methods of validation and that of the other sciences deserves special attention.

History is a study of the human past. The materials of history are artifacts (especially literary artifacts like diaries, official records, reminiscences, and letters) that serve as evidence for the reconstruction of the past. With the exception of archeology, some anthropological studies, and inferential studies from natural objects, such as historical geology, the other sciences have as their object the natural and social worlds as they are present to the researcher directly or indirectly through controlled observation. Verification in the nonhistorical sciences is the result of observation and experimentation; theories, in principle, can be repeatedly tested with like results. The verification of research in the behavioral sciences, for example, is related to the reliability and validity of its measuring instruments (e.g., control groups, inventories, testing). Unlike the research designs possible in some of the other sciences, historical events are nonrepeatable. History is thus recreated, not by repeating experiments in a laboratory nor by interviewing or testing self-responding subjects, but by the ability of the historian to reconstruct the past.

Natural scientists seek to explain a particular event as an instance of a universal law. The fall of a tree in a forest is subsumed under the general law of gravity. Behavioral scientists seek to understand the general principles of human behavior. Historians, in contrast, do not ordinarily explain historical events by reference to a body of general laws because each historical moment differs from any previous situation. Since the assassination of Abraham Lincoln was a unique event, historical explanation of it calls for more complete detail rather than the reference to a general theory of assassination. An understanding of John Wilkes Booth within the context of the Civil War is a more typical historical approach than is an attempt to see Booth in the light of similarities to Lee Harvey Oswald.

Scientific knowledge is cumulative. Current research builds on previous work; thus the explanatory and predictive uses of science are extended. History is not cumulative in the same sense. Although the past does not change, its meaning for us undergoes continuous revision. Human history must be written again and again, not simply because new materials force new understandings, but because the past is continually reevaluated from the present. History teaches, but what it teaches is partly tempered by the context in which the historian works.[4]

Religious phenomena can be studied scientifically—that is, through the methods of historians and social scientists. A scientific study locates religion in the context of the observable and knowable things of this world. It is concerned with carefully describing and analyzing what humans do when they perform religious acts. Perhaps some examples might provide a clearer conception of how religion can be studied scientifically. Sociologists of religion have made several efforts to measure religion as a dimension of public life in order to understand the relationship of religion to society. Church membership and frequency of attendance, for instance, have often served as gauges of the relative strength of religion in American culture. Such objective information may suggest some interesting parallels between the relative strength and stability of the churches and the larger society of which they are a part. How, for instance, are church attendance and financial support affected by division and disorder in the nation? In addition, religion is an object of historical research. Since religion is not so much something in general as it is something in particular, history is an invaluable way of reconstructing, as faithfully as possible, the unique character of each religion.

The Language of Science

The language of the sciences primarily addresses matters of empirical fact. In addition to their descriptive work, natural scientists seek to formulate laws or theories that serve as general explanations of the ways in which the world of nature works; behavioral and social scientists attempt to discover the general principles or uniformities that are operative in the human world. Scientists describe and explain such diverse phenomena as the relationship of the moon to the tides, the structure of atoms, the relationship of the heart to blood circulation, the causes of World War I, and the history of religion.

Because scientists strive for objectivity—that is, a commitment to let the evidence speak for itself—they often employ impersonal and unemotional language. Frequently, they seek to formulate their discourse in mathematical equations or to reduce the subjects of their discourse to logical relationships, such as, What steps are necessary for verifying that x was caused by y? While scientists often state their propositions in flat, matter-of-fact tones, historical narratives and psychosocial studies are much livelier because they must take account of human intention.

Although scientists use language to ask questions and point out formal or logical relationships, scientific statements usually provide information or knowledge about the world. For instance, the proposition, Salamanders are amphibians, provides information about the ability of salamanders to live in water and on land and, as is the case for all informative propositions, is either true or false. Since cognitive or informative statements are either true or false, we can appropriately ask how they are validated or verified. Science is a mode of discourse that insists on empirical verification of its cognitive claims; thus propositions are empirically verified through systematic observation rather than by proofs derived from logical necessity or by an appeal to sacred scripture.

Scientific Discourse and Religious Language

As indicated, the scientific way of seeing and speaking provides knowledge or information about the world. It has, as its guiding principle, systematic and dispassionate description of the world and the construction of formal models that parallel the relationships operative in the natural and social worlds. It also demands that its propositions and models be empirically verifiable. The cognitive character of scientific discourse raises the question of whether religious statements provide information or knowledge about the world, and, if they do, how they are validated. At least superficially, religious statements appear to provide knowledge about what is real. For example, the Hindu teaching that souls are eternal is assertive, as is the Buddhist doctrine that denies the reality of personal immortality. The statement, I believe in God, assumes that there is something to which the word God applies. The Muslim confession of faith, "There is no God but Allah, and Muhammad is his prophet," declares not only that there is a God but that Muhammad has a prophetic relationship to him.

For those who take such affirmations seriously, they are not mere **psychisms** intended only to express human feelings or prompt certain attitudes. They are assertions about reality. Nevertheless, the validation of the cognitive claims of religious statements presents serious problems. In fact, the philosophical point of view known as logical positivism or logical empiricism regards all talk about God, Tao, and such ineffable religious experiences as nirvana to be cognitively meaningless, since such talk refers to things that cannot be empirically verified. How, for example, is the proposition that God exists, to be verified, since it is neither empirically verifiable nor true by definition? The positivist's solution is to argue that religious language is emotive rather than cognitive, an expression of feelings and psychic needs. In this view, while the assertion that God exists appears to be an informative statement, it is better understood as an emotive utterance or a statement of value rather than a statement of fact.

Because the rules of evidence operative in scientific methods of validation are not readily applicable to truth-claims regarding what a person or a people regard as holy, philosophers have insisted that religious statements are a form of belief rather than knowledge. Belief statements may be true, but they do not constitute knowledge until the evidence is so conclusive that all reasonable doubt is overcome. Although religionists may acknowledge that theological propositions, such as God exists, are not factually descriptive in the same way that "All crows are black" is, they may want to insist that religious statements do have a **noetic** or cognitive quality that is more than a subjective commitment.

Not surprisingly, in an age that desires a scientific seal of approval, religionists occasionally appropriate the language and methodology of science to demonstrate the truth of their claims. Conservative Christians, in particular, have selectively used the scientific approach to buttress their conviction that the biblical story is either factually descriptive or defensible indirectly through empirical evidence. For example, some biblical archeologists diligently search for Noah's ark in order to corroborate the biblical text, while Christian astronomers attempt to provide evidence of the star that guided the Magi to Bethlehem. Scientists who are biblical creationists examine the fossil record and life's molecular structure in order to prove that the biblical account of creation is more plausible than evolution.

Christians are not alone in seeking the aura of scientific verification. Transcendental Meditation proponents regularly publish data intended to demonstrate empirically that meditation enhances health, and other religionists believe that biofeedback research offers empirical evidence of what sages and yogis have achieved through self-mastery.

The efforts of theologians and committed lay scientists to provide empirical evidence for their faith suggests that, although faith points to a mysterious and nonordinary dimension that is always beyond or something more than argument and evidence, belief in the holy is not unreasonable. Saint Augustine believed that faith seeks understanding; thus the noetic quality of religious language entails reasons, explanations, and evidence for the truth that is proclaimed.

We should note that contemporary behavioral and social scientists have, for the most part, retreated from logical positivism. They may concur that religious statements are beliefs rather than knowledge, but they are less likely to dismiss them as emotive and cognitively meaningless as the positivists do. J. Milton Yinger writes that "social scientists are less prone to assert all that is important about religion is available to the objective observer. This is, after all, an extra-scientific assumption, not itself demonstrable by scientific study."[5]

Limitations of the Scientific Way of Seeing and Speaking

The scientific way of knowing is an incredible human accomplishment. No other approach has proved equally fruitful as a way of understanding our natural and social environments; and yet to remain deaf to other ways of appropriating the world is dehumanizing. The language and method of science, with its emphasis on objectivity, precision, quantification, and empirical verification, needs to be complemented by an openness to expressions of feelings, commitment, and wonder. Science and mathematics may help build skyscrapers, formulate actuarial tables, and send spaceships to the moon, but the language of the heart does not speak in numbers. The scientific mode describes impersonally and objectively what is known and neglects the personal and individual character of existence. Its content is a world known as an object—a world in which feelings and evaluations are secondary.

Implicitly, science involves a commitment to the value of truth; nevertheless, because it is so narrowly circumscribed by adherence to natural explanations and a sticking to the "facts," it is a limited mode of discourse. Science offers information about such vital concerns as the pollution of the environment, the depletion of natural resources, and the magnitude of modern weaponry. It can suggest ways that resources can be conserved or alternatives developed, but on questions of value, of priorities, of choosing between industrial expansion or conservation, polluted or restored environments, an escalated arms race or disarmament, it is silent. Human expression is not exclusively a vehicle for conveying information or stating what is true. Familiarity with other more intuitive, existential, evaluative, and revelatory ways of knowing and speaking offers a corrective to the limits of science.

The language of science describes a natural world, a cosmos, of infinite complexity and intricate interdependence. To ask, What is the ultimate meaning of this complexity, this interdependence? is to transpose scientific discourse into a religious inquiry. Does the universe, as mirrored by science, require a unifying force such as the Tao or a creative intelligence (God) to adequately account for it? Does the design of the cosmos suggest a designer? When such questions are raised, humans have moved beyond the empirical limitations of science in the direction of ultimacy.

I would suggest you teach that poetry leads us to the unstructured sources of our beings, to the unknown, and returns us to our rational, structured selves refreshed. . . . Poetry is a verbal means to a non-verbal source.

A.R. Ammons
"A Poem Is a Walk"[6]

The Aesthetic Way of Seeing and Speaking

The aesthetic mode of perception, its way of seeing, notices things for their own sake rather than for their uses. The aesthetic experience of a landscape is one in which its colors and contours are perceived and valued as they are, without imagining how it could be otherwise or for what purposes such a landscape could be used. While the natural world has been a rich stimulus for aesthetic perception, perception for its own sake is even more evident in art, where poeisis, the making of things for their own sake, is a primary motivation. A painting, for example, is intended to be enjoyed for its internal structure—that is, the relationship of color, shape, and line in a finite space—rather than for either its conceptual significance or its usefulness.

Unlike the scientific approach, which is primarily cognitive, the aesthetic approach concentrates on the richness of perceptual experience. It delights in tonal and visual experiences and is only secondarily concerned with the classification and labeling of aesthetic objects or works of art. Where science adds to knowledge in order to manipulate and control, the aesthetic way of seeing asks us to see or hear the aesthetic object for itself. As art, the aesthetic object is something made in order to be seen (visual arts), heard (auditory arts), or read (literary arts). What art invokes is inseparable from the concreteness of the form itself; thus, a work of art cannot be translated into another form of expression without a loss of its intensity and meaningfulness. For example, the Austrian composer Gustav Mahler believed that his deepest spiritual yearnings could be given only musical expression:

> As long as my experience can be summed up in words, I write no music about it: my need to express myself musically—symphonically—begins at the point where the dark feelings hold sway, at the door which leads into the "other" world—the world in which things are no longer separated by time and space.[7]

While scientific language clearly refers to the natural world, ascertaining the referent of art is much more difficult. Science and mathematics are human creations, but their subjectivity is circumscribed—in the case of science, by the need to correspond empirically to the world of things and, in the case of mathematics, by a rigorous adherence to deductive proofs. There is a givenness to the natural world and a formal necessity to the world of logic and mathematics. Art is a human creation in a much more radical way. It is a created world—a world that has its basis in human experience but that does not lose its significance and value when the artist turns away from the natural world to create new tonal, visual, and conceptual worlds of meaning. Art imaginatively expresses human feelings and human meanings in a way that is always something more than imitative (even a portrait is an interpretation). Since art is rooted neither in the world of nature nor in logical relationships, it is freer to reach to the unknown. Salvador Dali's painting *The Persistence of Memory* illustrates the artist's ability to create new worlds of meaning.

Scientific discourse is informative and therefore true or false, while the language of art, in providing people with opportunities for aesthetic experience, lights up or illuminates existence and thus is more a disclosure of value than a factual description. Art discloses a way of being that is open and

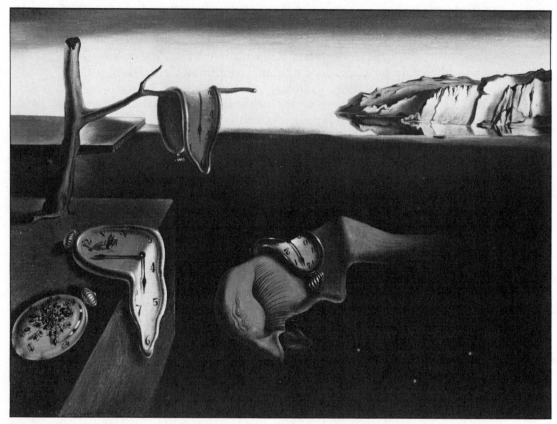

Salvador Dali, The Persistence of Memory. *1931. Oil on canvas, 9½" × 13". In this painting, the artist invites us to step out of our commonsense and scientific worlds into a dream world where chronological time is limp and broken, and space loses its sharp definition and geographical rootedness—a world in which time is unreal and space is infinite.*

Collection, The Museum of Modern Art, New York

sensitive to the natural and created worlds and, in doing so, drives us inward and puts us in touch with our feelings. Art, therefore, gives form to the emotions; it expresses attitudes, feelings, values. Art sensitizes and intensifies human experience. While science generalizes, art illuminates through the concrete and particular. In a few syllables, the Japanese poet, Matsuo Bashō (1643–1694), was able to express his longing to renew irretrievably lost friendships. Returning to Kyoto after a long absence, Bashō recalled the city as he had known it in his youth and the friendships that death had severed:

In Kyō I am,
and still I long for Kyō—
Oh, bird of time![8]

Art can evoke feelings and invites empathetic participation. In this haiku poem, the Japanese poet, Kobayashi Yatarō (1763–1827), who used the pen name Issa, helps us share in the sadness and wonder of growing old:

Now that I am old
Even tender days
of spring
See . . . can make me cry.[9]

Whenever the depths of human feelings are experienced, there is a groping toward the holy; thus some of the most powerful religious statements are expressed through art. Humans question the universe and their questions press beyond the scientific how of things to the why.

Religious language has much in common with the artistic mode. Both are personal rather than impersonal. They are languages of the whole self—heart as well as the head. Religious language, like that of art, is expressive. It can be a language of joyous praise like the Psalmist's invocation to sing a song unto the Lord and to praise God with trumpet, harp, dance, and cymbals; it may express agony and despair, as do Jesus' words from the cross, "My God, my God, why hast thou forsaken me?"[10] Whenever truth, beauty, or goodness are present in and through art, it is already pressing toward the ultimate. Likewise, whenever art cleanses, heals, restores, and sensitizes—in short, whenever it leads us to the ground of our humanity—it is religious.

Religious Ways of Seeing and Speaking

. . . we may define religious language as fundamentally referent to the ultimate, the unconditional, and the holy or sacred as these manifest themselves in human experience.
Langdon Gilkey
Naming the Whirlwind[11]

Religious language is not an exclusive vocabulary or separate language; it is a use of words in a distinctive way. It differs from other modes of discourse in that religious discourse points to the ultimate and nonordinary, whereas a scientific use of language refers to the natural world. Religious language is operative whenever the symbolic process points beyond itself to the ultimate. Four features of religious language are especially important in understanding religious ways of seeing and speaking: it is **double-intentional, paradoxical,** evaluative, and revelatory.

Religious Language as Double-Intentional

Religious language arises out of the human attempt to speak of ultimate existence. It is double-intentional in the sense that humans employ words used to speak of ordinary reality in such a way that they point to a nonordinary reality. If the sacred were entirely like ourselves or other things in the natural world, direct, rather than double-intentional, speech would be possible.[12] If, however, the holy is an ineffable and indefinable mystery that prompts humans to grope for words and symbols that point beyond the limits of language, then religious language must be double-intentional—that is, religious symbols must signify in the way that ordinary symbols do and, at the same time, must illuminate the ultimate as well. The twofoldness of human existence, our rootedness in the ordinary and our restless yearning for the nonordinary, is expressed through double-intentional metaphors. For example, in the Chinese classic, the *I Ching,* humans are seen as middle creatures stationed between heaven and earth. Here, *middle creature* is a double-intentional metaphor because it employs an experience common to all of us

Rock Garden of Ryoanji Temple, Kyoto, Japan. As a double-intentional symbol, the silence and emptiness of a Japanese garden point to something ultimate and nonordinary that lies beyond speech.

Photo courtesy Consulate General of Japan, New York, N.Y.

(that of being in between) in such a way that it points beyond the ordinary to our position in the cosmos. The imagery suggests that as middle creatures we unite in our being heaven and earth. Things can also be double-intentional; thus a Japanese garden, with its meticulously cared-for sand and solitary rocks, is a reminder that insights and transformed existence are manifested in silence.

Jesus was a master of double-intentionality, of talking about God in images of the ordinary. While conversing with a Samaritan (a member of a nonconforming Jewish sect) woman at a well, Jesus used the commonplace thirst for water as a metaphor for a spiritual thirst. In Jesus' metaphor the act of drinking water, which restores life to those who are thirsty, is compared by extension to a water that can forever quench a spiritual thirst. In another context, Jesus spoke of a shepherd's concern for a lost sheep in such a way that it served as an image of God's concern for the spiritually lost.

The language of Zen Buddhism is also rich in double-intentionality. The genius of Zen is that enlightenment or nirvana occurs within the ordinary. The truth of Zen is to be experienced and manifested in every aspect of the practical life; thus the graceful life of Zen is like a simple meal. A Buddhist metaphor compares the nonordinary and sudden character of enlightenment to an unruffled pond into which a frog jumps:

> *The old pond.*
> *A frog jumps in—*
> *Plop!*[13]

Sacred acts, like sacred words, are double-intentional in that they must point to the holy through such familiar activities as eating, drinking, gesturing, and speaking. In sacred rites the commonplace must point in two directions—to itself and beyond itself to the transcendent and enduring. For example, the washing of hands, as a holy rite, must point at once to the here-and-now and to the ultimate. The double-intentional nature of holy rites brings the familiar and habitual in contact with the holy. Holy acts and, in particular, holy rites are moments in which the nonordinary breaks into the ordinary—moments when the tyranny of the trivial is broken.

Religious Language as Paradoxical

Religious language is at least implicitly paradoxical. A paradoxical use of language is one in which contradictions are brought together in such a way that, instead of simply negating each other or becoming an absurdity, they express a profound truth. This paradoxical feature of religious language is amusingly illustrated by a passage from James Weldon Johnson's book *God's Trombones,* a collection of Negro sermons formulated in verse. Johnson told of a preacher who, after reading a rather cryptic Bible passage to his congregation, "took off his spectacles, closed the Bible with a bang and by way of preface said, 'Brothers and sisters, this morning—I intend to explain the unexplainable—find out the undefinable—ponder over the imponderable—and unscrew the inscrutable.' "[14] The preacher's conjoining of opposites is a vivid and explicit use of paradox.

Much of religious language is not, however, explicitly paradoxical. The statements that God exists or that the Noble Eightfold Path leads to enlightenment are not overtly paradoxical. The double-intentionality of the Buddhist Eightfold Path makes an analogy between a path, familiar in ordinary experience, to a spiritual path that leads to nirvana. Systematic analysis cannot completely remove an element of paradox in religious expressions, because sacred words and gestures must mediate between the known and the unknown, the instrumental and the ultimate, the speakable and the unspeakable, the temporal and the durative. The problem in speaking about nirvana is that nirvana is not a place and therefore, strictly speaking, no paths lead to it. Likewise, we are familiar with the existence of things, and the assertion that God exists is grammatically the same as the statement, Trees exist. The difficulty is that God is believed to be the ultimate ground of all things, the presupposition of existence. Can the ground of all things also be a thing?

Invariably, talk about the holy is driven to contradiction and paradox because it must speak of the infinite in terms of the finite. The sacred is always beyond the power of speech and the constrictions of definition, yet the other side of the paradox is that if the holy is to be known at all, it must be present in and through the symbolic or meaning-giving process. Humans and holiness meet in experience, and yet as Dionysus the Areopagite, a fifth-century Christian, wrote, "The simple, absolute and immutable mysteries of Divine Truth are hidden in the superluminous darkness."[15] Religious expression forces language beyond its ordinary uses and employs paradoxical expressions to speak about the unspeakable. Nirvana, for instance, is spoken of as ultimate enlightenment and, paradoxically, as nothingness or no-thing-ness. The *Tao Te Ching,* a classic rich in paradox, says enigmatically that the Tao does nothing, "yet through it everything is done."[16]

The double-intentional and paradoxical character of religious expression can be further illustrated by Abraham Heschel's remarks about the Jewish observance of Sabbath. In the Jewish tradition, Sabbath is a holy day—a day on which God draws near to his creation. Sabbath and Sabbath observance is a reminder of the two worlds, this world and the world to come. In Heschel's commentary, the joy of Sabbath is part of this world, while its holiness and peace are signals of the world to come. He wrote that "the seventh day in time is an example of eternity";[17] thus, paradoxically speaking, in Sabbath observance the eternal is drawn into time.

Religious Language as Evaluative

Religious language focuses on matters of value rather than matters of fact. Evaluative religious discourse is evident in the providing of instructions for living, in making commitments, or in raising questions that require moral or ethical reflection. Ultimate values provide norms by which individual and group life is guided and judged. For example, a Jewish interpretation of the story of creation in Genesis suggests that in the taking of a single human life a whole world is destroyed; killing a person destroys not only a single life but all those that might issue from it. The rabbinical tradition continues, "If anyone saves a single person, Scripture credits him as though he had saved a whole world."[18] The interpretation asks us to be sensitive to the ultimate value of each human life.

Evaluative religious language is often directive—that is, it commands or instructs. Traditionally, sacred duty is not so much reasoned moral deliberation as it is something commanded. The Ten Commandments are in the imperative form of "thou shall" or "thou shall not"; thus they prescribe Sabbath as a holy day and inveigh against adultery, lying, stealing, and murder. In the Gita, Arjuna is pictured as a warrior-prince, who, although obligated to lead his army in battle, was morally troubled because the war that he was to initiate pitted relatives against relatives, countrymen against countrymen. Arjuna told Krishna that he wished neither victory nor the slaying of his enemies. Lord Krishna responded by insisting that Arjuna's duty as a warrior-leader was to commence the struggle. The abandoning of duty, Krishna declared, would only bring evil to Arjuna and his people.[19] The validation of religious directives, sacred duty, is thus usually associated with a divine authority, such as Krishna, or is mediated through a sacred person or holy book. We should note, however, that some people may question and reject traditional authority when it is in conflict with moral reflection or matters of conscience. Certainly much that was traditionally taught concerning the male's spiritual and temporal rule of women has been modified or forthrightly repudiated by modern moral and theological arguments.

Unlike factual assertions, instructions or commandments are not, strictly speaking, either true or false. A more appropriate response to such directives is to question whether they are reasonable or unreasonable, performable or unperformable, legitimate or illegitimate. In the Sermon on the Mount, Jesus instructed his followers to love their enemies. The Buddha directed those who would serve him to do so by nursing the sick. Both assumed that their instructions could be carried out. The question was not whether Buddha's and Jesus' words were true, but whether they should be obeyed.

Evaluative discourse can be performative as well as directive—that is, words can be employed to do something. The taking of an oath, I do solemnly swear, is a thing done and not merely a description of reality. Performative statements change the situation; thus the words, I now pronounce you man and wife, directly change the relationship of the two parties, legally, morally, and perhaps spiritually. Mormons, for example, believe that marriages can be performed that are binding not only in time but for eternity. Since religious vocations require a commitment to a way of life, the context in which the commitment is made usually involves a ceremony in which a performative statement is made. For example, an initiate entering a Buddhist monastic community makes a threefold vow (I take refuge in the Buddha, I take refuge in the Teachings, I take refuge in the Community) in order to effect his or her passage from outsider to insider.

Religious Language as Revelatory

The point has been made that religious language is double-intentional, paradoxical, and evaluative. Religious language is also revelatory— that is, the religious way of seeing and speaking is something that is both a sacred disclosure and an invitation to see and model the social and psychological aspects of human existence in respect to what is ultimately real.

Revelation as Sacred Disclosure

The way the world appears to us is not entirely within our control. This has profound implications for religious ways of seeing and speaking that are more intuitive and revelatory than rational and empirical. From a religious standpoint the sacred is revealed or discerned in manifestations that seem more given than exacted, more waited on and listened for than willed or mastered. In theistic traditions, for instance, God takes the initiative in making himself known; thus he speaks to Moses out of a burning bush and to Job through a whirlwind. The holy can be known in more muted hierophanies. God was revealed to Elijah in "a still, small voice,"[20] and enlightenment, the Zen Buddhist reminds us, can be experienced in everyday activities and in the soft sounds that well up in the silence of meditation. The revelatory character of religious knowledge also implies that religious language is, in some situations, regarded as given rather than as a conscious human creation; thus, for example, the words of Muhammad recorded in the Koran are believed to have originated with Allah rather than with the prophet.

Because revelation and enlightenment cannot be forced, experiences of holiness are usually described as spontaneous, momentary, and self-confirming. The Zen scholar, D.T. Suzuki, described the liberating and revelatory character of satori (enlightenment) as being a moment of direct seeing, an intuitive apprehension, of things as they are. The experience, he insisted, transforms our normal way of seeing so that time and eternity are one.[21] Buddhist monks may spend years preparing for such an experience of ultimacy; a good part of their time may be devoted to controlling their appetites and to countless hours of disciplined meditation. Yet paradoxically, when the unity of being that is satori is experienced, it is abrupt or sudden and, though sought and prepared for, always a joyous surprise and a mysterious and amazing gift.

Revelation as Invitation and Discovery

In one sense, religious ways of seeing and speaking are sacred disclosures, something given; but in a second sense, they are human creations that invite us to discover an emotionally and intellectually satisfying view of life. In this second sense, religious symbol systems are **heuristic** or revelatory models that serve as an invitation to discover and know what is ultimately real. Religious discourse, whether sacred disclosure or conscious creation, is an invitation to discover, as a presupposition of all existence, an ultimate order through which human life can be unified.

As noted previously, science provides a picture of reality by employing symbols to correspond to relationships between entities in the natural world. Religious symbol systems are also models or maps of reality. In this sense, religion, like science, is cognitive—that is, a way of perceiving or knowing. However, scientific and religious knowledge differ profoundly. Scientific knowledge is factually descriptive and empirically verifiable. In contrast, the cognitive claims of religion are not so much about matters of fact as they are heuristic models for discovering what is ultimately real, for shedding light about the whole of existence. Reality isn't just a matter of facts; the manner in which facts are interpreted and the patterns that they are judged to form depend in part on the conceptual models through which they are filtered. Religious ways of modeling or arranging what is known provide a context in which the facts and the ambiguities of human existence are integrated and interpreted.

Religious language counters the fragmentary and commonsense character of what we know with an explanation of the whole of things. Religious models attempt to help us see patterns that are already there, but to which we may have been blind. A story from India illustrates the fragmentary nature of human understanding and suggests what a picture of the whole is like. Several blind men came upon an elephant. One grabbed the elephant's tail, a second felt the tusks, while a third companion caught hold of the trunk. Others busied themselves with the elephant's legs and sides. The blind people attempted to describe what they had ventured upon. None of their descriptions were entirely false, but each was true only up to a point. What they lacked was a vision of the elephant's wholeness. It is a vision of ultimate wholeness—that is, a comprehensive cosmic order—that religious ways of seeing invite us to discover.

As invitation and discovery, heuristic or revelatory religious language is also evident in the way in which religious questions center on things that concern us ultimately. The religious use of the interrogative is a device through which humans question their position in the cosmos. We can, like the biblical Job, take our case to the court of God and ask Why? of the universe. The religious voice can be painfully honest, like that of the psalmist who asked, "Why dost thou stand afar off, O Lord? Why dost thou hide thyself in times of trouble?"[22] The lamentation of the psalmist becomes, by extension, that of all humanity: Why must I suffer and die?

The test of religious questions is not simply whether they are answerable once and for all, but whether they are fruitful—that is, whether they lead from the ordinary to the nonordinary, from the instrumental to the ultimate. Perhaps Zen Buddhism more than any other tradition employs language playfully and humorously in order to serve the business of spiritual liberation. Questions **(koan)** and stories are cleverly used to transform and enlighten one's normal way of looking at things. For example, one Zen saying invites us to reverse our ordinary way of looking at things by suggesting it is the bridge that moves and the water that remains stationary.

Because Zen is so suspicious and critical of doctrinal discourse, it prefers linguistic forms that are enigmatic and revelatory. For example, the koan is a disconcerting form of questioning employed in the Rinzai Buddhist tradition. "What is the sound of one hand clapping?" and "Does a dog have the Buddha nature?" are two well-known examples.[23] Koan are perplexing problems because they are questions for which there are many correct answers but, paradoxically, no single right answer. The aim of these puzzling questions is the cultivation of intuition and insight in preparation for satori, rather than the formulation of correct responses. The instrumental nature of the koan is evident in the thirteenth-century Zen master Ekai's understanding of them as guides: "I meant to use the koan as a man who picks up a piece of brick to knock at a gate, and after the gate is opened the brick is useless and is thrown away."[24]

Koan, in a question and answer form, have been preserved as stories **(mondo)** that serve Zen students in their quest for liberation. Some of these stories invite a direct and intuitive understanding of Buddha's teaching that in the experience of ultimate existence the seeker must light his or her own way rather than look to others, including the Buddha, for deliverance. For example, on one occasion when a monk asked the master Ummon, "What is the Buddha?" he received the reply, "Dried dung."[25] The point of this mondo is that a person must sometimes say "no" to the Buddha in order to become a Buddha or, as another master, Joshu, humorously put it, "Wash your mouth thoroughly if you say 'Buddha.'"[26]

A religious question is unfruitful if it leads to shallowness; in fact, one of the objectives of the koan is to bring Buddhist students to a wariness and distrust of easy answers. Religious questions may be difficult to penetrate, even unanswerable, but they can be fruitful because they are valuable ways of remaining open to the possibilities of ultimate existence.

Like koan and mondo, religious language is often ambiguous, evocative, and contradictory. As revelatory or heuristic, religious language is intended to lure us beyond the fetters of literal-mindedness and the safety of the ordinary to an experience of the sacred. In the introduction to his play, *The Best Man,* Gore Vidal points out the difficulties that the storyteller faces: "It is infinitely harder to ask questions in such a way that the audience is led not to the answers (the promise of the demagogue) but to new perceptions."[27]

Concluding Remarks

Developing a feel for the different ways of seeing and the language appropriate to each is important. As Aristotle wrote in his *Nicomachean Ethics,* "It is the mark of an educated man to look for precision in each class of things just as far as the nature of the subject matter admits. It is obviously just as foolish to accept arguments of probability from a mathematician as to demand strict demonstrations from an orator."[28] Religious and aesthetic ways of seeing cannot obtain the empirical verification nor the formal validity of logic. Of course, their lack of precision and certitude is not an exclusive liability. As William James put it, "Objective evidence and certitude are doubtless very fine ideals to play with, but where on this moon-lit and dream-visited planet are they found."[29]

Religious language is discourse about the ultimate, the ground of all being, rather than something that can be proven through the rational-empirical approach of the sciences. Because Holy Being cannot be known in the same way that things are known, speech about the ultimate is often pressed to the breaking point of intelligibility; thus, religious language is double-intentional, paradoxical, evaluative, and revelatory. Like art, religious language is ambiguous, evocative, even occasionally contradictory. Its symbols are constantly in need of being revitalized and reinterpreted, and yet, in spite of its sometimes confusing imagery, religious discourse and sacramental act continue to manifest the holy.

The revelatory character of religious ways of seeing and speaking is both a disclosure and an invitation. As disclosure, the sacred manifests or reveals itself, and the manner in which it appears or is known is not entirely within our control. As invitation, religious disclosure offers heuristic models or symbol systems through which the sacred can be discovered or seen. Although religious language is not factually descriptive or verifiable through the methods of science, it does provide maps or models that offer a way of seeing, discovering, and knowing what is ultimately real.

Notes

1. Clifford Geertz, "Religion as a Cultural System," in Michael Banton, ed., *Anthropological Approaches to the Study of Religion* (London: Tavistock, 1966), p. 26.

2. Ibid.

3. J. Milton Yinger, *Sociology Looks at Religion* (New York: Macmillan, 1963), p. 12.

4. Allan Nevins, *The Gateway to History* (Garden City, N.Y.: Doubleday, Anchor Books, 1962), p. 33.

5. J. Milton Yinger, *Religion, Society and the Individual* (New York: Macmillan, 1957), p. 3.

6. A.R. Ammons, "A Poem Is a Walk," *Epoch* 18 (Fall 1968): 119.

7. Gustav Mahler, letter to Max Marschalk, quoted in Notes for Mahler's Symphony No. 2 in C Minor by Deryck Cooke, insert for CSA 2217/CMA 7217 Decca Record, Ltd., New York, N.Y.

8. Harold G. Henderson, *An Introduction to Haiku* (Garden City, N.Y.: Doubleday, Anchor Books, 1958), p. 43.

9. R.H. Blyth, *Haiku,* vol. II (Tokyo: Hokuseido Press, 1950), p. 50.

10. Mark 15:34.

11. Langdon Gilkey, *Naming the Whirlwind: The Renewal of God-Language* (Indianapolis, Ind.: Bobbs-Merrill, 1969), p. 295.

12. See Gilkey, *Naming the Whirlwind,* pp. 290–95.

13. R.H. Blyth, *Zen in English Literature* (Tokyo: Hokuseido Press, 1948), p. 217.

14. James W. Johnson, *God's Trombones,* 13th ed. (New York: Viking Press, 1950), pp. 4–5.

15. *Dionysius the Areopagite on the Divine Names and the Mystical Theology,* trans. by C.E. Rolt (New York: Macmillan, 1940), p. 196.

16. *The Wisdom of Laotse,* trans. by Lin Yutang (New York: Random House, 1948), p. 194.

17. Abraham Heschel, *The Sabbath* (New York: Farrar, Straus and Young, 1951), p. 74.

18. Mishnah: Sanhedrin 4:5 in *Likrat Shabbat: Worship, Study, and Song for Sabbath and Festival Services and for the Home* (Bridgeport, Conn.: Prayer Book Press, 1975), p. 95.

19. *The Bhagavad Gita,* Trans. by Franklin Edgerton (New York: Harper Torchbooks, 1964), pp. 6–7.

20. 1 Kings 19:12.

21. See D.T. Suzuki, *Essays in Zen Buddhism* (New York: Grove Press, 1961).

22. Psalms 10:1.

23. Isshu Miura and Ruth Fuller Sasaki, *The Zen Koan* (New York: Harcourt, Brace and World, 1965), p. 44.

24. Paul Reps, *Zen Flesh, Zen Bones* (Garden City, N.Y.: Doubleday), p. 88.

25. Ibid., p. 106.

26. D.T. Suzuki, *Studies in Zen* (New York: Delta Books, 1955), p. 168.

27. Gore Vidal, *The Best Man* (New York: Signet Books, 1960), p. ix.

28. *The Works of Aristotle,* trans. by W.D. Ross (Chicago: Encyclopaedia Britannica, 1952), vol. II, pp. 339–40.

29. William James, *Pragmatism and Other Essays* (New York: Washington Square Press, 1963), p. 202.

Chapter Seven
Religious Language as Story

Tell all the Truth but tell it slant—
Success in Circuit lies
Too bright for our infirm Delight
The Truth's superb surprise

As Lightning to the Children eased
With explanation kind
The Truth must dazzle gradually
Or every man be blind—

Emily Dickinson
"Tell All the Truth"[1]

Unlike scientific and mathematical ways of speaking, religious discourse is often expressed in story form; therefore a study of religious language would be incomplete without a consideration of sacred stories. As noted in chapter six, the dilemma of religious expression is that the holy cannot be spoken of in the same way as commonplace and ordinary things, but if humans are not to remain silent, they must point to the infinite and unspeakable through the finite and ordinary. In fact, if all talk about the holy is double-intentional and paradoxical, then the imaginative and made-up quality of stories is a particularly fruitful way of speaking about the mysterious and sacred ground of all existence. Certainly it is obvious that such story forms as myth, mondo, and parable have persistently recommended themselves to the religious imagination; the thesis of this text is that more direct forms of religious discourse, such as commentary, preaching, and theology, with their emphasis on rational and systematic discourse, are also implicit stories or metaphors rather than factually descriptive speech. One of Emily Dickinson's poems begins, "Tell all the Truth but tell it slant," for, in speaking about what is ultimately true, success lies in indirection.[2] Sacred stories are the slant or indirection through which humans grope toward ultimate existence.

When the holy is its subject, religious language is story—that is, creative fantasy and sacred disclosure. As a vision of ultimate existence, sacred stories are more imaginative and indirect than factually descriptive. This is not to argue that historical events are irrelevant to faith or that faith is make-believe; factual and historical data play a prominent role in faith. Moses and King David are not just legendary figures or characters in a fabulous tale; they are historical figures rooted in time and space. What gives their lives a story quality is the conviction that God played a part in their stories. Siddhartha Gautama was a commanding figure who lived centuries before the time of Jesus and whose insights have profoundly influenced the course of civilization. Yet, to claim that Gautama was an enlightened one, a Buddha, who was liberated by an experience of ultimate existence, is to give his life a transempirical story quality. The consideration of religious language as story begins with an examination of the imaginative and revelatory character of sacred stories and concludes with a consideration of two types of sacred stories: myth and parable. Theology, regarded as an implicit story form, is addressed separately in part IV.

Must then a Christ perish in torment in every age to save those that have no imagination?
George Bernard Shaw
Saint Joan[3]

Sacred Stories as Imaginative

Stories, like all artistic expressions, are both imaginative and conscious creations—that is, they are to some degree both nonfactual and inventive. The artistic imagination modifies and shapes the data of experience and the facts of the objective world to create a new world of meaning. The storyteller is inventive and fanciful; thus, stories always have a made-up quality even when the subject matter is vividly realistic.

Like stories in general, sacred stories are imaginative; they have a fantasy quality like that of art. Pablo Picasso, one of the giants of modern art, said of the inventiveness of art, "Art is a lie that enables us to realize the truth."[4] Like artistic creations, sacred stories are "lies," creative distortions, in which the truth appears. The artistic and religious imaginations are free to penetrate behind appearances to discover the reality hidden in them. Susan Feldmann, in her *African Myths and Tales,* repeats the following Sudanese dialogue between a storyteller and his audience:

> *"I'm going to tell a story," the narrator begins.*
> *"Right!"the audience rejoins.*
> *"It is a lie."*
> *"Right!"*
> *"But not everything in it is false."*[5]

The important thing about sacred stories, as this Sudanese dialogue discloses, is not whether they are literally true, but whether the truth is presented or conveyed through them. They are a form of indirect speech that, if taken literally, are likely to be misunderstood and yet, if they are dismissed as fabulous nonsense, the truth that is hidden in them remains undisclosed. Sacred stories are, in a sense, a form of play that has as its purpose, according to philosopher Susanne Langer, "not wishful distortion of the world, but serious envisagement of its fundamental truth; moral orientation, not escape."[6]

The Ashanti, a people of West Africa, traditionally begin their tales with a recognition of the imaginative nature of their stories: "We do not really mean, that what we are going to say is true."[7] In doing so, the Ashanti recognize that stories are different from reporting or giving directions. The nonliteral or metaphorical quality of stories does not mean, however, that they have neither value nor truth; the imagination, more than what is already known, is the vehicle for ecstatic and liberating ways of appropriating reality.

Sacred Stories as Revelatory

Since God in the mystery of His being transcends the world of our ordinary experience, He can only be known through His revelation of Himself within that world. Because He is transcendent, we cannot know Him by our own methods of discovery.

Langdon Gilkey
Maker of Heaven and Earth[8]

If sacred stories are imaginative, are the stories told by shamans, sages, prophets, and priests conscious creations like those of novelists and poets? Are sacred stories made up or given? From one way of seeing, sacred stories are lies or human inventions that disclose the truth; in another sense, they are divinely inspired stories that tell themselves. Perhaps such stories are both made up and given—that is, conscious creations that storytellers shape and form, yet, paradoxically, revealed to or dreamed by them.

Some forms of sacred stories (mondo, parable, theology) are more obviously inventive while other forms (myth, prophecy) are more visionary or revelatory. Mythic and prophetic forms of sacred stories are usually believed to be revealed, dreamed, or envisioned. Black Elk, the Lakota Sioux, spoke of his spirit-vision as something that seized him, which had, as it were, a life of its own. He wrote, "Nothing I have ever seen with my eyes was ever so clear and bright as what my vision showed me. . . . I do not have to remember these things; they have remembered themselves all these years."[9] The prophets of Israel spoke the words that God commanded; thus, their message was not simply their own. Amos, a prophet of the eighth century B.C., characterized himself as a Judean herdsman and gatherer of sycamore, commanded by God to speak His word to Israel. Typically, the Hebrew prophets prefaced their words, as Amos did, with "Thus saith the Lord" in order to emphasize the divine imperative. Similarly, the Sudanese storyteller, who traditionally begins his narrative by telling his audience that his story is a lie that clothes the truth, ends his story with, "I put the tale back where I found it," which emphasizes the givenness of the story.[10]

However, to the degree that sacred stories are flexible and designed to fit the circumstance of their telling and the skills of the storyteller, they are products of human inventiveness. Certainly theology and parable are primarily conscious creations, yet in a sense they are a response to divine revelation. Myths are often claimed to be given or dreamed, yet ethnographers have noted that a myth can be given variant tellings. Navahos with traditional values demand ritual exactness and are fearful if their sacred stories are not chanted or said properly. Peyote-inspired Navahos, however, seek spontaneity in their prayers and inventiveness in their stories.

The several varieties of sacred narratives include such well-known story forms as **myth** and parable. Of course, religious language includes nonstory modes of discourse: theology, which is speculative and rational; preaching, which is proclamative and evaluative; koan, which are puzzling and liberating; scripture, which is authoritative and revelatory; songs and poems, which are evocative and expressive; and commentaries, which are discerning and instructive. However, insomuch as each of the nonstory forms have the holy as their subject, they are subtle and implicit forms of story. Because we must limit the discussion, only two types of sacred stories are discussed in detail: myth and parable.

Myth

In terms of naked fact the poet's lines are false, but in terms of insight they are so profoundly true that they shout inspiration. So it is with myths. A myth is not a fairy tale at odds with reality; it is designed to communicate truth.
Milo C. Connick
The Message and Meaning of the Bible[11]

The word *myth* means tale or story. Scholars of religion commonly use the term *myth* in the way that story is used in this text; thus, to say religious language is mythic is the same as saying that it is story. While in this text religious language is understood as story or metaphor, myth is used in a more restricted sense to signify a particular variety of story.

As a type of story, myths deal with cosmic and exemplary time rather than historical time. The subject matter of myths is primeval origins, ancestral models, and paradigmatic lives, or expectations about the future and the end of time. Cosmic time stands outside history, beyond the reach of eyewitnesses, and is thus inaccessible except through the imaginative and revelatory dimension of sacred expression. Primeval origin stories, such as the Polynesian tale that the universe, including the gods, originated from an egg and those from the book of Genesis that speak of Yahweh's creation of the world in six days, the expulsion of Adam and Eve from the Garden of Eden, and the confusion of tongues at the Tower of Babel, are examples of myth.

In addition to speaking of a nonhistorical and cosmic time, myths usually include bizarre and fabulous phenomena, such as the creation of Eve from the rib of Adam and the talking serpent in the Garden of Eden, that are difficult to harmonize with modern ways of knowing and speaking about the world. One of the Hopi stories of origin communicates something of the fantasy character of myth. Tawa, the sun-source of life, placed ants and other insects in the earth. When dissension arose, Tawa sent Spider Grandmother to guide the insect-creatures to a new world closer to the surface of the earth where they might live more peaceably. As the insects emerged into the new world, their bodies changed to those of bears, rabbits, wolves, and other animals. Violence soon erupted, and the animals lost their sense of purpose. Spider Grandmother led the creatures from the second world to a third that lay just under the earth's surface. In the process the animals took the form of man and lived the way that humans do. Some of the people lost their way and abandoned their rituals and devotions. This time Tawa sent Spider Grandmother to those who had been steadfast, and she led them upward through a small opening to the surface of the earth. As they emerged, they were separated into Hopi, Zuni, Pima, and Navaho.[12]

The Hopi narrative illustrates some of the salient features of myth. The time of origin lies outside ordinary time, and the ancestors of the present-day tribes are exemplars, chosen ones, who know the meaning of life. In the Hopi myth, human ancestry stretches far behind the first Indians to a primeval nontribal people and finally to animals, insects, and the sun; thus the world of man and nature are one. The myth also has a fabulous character, including a spiritualized and humanized Spider Grandmother and a description of human origins, that cannot be easily coordinated with modern explanations.

Scholars differ on the value and function of myth. Some insist that myths are a premodern mode of human expression that no longer meets human needs and that cannot, in the light of modern scientific and rational ways of knowing and speaking, be taken seriously. Scholars who regard myths as outmoded have often insisted that such stories have primarily served a cognitive function; thus origin myths are regarded as speculative and prescientific explanations or etiologies of how and why things are as they are. How, for instance, did humans come to speak different languages? In the Genesis account, our primeval ancestors built a tower that reached the heavens in order that they might "make a name" for themselves. When the Lord saw what they had done, he was offended, and he disrupted their linguistic unity so that they could not understand each other.[13] The Toltecs of Mexico told a similar story; a group of people who had survived a great calamity built a tower to heaven where they hoped to obtain safety "only to have their tongues confused."[14] The theft of fire is also a common etiological motif explaining how humans obtained fire. In Greek mythology, Prometheus, who in one Greek myth was the creator of humankind, cared so much for his creation that he stole fire from the gods and gave it to humans. As punishment for his rebelliousness, Prometheus was bound with unbreakable chains to a lonely rock by order of Zeus, the lord of Olympus.[15]

From a second perspective, myths have a far more important function than that of assigning causes or explanations of how things began. In fact, some scholars argue that the truth of myth usually has little to do with etiology. Myth provides people with models for authentic action as well as an understanding of their position in the cosmos. Myths are thus not only **cosmological** but **ontological**—that is, concerned with the condition and being of human existence. The ontological character of myth is evident in such themes as our original state, experiences of alienation or separation, and the origin of death and suffering.

Although myths have a fantasy quality—that is, they are not factually descriptive or believable if taken literally—they should not be dismissed as untrue or irrelevant. Like all sacred stories, myths are valued by those who believe that truth is expressed through them. While myths are neither reliable history nor science, they may have important things to say; their subject matter revolves around the deep and abiding concerns of human origins and destinies. In short, myth focuses on our position in the cosmos and our understanding of who and what we are. This focus elicits and perhaps is better served by mythic and poetic forms of expression than by more intellectually constrained forms of speech.

Sacred myths are distinguishable from folktales and sagas. Folktales, including fairy tales like Sleeping Beauty and fables like How the Leopard Got Its Spots are different from myths in that they are primarily entertaining. They do not plunge into the depths of existence but offer instead diversion from the frustrations and conflicts of life. Legends and sagas are imaginative accounts rooted in historical events, whereas myths, although they may include historical elements, are more clearly nonhistorical. The Israelites' exodus from Egypt is, for example, a historical event encrusted in legend. In the biblical narrative the entire Hebrew struggle for liberation is what Martin Buber called a saga—that is, a historical event seen through the eyes of faith.[16] Myth expresses the meaning of life through fantasy-laden speech about cosmic time, whereas saga discerns divine activity in history.

While myths are in some ways creative fantasies, they are less consciously constructed than are other forms of sacred stories. Just as God's word is revealed to a prophet, the myth is believed to be given, found, or dreamed. In the context of faith, the givenness of sacred myths validates their authority and makes them true rather than simply entertaining. In some tribal cultures, myths are spiritual disclosures or visions that occur in dreams. For the Iroquois the wishes and commands of the spiritual world were conveyed in dreams that possessed an authority and authenticity that more conscious creations lacked.

Although myths appear to be unconscious creations, they are also made up and narrated according to the interests and talents of the storyteller. Myths are dynamic rather than static; several versions of the same myth quite commonly exist in a single tribal tradition. Paul Radin reported the case of two brothers who had learned a myth from their father; "the differences between these versions were remarkable and can be explained by the different temperaments, literary ability and interests of the brothers."[17] Conflicting accounts of the gods exist in the same cultural milieu; thus, variation of theme and subject matter is possible and acceptable without a loss of meaning and value. The storyteller is, in spite of the givenness of sacred myth, free to develop and adapt his story to fit the occasion of its telling.

Origin Myths

Of the several varieties of myth, only two types, origin and eschatological, or future-time, myths, are discussed in detail. Under the category of origin myths are stories that tell of the genesis of the cosmos and those that speak of the origin of human existence, including the motif of divine-human alienation.

Origin-of-the-World Myths

Creation-of-the-world, or how-the-world-began, myths are common to many traditions. According to a myth of the Yoruba of Nigeria, the world was initially marshy and watery. The sky was the home of the gods. The principal or supreme deity, Ol-orun, directed Great God, Orisha Nla, to make firm ground. Nla was given a snail shell that contained loose earth, a pigeon, and a five-toed hen to facilitate his task. He threw the dirt down upon the marshy surface, whereupon the hen scratched the dirt until dry land was formed. The creation of earth was accomplished in four days and the fifth day was given over as a day of worship to its creator, Orisha Nla.[18]

In one of the Greek creation myths, Mother Earth emerged from chaos and gave birth to her son the Sky (Uranus). From the fertility of Mother Earth and the gentle showers of the sky came plants and animals, rivers and lakes. Earth and Uranus subsequently gave birth to the Titans. Mother Earth, provoked by the behavior of her husband, called upon the godlike Titans to attack their father. Led by the Titan Cronus, they surprised the sleeping Uranus and castrated him. His father emasculated, Cronus married his sister Rhea. Fearful of his own offspring, Cronus swallowed the children of his union with Rhea. Enraged, Rhea secretively gave birth to her third son, Zeus. When her husband came to devour the infant, she cleverly wrapped a stone in the fashion of infants, and Cronus, mistaking it for the child, swallowed it. The myth concludes with a fully grown Zeus subduing his father and forcing him to vomit up the gods and goddesses he had swallowed.[19]

Human Origin Myths

In addition to telling how the universe began, some myths speak of human origins. In the Yoruba creation story, Orisha Nla, after creating the earth in four days, molded a clay image of man that the supreme deity Ol-orun gave life. The Ewe-speaking tribes of Togo, in West Africa, tell the story that in the beginning God fashioned a man from clay and later molded a woman. When the two looked at each other, they laughed, prompting God to send them out into the world.

There are two human-origin stories in the Bible. In the first creation story, Genesis 1–2:3, male and female are made in the image of God. This account, which shares the relatively common mythic theme that divine and human existence were originally both male and female, suggests that femininity is as much a likeness of God as masculinity. In the second creation myth, Genesis 2:4–25, God formed Adam from the dust of the earth and breathed life into His sculpture. After failing to find a helpmate for man among the beasts and birds, God formed woman from one of Adam's ribs. In this account woman is a second-order creature who is to be an obedient helpmate for man.

Myths of the Origin of Alienation and the Loss of Paradise

One ontological motif evident in myths of origin is that of the separation between God and humans. Sometimes God is believed to have withdrawn. The Bantus say that "God, after making man, pays no attention to him."[20] In an Ashanti myth, Onyankopon originally lived on earth. While

Michelangelo Buonarotti, The Creation of Man (detail), *Sistine Chapel, Vatican City. In Michelangelo's vision of the primal event, God brings life to Adam by the touch of his finger, while Eve clings to God's side. Adam's likeness to God is made explicit by Adam's power and beauty—a power and beauty that even God's presence cannot dwarf.*

Photo: Alinari/Florence, Editorial Photocolor Archives

mashing yams, an old woman repeatedly struck the god with her pestle. Annoyed, Onyankopon took himself up into the sky where the people no longer had direct access to him. Dismayed, the old woman advised her children to build a tower so that the sky-god might be reached. Mortar by mortar the tower rose until only one more was needed to reach the top. Since not a single additional mortar could be found, the old woman instructed them to take the bottom mortar and place it at the top. The tower promptly collapsed, killing many people and leaving the sky to Onyankopon.[21]

The mythic separation of the divine and human is often associated with a loss-of-paradise theme. Ancestral man is commonly seen as living in a blissful and harmonious state—a paradisiacal dwelling place of both the divine and the human. The loss of paradise is one of the themes in the Adam-and-Eve myth. The consequence of the primeval couple's disobedience is their expulsion from the Garden of Eden into a world in which they and their progeny must suffer and die. Such stories reflect the awareness that human existence is in some very basic way unsatisfactory.

Another variation on the theme of the loss of paradise and the origin of death and suffering is that of the perverted or falsified message. In this form, the gods intended that humans should have eternal life, but the message is either never delivered or, through ignorance, misunderstood. The Akamba of Kenya tell a story of why humans die. God, the creator of humans, did not wish that they should completely die but desired that, after death, they should rise again. God frequently spent time with the chameleon and the weaverbird. He observed that the chameleon spoke the truth, whereas the weaverbird was a great liar. God sent the chameleon, as his messenger, to tell humans that they would rise again after they died. The chameleon traveled slowly, and when he arrived could get no further into his message than to say, "I was told, I was told . . ." Meanwhile, the much swifter weaverbird arrived and spoke, "Truly, we were told that men, when they are dead, shall perish like roots of the aloe." The chameleon then spoke and tried to rectify the weaverbird's lie, but the magpie interjected that the first speech was true; that is how it came to be that men die and do not rise.[22]

The perverted message is an example of the mythic theme of the presence of deception and trickery associated with creation and the ensuing ambiguity of human existence. The trickster is a common figure. Among the Indians of North America, the trickster is often a raven or coyote. In a Navaho myth, Coyote was blamed for bringing death into the world:

> During one long hard winter Coyote saw that there were too many people and not enough food, and he said that Death must be allowed to take away the old ones. Everyone was horrified and said, "This is the worst idea Coyote ever had." But Coyote said the people who died would come back when there was enough food and he explained how to build an arrow path to the sky. So the people agreed. But when some had died and the path of arrows was prepared for their return, cunning Coyote grabbed the last one and pulled all the arrows down out of the sky. That is why there is now no way for the dead to return to earth.[23]

Sexual alienation is also a mythic theme. Women, for instance, are often instruments of destruction in loss-of-paradise stories. In the Ashanti myth an old woman's careless abusiveness and ignorance prompted Onyankopon to make his home in heaven. Christians and Jews have used or misused the Adam-and-Eve myth to portray Eve as a willing and seductive tool of the wily serpent. The dubious value of women is an explicit feature of one of the Greek creation myths. As was mentioned, Zeus punished Prometheus because he had given fire to humans. Zeus' condemnation of the rebellious one was not sufficient; he sought to punish all people as well. Zeus' revenge was to make the first woman, the beautiful and alluring Pandora. In one variation of the tale, Pandora was given a box, which she was forbidden to open. Her curiosity got the best of her, however, and when she opened the box all sorts of evil escaped to plague mankind. By the time Pandora succeeded in closing the box, only one thing remained inside, and that was hope; thus, life's hardships were Pandora's dowry.

Eschatological Myths

Eschatological, or future-time, myths are concerned with human destiny, the counterpart of the concern with cosmic beginnings. In loss-of-paradise stories, the divine is either obscured or separated from the human; thus the focus of eschatological myths is on the return of the eternal, a restoration of unity, and an abolition of all forms of alienation. Often this expectation is expressed in stories of saviors who are coming to disclose new pathways to the divine or who will, in their own person, reestablish a new heaven and a new earth. Such stories take two primary forms: either profane time is cyclically or periodically brought to an end by a return of the eternal, or the movement of time is unique and brought to a close only once. In the

Edward Hicks, The Peaceable Kingdom. *The expectation of a time of peace and harmony is evident in Edward Hicks's treatment of Isaiah's vision of a time when a little child shall lead wolf, lion, and leopard to lie down with domestic animals. As a foreshadowing of such a time, William Penn is depicted concluding a peace treaty with the Indians.*

Photo courtesy Worcester Art Museum, Worcester, Massachusetts

academic study of religion, **eschatology** is the technical word for the expectation of what is to come, of what lies beyond. The eschatological imagination abounds in visions and prophecies of the last days. In the broadest sense, eschatology is a hope that the eternal will make itself known in the future.

End-of-Historical-Time Myths

The myth of the end of a single and unique historical time is found in faiths, such as Judaism and Christianity, where time is seen to have only one beginning and one end. Judaism has been a faith suspended between the exodus from Egypt and the disclosure of the Torah at Sinai and the eschatological hope of a Messiah, the anointed of God, who is yet to come. For the Jews, the messianic age to come will be one in which, as the prophet Isaiah proclaimed, the nations "shall beat their swords into plowshares and their spears into pruning hooks; nation shall not lift up sword against nation, neither shall they learn war anymore."[24]

Christianity is a faith that proclaims Jesus of Nazareth as God's Christ, his anointed, and yet looks not only backward to the time of Christ's advent, crucifixion, and resurrection but expectantly to a future act of God. One form of this future hope involves a scenario in which the present evil age is brought to a cataclysmic end by a Second Coming of Christ. In the apocalyptic vision of John of Patmos, the present age is ruled by Satan and is evil beyond redemption. Just as Satan is opposed to God, an Antichrist is to appear in opposition to Christ. The horror of the last days, with their famines, pestilence, war, and death, is to be closed by a final mighty struggle between the forces of righteousness led by Christ and the legions of evil commanded by Satan. Ultimately, Satan and the Antichrist are to be subdued and thrown in a lake of fire where they and their worshippers will be eternally punished. The righteous are to be gathered in a New Jerusalem, where humans can once again rapturously live in the presence of God.

Although messianic movements are atypical of tribal peoples, they are not unknown to them. In times of stress American Indians have responded to the call of prophets who have heralded a new age, the restoration of tribal glory, and the repulsion of the white man. From 1888 to 1890 Jack Wovoka, a Nevada Paiute, preached the Ghost Dance religion. In a trance Wovoka was shown by the Great Spirit the place where all Indians who had died were again young and happy. A Ghost Dance, performed by the living, was to restore the dead to earthly life and usher in a revival of Indian glory. The Ghost Dance spread quickly to other tribes, including the Arapaho, Cheyenne, and Sioux. Among the Sioux Wovoka's prophecies were associated with an eschatological hope that the performance of the dance would not only lead to restoration of the Indian way and of their ancestral dead but would also trigger an annihilation of the whites. The expectations that buoyed the Ghost Dance religion were shattered by the death of Sitting Bull and more than 150 other Sioux in the massacre at Wounded Knee, South Dakota, in 1890.

In spite of the repeated disappointment of the faithful, messianic myths have a surprising capacity for periodic renewal. In Christendom, the time of the Lord's return or the Messiah's advent, attended by the end of the evil age and the restoration of the righteous, has been repeatedly proclaimed. The Anabaptists anticipated the Parousia (the return of Christ) during the Peasants' War of 1525. William Miller, an influential figure in the American Adventist movement, proclaimed on scriptural grounds that the Parousia would take place between March 21, 1843 and March 21, 1844. Hundreds of Adventists sold or disposed of their property and otherwise settled their affairs in expectation of the end. Not surprisingly, in the face of the violence and suffering of the twentieth century, apocalypse-minded Christianity has enjoyed a revival.

Myths of Cyclical Renewal

In contrast to sacred stories in which the last days signal the abolition of a single historical time and the ushering in of a new age that lies beyond history are myths in which time moves in a circle, and ages are periodically ended and new ones begun. The conviction that life moves in a circle and that the ages of man are repeatedly destroyed and reconstituted is a fairly common motif in Asian mythology. For example, devotees of India's popular cult of Vishnu believe that on numerous occasions Vishnu has been embodied in such animal forms as a fish and a tortoise as well as in the divine-human exemplars, Rama and Krishna. In this myth Vishnu comes near, only to withdraw again. The devotees of Vishnu look to a future avatar, Kalki, who is to come at the end of the present age to set a new age in motion. Some Buddhist groups expect a Maitreya Buddha, a looked-for one, who is to inaugurate a new age.

There are many variations on the cyclical motif of the repeated regeneration of a sacred cosmos. In one quite common mythic form, the return of the eternal is reflected in the daily eclipse and rise of the sun deity who dies and rises again each day, whose movement is seen in the rhythm of the seasons and in the withdrawal of the old year and the birth of the new. In such a mythic cosmos, the gods die and rise only to return again, and the cycle of human life follows the same cosmic rhythm from birth to death to rebirth.

Still another example of the cyclical motif is evident in the myth and ritual practice of the Greek mystery cult of Demeter and Persephone, which celebrated the periodic renewal of the cosmos. The cult of Demeter, a goddess of the earth and growing things, had its center in the small Greek town of Eleusis. According to the Eleusian myth, Persephone, the beautiful daughter of Zeus and Demeter, was abducted by Hades, the lord of the dead. For nine days and nights, the grieving Demeter searched for her daughter. After discovering the abduction and rape of her beloved Persephone, Demeter transversed the earth in sorrow and anger; she made the fertile land barren and endangered human survival. As conditions worsened Zeus dispatched a messenger to his brother, Hades, asking for the return of Persephone. Eventually, Zeus succeeded in securing a compromise that averted the extinction of human life. According to the agreement Persephone was to spend three months in the company of Hades, a time in which Demeter's grief manifested itself as winter, and nine months with her mother; thus the cycle of the seasons paralleled the annual separation and subsequent reunion of the divine mother and daughter.

Interpreting Myth

Myths are telling us . . . of matters funda-mental to ourselves, enduring essential prin-ciples about which it would be good for us to know; about which, in fact, it will be necessary for us to know if our conscious minds are to be kept in touch with our most secret, motivating depths.

Joseph Campbell
Myths to Live By [25]

How are these strange stories to be understood? Are they to be dismissed as interesting but credulous prescientific explanations, or should we look to them for deeper ontological meanings? Following the work of Rudolf Bultmann, a New Testament scholar, the interpretation of myth has often been characterized as demythologizing. In Bultmann's usage de-mythologizing involves unpacking the meaning of myths so the truth contained in them can be more clearly discerned. "Its aim is not to eliminate the mythological statements, but to interpret them. It is a method of hermeneutics." [26]

Myth as Disclosure of Ultimate Existence

In distinguishing between the principal hermeneutics, or interpretations, of myth, perhaps we should begin with the view that myths are important expressions of our experience of the sacred. Thus myth and ritual are primarily ways of responding to the holy. Walter Otto wrote, "At the center of all religion stands the appearance of God. That He has come, that He is present—this gives meaning and life to all of religion's primal forms." [27]

In Otto's image, the myth of the holy is the commanding myth of all religious experience.

Taking a similar position, Mircea Eliade sees myth as speech about the sacred center of all authentic existence. Eliade argues that myths provide exemplars of authentic life, precedents for action. The thrust of such stories is to re-create vital life, as Vedic literature directs, by doing "what the gods did in the beginning."[28] Eliade carries his analysis a step further when he contends that myths provide something more than models of authenticity. Humans tell stories because something sacred prompts them; thus myths communicate something of the ultimate nature of both the divine and the human. In Eliade's view, myths reveal the paradox of the sacred—namely, that opposition or conflict is part of the sacred. The Greek god Dionysus is both terrible and attractive. Demeter is the source of all bountiful life, yet her sorrow and anger condemns men to harsh winters of the soul. In one of the Hindu cults, the male aspect of divinity is known as Shiva, while the female dimension is called Kali; the two form a divine unity. In the Bible, Yahweh sends Moses to lead the children of Israel out of bondage, and yet, while Moses is obediently on his mission, the Lord seeks to kill him. In Eliade's hermeneutic the mythical pattern is one in which the sacred is seen in such polarities as those of male-female and creator-destroyer, and yet, Eliade adds, the sacred is also paradoxically that which reconciles all opposition.[29]

Myth as Projection of the Unconscious

A second hermeneutic, associated with depth psychologists like Sigmund Freud and Carl Jung, sees myth as a relatively unconscious projection. Jung wrote that "the primitive mentality does not invent myths, it expresses them. Myths are the original revelation of the pre-conscious psyche, involuntary statements about unconscious psychic happenings."[30] Myths are a public form of dreams and thus share in the fantasy and symbolic character of dreams. The depth-psychological interpretation offers an explanation for the universal features and widespread distribution of similar mythic motifs. For instance, flood stories and stories about those who survived the flood, such as Noah and his family in the Bible and Utnapishtim and his wife in the Gilgamesh epic, are found among several Mediterranean cultures and are common to American Indian tribes as well. From a Jungian perspective, the similarity of myths is indicative of inborn tendencies or permanent features of the human psyche; thus recurrent symbols or images, such as water, the earth-mother, the hero, the number four, and the divine child, are manifested in myths and dreams. In this light, myths are terribly important because they are public dreams that bring us in touch with the unconscious depths of human existence. Myths express the inner or psychic life of man.

The Greek creation myth, mentioned previously, lends itself to the hermeneutical approach of depth psychology. It is at first glance merely an incestuous and bloody fantasy. The sky deity (Uranus) is castrated by his son (Cronus). Cronus mates with his sister (Rhea) and devours each of his offspring in their infancy. Zeus' life is spared when he is hidden by his mother. Eventually Zeus forcibly subdues his father. From a Freudian perspective, the myth projects in story form the unconscious hostility that exists between father and son. Like the story of Oedipus, who killed his father and married his mother, the Greek creation myth is a riot of sexual and filial conflict. In Freudian terms all fathers threaten to swallow up their offspring psychically and must, like the giants of mythology, be slain if their progeny are to be free. Such myths can still move modern man, Freud argued, because the conflicts between father and son are real. Oedipus' fate, as well as that of Uranus and Cronus, Freud wrote, "moves us only because it might have been our own, because the oracle laid upon us before our birth the very curse which rested upon him. It may be that we are all destined to direct our first sexual impulses toward our mothers, and our first impulses of hatred and violence toward our fathers: our dreams convince us that we are."[31]

Myth as Validation of the Social Order

Anthropology, more than any other discipline, is a storehouse of detailed studies and interpretations of myth and ritual, particularly those of primitive cultures. One anthropological hermeneutic stresses the social and economic context in which the stories are told and minimizes the importance of their content. According to Bronislaw Malinowski, the key to understanding myths rests in understanding their social context, the situation in which they are told or performed, rather than in the details of the stories themselves. What myths explain is of minor consequence. He proposed that "the function of myth is to strengthen tradition and endow it with a greater value and prestige by tracing it back to a higher, better, more supernatural reality of initial events."[32] Myths are thus told or acted out in ritual primarily to validate or reinforce tribal morality and socially adaptive responses. Malinowski's major ethnological fieldwork was in the Trobriand Islands among the Melanesian tribes of New Guinea. One important Trobriand myth establishes the land rights and social status of each clan. According to this myth the ancient ones lived in the underworld before they emerged on the surface of the earth. Each clan came through a particular hole; thus the land surrounding it is the clan's ancestral and rightful home. The order of emergence determined the clans' ranking, with the highest rank conferred on the first.

Myth as Mediation of Conflicts and Contradictions

A second anthropological approach is represented by the work of Claude Levi-Strauss. In Levi-Strauss's words, "The purpose of myth is to provide a logical model capable of overcoming a contradiction."[33] Myths reflect binary opposition—that is, conflict between opposing ways of life and cultural roles; thus, they typically have as their themes male and female antipathies, generational conflicts between old and young, anxieties about the boundaries of life and death, antagonism between natural desires and cultural restraints. Levi-Strauss saw contradiction and conflict as a fundamental characteristic of human existence. Myths reflect this opposition and offer resolutions for overcoming or disguising the dichotomies between good and evil, darkness and light, reason and emotion, the above and the below, nature and culture.

One primary form of opposition is between the settled life of the village (culture) and the nomadic life of the desert or forest (nature). This tension pits the unorthodox life-style of the inhabitant of the desert or forest against the more secure and settled life of the villager. Villagers' lives revolve around customary practice; they till the soil and raise crops. The fireplace and cooked food is symptomatic of culture. By contrast, the people of the desert or forest travel light. They are first hunters and gatherers and, eventually, herders. Their food is often consumed raw and on the spot. Seen in a Levi-Straussian perspective, the Cain-and-Abel myth is much more than an explanation for the origin of murder. Cain is a tiller of the ground and Abel is a keeper of sheep. Both make offerings to God. Abel's animal sacrifice is accepted by God, but He has no regard for Cain's gift from the fruits of the earth. In anger, Cain slays his brother. As an example of binary opposition, the story is a conflict between the shepherding values of Abel and the agricultural values associated with Cain.

Perhaps one more example of the binary nature of myth will suffice. The Trobrianders believe that there was a time when people did not die. In that time humans stayed young by periodically shedding their skins like snakes. According to one myth, the situation was changed in this manner: A grandmother, her daughter, and granddaughter were together on the beach. The grandmother entered the water and shed her skin. When she returned to shore, the granddaughter did not recognize her and rejected her as a youthful stranger. The grandmother promptly returned to the sea and put on her old skin. Angered by the girl's failure to recognize her, the grandmother insisted that all humans must die.[34] The story's principal conflict is between generations. The young ignore and reject the old, and, in retaliation, the old are avenged by death. The myth also provides a way to mediate or accept the harsh inevitability of death. Myths mediate the binary conflicts of human existence, British philosopher G.S. Kirk argued, "by simply obfuscating it, or making it appear abstract and unreal, or by stating in affect terms that it is insoluble or inevitable, part of the divine dispensation or natural order of things, or by offering some kind of palliative or apparent solutions for it."[35]

Parable

Parable is paradox formed into story.
John Dominic Crossan
Raid on the Articulate[36]

Parables are imaginative narratives about conditions common to human experience. Unlike myth, which has a fantasy quality, parable is rooted in the familiar; while the contents may be consciously created, they have the ring of truth. In the parable of the prodigal son, Jesus told of two brothers and their father; in doing so he may have had no specific father and sons in mind, but the parable is clearly grounded in the familiar rather than the fantastic. In anticipation of an inheritance, the younger son asked for and received it from his father. The son soon squandered his fortune. Hungry and impoverished, the young man resolved to return to his father's house. When the father heard of his son's return, he told his servants to prepare a feast "for this my son was dead, and is alive again; he was lost, and is found."[37] The parable ends on an even more realistic note, for when the elder brother observed the music and dancing, he complained to his father that his steadfastness had never been rewarded with a party.

The parable engages the hearer. It asks that he or she be a participant in the truth disclosed in the story. The importance of a parable is related to the effect it has on those who hear it. Its telling can be a saving or redeeming event when truth is appropriated through it. In the parable of the good Samaritan, Jesus was asked by a lawyer to explain further the scriptural command to love your neighbor. "Who is my neighbor?" the lawyer inquired. Jesus responded:

> *A man was going down from Jerusalem to Jericho, and he fell among robbers, who stripped him and beat him, and departed, leaving him half-dead. Now by chance a priest was going down that road; and when he saw him he passed by on the other side. So likewise a Levite, when he came to the place and saw him, passed by on the other side. But a Samaritan, as he journeyed, came to where he was; and when he saw him, he had compassion, and went to him and bound up his wounds, pouring on oil and wine; then he set him on his own beast and brought him to an inn, and took care of him.*[38]

After telling his story, Jesus engaged the lawyer as participant in the story by turning the question back to him: "Which of these three, do you think, proved neighbor to the man who fell among the robbers?"

One type of parable provides models of how to act. The parable of the good Samaritan asks that we respond to those we come in contact with in the loving spirit of the Samaritan. The prophet Nathan used a parable to help King David see more clearly the sin that he had committed against Uriah the Hittite. David, because he desired Uriah's wife, Bathsheba, had conspired to have Uriah killed in battle. Nathan's parable concerns two men, one rich and the other poor. The rich man had large herds and flocks, but the poor man had only one lamb, which was lovingly raised by his entire family. A traveler came to the rich man for hospitality; the rich man was reluctant to slaughter one of his animals but "took the poor man's lamb." Hearing the story, David was angry and demanded to know the identity of the rich man that he might punish him as well as make restitution to the poor man. Nathan then replied to the king, "You are the man."[39]

Parables as Double-Intentional and Revelatory

Parables are invitations to look at reality in a different way or to discover something about ourselves and our place in the cosmos. The parable of the prodigal son is, on one level of understanding, a story of the relationship of a father and his two sons. On another level it suggests that God, like the father of the story, is compassionate and forgiving. God rejoices when those who have squandered their spiritual legacy, like the prodigal, return to him.

The Zen tradition is rich in delightful stories. One parabolic story is of two monks, Tanzan and Ekido, who, in their travels, met a lovely girl in a silk kimono who was deterred from crossing a road because it was so muddy. Tanzan unhesitatingly took the girl in his arms and carried her over the mud. Ekido said nothing until they arrived at a temple where they were to spend the night. Finally Ekido said, " 'We monks don't go near females especially not young and lovely ones. It is dangerous. Why did you do that?' Tanzan replied, 'I left the girl there. Are you still carrying her?' "[40]

A second Buddhist story, "The Parable of the Mustard Seed," communicates something of the universality of suffering and the impermanence of all living things. The story, like all parables, is personal and concrete, but also speaks about the nature of all existing things. Kisa Gotami came from a poor family. After her marriage, according to Indian practice, she went to live in the home of her husband's family. There she was treated contemptuously until she gave birth to a son. Her child brought her the respect and acceptance she desperately wanted. When the boy was still a child, he died. Unable to part with her son, Kisa carried him on her side and sought a medicine that might restore him. In this manner she came to the

Buddha and sought his help. Buddha directed the woman to go to each house in a nearby city and "in whatever house no one has ever died, from that house fetch tiny grains of mustard seed." When Kisa found no homes, no families that had escaped death and suffering, she was able to place her son's body on the cremation pyre. "Dear little son, I thought you alone had been overtaken by this thing which men call death. But you are not the only one death has overtaken. This is a law common to all mankind."[41]

Parables as Paradoxical and Evaluative

Parables, like myth, can be paradoxical; they juxtapose the ordinary and nonordinary and reverse normal human expectations. The parables of Jesus often reverse the normal order of things: A man gives a banquet to which he invites his friends, but each excuses himself as too busy to attend. In anger, the man sends his servants into the streets to "bring in the poor and maimed and blind and lame."[42] In this parable, the question is, "Who shall eat bread in the kingdom of God?" Jesus' story juxtaposes a situation from ordinary experience (the banquet) with indirect speech about the kingdom of God. The expected participants in the banquet and the kingdom (friends of the powerful) have forfeited their places at the table through indifference and misplaced priorities. Much to their surprise, their places were taken by unlikely guests. The paradoxical reversal is that in God's kingdom the last shall be first. Like the parable of the banquet, the good Samaritan story has a paradoxical quality: the pious ones who were expected to respond to the battered and beaten traveler failed to do so, while the Samaritan, an ancient adversary of the Jews, responded to his plight.

Parables rupture the ordinary by reversing its order. Perhaps the most profound parabolic proposition is that the way to the self is through the loss of self. The Japanese Sōtō Zen master, Eikai Dōgen, expressed the paradox this way: "To study the Buddha way is to study the self. To study the self is to forget the self. To forget the self is to be enlightened . . . ."[43] One of Jesus' sayings has a similar ring: "Whoever would save his life will lose it, but whoever loses his life for my sake, he will save it."[44] Jesus' enigmatic words are no more parabolic than was his life; Jesus' personal story is similar to the parable he told of the mustard seed. The mustard seed, though small at the time of its planting, grew until it became "the greatest of shrubs."[45] Jesus began and ended his life as a relatively unknown Galilean, yet his life has come to have an unparalleled influence on the spiritual and intellectual life of the West. As a messianic figure, he entered Jerusalem "triumphantly" on the back of an ass. He was hailed as king, but ruled only by the power of love. Constantly he reversed roles; the master washed his disciples' feet. The first, he said, shall be last and the last shall be first. Paradoxically, Christians proclaim that Christ's crucifixion leads not to defeat and death but to resurrected life, not only for him but for those who follow him.

Be it known that the sense of this work is not simple, but on the contrary it may be called polysemous, that is to say, of more senses than one.

The Truth of Sacred Stories

Dante Alighieri
Convivio[46]

Sacred stories are polysemous—that is, they support multiple layers of meaning. Jesus' parable of the prodigal son is in one sense the story of a father and his two sons; in a second sense, the father points to God's compassion for all prodigals. Still another layer of the parable's meaning suggests that God's kingdom reverses the conventional order of things, for it is the prodigal for whom a banquet is prepared, while the righteous son, incapable of celebration, looks on in dismay. Because sacred stories are polysemous, they cannot be understood or interpreted in a single way. However, not every interpretation is legitimate; the form and content of stories support some interpretations more convincingly, more conclusively, than others. One value of considering religious language as story is that it avoids focusing on the question of whether a story is true or false and simply invites a joyful and serious participation in the texture and levels of meaning implicit in it.

One way of dealing with the truth of sacred stories is to ask whether they are living or dead, meaningful or meaningless. Protestant theologian Reinhold Niebuhr once said, "Religion is poetry which is believed."[47] The truth of sacred stories is not so much a property of the stories as it is something that is made true in experience. Faith has a lived-through quality; thus, the truth of sacred stories is less a matter of logical proofs than it is a matter of a personal experience of the sacred. Sacred stories are dead when the holy is no longer heard through them. They become, like Greek mythology, curious and entertaining tales in which the numinous quality of the gods has been eclipsed. In her poem, "The Dead Pan," Elizabeth Barrett Browning spoke of the death of the gods of Hellas, a poetry no longer believed:

> *Gods of Hellas, gods of Hellas,*
> *Can ye listen in your silence?*
> *Can your mystic voices tell us*
> *Where ye hide? In floating islands,*
> *With a wind that evermore*
> *Keeps you out of sight of shore?*
> *Pan, Pan is dead.*[48]

The Greek gods have been replaced by stories of the Buddha, of Christ, of Moses, of Joseph Smith, and of Karl Marx. But the vitality of these stories is, like those of ancient Greece, dependent on the receptiveness of people. Nietzsche's madman proclaimed, "God is dead! And we have killed him! How shall we console ourselves, the most murderous of all murderers? The holiest and the mightiest that the world has hitherto possessed, has bled to death under our knife—who will wipe the blood from us?"[49] When human hearts and minds no longer have a story to tell or give assent to, the inner life becomes the altar on which new gods are slain. The movement of sacred stories and symbols is, as French philosopher Paul Ricoeur argued, one of "forgetfulness and restoration"[50]—a movement of death and re-creation. Elie Wiesel prefaces his novel *The Gates of the Forest* with this story of forgetfulness and restoration:

> *When the great Rabbi Israel Baal Shem-Tov saw misfortune threatening the Jews it was his custom to go into a certain part of the forest to meditate. There he would light a fire, say a special prayer, and the miracle would be accomplished and the misfortune averted. Later, when his disciple, the celebrated Magid of Mezritch, had occasion, for the same reason, to intercede with heaven, he would go to the same place in the forest and say: "Master of the Universe, listen! I do not know how to light the fire, but I am still able to say the prayer," and again the miracle would be accomplished. Still later, Rabbi Moshe-Leib of Sasov, in order to save his people once more, would go into the forest and say: "I do not know how to light the fire, I do not know the prayer, but I know the place and this must be sufficient." It was sufficient and the miracle was accomplished. Then it fell to Rabbi Israel of Rizhyn to overcome misfortune. Sitting in his armchair, his head in his hands, he spoke to God: "I am unable to light the fire and I do not know the prayer; I cannot even find the place in the forest. All I can do is to tell the story, and this must be sufficient." And it was sufficient.[51]*

The truth of sacred stories can be understood in another sense. Return, for a moment, to the story of the blind men and the elephant. Each person understood the elephant in a limited and grossly inadequate way, but was their information false or merely incomplete? Take a closer look at the elephant. An elephant can be known by several reality-organizing models. On the submicroscopic level the elephant is an atomic reality. Physics can reduce the giant pachyderm to mass and motion. An elephant can be studied genetically; the elephant's genes can be analyzed in terms of their chemistry as well as in terms of the ways that genes determine inherited characteristics. What is true of the genetic character of the great beast does not negate what can be said of its physiology. Bone structure, epidermis, and organ systems are still another facet of its reality. The elephant is not, however, just a physical reality; it has a social and environmental reality. Naturalists are interested in its eating habits and impact on the environment. Its ivory tusks are valued in the marketplace. Imagine that the elephant has been domesticated and is employed by a Thai lumberman in moving logs. Is the lumberman's understanding of the animal—as an economic asset (it must be fed but is also productive), as strong (and therefore potentially dangerous), and yet as obedient to instruction—less true than the more physical explanations? And what is to be made of the Thai children who love to play games with it and, for that matter, the child in us all who is delighted and awed by the clumsy majesty of an elephant?

The example of the elephant indicates that there are different organizing models for understanding reality. Which organizing model is true? Is just one model true, or does each one complement rather than invalidate the others? The organizing models for understanding the different levels of reality can be compared to homolographic projections, or map-like transparencies, that can be laid over each other to add another dimension. Each homolograph adds breadth and depth to human understanding. Within each organizing model competing theories are proven or disproven by their capacity to account for the phenomena in question. Are sacred stories important transparencies, homolographic projections, that can be placed over other stories since what they point to is the ultimate ground of all transparencies, of all organizing models?

Concluding Remarks

Religious language often takes the form of a story, which can be seen in such explicit story-forms as myths and parables. However, this text contends that all religious language, because it is discourse about that which transcends the empirical, is implicitly sacred story or double-intentional metaphor. Because sacred stories touch what is fundamental in human experience, they have a way of persisting even in a literal-minded and scientific age that is not very receptive to stories. The story quality of religious language, Paul Ricoeur wrote, "has a way of *revealing* things that is not reducible to any translation from a language in cipher to a clear language."[52] Perhaps when we, like Rabbi Israel of Elie Wiesel's story cannot light the fire or find the place in the forest, then all that is left is to tell the story—unless, of course, we no longer have the capacity to believe in stories.

Notes

1. In Oscar Williams, ed., *A Little Treasury of Modern Poetry,* rev. ed. (New York: Scribner's, 1952), p. 53.

2. Ibid.

3. George Bernard Shaw, *Saint Joan* (Baltimore, Md.: Penguin Books, 1951), p. 154.

4. *Picasso* (McGraw-Hill film, 1968).

5. Susan Feldman, *African Myths and Tales* (New York: Mentor Books, 1964), p. 153.

6. Susanne K. Langer, *Philosophy in a New Key* (New York: Mentor Books, 1964), p. 153.

7. Feldman, *African Myths,* p. 12.

8. Langdon Gilkey, *Maker of Heaven and Earth* (Garden City, N.Y.: Doubleday, 1965), p. 103.

9. John G. Niehardt, *Black Elk Speaks: Being the Life Story of a Holy Man of the Oglala Sioux* (New York: Pocket Books, 1972), p. 36.

10. Feldman, *African Myths,* p. 12.

11. Milo C. Connick, *The Message and Meaning of the Bible* (Belmont, Calif.: Dickenson, 1968), p. 85.

12. Donald G. Pike, *Anasazi: Ancient People of the Rock* (Palo Alto, Calif.: American West, 1974), pp. 43–44.

13. Genesis 11:3–9.

14. Theodor H. Gaster, *Myth, Legend and Custom in the Old Testament,* vol. I (New York: Harper & Row, 1969), p. 136.

15. Edith Hamilton, *Mythology* (Boston: Little, Brown, 1942), p. 91.

16. Martin Buber, *Moses, the Revelation and the Covenant* (New York: Harper Torchbooks, 1958), pp. 13–19.

17. Paul Radin, *Primitive Man as Philosopher* (New York: Dover, 1956), pp. 53–54.

18. Geoffrey Parrinder, *Religion in Africa* (Baltimore, Md.: Penguin Books, 1969), p. 30.

19. Robert Graves, *The Greek Myths,* vol. I (Baltimore, Md.: Penguin Books, 1955), pp. 37–39.

20. Mircea Eliade, *Patterns in Comparative Religion* (New York: World, 1963), p. 49.

21. Feldman, *African Myths,* pp. 41–42.

22. Ibid., pp. 107–09.

23. Jean Savage, "Theme and Variations on the Trickster Myth," unpublished essay, Sierra College, Rocklin, Calif., May 1978, pp. 6–7.

24. Isaiah 2:4.

25. Joseph Campbell, *Myths to Live By* (New York: Viking, 1972), p. 26.

26. Rudolph Bultmann, *Jesus Christ and Mythology* (New York: Scribner's, 1958), p. 18.

27. Walter Otto, *Dionysus Myth and Cult* (Bloomington: Indiana University Press, 1965), p. 27.

28. Eliade, *Patterns in Comparative Religion,* p. 417.

29. Ibid., p. 419.

30. In G.S. Kirk, *Myth: Its Meaning and Functions in Ancient and Other Cultures* (Berkeley: University of California Press, 1970), p. 279.

31. Sigmund Freud, "The Interpretations of Dreams," in *The Basic Writings of Sigmund Freud,* trans. by Dr. A.A. Brill (New York: Modern Library, 1938), p. 308.

32. Bronislaw Malinowski, *Myths in Primitive Psychology* (Westport, Conn.: Negro Universities Press, 1971), pp. 91–92.

33. Claude Levi-Strauss, *Structural Anthropology,* trans. by C. Jacobson and B. Schoepf (New York: Basic Books, 1963), p. 229.

34. Malinowski, *Myths in Primitive Society,* pp. 61–62.

35. Kirk, *Myth,* p. 258.

36. John Dominic Crossan, *Raid on the Articulate: Comic Eschatology in Jesus and Borges* (New York: Harper & Row, 1976), p. 93.

37. Luke 15:11–24.

38. Luke 10:30–34.

39. 2 Samuel 12:1–7.

40. Paul Reps, *Zen Flesh, Zen Bones* (Garden City, N.Y.: Doubleday), p. 18.

41. E.A. Burtt, ed., *Teachings of the Compassionate Buddha* (New York: New American Library, 1955), pp. 44–45.

42. Luke 14:16–24.

43. *The Way of Everyday Life: Zen Master Dogen's Genjokoan with Commentary by Hakuyu Taizan Maezumi* (Los Angeles: Zen Center Publications, 1978), unnumbered.

44. Luke 9:24.

45. Matthew 13:31–32.

46. In Evelyn Underhill, *Worship* (New York: Harper Torchbooks, 1957), p. 28.

47. In Robert H. Ayers, "Religious Discourse and Myth," in Robert H. Ayers, ed., *Religious Language and Knowledge* (Atlanta: University of Georgia Press, 1972), p. 89.

48. *Poetical Works of Elizabeth Barrett Browning,* 12th ed. (New York: Thomas Y. Crowell, 1974), p. 408.

49. Friedrich Nietzsche, "Joyful Wisdom," in *The Complete Works of Friedrich Nietzsche,* vol. X (New York: Russell & Russell, 1964), p. 168.

50. Paul Ricoeur, *The Symbolism of Evil,* trans. by Emerson Buchanan (New York: Harper & Row, 1961), p. 349.

51. Elie Wiesel, *The Gates of the Forest* (New York: Holt, Rinehart and Winston, 1966), preface.

52. Ricoeur, *Symbolism of Evil,* p. 163.

Chapter Eight
Holy Rites

Ritual is a symbolic mode of communication, of "saying something" in a formal way, not to be said in ordinary language or informal behaviour. This idea of "not to be said" in an ordinary way means that a special character of ritual is its reserve, its apartness, its "sacred" quality.

Raymond Firth
Symbols Public and Private[1]

Holy words and sacred stories are only one aspect of religious expression. Gesture and **ritual** are also primary modes of religious expression as well as indispensable forms of human action. Every society organizes human existence into formal patterns through which group or individual action takes place. Rites are something done; they are visual and tactile performances, movements of coordinated gestures, words, and symbolic objects, which impinge on the entire spectrum of the senses in complex ways that words and concepts by themselves do not.

149

Ceremonies are ubiquitous. They can be occasions for pomp and pageantry, such as the inauguration of a president or the coronation of a monarch, or they can be more subtle and commonplace, such as a greeting or a handshake. They can be explicitly religious, such as the Jewish rite of circumcision, or they can be secular, such as the flip of the coin at a football game or the conferring of degrees at a graduation from a public high school or college.

Sacred rites differ from secular or profane ceremonies in that they are intended to link the ordinary and the nonordinary. Holy rites charge the commonplace and instrumental world with ultimate meaning. Clifford Geertz has used "leaping" as a metaphor for understanding the sacred dimension of ceremonies. Through sacred ritual humans leap into the framework of the sacred. When the ritual ends and the communicant returns to the ordinary world, the person is, as Geertz notes, changed "unless, as sometimes happens the experience fails to register. . . . And, as he is changed, so also is the commonsense world, for it is now seen as but the partial form of a wider reality which corrects and completes it."[2]

We should note that the elements of ritual, like sacred stories, are polysemous, or what anthropologist Victor Turner labeled "condensed symbols," capable of several layers of meaning. Among the Ndembu of northeast Zambia, white is a condensed symbol that suggests divinity, purity, good luck, and fertility. At one point in the *Isoma* rite, a ceremony to remove the affliction or curse that prevents a couple from having a child, a white pullet is given the female patient. The wife holds the white pullet to her breast as a mother holds a child. The pullet symbolizes her transition from defilement to purity. As a condensed symbol, it also suggests that a proper relationship to the ancestral spirit world has been reestablished and that good fortune and fertility will follow.[3]

For the Jewish community, a thing so simple as the prohibition of pork has been a condensed symbol for the Jewish faith. In the second century B.C., the Greeks, led by Antiochus IV, attempted to force their culture on the Israelites. Resistance often meant death. Under Antiochus's repressive leadership, swine were immolated on the altars of the Temple of Jerusalem, and stern measures demanded that the Jews abandon and break Yahweh's instruction. In such a context the refusal to eat pork became a symbol not only of Jewish allegiance to Yahweh but of their resistance to foreigners like Antiochus who, in attempting to make them conform to Greek values, forced them to defile their bodies, repudiate the Torah, and profane the Temple. Prohibition of pork was, in a sense, a shorthand notation for the Hebrew faith, just as abstinence from eating meat on Friday served for many decades as a condensed symbol of an allegiance to Roman Catholicism.[4]

Ritual is the language of religion. It brings into our daily life the invisible world of the spirit and the unseen presence of God.

Morris Adler
Likrat Shabbat[5]

The Primary Features of Holy Rites

Since an understanding of ritual is important in a study of things religious, taking a close look at it is imperative. A good point of departure is to examine the principal features of holy rites. Holy rites resemble each other in at least four ways—namely, they are sacramental, performative, repetitive, and social.

Ritual as Sacrament

In the broadest sense of the term, all moments in which the holy is present are sacraments. Simone Weil suggested that "contact with God is the true sacrament."[6] In Weil's sense the experience of the holy is a sacramental event that is not restricted to the performance of specific rites nor limited to special times or places. Sacrament is contact, and contact with the holy can be experienced in just about any event, person, or thing. For example, in the Zen experience spiritual awareness is possible in such simple activities as planting seeds or washing dishes. In Jewish practice each day and all its activities are to be sanctified by God's presence. Nothing is to be left untouched. Eating, drinking, working, speaking, playing—in short, all of life—is to be touched by the holy.

Although the sacred is manifested in many ways, in practice what is labeled a sacrament has assumed specific and concrete ritual form. The explicit and restrictive character of the sacramental is exemplified by Christian practice. In the early Christian church, Saint Augustine applied the term sacrament to the Creed, the Lord's Prayer, Holy Communion, and baptism. As late as the twelfth century, Hugh of Saint Victor enumerated thirty sacraments. At the Council of Florence in 1439 and again at the Council of Trent in the sixteenth century, however, the sacraments of the Roman Catholic Church were officially declared to be only seven in number: baptism, confirmation, matrimony, communion, ordination, penance, and anointing of the sick. Protestant practice has commonly limited the number of sacraments to two: baptism and communion.

Although holiness can be thought of as everywhere, in the sacrament it is focused in a particular ceremonial process; thus the sacred is made present through gestures, words, and objects. Because they are performed, sacraments are tangible. Contact with the holy is made with the body as well as the mind—that is, the holy is present visually and tactilely as well as conceptually. The Sufis, for example, believe that Allah is present in the motion of the holy dance; as the Sufis dance, they become filled with Allah's presence. The dancer and the dance become an activity of God.

In the sacramental act, the divine power is embodied in a material process. *Chijikijilu* is the Ndembu word for ritual elements that unite the known and unknown. The word means "landmark" or "blaze" and is associated with the trail markings that hunters make to find their way back from unfamiliar areas. The *chijikijilu* are the elements of Ndembu ritual (songs, gestures, articles) that unite the invisible with the visible or embody and make intelligible a mystery.[7]

Two specific examples should clarify what is meant by sacrament as an embodied sacred presence. In the *Isoma* rite two holes with a connecting passageway are dug in the earth, and the couple to be healed take their place in them. One of the holes is said to be hot; it enables the Ndembu to envision death and the curse that prevents the couple from having a child. The second hole is said to be cool and signifies life. The patients move from death to life, from misfortune to health, by ritually crawling from the hole of misfortune, through the umbilical-like passageway, to the hole of restoration; thus the holes dug in the earth sacramentally embody or make visible the curse and its remedy.[8]

The Christian sacrament of Holy Communion is a second example of a sacred presence manifested in a tangible and material process. For many Christians the mystery of the Mass or Eucharist is that, in the proper ritual

Celebration of Holy Communion. Every day and every hour, somewhere in the world, Christians celebrate Holy Communion.

Photo by John Pini

context, Christ is present to the communicant through the material elements of bread and wine. The preamble to the *Constitution on the Sacred Liturgy* issued by the Second Vatican Council (1965) makes this embodiment emphatic: Christ "is present in the sacrifice of the Mass, not only in the person of His minister" but also in the Eucharistic elements, the bread and wine.[9] The Christian message is that Christ died, Christ is risen, Christ will return; the sacrament mysteriously embodies and makes present this message. As a presentational symbol, Holy Communion is a re-presenting of Christ's redemptive work, through which the recipient is united to Christ and enabled to conform to the pattern of His existence.

When sacraments are treated as presentational symbols, the elements of the sacrament are not entirely separable from their signification; thus, for example, in Holy Communion Christ is believed to be present in the bread and wine. His presence, if not a material one, is nevertheless believed to be actual or real. The bread and wine are not physically or in a scientific sense changed, but, in the sacrament, faith enhances the senses so that the communicant perceives the divine presence through them.[10] To affirm the efficacy of the sacraments is to believe and to experience the divine presence in them.

Where ritual acts and elements are viewed as representational rather than presentational symbols, the sacramental elements are separated from their signification; their value is primarily in their meaning to the mind. The distance separating ritual as sacrament or as symbolic reminder is evident in Christian practice. Where Holy Communion is primarily an act of remembrance, the liturgical focus is on the ministry of the word—the sermon. In contrast, the dramatic climax of the Catholic Mass is neither scripture nor sermon, but rather the moment in which the priest, acting in the place of Christ, consecrates the elements so that the body and blood of Christ is re-presented to the people through a transformation of priest, bread, and wine. Seen as a sacred presence, the Mass is an act of God, "a divine event, eternity breaking into time,"[11] as Carl Jung described it.

Ritual as Performative

The ceremonial act is a context in which words, gestures, and objects are employed to do things.[12] They may, for instance, alter or change the status of the participants. The presidential oath is a ritual act in which a president-elect becomes the president of the United States. As such, the presidential oath is an essential act. Neither victory in a presidential election nor an inauguration is necessary; vice-presidents and others in the order of succession can, in the event of the death or resignation of the president, be sworn in without benefit of either. The change of status is effected through the oath. Significantly, the presidential oath to carry out the duties of the office is made to God, which gives a superempirical validation to what otherwise might be viewed as a wholly secular ceremony. In doing so, the American nation and its sociopolitical process is sanctified.

Perhaps installation ceremonies are the most obvious example of ceremonies that change the status of the participants. For example, in the Sinhalese Buddhist community, the transition from secular life to the priesthood is marked by the symbolic breaking of connections with society. The initiate's head is shaved and his body is smeared with mud so that the taint of ordinary activities might disappear. After a ritual bath the newly created monk dons his robe and takes a new name indicative of his new status and spiritual birth. Likewise, for most Christian bodies, baptism is a necessary incorporation rite before membership in the church is conferred.

Rituals have an obligatory quality. Americans conventionally stand when the National Anthem is played; the subtle coercion of custom as well as respect for the symbols of song and flag require it. The Ndembu word for ritual, *chidika,* can be translated as acts that are performed as an obligation or special engagement. The Confucian tradition notes 300 major rites and 3000 minor ones, which are to be observed in their proper context. *Li,* the Confucian term for ceremony, is appropriately understood as the performance of those procedures that are proper to ceremonies. In the Confucian view, humanity is molded and expressed through a respectful performance of conventional rites; humaneness within is fostered by an attention to proper conduct. Herbert Fingarette, a philosopher, writes in his *Confucius: The Secular as Sacred,* "men become truly human as their raw impulse is shaped by *li.*"[13] Like Confucianism, Hinduism stresses ritual. *Rta* is the Vedic word for the order of things, and *rta* is believed to be manifested and sustained through rites. The proper performance of ceremonies assures the prosperity and continuity of the order of things, whereas pollution or nonobservance dislocates the cosmos and endangers the life of the community.

On what does the performative power of ritual depend? In what sense do ritual words and gestures do things? From one perspective, the procedures and elements proper to ceremonies are sufficient to accomplish their ends; thus, the efficacy of ritual is not entirely dependent upon either subjective states or conscious understanding. The magical or efficacious power of *li* enables a person to accomplish his will directly through ritual and gesture; as Fingarette observed, "one simply wills the end in the proper ritual setting and with the proper ritual gesture and word; without further effort on his part, the deed is accomplished."[14]

The presidential oath is a case in point, for it is the oath that confers the change in status and not the subjective conceptions of the chief justice or the president-to-be. Observe also how effortlessly the traditional gestures of greeting, such as the handshake, the embrace, or the bow, create a condition in which cordial exchange is possible. As anthropologist Mary Douglas noted, "only a ritual structure makes possible a wordless channel of communication that is not entirely incoherent."[15] In this sense, the ritual conventions of a society almost imperceptibly, even magically, make communal life possible. The connection between *li* and humaneness is especially emphasized in Confucianism, which stresses that good manners, communicated through ceremonial gestures, produce and exemplify good will.

The insistence that rituals are efficacious in themselves is evident in the following examples. Advocates of Pyramid Power maintain that structures in the form of a pyramid trap beneficial energy. They believe that the well-being of a person who assumes a position within a pyramid structure will be materially enhanced without any further effort or even an understanding of the energy process involved. In this example the pyramid structure is a ceremonial element that reportedly, in itself, makes available a sea of "biocosmic" power. Transcendental Meditation claims that the ritual practice of twice-daily periods of meditation produces dramatic results; practice involves assuming a comfortable position, closing the eyes, and reciting a mantra during each meditation period. There is evidence that such a simple technique, even if imperfectly understood, can produce significant physiological changes, including lowered blood pressure, prevention of cardiac arrest, and profound relaxation. In the Buddhist denomination, Nichiren Shōshū, the devotee is given a *gohonzon,* a mandala of the eternal Buddha or Buddha-nature, to gaze upon. Individual happiness is believed to be obtained by chanting "Nam-myōhō-renge-kyō" before the *gohonzon.*

Do rituals really work? Can rituals be beneficial without being understood? How can legitimate claims about the efficacy of rituals be distinguished from fraudulent ones? Is it possible to distinguish between a magical and a sacramental rite? Certainly ceremonies work when their performance changes the status of the participants; for example, installation rites clearly do something. They also work in the Confucian sense of providing a context for an experience of community. Community and civilized life cannot exist without shared rites and symbols. Such a deceptively simple thing as shaking hands with strangers is a powerful ceremonial gesture. The greeting of strangers is often unsettling. Should they be ignored, abused, or greeted? The handshake establishes a nonthreatening physical contact and provides a ritual context for courteous interaction through which the psychic distance separating strangers can be bridged. As a ceremony the handshake provides the cues and creates the conditions in which humane interaction is possible.

Besides their social effectiveness, rituals work psychologically to produce desired subjective states. In one perspective, the inner space of the participant rather than the objective and material elements constitutes the most important arena in which rites work. Buddhist rituals and prayers, for example, are not ordinarily intended to be seen or heard by the Buddha, but their performance can have beneficial subjective effects. Ceremonies can also be a channel for expressing joy or grief or can help facilitate meditative states. Rites are more likely to be effective if they are performed sincerely. Chanting and gazing at a *gohonzon* work, in part, because they are believed in and not just because of their objective power. Likewise, baptism and Holy Communion provide psychic rewards, including those compensations that come from group participation, even if they are not objectively efficacious.

From the magical and sacramental perspective, rites are at the same time subjectively and objectively efficacious. Sincerity and commitment are important factors, but a sacrament is not intended exclusively to nourish inner states. In the full sense of its meaning, a sacrament involves a sacred presence and a ritual efficacy. Power is available in the sacramental act. Seen as magical, rites provide humans with the elements (words, gestures, objects) that allow them to control, manipulate, and otherwise benefit from nonordinary power. Seen as sacramental, rites involve a divine presence whose transforming power is present as a gift rather than as the result of human coercion. A sacrament is paradoxically an act of God, who makes himself present in the ritual elements, and a human act through which human activities are instruments of the re-presentation of the holy. In speaking of Holy Eucharist or Holy Communion, Mary Douglas summed up what might be justifiably said of the performative character of all sacraments: "Symbolizing does not exhaust the meaning of the Eucharist. Its full meaning involves magical or sacramental efficacy. . . . The crux of the doctrine is that a real, invisible transformation has taken place at the priest's saying of the sacred words and that the eating of the consecrated host has saving efficacy for those who take it and for others."[16]

Ritual as Repetitive

Ritual is repetitive; it is action that is definite, structured, and repeatable rather than spontaneous and unique. Because of their regularity rituals are usually conventional and traditional, even though their repetitiveness and compliance with tradition is open to modification. The repetitive character of ritual is necessary because gestures communicate best when they are familiar, and because rites are linked to the past.

Stereotyped or habitual gestures have more symbolic and expressive richness than do random and unfamiliar ones. Just as linguistic communication is facilitated by following ordinary usage, so also the symbolic import of body language is enhanced through repetition. If rites are a point of contact with the sacred, they must be familiar enough to the participants that they can unobtrusively serve this function. In this sense, ritual is like a musical composition. If attention is drawn away from the piece by discordant notes, then its structural integrity and expressive power is in danger of being subverted by the fragmentary and unfamiliar.

Holy rites are also reiterative because they are dramatic re-presentations of those momentous and exemplary past events in which the sacred has been focused. As Mircea Eliade notes, "Every ritual has a divine model, an archetype." [17] The past time of ritual serves as a model for authentic human existence. It is a momentous time—a sacred time renewed in ritual, from which a people draw their sense of self-understanding and community. Holy drama is a dramatic performance in speech and gesture, which incorporates the meaningful past in the present through regular or periodic repetition.

The reiterative quality of ritual makes it a primary mode for preserving the authority and example of predecessors. If, for instance, tribal peoples are asked why a rite is done or told in such a way, the most typical answer is that the ancient or holy ones arranged or did it in that way. In the Christian tradition, Christ is the authority for the sacraments. As Christ did, so must his people do; the sacraments are performed because they are believed to have been instituted by him. The Muslim obligation to fast ritually during the month of Ramadan is likewise to be observed because it is a practice stemming from Muhammad. Just as Muhammad and Christ are the predecessors to be imitated by Muslim and Christian, so also the Vedas offer the gods as divine models for Hindus: "Thus the gods did; thus men do."[18] Metaphorically speaking, sacred rites are the dramatic vehicle or time machine through which the past is re-presented.

The repetitive character of ritual makes it particularly suitable to act as a double-intentional metaphor through which the common points to the sacred. Through traditional practice each element of ritual can become charged with meaning. Islamic practice, for example, calls for each Muslim to pray five times each day. The physical aspects of the prayers have assumed a well-defined import through repetition. Before the prayer is commenced, the worshiper purifies himself by a ceremonial washing or bathing. The majestic power of Allah commands humility and submissiveness; thus the Muslim kneels during the course of his prayers and touches the earth with his forehead. The body is further positioned so that the head and heart face in the direction of Mecca, the holy city where Allah's revelation to his prophet, Muhammad, was initiated and consummated.

How a people's vital roots, their contact with the holy, are re-presented in ritual can be conceived of in two ways. In one outlook sacred rites are re-creative or sacramental—that is, the past is actually re-presented through imitating the way the ancestors or gods acted in the beginning. From a second perspective sacred rites are symbolic reenactments through which charter events are commemorated or remembered.

Holy Rites as Re-creative

Those who see rites as re-creative believe that an imitation of charter events and divine models constitutes an actual reenactment; thus, sacred myth and ritual is sometimes understood as the real world, the source of true being, and the actual, ordinary world is real only insofar as it reflects the sacred. Mircea Eliade described this conception of being: "an object or an act becomes real only insofar as it imitates or repeats an archetype. Thus reality is acquired solely through repetition or participation."[19] The principle of imitative or mimetic rites is that like produces like. As the gods gestured forth the world, so also, in imitating such gestures, humans sustain and renew the order of creation. Humans are not spectators but rather participants through rituals in the drama of cosmic events. Re-creation is participation; thus, for example, the marriage rite can be seen as an imitation of the cosmic marriage between heaven and earth. In ancient India's matrimonial rite, the husband said to his wife, "I am Heaven. Thou are Earth."[20]

Some of the religious practices of the Huichol Indians of Mexico have this re-creative or sacramental quality. Each year, during the dry season, some of the approximately 9,000 Huichols make a pilgrimage in small groups to Wirikuta, the land of their ancestors. In one sense, the purpose of the journey is merely the gathering of peyote, a hallucinogenic plant that produces visions and stimulates dancing and singing. But its double-intentionality, its transsignification, is important. The pilgrimage is a ritual act that enables the pilgrims to return to the land of their origins, to the sacred space from whence their ancestors came. They hope to revitalize, to re-create, their lives by returning to what they regard as the center of creation.

The Huichol pilgrimage to Wirikuta is led by a tribal shaman, a specialist in the sacred, who has prepared himself spiritually to lead his companions from the ordinary to the nonordinary. The journey begins at the Gateway to the Clouds, the first threshold to be crossed over on the way to Wirikuta. Initiates, those who have never been to the sacred place, are blindfolded so that they might be safe, for the holy ones are dangerous as well as the source of life. At a point early in the pilgrimage, a water ceremony is performed by the shaman. The water is a condensed symbol and is the first of the holy ones made present to the companions. Water is addressed as Our Mother—a divine Mother to whom an offering is given and to whom supplication is made, particularly for the gift of children. It is also a restorative, to be taken home in gourds or bottles so that friends and relatives who have stayed behind might be nourished by drinking it. Water is curative, and the shaman may use it in healing. Water is all of these things, yet in the ritual context it is much more. It is a purifying element that cleanses the pilgrims of their impurities, and it is an instrument of transformation through which the companions shed their usual identities and take on those of their ancestors. As the shaman pours water on each pilgrim's head and removes the initiates' blindfolds, they become their ancestors. At this point the shaman also ceases to be merely himself and becomes the first *marä akáme,* the first ancestral shaman. The presence of the ancestors is re-created in the rite, and the identities of each of the participants are transformed so that they might do what was done in the beginning. Ordinary time is abolished, through the rite, by the eternal or timeless.

The final act of incorporation is the gathering and eating of the peyote known to the Huichols as "our elder brother," *Kauyumarie.* Peyote is both a plant to be eaten and an elder brother whose spirit gives the Huichol life, and who is one way that contact with the gods is made possible. The pilgrimage is a sacramental feast in which the sacred is made present in the eating of peyote and in a festive celebration punctuated by visions, music, dance, and song. The shaman addresses the peyote, "We shall eat your flesh, your body, my Elder Brother." As they eat of the sacramental feast, they are transported into an ecstatic state in which they are made one with the ancient ones, the holy ones.[21]

Holy Rites as Commemorative

Commemorative rites are recollections rather than re-creations of momentous events. Their chief aim is to fix the paradigmatic event and its significance in the mind. Unlike re-creative or presentational rites, the participants in commemorative ceremonies do not assume the identities of either gods or paradigmatic predecessors. The participants know that the rite's mimetic gestures are a form of role playing rather than an actual transformation of reality. For example, when Holy Communion is seen as commemoration only, its performance is intended as a reminder of the Last Supper as a historical event and of its significance in God's plan of salvation rather than as a sacrament in which Christ is re-presented.

Tribal peoples perform both re-creative and commemorative rituals. While the pilgrimage of the Huichols with its holy meal is an example of a sacramental re-creation, the Warramunga of Australia perform a ceremony that dramatically commemorates their mythical ancestor. This ancestor, Thalawalla, formed the land; from his body ultimately came the seeds from which each member of the clan germinated. The commemoration takes the form of retracing through symbolic gestures and designs the travels and creative acts of Thalawalla in the same order that he performed them. The officiants do not become embodiments of the ancestor. As Emile Durkheim pointed out, they know that they are playing a role "whose only object can be to render the mythical past of the clan present to the mind."[22]

Celebration of Passover. Through the Passover meal, Jews commemorate their liberation from slavery in Egypt and reaffirm the preciousness of freedom.

Photo: The Bettman Archive, Inc.

The Jewish Passover *(Pesach)* festival is a beautiful commemoration in word and gesture of God's liberation of the Israelites from bondage in Egypt. The celebration is intended to fix the significance of the Exodus so indelibly in the Jewish consciousness that in each generation "a man is bound to regard himself as though he personally had gone forth from Egypt."[23] At the center of the festival is a family service in which the Passover meal is eaten. The order of the family service, called a seder, is contained in the Haggadah, the book that contains the seder and the Passover narrative. Haggadah is the Hebrew word for telling, and the Passover liturgy is based on the biblical directive, "And you shall tell your son . . . of what the Lord did for me when I came out of Egypt."[24]

Seder begins with a benediction (kiddush) over wine, thanking God for the gift of the Holy Sabbath and for Passover, the "season of our freedom." The father, or the one conducting the seder, washes his hands in imitation of a ritual gesture the priests performed when Passover was celebrated in the Temple of Jerusalem. Parsley is dipped in water and eaten as a reminder of the tears and hunger of slavery. Unleavened bread is eaten, as was commanded of the Israelites in the time of Moses. Candles are lit, usually by a woman, who also pronounces a benediction, "Blessed art Thou O Lord our God, King of the Universe, who has sanctified us by Thy commandments and commanded us to kindle the festival lights."[25] In another prayer, the poor and homeless are invited to join in the seder meal: "This is the bread of poverty, which our ancestors ate in Egypt. All who are hungry, let them come in and eat. All who are needy, let them come in and celebrate the Passover. Now we are here; next year may we be in the land of Israel! Now we are slaves; next year may we be free men!"[26]

The main body of the service is the retelling of the Passover story of the miraculous liberation of the Israelites from slavery in Egypt. The parent must tell the story to the children on each Passover so that its reality and its significance will not be lost. The story is told in response to four questions, taken from the Haggadah, which the children traditionally ask:

"Why is this night different from all other nights?"

"Why on this night do we eat bitter herbs?"

"Why on this night do we dip them in salt water and haroseth?"

"Why on this night do we hold this seder service?"[27]

The parent replies to the four questions by telling of the Exodus. Subsequently a festive meal is eaten, and the seder is concluded with a final benediction.

The rite represents the significance of Passover. It does not re-create or reincarnate the ancestors in the participants, nor is God present in the meal. Through the Passover commemoration the Jewish people forge a link to their past and learn something of the meaning of their Jewishness.

Ritual as Social

Holy rites are social and dialogical rather than private and exclusive. Of course, private as well as public rites exist. Prayer, for instance, can be spontaneous and private as well as formal and public. But even private prayers are often shaped by conventions as to how one prays and by recitation of ritual prayers, such as the Paternoster, "Our Father Who art in heaven . . ." and the Ave Maria, "Hail Mary, full of grace . . . ." Even when holy rites are domestic or private rather than public and collective, their intent is communal in that they preserve cultural values and seek contact with ultimate existence. Holy liturgies can be performed by solitary officiants. Each day the male head of a Hindu household performs domestic rites in which he functions as a priest. Nevertheless, the householder's rites also have a communal character because they are not performed exclusively. Similar rites are performed in thousands of other homes; thus, the householder is part of a believing and gesturing community that has endured for centuries. Though performed by a solitary individual, the rite is not only a way of giving thanks to a deity; it is also performed on behalf of the officiant's family and home.

Collective Rites

The social and interactive character of ritual is most obvious when rites are public and collective. Collective rites are occasions for group drama; this is especially apparent in rites celebrated by an entire people. For instance, the *Apo* ceremony of the northern Ashanti of Ghana is a New Year's feast of eight days in which the entire tribe joins in song, dance, and comic gestures, including the lampooning of the powerful. The rite is intended to cleanse away individual and communal impurities, including those of divisiveness and ill-feeling, that have accrued during the year.

Just as the *Apo* ceremony unites a tribal people in a common festival, so also the Christian calendar unites Christians throughout the world and influences the pattern of collective and public rites in countries where Christian influence has predominated. The calendar of faith begins with Advent, the four Sundays before Christmas. The liturgy of Advent heralds the coming of the Christ child. From Christmas to Easter, Christ's life is remembered, especially in the Lenten preparation for the re-presentation during Holy Week of the Crucifixion and Resurrection. The remainder of the Christian year, from Pentecost to Advent, commemorates not a single life, but human life as it is reflected in the Bible and in the history of the church. Besides the high holy days of Christmas and Easter, each Sunday, each Lord's Day, is a day of congregational worship that stands like Easter as a reminder of Christ's resurrection. No matter how small or isolated a Christian congregation is, it knows that it is part of a universal collective body that shares common beliefs and holy days.

The mass of people that rituals can bring together is, on occasion, almost overwhelming. The intoxication of collective action creates a group psychology capable of sweeping up the participants so that they become engulfed in the drama and fully incorporated in the celebrating community. In the *Kumbh Mela,* a festival held in India once every twelve years, millions of Hindus make their way to the Ganges, the holy river, to bathe in its spiritually liberating waters. Nearly ten million Hindus made the pilgrimage to the festival held in 1977.

Ritual as Shared Experience

Besides the obvious social aspect of collective rites, ceremonies are social in a second and more profound sense. Ritual is one of the principal vehicles that bind people together in a community of shared interest and tradition. Ritual and ritual elements provide group-associational patterns through which people learn what is expected of them and to whom or what they belong. Communities are formed around and sustained by shared rites and symbols. Where common symbols are weak or nonexistent, an experience of community is unlikely.

In religious groups with a strong sense of community, ritual practice even more than belief provides cohesiveness and sets group members apart from others who do not share their customs. The Jewish community is a good case in point. The Jews are admonished, "do not set thyself off from the community," and they are incorporated into the House of Israel principally through **orthopraxis** (correct practice) rather than **orthodoxy** (right beliefs). To be Jewish is less a matter of individual confessions of faith than observance of traditional ways of dealing with human existence.

Jewish worship takes place in the home or synagogue and is primarily corporate. This is exemplified by the corporate character of Jewish prayer on Yom Kippur, the Day of Atonement. The Jew observes this, the most solemn of high holy days, by fasting and through prayers of repentance and supplications for forgiveness. The prayers *(tefillah)* of Yom Kippur are prayed "we" rather than "I." They seek reconciliation and forgiveness for a community and not just the cleansing of an individual. "What shall *we* say before You, who dwell on high" a prayer of confession begins and concludes with the entreaty "May it therefore be Your will, O Lord our God and God of our fathers, to forgive *us* for *our* sins, to pardon *us* for *our* iniquities, and to grant *us* atonement for all *our* transgressions."[28] [Italics added.]

That the personality or melody of a faith is communicated in its ritual is certainly evident in the Jewish faith. At the center of Jewish worship is God who has blessed the Jews with a holy day (Sabbath) and a holy book (Torah) and who has made them a holy people. Jewish ritual is an important context for acting out what God has commanded, for life is sanctified or hallowed through ritual. The Jewish prayer book *(Siddur)* is the primary instrument for the liturgy of the synagogue. It reflects not only Jewish values but their tensions as well. Jewish worship is primarily directed to giving thanks and praise to God, "O give thanks to the Lord, for He is good." Seared deep into Jewish consciousness, however, and reflected in the prayerbook, is the time of slavery in Egypt, the centuries-old story of persecution in Europe, and finally the horror of the Holocaust, in which over 5 million Jews were systematically imprisoned and murdered. The sanctifying of life, of drawing God near, through the ritual process mediates but does not entirely resolve the experience of his absence in Auschwitz, Buchenwald, and Dachau.

The poetry of the liturgy and the colorations of the ritual context set the heart dancing or, conversely, make the participant feel uncomfortable and out of place. Witness the typical reaction of outsiders to faiths with differing liturgies. For example, the ceremonial richness of Catholic liturgy has a very different tonal quality from that of most Protestant bodies. A young Catholic reported this reaction to her first experience with United Methodist worship: "I felt very strange inside the church. It really looked empty compared to my church. There were no windows or candles or statues—just rows and rows of pews."

Ritual renews and fortifies our sense of linkage with a tradition and our continuity with a community spanning centuries. . . . Woven into the daily texture of his life, ritual is a reminder to man of who he is, and what his supreme goals and duties are.

Morris Adler
Likrat Shabbat[29]

The Purposes of Holy Rites

As indicated in the previous section, holy rites are meeting places, points of contact with the holy. They are visible, tangible, repeatable patterns through which the holy is drawn near and focused. Some ceremonial acts are performed solemnly with hushed sounds and subdued gestures, while others are jubilant, even intoxicating. Rites associated with sickness, famine, death—in short, all that endangers life—are usually, like tragedy, dramas in which some stain is removed and the correct order of things is reestablished. Four primary themes and purposes of sacred rites are purification, supplication, praise, and thanksgiving.

Rites as Purification and Supplication

Supplication and purgation—seeking help and expiation of guilt—are common modes of expressing human needs and are found in the religious life of all peoples. Rites and prayers of supplication seek either divine help or the avoidance of divine wrath by acts of expiation, of purification. Human dependence, the need for help, is expressed simply, yet eloquently, in this prayer of a woman from the Watja tribe of Africa: "O divine power, I know thee not. But thou knowest me; I need thy help."

In practice, supplication and purification are closely linked. For instance, in some rituals sacrificial offerings, believed to embody the impurities of a group, are placed in a fire so that the flames, identified with God, might burn away guilt. Water, like fire, is also a natural symbol of purification; thus, for example, the Muslim's prayer is preceded by a symbolic cleansing in preparation for communion with Allah.

Purity of the body has been regularly associated with the drawing near of the sacred. Sexual abstinence, fasting, pilgrimage, and other forms of self-denial are practiced to obtain divine favor or as expiation for sin. Mortification of the flesh is not uncommon; thus the body may be beaten, lacerated, suspended on hooks driven through the flesh, or otherwise abused. Lent and Ramadan are times of abstinence and self-denial. During Ramadan Muslim faithful are not to take either food or drink from sunrise to sunset through the entire month. For Christians the Lenten season is one of physical austerities and prayer in preparation for the celebration of Christ's crucifixion and resurrection; the physical deprivations of Lent help the communicant focus on the suffering of Christ. Formerly Lent was observed by abstinence from eating meat for a period of forty days before Easter Sunday, excluding Sundays, which are feast days. Now, however, Catholic Christians are obligated to observe only two fast days: Ash Wednesday, which marks the beginning of Lent, and Good Friday, the day of Christ's crucifixion.

Rites of supplication and purification need not be as solemn as the previous examples suggest. Just as holy dramas performed in the tragic mode remove stains and flaws, so also comedy heals and restores by laughter. The *Apo* rite of the Ashanti, an eight-day feast that takes place prior to their new year, is a good example of the curative power of comic rites. At this time the powerful are humbled and the humble, in anthropologist Victor Turner's words, "are exalted through the privilege of plain speaking."[30] *Apo* is an occasion when direct and unflattering speech, in a festive context of song and dance, joy and mirth, is intended to cleanse both the speaker and those who are made fun of. As a testimony to the cleansing and healing power of *Apo*, Turner quotes an Ashanti high priest of the god Ta Kese:

> *You know that every one has a* sunsum *(soul) that may get hurt or knocked about or become sick and so make the body ill. Very often, although there may be other causes, e.g., witchcraft, ill health is caused by the evil and the hate that another has in his head against you. Again, you too may have hatred in your heart against another, because of something that person has done to you, and that, too, causes your* sunsum *to fret and become sick. Our forbears knew this to be the case, and so they ordained a time, once every year, when every man and woman, free man and slave, should have freedom to speak out just what was in their head, to tell their neighbours just what they thought of them, and of their actions, and not only to their neighbours, but also the king or chief. When a man has spoken freely thus, he will feel his* sunsum *cool and quieted, and the* sunsum *of the other person against whom he has now openly spoken will be quieted also. The King of Ashanti may have killed your children, and you hate him. This has made him ill, and you ill; when you are allowed to say before his face what you think you both benefit.*[31]

Rites as Praise
and Thanksgiving

Just as supplication and purification are human responses to holiness, so also are thanksgiving and praise. In fact, rites are ordinarily a mixture of purification, supplication, thanksgiving, and praise. The Muslim month of Ramadan, the month of solemnity and austerities, is brought to an end by a joyous day of feasting. Fast gives way to festival, expiation to thanksgiving. The *Apo* ceremony of the Ashanti is a time of dancing, singing, and laughter. In the Jewish faith, God is praised by joyful living: "Make a joyful noise unto the Lord, all ye lands. Serve the Lord with gladness: come before his presence with singing."[32]

Holy rites are sacrificial; in fact, thanksgiving is exemplified in the practice of sacrificial giving. Sacrifice is an offering of a gift to the holy in thanks for what has been received. Reciprocity is the formula of sacrifice. It can be direct and material as in this Papuan prayer and offering: "Compassionate father, here is some food for you. Eat it, and be kind to us on account of it."[33] Something is given; something is received. Sometimes animal life or, more rarely, human life is sacrificed. One of the tragic stories of human sacrifice is that of Jephthah, the Israelite who sought God's help in battle. Jephthah vowed, "If thou wilt give the Ammonites into my hand, then whoever comes forth from the doors of my house to meet me, when I return victorious . . . I will offer him up for a burnt offering."[34] When the victorious Jephthah returned home, it was his daughter, his only child, who ran from the house to meet him.

A Shinto rite, the Great Food Offering, illustrates the mixed character of ritual expression. The rite is traditionally performed soon after the Japanese mikado takes his throne. Shinto priests first purify the sacred place and the celebrants in order to receive the *kami* (spirits). Properly cleansed, they pray to summon the *kami,* and offerings are given. Prayers, chants, and other gestures are then performed, praising and seeking the *kami's* blessing. After the *kami* are invited to retire, a joyous communal feast is celebrated.

The Great Food Offering is a major public Japanese rite, but the same complex richness of ritual expression can be found in simpler ceremonies. For example, Aylward Shorter describes a healing rite for an injured boy of the Nuer people of the Sudan. The rite primarily seeks divine aid for the boy, but since supplication involves giving thanks for what is to be received, the Nuers sacrifice a ram to their deity, Kwoth. Before the gift is given, the ram is first consecrated or purified by placing ashes on its back and by cleansing its tethering peg with water. A prayer is said, which begins with an invocation seeking God's presence, followed by telling the wounded boy's story. The petition, the primary occasion for the rite, is made: " 'Let the wound heal, let it be ransomed.' " The prayer concludes by praising Kwoth's greatness: " 'For you are God of our home in very truth.' "[35]

Ritual and Antiritual

Rite brings out . . . the harmony and beauty of social forms, the inherent and ultimate dignity of human intercourse . . . the moral perfection implicit in achieving one's ends by dealing with others as being of equal dignity. . . . to act by ceremony is to be completely open to the other; for ceremony is public, shared, transparent.

Herbert Fingarette
Confucius: The Secular as Sacred[36]

Although ritual has been an indispensable feature of religious symbol systems, modern sensibilities have questioned the capacity of traditional rituals to serve as instruments of worship and spiritual liberation. In the remaining section of this chapter, we consider different assessments of the value of sacred rites.

Moderns are often suspicious of and hostile to rituals. Ritual has become, as Mary Douglas noted, "a bad word signifying empty conformity."[37] Certainly a distrust of ritual has been a persistent theme in the American experience. The democratic impulse, with good reason, has been chary of and inhospitable to imperial pomp and societal structures that place kings and aristocrats over commoners. American Protestantism, shaped by its anti-Catholicism and the character of life on the American frontier, has countered the sacramental and hierarchical formalism of Catholic rites by stressing liturgical simplicity and private religious experience. The revolt against religious formalism is taken a step further by those who dismiss claims of the efficacy of sacred stories and rites and who equate them with the magical emphasis on the faithful execution of prescribed gestures, formulas, and incantations.

The major dislocations of the sixties and early seventies, the struggle for racial and sexual equality, and the Vietnam War deepened the contempt for traditional rituals and symbols. "All men are created equal," Thomas Jefferson wrote in the Declaration of Independence, and in doing so he struck a moral chord that has informed American values. The Statue of Liberty beckoned Europe's poor to the land of the free; it stood as a symbol of America as a land of opportunity and as a melting pot of ethnic diversity. The experience of the sixties, however, raised to consciousness a radically different perception of America. In American practice, equality was a mockery. Blacks, browns, and women were caught in a web of discriminatory practices. The country's history was stained by racism, and nowhere was this more evident than in the inequalities of America's justice system, where minorities and the poor found justice anything but blind to the realities of status and color. Public success in the land of opportunity seemed for white males only and particularly for those who were Anglo-Saxon and Protestant. The schools conformed blacks, browns, and American Indians to the image of the WASP. Women were sandwiched into submissive roles as wives and homemakers. In Vietnam, the government's military might, in the name of stopping the communist peril in Asia, allied itself with a corrupt minority regime. At one point in the war, the United States' executive and military leadership appeared to have embraced the paradox that in order to save Vietnam, it might be necessary to destroy it. Watergate was the final denouement; it revealed that those associated with the highest office of the land were guilty of breaking the law they had sworn to uphold.

Amidst such dislocations, the ritual elements that formerly served to unite the nation (the flag, the national anthem, the Pledge of Allegiance) and the traditional Christian liturgies, America's dominant religious tradition, experienced a perilous passage. The old rituals and symbols became divisive rather than unifying. As American unity unraveled Americans sought their identities either in countercultures that provided alternative supporting communities with new rituals and symbols or in expressions of individuality.

The more politically active and ideologically minded condemned as coercive and repressive those rituals that reinforced traditional values. They perceived that no break with tradition is possible unless the habitual and routine is broken. Courtesies to women were seen as symptomatic of male oppression. Christian reformers sought and are still seeking changes in those Christian rites and priestly communities that are exclusively or predominantly male. The suit and tie, short hair, and neatness symbolized conformity to the values of a corrupt system. Long hair, denims, and drugs symbolized liberation. Add a beard, foul language, and militant gestures, and the ritual posture of a revolutionary is created. Good manners and public propriety were dismissed as mindless conformity to middle-class morality and were replaced by such new rituals as a politics of confrontation.

Where ritual was not denounced as a tool of repression, it was often declared empty, monotonous, and dead. Spontaneity, novelty, even inarticulateness, if it came from the heart, was preferred to the structured, formal, and well-rehearsed. The cult of the individual sought to follow Jerry Rubin's advice, "Do it!" Doing your own thing is, of course, the very antithesis of doing ceremonies. The repetitive and structured character of ritual was judged boring, while the unstructured and spontaneous were exciting. The now generation concurred with Henry Ford's judgment, "History is bunk." Rituals, the principal dramatic mode for preserving traditions and commemorating the historically momentous were out; happenings were in. Uniqueness was judged the exclusive mark of creativity. Inward states were eagerly sought and were juxtaposed to outward states that were judged mechanical and superficial. Timothy Leary and the hippies recommended turning off, dropping out of society, and tuning in to a psychedelic world available through drugs. Encounter groups, marathon therapies, and other experiments sought ways of making people open to each other. Rituals were condemned for fostering a lack of feeling and commitment. Thomas Harris, author of *I'm OK, You're OK,* concluded that rituals are relatively impersonal uses of time that can keep humans apart because they require no risk or commitment. "There are worship rituals, greeting rituals, cocktail party rituals, bedroom rituals. The ritual is designed to get a group of people through an hour without having to get close to anyone."[38]

How can ritual be defended against the charges that it is repressive and coercive or that it is empty and unfeeling? The two charges are quite different. Where rites are judged repressive and coercive, they are perceived as a powerful societal force that requires opposition. Where they are merely empty and unfeeling, they are best countered by indifference.

The ritualist and the antiritualist agree on several points. Ceremonies are repetitive; they do reinforce and conserve traditional values. But the ritualist would like to argue that these qualities should not be summarily dismissed. To demand that ritual be spontaneous and unstructured is to insist that it be something other than what it is. Sacramental contact is made through reiteration and re-creation. It is the structured nature of ritual, in which one thing follows another effortlessly, that creates an openness to the holy and to an experience of community. Nothing may happen in the ritual, it may be flat and empty, precisely because an individual is unwilling to be enlisted as an actor who participates willingly and thankfully in the drama. Rituals are repetitive, even habitual, but they are not necessarily performed mindlessly, without feeling or commitment. Authentic ritual, true *li,* is alive and noncoercive when those who participate in it respect its form and draw meaning from its performance. Holy Eucharist, for example, is communion when it involves feeling, commitment, and openness to the sacrificial mystery, the presence of Christ in the elements of the Mass. Its transsignification is lost only for those who participate insincerely and mechanically.

A strong case can be made for the indispensable role that rites play in the creation and preservation of civilization. In addition to the study of history, the ritual process is the principal way that a people's past, and all that is sacred in it, is made present. In his study of Confucius's understanding of *li,* Herbert Fingarette makes a persuasive case for the capacity of ritual to conform man's raw impulses to those of a social being:

> *Only as we grow up genuinely shaped, through and through, by traditional ways can we be humans. . . . Shared tradition brings men together, enables them to be men. Every abandonment of tradition is a separation of men. Every authentic reanimation of tradition is a reuniting of men.*[39]

Rites preserve the reasonable conventions of society. Without good manners and common courtesies—that is, without the ritual context—humans are too often loutish and abusive. A people unmindful of its traditions, disrespectful of ritual, is a fragmented, even solipsistic, collection of individuals rather than a shared community. Where people are bound together in a closely knit community, ritual is strong. The more unstructured and fragmented the culture, the less ritualistic.[40] At its worst, ritual is an instrument of repression, and at its best it is both a sacramental presence and an experience of a human community.

In an age of rapid social change, the survival of traditional ritual forms or even of a sense of history is problematic. New understandings and changing social conditions force old forms to their breaking points and demand new rituals and symbols. It is a difficult time for liturgists. Traditionalists want to follow the old ways, while nontraditionalists maintain that reforms have not gone far enough. Some demand a shift from vertical worship of a transcendent Being to horizontal liturgies that stress interaction between the celebrants. Eyes and gestures that formerly reached heavenward must now be redirected to one's neighbors. And yet, in spite of all the stresses, somehow, as Ernesto Cardenale, a Nicaraguan priest, points out, people still turn to holiness, still seek ultimate existence:

> *Right now there is no "correct" way to worship*
> *the Lord; no such thing as sacred music exists;*
> *hardly any religious symbols can be recognized . . .*
> > *but people do sing praise*
> > > *and pray*
> > > *and cry hurray . . .*
> > *and they congregate to sing praise*
> > > *and pray*
> > > *and cry hurray . . .*
> > > *and*
> > > *ask for justice*
> > > *seek liberation*
> > > *break bread*
> > > *drink wine.*[41]

Concluding Remarks

Ritual is a primary mode of religious expression—one that unites words and gestures to form a sacred drama. Like all ceremonies sacred rites are performative, repetitive, and social. They differ, however, from other ceremonies in that they are a play of words and gestures through which the holy draws near or is made present. Through such rites people individually and in groups, act out their supplications, seek purification of their defilements, and celebrate in praise and thanksgiving the gift of transformed existence.

Notes

1. Raymond Firth, *Symbols Public and Private* (Ithaca, N.Y.: Cornell University Press, 1973), p. 176.

2. Clifford Geertz, "Religion as a Cultural System," in Michael Banton, ed., *Anthropological Approaches to the Study of Religion* (London: Tavistock, 1966), p. 38.

3. Victor Turner, *The Ritual Process: Structure and Anti-Structure* (Chicago: Aldine, 1968), pp. 11–25.

4. Mary Douglas, *Natural Symbols* (New York: Pantheon Books, 1970), p. 11.

5. In *Likrat Shabbat,* compiled and trans. by Rabbi Sidney Greenberg (Bridgeport, Conn.: Prayer Book Press, 1975), p. 85.

6. Simone Weil, *Waiting for God,* trans. by Emma Craufurd (New York: Harper & Row, 1973), first published by G.P. Putnam's Sons in 1951, p. 214.

7. Turner, *The Ritual Process,* p. 15.

8. Ibid., pp. 18–24.

9. In James Hitchcock, *The Recovery of the Sacred* (New York: Seabury Press, 1974).

10. John Macquarrie, *Principles of Christian Theology,* 2nd ed. (New York: Scribner's, 1977), pp. 478–81.

11. In S.P. Nagendra, *The Concept of Ritual in Modern Sociological Theory* (New Delhi: Academic Journals of India, 1971), pp. 108–09.

12. See Herbert Fingarette, *Confucius—The Secular as Sacred* (New York: Harper Torchbooks, 1972), p. 14.

13. Ibid., p. 71.

14. Ibid., p. 3.

15. Douglas, *Natural Symbols,* p. 5.

16. Ibid., pp. 47–48.

17. Mircea Eliade, *Cosmos and History,* trans. by Willard Trask (New York: Harper & Row, 1959), p. 21.

18. Ibid.

19. Ibid., p. 34.

20. Ibid., pp. 2–3.

21. See film, *To Find Our Life,* produced and directed by Peter Furst, Latin-American Center, University of California at Los Angeles, 1969.

22. Emile Durkheim, *The Elementary Forms of the Religious Life* (New York: Free Press, 1951), pp. 416–20.

23. Abraham Millgram, *Jewish Worship* (Philadelphia: Jewish Publishing Society of America, 1971), p. 307.

24. Exodus 13:8.

25. Frances Fowler Allen, "When Jew and Christian Meet," *United Methodists Today* (Nashville, Tenn.: United Methodist Publishing House, June 1975), p. 40.

26. Millgram, *Jewish Worship,* p. 306.

27. Ibid., pp. 307–09.

28. Richard Comstock et al., *Religion and Man: An Introduction* (New York: Harper & Row, 1971), p. 518.

29. In *Likrat Shabbat,* p. 85.

30. Turner, *The Ritual Process,* p. 179.

31. Ibid.

32. Psalm 100:1–2.

33. See Jan de Vries, *The Study of Religion: A Historical Approach,* trans. by W. Kees Bolle (New York: Harcourt, Brace and World, 1967), pp. 200–02.

34. Judges 12:30.

35. Aylward Shorter, *Prayer in the Religious Traditions of Africa* (New York: Oxford University Press, 1975), pp. 21, 61.

36. Fingarette, *Confucius,* p. 16.

37. Douglas, *Natural Symbols,* p. 1.

38. Thomas Harris, *I'm OK, You're OK* (New York: Harper & Row, 1969), p. 116.

39. Fingarette, *Confucius,* p. 69.

40. Douglas, *Natural Symbols,* pp. 70–74.

41. In *Sing and Pray and Shout Hurray!* compiled by Roger Ortmayer (New York: Friendship Press, 1974), p. 7.

Chapter Nine
Patterns and Types of
Holy Rites

*Religious ritual is an agreed pattern of ceremonial
movements, sounds, and verbal formulas, creating
a framework within which a corporate religious
action can take place.*

Evelyn Underhill
Worship[1]

The exploration of the conceptual and ritual dimensions of religious
expression has entailed an examination of the symbolic character of human
expression and an introduction to religious language and sacred rites. In
chapter eight, the focus shifted from religious language to an analysis of the
general features and purposes of sacred rites. This chapter completes the
study of the ritual dimension with a consideration of the dramatic character
of holy rites, a description of what some scholars have identified as a ritual
pattern or process, and an identification of varieties of sacred rites.

Tis said, it could be very harmful
To make profession of disguise
And see and act through others' eyes;
If this is very often done,
A man becomes the other one.

Wolfgang von Goethe [2]

Just as story is a useful category for understanding religious language, drama is a useful metaphor for holy rites. Drama, like ritual, is performed. The derivation of both terms indicates activity. The word *ritual* is derived from a Greek term meaning "a thing done," and *drama* is a derivative of a Greek verb meaning "I act" or "I do." A drama is a staged production uniting words, gestures, and material supports to express ideas and emotions. Ritual has the same ingredients; thus the major religious celebrations combine the poetry of myth and song with gesture and dance. The highest forms of ceremonial expression are sacred dramas. The experience of holiness has incited man to respond, as Evelyn Underhill observed, "not by a single movement of the mind, but by a rich and complex action in which his whole nature is concerned and which has at its full development the character of a work of art."[3] The dramatic and evocative character of ritual prompted Susanne Langer to characterize ritual as "a symbolic transformation of experience that no other medium can adequately express."[4]

Stages and playgrounds are self-contained and contrived worlds that, in setting aside the common and routine, catch us up in the make-believe world of drama and game. Holy rites share with drama the quality of make-believe, for they involve stepping out of the ordinary in order to entertain a holy presence. Holy rites are the play and playground where, as Karl Kerenyi suggested, "something divine must be added, whereby the otherwise impossible becomes possible"[5] — where the celebrants make contact with the holy and in the drama of the ritual put on the mask of God.

In assuming roles and bringing characters to life, actors create a world of meaning that their audiences may empathetically enter; thus drama, in evoking laughter and tears, cleanses and heals the human spirit. Participants in holy rites perform their roles for a sacred audience. In the ritual drama the participants re-present the meaningful or exemplary past through remembering or re-creating the sacred gestures and words of the gods or of paradigmatic predecessors. In both types of drama, the actors become, as Goethe's poem suggests, identified with the one whom they are representing; thus as actors lose themselves in their roles, the celebrants in holy rites lose themselves in the sacred.

Drama calls for a suspension of disbelief. In order to enter fully a play or rite, the participants must be able to suspend the ordinary and conventional. Mary Chase's play, *Harvey,* asks the audience to share in the delightful fantasy world of Elwood P. Dowd and his six-foot-tall rabbit companion, Harvey. The play offers two images of reality. One image demands that humans be materially successful, which, in turn, requires that they be smart, aggressive, callous, and insensitive. Elwood's psychiatrist asks him to be a responsible part of this conception of reality. The play places the second image of reality, the one chosen by Elwood, alongside the first. Rather than opt for success erected on indifference to others, Dowd chooses to be pleasant, affectionate, and considerate. His struggle between the two visions of reality is reflected in his reply to the psychiatrist: "I wrestled with reality for forty years, doctor, and I am happy to state that I finally won out over it. . . . My mother used to say to me, 'In this world, Elwood, you must be oh, so smart, or oh, so pleasant.' For years I was smart. I recommend pleasant. You may quote me."[6]

Playground, stage, and rite are instruments for the creation or re-creation of different visions of reality. Elwood's world is an invitation to humaneness—an invitation that the play helps us to see with a clarity of vision that is often blurred in day-to-day living. Holy rites are intended to suspend the ordinary in order to re-create a sacred place and a sacred presence. Holy dramas are fantasies that, like Elwood's rabbit, can liberate us from the tyranny of ordinary reality by serving as an invitation to a vision and experience of a sacred cosmos.

Perhaps the simplest and purest forms of dramatic expression are dance and pantomime, because they employ only gestures and movements. Dance and pantomime have played significant roles in holy drama, especially in tribal faiths. Humans put on the masks of the gods and, in imitating their movement or rhythm, make the gods present. Power over prey is believed to be obtained through hunting dances. In war dances, the enemy is ritually portrayed and symbolically overcome. In dances of love, lovers are opened to each other.

Dance and gesture are, of course, not limited to the holy dramas of tribal faiths. In many traditions the holy is believed to be present in the dance. Shiva, one of the great gods of India, is also known as Nataraja, Lord of the Dance. The movement of the universe is Nataraja's dance. The gods of the Greeks also danced. Dionysus, the mad, intoxicating god associated with wine, was said to set people dancing and, in dancing the dance of his cultic ritual, the celebrants become god-intoxicated. It was the gods of ancient Greece, like Dionysus, that prompted Nietzsche to exclaim, "I would believe only in a god who could dance . . . who would dance his dance through me."[7] The spiritual home of the Muslim dance is found among the Sufi. In the spinning and whirling of the Sufi dance, the participants experience a disorientation, a loss of self, in which the celebrants feel transported, as if they were standing outside of themselves. The Sufi poet,

Circumcision Ceremony of the Wagogo Tribe, Tanzania. Among tribal peoples, dance and song are primary vehicles for the performance of their sacred stories and rites.

Photo by George Rodger, Magnum Photos

Jalal al-Din al-Rumi (d. 1273), said, "Whoever knows the power of the dance resides in the god, for he knows how love kills."[8] In the rhythm of the dance, the self is obscured so that the soul can be filled with god.

A Hero ventures forth from the world of
common day into a region of supernatural
wonder; fabulous forces are there encountered,
and a decisive victory is won; the hero comes
back from his mysterious adventure with power
to bestow boon on his fellow men.

Joseph Campbell
The Hero with a Thousand Faces[9]

A Ritual Pattern

Although scholars do not agree on the subject, some have identified a ritual process that unfolds in three stages. The successive stages of the ritual process have been the subject of several anthropological studies, including those of Arnold van Gennep and of Victor Turner, who described the ritual structure as beginning with a rite of separation, entering a transition or **liminal** period, and concluding with an act of incorporation. Depth psychologists, particularly those influenced by Carl Jung, have also discerned three ritual stages. For example, Joseph Campbell maintains that the three phases of the ritual process are a manifestation of a universal cosmic force present in all of us. The triadic structure of separation, initiation, and return is what Campbell refers to as a monomythic pattern—that is, a pattern of social, psychological, and cosmic separation, struggle, and reintegration manifested throughout the world in sacred stories, rites, and dreams.[10]

The three phases of the ritual process are best illustrated by looking closely at a specific ritual performance. Peter Farb describes a rite of initiation to adulthood of the Luiseño Indians of southern California. Those who were to make the transition from adolescence to maturity were first set apart in a special place and were given a drink made from the roots of jimsonweed. The drink prompted visions and what they experienced as a sacred presence. "Later the initiates had to descend into a pit dug in the ground, symbolic of death, and then climb out again, supposedly indicating rebirth."[11] During the rite, the youths endured physical ordeals and were taught Luiseño values and norms of adult conduct.

The Luiseño rite follows the pattern or process that Turner, van Gennep, and Campbell believe is present in most fully developed holy rites. The pattern of ritual drama is like a three-act play. In act one, the participants in the ritual are separated from the profane world—that is, they enter a sacralized, set-apart world. In the case of the Luiseño, the initiates were placed in a special enclosure where sacramental contact was made.

Act two is a time of transition during which the initiates are suspended between what is being left behind and what they are not yet fully part of. Liminal, meaning threshold, is what van Gennep labeled the second phase. It is a period of crossing over a threshold or passing through a doorway leading from one way of being to another; thus it is a time in between, like that between waking and sleeping. The movement from the death of the old and the birth of the new is symbolized in the Luiseño rite by the initiates' descent into and ascent from the hole in the earth.

In act three, the initiates are reincorporated into communal life. The perilous passage from one stage to another is accomplished. In the case of the Luiseño initiates, adult status with its privileges and responsibilities is conferred. The communicants reenter the profane and the secular, but they return, by virtue of the performance of the ritual process, with their lives changed. It is the rite that changes the status and transforms the lives of the participants. Incorporation phases, since they are births of transformed or changed beings, are often times of jubilation and celebration.

The triadic structure of ritual is therefore one of separation, transition, and incorporation. Most momentous occasions in the human life cycle are marked by rites that reflect this common pattern. In traditional Jewish practice, for instance, the incorporation of two families and two people in the marriage rite was preceded by an engagement followed by a betrothal period. The engagement set the prospective bride and groom apart from the social pattern as they had known it. A betrothal period, the liminal phase, followed; it was formerly a year in length. The betrothal period was traditionally a time of struggle, assessment, and anticipation, in which the enormous consequences of marriage were faced.

Pregnancy and childbirth have prompted the same ritual pattern. In many tribal cultures, the first signs of pregnancy trigger the process, and the pregnant woman is isolated from the ordinary course of life. Her person is taboo—that is, it is in the circle of sacred existence and is withdrawn from the common and profane. The period of pregnancy is one of transition. It calls for ritual acts that facilitate an auspicious childbirth. In India, for instance, a Vedic practice calls for a "parting of the hair" ceremony sometime between the fourth and eighth month of pregnancy. The husband takes a position behind the mother-to-be and parts his wife's hair, moving from the forehead back. The rite is believed to help insure a safe delivery. The final ceremonial phase is associated with childbirth. The rite incorporates the mother into her new role and makes a place for the child in the community.

The ritual structure is rooted in profound natural, individual, and communal experiences. Joseph Campbell has pointed out a similar pattern in the adventures of the archetypal hero and by extension in the transformational experiences of all humanity since, in the depth-psychological approach, archetypal heroes are projections of us all. Heroes are initially separated from ordinary reality and enter a supernatural region. Before they can become whole, they must endure and triumph over hardships. The time of transition is a time in between, during which heroes are initiated, usually in the form of tests, before they can cross the threshold and return to profane life.[12] The pattern is analogous to dying and rising—a life-death-rebirth triad. The crucifixion and resurrection of Christ ritually celebrated each year as the culmination of Holy Week reflects a similar pattern. The crucifixion, Christ's death, is the point of separation. The liminal phase is the ambiguous time in between the death on the cross and the resurrection on Easter Sunday. In this time, according to Christian mythology, Christ descended into hell and broke Satan's rule and the dominion of death. Easter is the time of his return, his resurrection, his reincorporation among the living.

Victor Turner has pointed out that the phases of ritual separation and incorporation are relatively structured, while that of liminality is ambiguous and unstructured. In the first phase, the participants are isolated from the profane world and enter a separate sacred mode; what must be done to mark off a sacred cosmos is known and acted upon. In the incorporation phase, the participants are restored to ordinary individual and group life. For example, in the *Isoma* rite to restore a couple's reproductive power, the final phase does not take place until the patient has successfully given birth and raised a child to the toddler stage; until then she lives apart from ordinary social interaction. The incorporation rite restores her to the normal Ndembu pattern. Since the ceremonial return often marks a change of status, as it does in the *Isoma,* it is an occasion for a festive celebration. As an incorporation rite, Easter Sunday is also, like the *Isoma,* a reestablishment of structure. It celebrates the triumph of life over the ambiguity of death and God's victory over Satan. The Lenten season is primarily liminal—a nonordinary time of fasting, prayer, and spiritual preparation that Easter brings to an end. Community life and personal life can now return to normal, buoyed by its experience of resurrected life.

Liminality and Communitas

The liminal or transition phase of the ritual process is an ambiguous in-between time when the celebrants have left behind some fairly well defined condition and have not yet been incorporated into their new roles. In such an ambiguous state, Victor Turner notes, initiates lack status and sharply defined social roles. Often, for example, they wear nothing that might indicate distinctions of rank or class or that would otherwise serve to set them apart from their fellow neophytes. Typically, they dress alike or even go unclothed. In early Christian practice, for example, candidates, whether prince or pauper, were sometimes baptized naked. The thrust of liminality is thus in the direction of anonymity, equality, homogeneity, and statuslessness—qualities that are ritually facilitated by uniform dress, abolition of rank, obedience, submissiveness, and suspension of routine patterns of living.[13]

One example of the movement of liminality toward equality and statuslessness is illustrated by the Ndembu rite for installing a new chief. The position of chief, Turner points out, is a condensed symbol for the total Ndembu community and its tribal land; the fecundity and well-being of the land and its people are tied to the office. Before the chief-to-be is elevated to his new status, he is first ritually stripped of his status. In a sense, the highest tribal office can only be conferred after the chief-to-be experiences the anonymity of the least of his people. The liminal aspect of the rite begins with the building of a small grass hut. It is called a *kafu,* derived from the Ndembu expression for "to die"; in the *kafu,* the chief-to-be "dies from his commoner state."[14] The chief-elect is dressed in a ragged waist-cloth that is symbolic of his statuslessness; he assumes a posture of shame or modesty to emphasize his submissiveness. During the liminal phase he is insulted and made fun of but must not rebuke or otherwise respond in anger to his revilers. He must sit in silence, with downcast head, as a sign of his patience and humility.[15]

In the liminal phase, initiates prepare, sometimes quite arduously, for the act of incorporation. Candidates for Christian baptism, for instance, traditionally readied themselves by prayers, fasting, confession of sins, and all-night vigils. The crossing of the threshold from a previous condition through a mode of statuslessness to incorporation into a new and usually elevated status can require painful trials and ordeals. The crossing-over through ordeal and pain focuses the initiate's attention on the meaning of the process and fixes it in his or her consciousness. Pain and, in particular, mortification or wounding of the flesh has often accompanied rites that initiate youths to adult life. The circumcision rite for young males is one very common example. Turner notes that Tsonga boys are beaten, forced to sleep naked in the cold, forbidden water, and required to eat nauseating food.[16] Most transitional stages, such as pregnancy and betrothal, are accompanied by only mild ascetic practices, but they are ritually marked in some fashion that makes the momentous process an unforgettable one.

The ritual pattern (separation, liminality, incorporation) is, in Turner's analysis, a dialectical movement from structure to antistructure to a reincorporation of structure.[17] The Ndembu chief-to-be is isolated from the normal pattern of his life. He is separated from the structured world, with its relatively well defined roles and norms, and placed in a sacred cosmos. In its liminal phase, the ritual process, like the play, suspends the ordinary and routine. In the case of the Ndembu, the first, the chief-elect, is ritually made to be the last; thus all indication of his status is removed and he is made fun of and likened to a slave. The liminal phase serves as a crack or break in the structure of society and facilitates experience of what Victor Turner calls **communitas.**

Communitas refers, as Turner describes it, to a communion of individuals who share a common humanity.[18] Communitas is a relationship with others, to use Martin Buber's expression, a meeting of "I and Thou." The meeting, the relationship with the other as a Thou, is direct, personal, and nonmanipulative. In Buber's words, *"If I Face A Human Being As My Thou,* and say the primary word *I-Thou* to him, he is not a thing among things, and does not consist of things."[19] Communitas, I and Thou, is the very opposite of knowing others only objectively and impersonally. Communitas, like the liminal phase of ritual, is "a moment in and out of time" and "in and out of secular social structures" when humans experience their existence and that of others as a Thou.[20] In fact, Turner argues, the experience of a shared humanity makes society, structured life, possible.

The Ndembu's reviling of their chief-elect, who moves from lower to higher status through a phase of statuslessness, reveals something of the capacity of the ritual process to make an experience of communitas possible. Turner has recorded the remarks that begin the time of reviling. They are so indicative of the power of the rite to shape the chief in the form of a Thou, who will not lay aside his humankindness once he is installed in office, that they are repeated here:

> *Be silent! You are a mean and selfish fool, one who is bad-tempered! You do not love your fellows, you are only angry with them! Meanness and theft are all you have! Yet here we have called you and we say that you must succeed to the chieftainship. Put away meanness, put aside anger, give up adulterous intercourse, give them up immediately! We have granted you chieftainship. You must eat with your fellow men, you must live well with them. . . . We have desired you and you only for our chief.*
>
>   *. . . today you are born as a new chief. You must know the people . . . You must give up your selfish ways, you must welcome everyone, you are the chief!*[21]

Communitas and Rites of Status Elevation

The installation of the Ndembu chief is a status-elevation rite. During the liminal phase of such rites, the candidates are ordinarily stripped of their status and made to endure trials and ordeals in preparation for crossing over the threshold into a higher status. Wounding is not uncommon. For instance, before the reviling of the Ndembu chief-elect begins, he is cut on the underside of his left arm. He is further physically harassed by being kept from sleep during the entire night of reviling and is periodically hit on the buttocks. The trials and ordeals do several things. They fix in consciousness the importance of the passage, of the change in status. More important, they are elements in the ritual process, a kind of ritual simulation-drama that, in humbling the initiates, facilitates communitas. In a sense, the installation of the Ndembu chief shapes the candidate in the form of a just ruler.

Communitas and Rites of Status Reversal

In rituals of status reversal, those who are already in positions of power reverse roles and experience, through a ritual simulation, the status of the weak. At the same time that the strong are made weak, the weak and the lowly are ritually given power over their social superiors. One example should suffice. The *Holi* festival, celebrated in parts of India every March, is a riot of status reversal. The ritual is associated with the god, Krishna, who has himself experienced several reversals of status—that is, incarnations in which he is believed to have assumed human or animal form. Just as Krishna, the most high, has become man or beast, so also in the *Holi* festival the powerful become identified with the weak, and the socially marginal are elevated. "Under the tutelage of Krishna, each person plays and for the moment may experience the role of his opposite; the servile wife acts the domineering husband, and vice versa; the ravisher acts the ravished; the menial acts the master; the enemy acts the friend; the strictured youths act the rulers of the republic."[22] Men from the Brahman caste, village leaders, are set to flight by the sweeper of their restrooms; wealthy men are jeered and struck by the wives of low-caste laborers and artisans; women are elevated over men and given license to jeer their husbands; bullies are bullied in return; moneylenders are harangued and burlesqued. In short, the *Holi* annually reverses the social order, if only momentarily, and in doing so makes an experience of communitas possible by allowing, even demanding, that it be acted out passionately and jubilantly.[23]

Communitas is, then, an experience that breaks down, but does not destroy, the structures that divide and separate human existence. In the *Holi* and other rites of status reversal, weak are made strong and strong are made weak. In the gospel of John, Jesus acted out the same pattern when he washed his disciples' feet. The master became the servant; the ruler, the ruled. During Holy Week, the pope sometimes visits an Italian prison and washes the feet of some of society's dispossessed. The high is made low, and the low is elevated. A holy, cleansing power was made present to the Sioux Indian through comic rites. In the *Heyoka* ceremony, sacred fools made the Sioux laugh by doing everything backwards or upside down. Through the *Heyoka,* the Sioux were better able, as Black Elk put it, "to see the greenness of the world, the wideness of the sacred day, the colors of the earth, and to set these in their minds."[24] In rites of status elevation, communitas is achieved by a passage to status through a liminality of statuslessness.

An experience of communitas is, of course, possible outside of the explicit ritual process. At the courts of kings and queens, fools and court jesters had license to make fun of the mighty. Woody Allen and Mort Sahl, to name but two, do the same for Americans today. However, an age so suspicious of ritual is likely to experience a poverty of liminality, of cracks in the structure, through which communitas is possible.

An experience of statuslessness, of antistructure, with its possibilities for communitas is perhaps part of the tilt of some modern seekers eastward to Asia. Taoist wisdom, for example, sees clearly the power of the unstructured and passive. It exalts the humble self. "There is nothing weaker than water. But none is superior to it in overcoming the hard. . . . Weakness overcomes strength and gentleness overcomes rigidity."[25] If the power of weakness is one of the themes of the *Tao Te Ching,* is it not also a message of Christmas? Nothing is so weak, so dependent, as an infant, and yet the

Christ Washing the Feet of the Apostles, *attributed by the Kress Foundation to Bernardo Butinone. In this example of communitas, Christ reverses the master-servant role by washing his disciples' feet. Christian groups, such as the Seventh Day Adventists, continue to emulate Christ's example through their practice of a foot-washing ceremony. The rite makes an experience of a sense of community and a common humanity possible.*

Collection of the University of Nebraska Art Galleries, Lincoln, from the Kress Foundation

liminality of Christmas celebrates a poor and fatherless child as the embodiment of God. In his poem, "For the Time Being, A Christmas Oratorio," W.H. Auden suggests, "To those who have seen The Child, however dimly," each Christmas, in spite of its counterfeiting distractions, is a reminder of "the stable where for once in our lives/Everything became a You and nothing was an it."[26]

To this point, the study of holy rites has entailed an examination of general features (rites as sacramental, performative, repetitive, and social), some distinctions as to their purposes (supplication, purification, praise, and thanksgiving), and a look at a ritual pattern (separation, liminality, and incorporation). In the process several types of rites were introduced, including re-creative and commemorative rites and rites of status elevation and status reversal. Only two additional typologies demand special mention: life cycle and seasonal rites.

The life of an individual in any society is a series of passages from one age to another and from one occupation to another.

Arnold van Gennep
The Rites of Passage[27]

Life Cycle Rites

Every community of faith marks, in a ritual context, momentous changes of status or condition. The critical moments of human existence, the points of biological, psychological, and communal stress and transition, are times of ambiguity and anxiety, of moving from the familiarity and security of one way of being to an unfamiliar and intimidating new mode of being. **Rites of passage,** or as Victor Turner calls them, life-crisis rites, provide a context in which the perilous passage can be safely made, as well as a dramatic signal of the importance of the change in the life of both the individual and the community.

Birth, puberty, marriage, and death are the critical junctures in human experience that are, almost universally, occasions for ceremonies, even though all rites in which a change in status or condition is facilitated, including installation rites for presidents, popes, and priests, are rites of passage. Some Hindus, for example, still ceremonially observe as many as sixteen sacred transitional events, and five of the seven sacraments observed by Roman Catholic Christians are rites of passage in which changes in status are effected and sacralized. Because installation rites have already been explained, only those rites of passage associated with birth, initiation to adulthood, marriage, and death are given further attention here.

Life cycle rites play a prominent role in most religions. Among the Coast Salish Indians of British Columbia, for instance, a masked dance was traditionally performed on each of life's milestones. One of the Coast Salish group, the Katzie tribe, believed the creator deity, He Who Dwells Above, established the masked rite to increase their joy and to comfort them during times of grief. They believed the ceremonial wearing of the mask made present a fortuitous and protective power, while the failure to perform the rite left the Katzie powerless or rudderless during the dangerous times of transition. According to the Katzie medicine man, Old Pierre, the god He Who Dwells Above directed the Coast Salish Indians to perform the masked dance:

"Wear this mask when grief and sorrow overtake you, and it shall bring you joy again. Whenever a child is born in your family put on the mask, shake the rattle and chant the prayer that I will teach you, so that the child may grow and prosper. Whenever again one of your daughters reaches woman-

hood wear it and pray four days in succession, so that her new blood may strengthen her and enable her later to bring forth healthy children. Wear it and pray whenever one of your daughters marries and sits for the first time beside her husband. Finally, when I take someone from you—for you shall not live for ever—pray again, beseeching me to care for the soul that has left you, to grant it a happy resting-place, and to spare for a short time longer those who remain behind."[28]

Birth Rites

Life's perilous passage begins with conception and is sacralized by ceremonies associated with pregnancy, childbirth, and child rearing. In one sense, birth rites are rooted in the precariousness of human existence. Will the child survive? Will the mother survive? Will they be healthy? The dangers are very real, especially where modern technology and care are unknown. Rituals enable humans to take an active role in obtaining safe passage.

The fragile and dependent nature of human existence is nowhere more evident than in conception and birth. Parts of the Hindu ritual process associated with birth are primarily intended to insure the continuation of life. In the later stages of pregnancy, the "parting of the hair" ceremony is believed to facilitate a safe delivery. On the day of birth, a ceremony to promote a long life is performed. In the sixth month another milestone is reached and ritually observed when the child eats solid food for the first time. Birth ceremonies, however, involve more than a survival of biological life. Rituals are communal and mark an infant's incorporation in a human family rather than simply an entry into biological life. Infants enter the natural world through childbirth, but they enter human existence, the world created by man, through rites. The Jewish covenant of circumcision, the circumcision of male infants on the eighth day of their lives, shares in the joy of the parents in giving birth to a son, but it also, and more importantly, joins the infant to a supportive and loving community of faith.

Initiation Rites

After birth, the next major biological and psychological dislocation in the human life cycle is that of the transition from childhood to adulthood. These are the difficult years when each person must establish his or her own identity separate from that of his or her parents. Even in the best of times, it can be a troublesome passage. In disjointed times and divided communities, serious identity crises may be the rule rather than the exception. In the broadest sense, initiation rites mark a change of status from childhood to adolescence or adulthood (puberty rites) and admission into relatively restrictive societies or positions (installation rites).

In a narrow sense, initiation rites have been equated with puberty rites that mark the difficult passage to sexual maturity. Certainly many initiation rites have a sexual component and often roughly coincide with the onset of puberty. Adult life involves an explicit sexuality and assumption of sexual roles that set male and female apart in ways that childhood does not. Children may express a bisexuality that the passage to adulthood suppresses. Pain and, in particular, sexual wounds are often an element in puberty rites. In some cultures, young males are circumcised, sometimes quite cruelly and always painfully, as a condition for passing through the threshold to the privileges and responsibilities of adulthood. Tribal women may avoid sexual union with males who have not yet had their sexual maturity confirmed ritually. More rarely, young women are ceremonially wounded in the vaginal area.

In his book *Symbolic Wounds: Puberty Rites and the Envious Male,* Bruno Bettelheim focuses on the pain and, in particular, the sexual wounding that so often accompanies the transition from childhood to adulthood. Other rites follow a pattern of separation, transition, and incorporation, but why is the liminal phase of puberty rites, and, to a lesser extent, of installation rites so much more violent? Victor Turner suggests that the trials and ordeals of liminality are humbling elements in the ritual process that contribute to communitas—that is, an experience of a common human bond. Some stress that liminality is a time of learning, of being initiated into new roles, and that ordeals and pain fix the significance of the event indelibly in the mind. Bettelheim offers another perspective; he finds that circumcision and other sexual wounds associated with puberty rites reflect a deep-seated human desire to possess the characteristics of their sexual opposites. Sexual wounds, male or female, seem, Bettelheim writes, "to originate in the great biological antithesis that creates envy and attraction between the two sexes."[29] In this view, the individual human psyche is both male and female, anima and animus, rather than exclusively male or female. Circumcision symbolizes the male desire to possess a vagina—that is, to be both masculine and feminine. The wounding of the penis, Bettelheim argues, identifies boys with the structure of their mother's vagina and her menstrual bleeding. Circumcision and other male sexual wounds are thus symptomatic of vagina envy, the male's desire to have the sexual apparatus of women.[30]

The sexual component emphasized by Bettelheim distorts the broader significance of initiation rites. In fact, initiation rites often do not correspond to the advent of puberty and are, in many cases, more clearly social than sexual. Even where sex is prominent, puberty rites function to socialize sex and direct it into socially acceptable expression. Initiation rites continue the humanizing process initiated at birth and embody, in particular, the movement to full participation in adult life, which inescapably entails a sexual factor. This is true of the Jewish practice of bar mitzvah, which, although paralleling the onset of puberty, primarily initiates boys at age thirteen to full participation in the religious life of the community.

Like bar mitzvah, the initiation rituals of other religions stress maturity in matters of faith. The Catholic sacrament of confirmation does not incorporate the celebrant into the body of Christ, the Church; baptism does that. But confirmation does signal a mature reflection and conscious commitment to the baptismal faith. While traditionally all Hindu children are born into a caste, in a sense the children of the three upper castes are casteless until they have ritually crossed over the threshold leading from childhood to the student stage of life. It is through the *upanayana* rite that boys of the Brahman, Kshatriya, and Vaisya castes are initiated into the responsibilities and knowledge relevant to their status. According to ancient Vedic practices that continue with some modifications today, Brahman-caste youngsters are to begin *upanayana* during their eighth year; if the training runs its full course, it requires twelve years to complete. *Upanayana* is initiated by a ceremony that unites the boy with a guru, a spiritual father, who is to impart his knowledge in exchange for the youth's service in securing food and maintaining a sacred fire. During *upanayana* the youth is given a sacred thread that he wears on his left shoulder for the rest of his life. The thread symbolizes his spiritual birth. At one point in the rite, the boy hears scripture, a passage from the Vedas, for the first time and is obligated to recite the sacred text in his daily devotions for the remainder of his life. After the youth has been shaped as a Brahman by his spiritual studies and disciplines, he participates in a rite of return through which he leaves his guru and takes his place in the adult community. The rite of return, of incorporation into communal life, involves a ritual bath taken in the presence of women. It symbolizes the passage from the celibate student phase to that of one prepared to be head of a household and to participate in full adult living.

Marriage Rites

Marriage is still another critical change. In spite of its festive and joyous character, marriage involves considerable stress and actual dislocation in that it unites not only the marriage partners but families and class as well. A change of residence, leaving home, is normally part of it. In traditional Vedic practice, the husband-to-be takes leave of his home by eating a last meal with his mother. Marriage is so serious that it usually is accompanied by a change of name, which, like the name given at birth, is inseparably linked to one's identity.

As a rite of passage, the marriage ritual usually begins with the separation and liminality of engagement and betrothal and culminates in the wedding celebration. One example of the marriage ceremony will suffice. The Jewish faith is rooted in family life. Normally a person is born Jewish, rather than converted, and is nourished in the faith in a family context. Israel is appropriately likened to a house, a family of faith. The hallowing of marriage, and of the children that are to issue from it, is therefore of incredible import. The Talmud teaches, "Any man who has no wife lives without joy, without blessing, and without goodness."[31]

In modern Jewish practice betrothal, which was traditionally a separate phase, is now part of the wedding ceremony. The wedding usually begins with the entries of the groom, escorted by his father and father-in-law, and the bride, escorted by her mother and mother-in-law; it is, after all, a ceremony uniting families. The bride and groom meet under a canopy *(huppah)* supported by four rods, which symbolizes the bridal chamber where the marriage is sexually consummated. Under the canopy, the sanctification *(kiddushin)* of the marriage begins when the rabbi pronounces the benediction (blessing) of betrothal over a cup of wine. The couple share the wine as a symbol of their commitment to a shared life. The consecration continues by the groom's giving a gift, a wedding ring, to his bride and the recitation of the words, "Behold, thou art consecrated unto me by this ring, according to the law of Moses and Israel."[32] A marriage contract, delineating mutual obligations and providing protections for the bride in the event of divorce or widowhood, is read and signed before witnesses. The rabbi blesses a second cup of wine, which the couple share as they are henceforth to share the cup of life. At the end of the ceremony, a glass is broken as a reminder, even during the moment of joy, of the suffering that Israel has endured. The joy of the occasion is then celebrated with a feast and other festivities.

The momentousness of marriage is further emphasized by its relative permanence, religiously speaking. Many faiths see it as a relatively indissoluble union and either prohibit divorce or make it difficult to obtain. Mormons stress the importance of marriage so much that they perform a rite that is intended to seal marriage for eternity. Marriage for an ordinary life span is possible, they believe, but a celestial marriage performed in a Mormon temple is preferable.

In practice, marriage often is predicated on assumptions that reflect Saint Thomas Aquinas's characterization of woman as a "misbegotten male."[33] Marriage, for instance, is of such moment that Mormon women are taught that there can be no salvation for them outside of marriage. Although the contractual element in Jewish weddings may serve as a vehicle for sexual equality, Jewish women, like the women of most faiths, have been legally and religiously inferior to their husbands. Traditionally, Jewish husbands could obtain a divorce while their wives could not. The female role was narrowly prescribed in terms of child-rearing and maintaining a home. The Torah teaches that women are physically impure and are not to be touched during menstruation or for seven days thereafter; the wife must take a ritual bath to purify herself before intercourse can resume. Even the birth of male and female children is marked by female inferiority. As prescribed in Leviticus, a woman is unclean for seven days following the birth of a male child, but she is taboo for fourteen days if she bears a daughter.[34]

Rites of Mourning

The perilous passage, the final milestone to be passed over, is death. It is the most feared crossing-over because it leads to an uncharted country from whence, as Hamlet says, "no traveler returns." In most faiths there is a conviction that life does not stop with the death of the body, that survival after death is a dimension of reality. Speaking of tribal faith, philosopher Ernst Cassirer described the deep and abiding conviction that life goes on: "If anything is in need of proof it is not the proof of immortality but the fact of death. And myth and primitive religion never admits these proofs."[35] The message of the pyramids and the elaborate Egyptian ritual process associated with death is the assurance that the dead live.[36]

The threshold that leads "through the valley of the shadow of death" to a different mode of existence has prompted a bewildering panoply of ritual practice. The context of such rites extends from life-endangering situations—illness or injury—to funeral and memorial services where contact between the living and the dead is continued. Apprehension and fear of the departed manifests itself in ritual acts intended either to placate or nullify the danger. Stakes are sometimes driven through the deceased's body so that the spirits might not be set free to haunt the living. Sometimes the body is removed through a window and the path to the home swept clean so that the spirit will not find his or her way back to the family's door. The ambiguous relationship of the dead and the living is evident in the practice of the Coast Salish Indians. The Coast Salish group fear the ghost or shades of their dead, which, they believe, exist invisibly in their lands and might harm the living. When one of the tribe dies in the home, the body is carried out by removing a board from the back wall of the house, because the Salish believe only the living should come through the doorways of their homes. After the body is removed and ritually washed by priests, prayers are said to remove impurities in the home and the board is returned. Two or three days after the funeral, the mourners ritually bathe in a river to complete their purification before they are reincorporated into ordinary life.[37]

Sacred rites normally involve grieving for the deceased, as is the case in the Jewish rite of mourning. If death is expected, the family joins the patient in reciting a confession of sins: "May my death be an atonement for all the sins, iniquities, and transgressions of which I have been guilty against Thee"[38] and concludes with the Shema, the Jewish affirmation of faith, "Hear O Israel, the Lord our God, the Lord is One: and thou shall love the

Lord your God with all your heart, and with all your soul, and with all your might."[39] During the funeral, eulogies for the deceased are spoken. While the corpse is carried to the place of burial, the ninety-first Psalm is repeated, and, at the grave site, God's justice is proclaimed: "The Lord gave, and the Lord hath taken away; Blessed be the name of the Lord."[40] As the mourners close the grave with earth, they may express their grief by tearing their clothing. The mourner's prayer (Kaddish) is recited; it is a song in praise of God that does not mention death. After the service, the grieving family is customarily greeted by the words, "May God comfort you." For one week following the service, the immediate family sit on low stools, befitting their grief. During this week, candles are kept burning, prayers are recited, the hair may be cut, and mirrors are covered. In successive years, on the anniversary of the day of death, a memorial service is held. A candle is kept lit for twenty-four hours; the family remembers their loved one and they reflect on their lives in the light of their relationship to the departed. The Kaddish of mourning praising God is again recited, as it was on the occasion of the funeral.

Besides their function as a vehicle of mourning, death rites are often believed to affect the dead as well as the living. From one perspective, the dead are dependent upon the living, and rites are the most important service that the living perform for the dead. Mormons, for example, practice baptism of the dead. They believe that baptism is essential to salvation; thus those who have died outside the faith and without an opportunity to embrace it still have a chance after death to respond to the Gospel. The baptism for the dead is performed for the deceased by a living person who acts as their proxy. Although the rite itself is not sufficient to guarantee salvation, which requires faith and repentance, it is a necessary condition. Because death does not close the door of salvation, Latter Day Saints, not surprisingly, have an enormous interest in genealogy.

In Hinduism, *Shradda* rites are performed to reconstruct ritually the body of the deceased and to facilitate its spiritual birth. Ordinarily, the funeral rite begins with bathing the body, preferably in the sacred Ganges River. After purification, the body is cremated, often with the eldest son presiding as the priest. When possible the ashes are placed in the Ganges in order to insure salvation; often ashes are brought in jars from great distances so that they might be returned to the sacred source of life. The most important stages of the *Shradda* rites, the reconstitution of the spiritual body, are performed during the twelve days following the cremation. Each day a part of the deceased's body is ritually reconstructed until, on the tenth day, the spiritual body is completed and is ready to join the spirits of other ancestors. On the twelfth day, three generations of ancestors (for example, a deceased father, his father, and his grandfather) are symbolically united by a pressing of rice to form a rice ball. When the rite is completed, the son is free to return to ordinary life. Each year memorial services of prayers and food offerings maintain the contact between the living and the dead. In death, as in life, Hindu women are dependent on male family members. *Shradda* rites can be performed only by a male and thus, for either parent to die without a son is to be set afloat in the liminality of death without help from the living.

Seasonal Rites

The ritual act has all the formal and essential characteristics of play . . . particularly in so far as it transports the participants to another world.

Johan Huizinga
Homo Ludens[41]

Return for a moment to the metaphor of drama, and, in particular, to ceremonial dramas in which contact with the sacred is made. Rites-of-passage dramas are set in the cycle of human existence and the crucial changes in status that are part of a person's movement from birth to death to life. Although the rites may be collective, they are done chiefly for individuals. The actors in life-crisis rites play themselves and are modeled through the process in the ideal forms of their predecessors. Seasonal rites are performed on a different stage. Their subject is the movement of the cosmos; thus, they are calendrical or seasonal dramas that coincide with the movement of the seasons and the renewal of the year. The actors in such dramas do not play themselves, or even human beings for that matter, but re-create the roles of cosmic actors and forces. Seasonal dramas are performed to renew and revitalize the cosmos. Since their scope touches everyone, seasonal rites almost always call for the participation of whole societies or entire groups.

Seasonal dramas are re-creative rather than commemorative, sacramental rather than representational; thus in the ritual process the microcosm recreates the macrocosm. In cosmic faiths, the movement of time is cyclical—a circular movement of periodic beginnings and endings reflected in the biocosmic rhythm of nature. The sacred rhythm of the universe is celebrated through a calendar of rites that closely parallels the alternation of the seasons and the passing of the year and the onset of the new. Seasonal festivals reflect nature's alternation between plenty and scarcity, fertility and barrenness, life and death. In the cult of Demeter, for example, the fertility and fortune of earth and humans are inseparable from the struggle between Demeter and Hades. The reunion of Demeter and Persephone is a time of plenty that is celebrated by a harvest festival. Their separation is a time of scarcity, and the rites that are performed are intended to ease the transition from the harshness of winter to the reuniting of the goddesses in the spring.

A clear example of what is meant by a seasonal drama is embodied in the Babylonian festival of the new year. Through the festival the Babylonians celebrated the victory of divine order over chaos as it happened in the beginning on the day of creation. The participants in the drama were not merely commemorating the primordial conflict; on the contrary, in repeating the yearly festival through mock battles and other ceremonial acts, they believed that they sustained and renewed the cosmic order. Just as their god, Marduk, triumphed over the sea monster Tiamat (chaos) and created the earth from its vanquished body, so also the Babylonian king played the deity in a re-creation of the struggle. What the god did in cosmic time, the king represented and continued at the beginning of each year. In a sense, the rite abolished or suspended trivial and ordinary time by incorporating the living in the eternal. The new year festival took place over twelve days. During the rite, the Babylonian creation myth, the *Enuma Elish,* was recited several times in Marduk's temple. Like the mock battles and gestures, the saying of the myth was believed to be instrumental in renewing the cycle of nature and the life of man; thus, in cosmic drama, myth and gesture recreated and sustained the ultimate order.

Concluding Remarks

Ritual is one of the primary ways that humans, the middle creatures, mediate between ultimate and ordinary existence. Rites are intended to shape or consecrate human existence, both individual and group, in the ways it ought to be (for example, wise and benevolent leaders, mutually supportive spouses, responsible adults, healthy infants, orderly and humane social structures, and a bountiful earth) and to purge what ought not to be. The ritual process, particularly during the liminal phase, breaks down social conventions that separate us and allows us to experience a sense of community or communitas. Rather than being boring and trivial, as some moderns suppose, rites have been primary instruments through which ultimate existence is experienced and celebrated.

Notes

1. Evelyn Underhill, *Worship* (New York: Harper Torchbooks, 1957), p. 32.

2. In Gerardus van der Leeuw, *Sacred and Profane Beauty: The Holy in Art* (London: Weidenfeld and Nicholson, 1963), p. 105.

3. Underhill, *Worship,* p. 23.

4. Susanne Langer, *Philosophy in a New Key* (New York: Mentor Books, 1964), p. 52.

5. In Adolf E. Jensen, *Myth and Cult among Primitive Peoples,* trans. by Marianna Choldin and Wolfgang Weissleder (Chicago: University of Chicago Press, 1963), p. 52.

6. Mary Chase, *Harvey,* in Mary Sherwin, ed., *Comedy Tonight* (Garden City, N.Y.: Doubleday, 1977), p. 488.

7. *Thus Spake Zarathustra,* in Oscar Levy, ed., *The Complete Works of Friedrich Nietzsche,* vol. XI (New York: Russell & Russell, 1964), p. 45.

8. In van der Leeuw, *Sacred and Profane Beauty,* p. 62.

9. Joseph Campbell, *The Hero with a Thousand Faces* (Princeton, N.J.: Princeton University Press, 1968), p. 30.

10. Ibid.

11. Peter Farb, *Man's Rise to Civilization* (New York: Dutton, 1968), p. 72.

12. See Campbell, *Hero with a Thousand Faces.*

13. Victor Turner, *The Ritual Process* (Chicago: Aldine, 1968), pp. 97–101.

14. Ibid., p. 100.

15. Ibid., pp. 100–01.

16. Ibid., p. 169.

17. Ibid., pp. 150–203.

18. Ibid., p. 96.

19. Martin Buber, *I and Thou* (New York: Scribner's, 1958), p. 8.

20. Turner, *The Ritual Process,* pp. 96–97.

21. Ibid., p. 101.

22. McKim Marriott, in Turner, *The Ritual Process,* p. 187.

23. Ibid., pp. 185–88.

24. John G. Niehardt, *Black Elk Speaks: Being the Life Story of a Holy Man of the Oglala Sioux* (New York: Pocket Books, 1972), p. 163.

25. *The Wisdom of Laotse* (New York: Modern Library, 1948), p. 306.

26. *The Collected Poetry of W.H. Auden* (New York: Random House, 1966), pp. 465–66.

27. Arnold van Gennep, *The Rites of Passage,* trans. by M. Vizedom and G. Caffee (Chicago: University of Chicago Press, 1960), pp. 2–3.

28. Wayne Suttles, *Katzie Ethnographic Notes: The Faith of a Coast Salish Indian* (Victoria, B.C.: British Columbia Provincial Museum, 1955), pp. 11–12.

29. Bruno Bettelheim, *Symbolic Wounds: Puberty Rites and the Envious Male* (New York: Collier Books, 1968), p. 147.

30. Ibid., p. 45.

31. In Abraham Millgram, *Jewish Worship* (Philadelphia: Jewish Publishing Society of America, 1971), pp. 326–27.

32. Ibid., p. 328.

33. In Mary Daly, *The Church and the Second Sex* (New York: Harper & Row, 1968), p. 49.

34. Leviticus 12:1–5.

35. Ernst Cassirer, *An Essay on Man* (New Haven, Conn.: Yale University Press, 1944), p. 84.

36. James H. Breasted, *Development of Religion and Thought in Ancient Egypt* (New York: Scribner's, 1912), p. 91.

37. Suttles, *Katzie Ethnographic Notes,* pp. 83–84.

38. Millgram, *Jewish Worship,* p. 331.

39. Deuteronomy 6:4.

40. Job 1:21.

41. Johan Huizinga, *Homo Ludens* (Boston: Beacon Press, 1955), p. 18.

Photo by Burt Glinn, Magnum Photos

PART III
THE PERSONAL
AND SOCIAL
DIMENSIONS OF
RELIGION

At this point you can look back on where you have been and assess where your study of religious phenomena is leading. The initial preparation for your voyage of discovery included a recognition of the problems involved in defining religion, a distinction between the academic and theological approaches to the study of religion, and an overview of the historical development of religion and the relationship of religion to magic. With the preparatory operations completed, you plunged more directly into the study of religious phenomena by becoming familiar with the concept of the holy and the symbolic character of religious expression.

Part II introduced the conceptual and ritual dimensions of religion by distinguishing between symbols that function signally, representationally, and presentationally. It also compared aesthetic, scientific, and religious modes of discourse and argued that religious language is double-intentional, paradoxical, evaluative, and revelatory. It concluded with a description and analysis of different types of sacred stories and rites.

Part III shifts the emphasis from the symbolic character of religious expression to its personal and social dimension. In part III, the personal dimension of religion focuses on those experiences in which individuals, either in solitude or in concert with others, experience a sacred presence. All religious beliefs, sacred rites, and holy communities are, at least in part, reflections of experiences in which the lives of individuals and groups have been transformed by ultimacy. Chapter ten initiates the study of the personal dimension of religion by distinguishing between experience and religious experience and by comparing and contrasting three ways in which humans have experienced and conceptualized their sense of ultimacy. Chapter eleven discusses the spiritual birth of two different types of religious personalities: troubled and untroubled selves. It concludes with a description of some of the paths believed to lead to ultimate liberation.

Religion is social as well as personal. The statement, One Christian is no Christian, applies to all religions. Jew, Muslim, Mormon, and Sikh are religious in community rather than in isolation. The social mode of religion is reflected in the human desire to organize human relationships and social structures around the sacred. Chapter twelve examines some of the ways in which religion influences and is influenced by society. It also distinguishes between natural and voluntary religious groups, examines conflict in holy communities, and touches on different patterns of religious governance, leadership, and social stratification.

Chapter Ten
Patterns of Religious Experience

Having left son and wife, father and mother,
wealth and corn and relatives, the different objects
of desire, let one wander alone like a rhinoceros.

Sutta Nipata[1]

The rhinoceros, quietly standing alone, is, in the Buddhist faith, a symbol of the monk who must work out his own salvation; it is an image of a private and personal struggle. The individual nature of religious experience influenced Alfred North Whitehead's understanding of religion as "what the individual does with his own solitariness."[2] Something about the intensity and compelling nature of personal religious experience invites such a definition. The story of religion is filled with biographies of those who were alone in their struggles: Muhammad, silently brooding in a cave, visited within his own heart by an angel of God; the Buddha, rejected and derided by those who disdained what they considered his self-indulgence, seated in isolation under the tree of his enlightenment; Joseph Smith, the founder of Mormonism, following the angel Moroni through the woods of western New York to a cache of gold plates; and Jesus, as we see him in those graphic moments of aloneness, struggling with temptation in the desert, agonizing in the Garden of Gethsemane, and finally betrayed and abandoned on the cross.

While such powerful images are important, a definition of religion in terms of the solitary and personal nature of religious experience distorts the realities of the religious life. Religious experience, like all experience, is personal, but the life of the spirit is nourished by a supportive community and a set of symbols, including holy words and holy rites. In the study of the conceptual and ritual dimensions of religion, the personal aspect inherent in participating in holy rites and telling sacred stories was, at times, overshadowed by the need to analyze and describe the general features and varieties of religious language and ritual. We need to emphasize, however, that holy words and rites are hierophanies through which the sacred is manifested and are also ways of acting out and eliciting personal experiences of ultimacy.

One way of understanding the relationship of the personal dimension to other dimensions of religious expression is to contrast the objective character of religion with the personal character of religious experience. Seen in this light, the ways people seek and respond to holiness have an external and an inward aspect. On the one hand, religion is manifested in objective and external forms of religious expression. The outer character of religious action is embodied in a multitude of different religions, each with a distinctive set of beliefs, rituals, social structures, sacred places, times, and things. On the other hand, religious experience points to the impression that contact with the holy makes on individual and group life. The inner character of religious experience refers not only to subjective feelings but to events, including ceremonies, in which people are affected by an experience of ultimate existence.

The study of the personal dimension of religion begins in this chapter with some remarks about the nature of religious experience. It also includes a discussion of three different patterns of religious experience—the experience of the holy as transcendent, as immanent, and as a mystical unity that goes beyond the dualism of transcendence and immanence.

While the primary emphasis in chapters ten and eleven is on the dynamic and constructive qualities of religious experience, religious actions can obviously be routine or destructive. Religion can be ecstatic and liberating for those who feel touched by the sacred, but it can also be a dull and perfunctory habit. A person may find participation in sacred ceremonies meaningless and boring, yet may, for some reason, continue to participate. In addition to the routinization that all religious acts and symbols are susceptible to, on some occasions contact with nonordinary power takes a destructive turn. Fanaticism, holy wars, holocausts, self-immolation, and mass suicides are forms of human behavior that have sometimes been justified by religious symbol systems and reportedly commanded by sacred voices, whether divine or human. The intent here, however, is to concentrate on the experiences of those people, as William James put it, for whom "religion exists not as a dull habit, but as an acute fever,"[3] and for whom such experiences are more liberating than destructive. Perhaps a good place to begin is to distinguish between experience and religious experience.

The Nature of Religious Experience

Religious experience is a response to what is experienced as ultimate reality.

Joachim Wach
Types of Religious Experience[4]

Broadly conceived, experience is anything humans are aware or conscious of in such typical activities as thinking, imagining, perceiving, feeling, and willing. Experience has a lived-through quality; it is personal, though not necessarily simply private and subjective. Nations, families, contracts, or religious communities are impossible unless shared experiences are possible.

Since humans know reality through experience, its relevance for religion is obvious. Personal and shared experiences must serve as the point of contact with the sacred. Every act of worship, religious belief or holy community is an interpretation of experience. If religion is to be understood as seeking for and responding to what is holy, then religious experience is understood here as that dimension of human experience in which individual and group life has been touched and perhaps transformed by an experience of ultimacy.

Since, as was argued in chapter four, descriptions and definitions of the holy are always inadequate, at least from a religious perspective, perhaps a consideration of those ecstatic moments in which humans have been directly touched by an experience of ultimacy can add to our understanding of what is implied by the holy and shed more light on the nature of religious experience. The unconditional character of ultimacy, for example, is evident in religious experiences that elicit response from a person's entire being, and the nonordinary power of the holy is manifested in the ecstatic and liberating quality of religious experience.

Religious Experience as a Total Response to Holiness

The experience of holiness is, according to sociologist of religion Joachim Wach, the most intense human experience and therefore calls forth "a total response of [an individual's] total being."[5] In experiencing holiness humans come into contact with all that is vital. **Faith** is often used as a symbol for the personal and committed nature of religious experience. Because faith is an action word that suggests vitality and involvement, it will be used in this context as a synonym for religious experience. Faith addresses the whole person; it is, in Paul Tillich's words, "the most centered act of the human mind. It is not a movement of a special section or a special function of man's total being. They are all united in the act of faith."[6] As a total response to the sacred, faith or religious experience involves the interplay of human intellect, will, and feelings; thus faith has cognitive, conative, and affective dimensions.

In the cognitive dimension, faith or religious experience involves wondering, interpreting, knowing, and believing. As a direct experience of the holy, the cognitive dimension of faith is primarily a knowledge of rather than a knowledge about the holy. It is a direct-seeing and self-confirming experience of ultimacy. Faith, in this sense, is deeper than words. But faith also moves from the wonder of the experience to an interpretation of it; thus faith is also that which is believed. Faith seeks understanding and must, therefore, in spite of the divine mystery, always be in some sense intelligible. As belief, as interpretation, faith has an intellectual quality. We can believe in the truth of faith without being able to give sufficient reason, but faith must always be supported by at least some reason. Faith as belief must be intelligible, discriminating, and even critical if it is to be something more than sentimentality. Belief is part of the cognitive content of religious experience, but faith is never just believing.

In the conative dimension, faith involves choosing, promising, trusting, and willing. We all must act; even inaction, the Gita teaches, is a form of choosing. Religious experience understood as a condition of being totally affected involves choosing and trusting. For example, the Buddhist monk makes a threefold commitment to the Buddha, to the doctrine, and to the Buddhist community. Body and mind are disciplined. Hours are spent in meditation to develop spiritual maturity. Buddhism is not, however, just an inward looking. As Hui-neng, a seventh-century Chinese Buddhist, observed, "If you think of the Tathagata (the Buddhas) as only sitting, you are tracing the path of heresy."[7] Religious experience as commitment involves trust, for it is an act of surrendering oneself to that which is greater than self. People may place their trust in the sacred even though they are incapable of giving sufficient reasons for their trust, as is evident in the fidelity of Job who, in spite of the incomprehensibility of his suffering, cried out, "Though He slay me, yet will I trust in Him."[8] Trust, however, can be misplaced, beliefs can be wrong; thus faith or religious experience is always a risk, a leap, to use Sören Kierkegaard's image, beyond the insufficiency of evidence. Kierkegaard said that "without risk there is no faith."[9] Willing and trusting are part of the conative dimension of religious experience, but faith is not just willing and trusting.

In the affective dimension, faith is emotional and passionate. The affections, the feelings, are keenly awakened in moments of spiritual birth when the holy is intensely and ecstatically experienced. Richard R. Niebuhr compared affection to the qualities of tonality and resonance;[10] joy, bliss, love, bitterness, anger, and tranquillity are tonal qualities. Buddha is the Compassionate One because compassion was the tonal quality, the resonance, that permeated his being. The emotional depth of faith is sometimes figuratively described as the peace that surpasses all understanding, or as being beside oneself with joy, or simply as bliss. It may be a feeling, a place where trust and assent join in an awareness that there is a sacred depth, which is loving and caring. In Paul Tillich's words, it is like a voice saying, "You are accepted. You are accepted, accepted by that which is greater than you, and the name of which you do not know."[11] Feelings are the affective dimension of religious experience, but faith is not simply emotion.

As indicated, religious experience, understood as total response of our total being, means that no human faculty (intellect, feeling, or will) is untouched. Faith, in this sense, seeks wholeness. But total response also suggests something about the depth and breadth of the religious life. If the experience of ultimacy stakes a claim to the whole person, it should be evidenced by fulfilled human existence. Perhaps there has been no more devoted and committed servant of the sacred in the twentieth century than the Hindu Mohandas Gandhi. His life is an eloquent example of being totally claimed by God. Gandhi's experience, including his study of the Gita, led him step by step to nonpossessiveness. In a passage in his *Autobiography,* Gandhi spoke of his struggle, after divesting himself of his property, to surrender himself further:

> How was one to divest oneself of all possessions? Was not the body itself possession enough? Were not wife and children possessions? Was I to destroy all the cupboards of books I had? Was I to give up all I had and follow Him? Straight came the answer: I could not follow Him unless I gave up all I had. . . .I understood the Gita teaching of non-possession to mean that those who desired salvation should act like the trustee who, though having control over great possessions, regards not an iota of them as his own.[12]

The holy never takes command of most of us as it did Gandhi. As Buddha taught, we hold on desperately to our selves and our possessions. Our glimpses of ultimate existence are so muted that our potentialities are only partially fulfilled or realized. Many people have had ecstatic and life-transforming experiences of the sacred, but such moments have rarely commanded their total being more than momentarily. All too quickly we retreat to private and profane existence. The fullness of the divine unveiling to Moses and Muhammad, Jesus and Buddha, Gandhi and Black Elk is relatively rare. Most of us approach the sacred by following in the steps of those people whose lives stand as paradigms of total response and by repeating the holy words and holy acts that have come down to us through our religious traditions.

The Ecstatic Quality of
Religious Experience

If an experience of holiness can claim one's total being and thus indirectly point to the unconditional character of ultimacy, then perhaps the ecstatic, liberating quality of faith is indicative of the nonordinary power of Holy Being. Ecstasy is a feeling of being outside oneself. It is a state, as Sam Keen observed, "accompanied by joy, enthusiasm, a sense of being a part of a moving reality that is greater than the self."[13]

In one form of faith the ecstatic experience of holiness, of transcending self, is relatively controlled. It is manifested as a liberating peace or enlightenment that issues from the depths of meditation or through the controlled gestures of ritual. Alternatively, contact with the sacred can be relatively uncontrolled—an effervescent and intoxicating experience. Effervescence issues from the overpowering and exalted character of the encounter and manifests itself in spontaneous and enthusiastic outpourings of the spirit.

✓ *Ecstasy and Effervescence*

Effervescent religious experience is exhibited in relatively uncontrolled behavior. In such moments people are so filled or possessed by the sacred that they no longer exercise control over their bodies or minds. Not

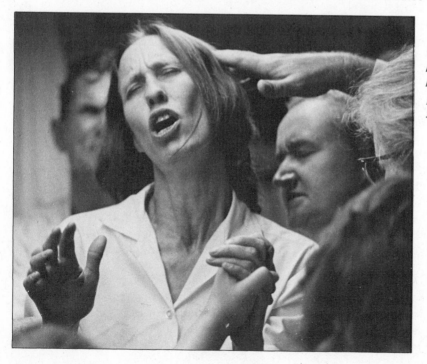

Revival Meeting in West Virginia. Charismatic Christians experience the presence and healing power of the Holy Spirit.

Photo by J.R. Holland, Stock, Boston

uncommonly, devotees' bodies are involuntarily moved to jerking or shaking. In moments laden with emotion, the ecstatic ones may break out in dance, toss their heads, or whirl around and around. They may roll or run about or become immobilized or entranced. The tongue also responds to the consuming fire of the spirit; the tongue is like a flame that bursts forth with holy shouts, inspired exhortations, sacred songs, or a speaking in incoherent, spirit-filled tongues. Visions, dreams, trances, speaking in tongues (glossolalia), and hallucinogen-induced changes in consciousness have all been part of the ecstatic and sometimes bizarre signs of faith.

Effervescence is common to many religious traditions and is kindred to spontaneous and enthusiastic outpourings of emotion that occur outside the context of faith. For example, the devotees of Dionysus sought ecstasy through the dance, and in one form of the Tantric tradition of India, male and female worshipers seek union with the divine power of Shiva-Shakti through a ritual that culminates in sexual union. Christian revivalism is also associated with physical and spiritual enthusiasm, and Pentacostalism in particular prizes gifts of the Holy Spirit, such as glossolalia. One of the most memorable revival meetings was held at Cane Ridge, Kentucky in August of 1801. Cane Ridge was likened to the outpouring of the Spirit at Pentecost. There is considerable disagreement, then and now, as to the value of what transpired. Whatever the judgment, the frontiersmen responded to the heady mixture of preaching fervor and the import of the social occasion with emotional outbursts and physical agitations. Barton Warren Stone, a Presbyterian minister who called for the Cane Ridge gathering, later described some of the eccentricities that were part of the excitement:

> The bodily agitations or exercises, attending the excitement in the beginning of this century, were various, and called by various names. . . . The falling exercise was very common among all classes, the saints and sinners of every age and of every grade, from the philosopher to the clown. The subject of this exercise would, generally, with a piercing scream, fall like a log on the floor, earth, or mud, and appear as dead. . . .
>
> The jerks cannot be so easily described. Sometimes the subject of the jerks would be affected in some one member of the body, and sometimes the whole system. . . . When the whole system was affected, I have seen the person stand in one place, and jerk backward and forward in quick succession, their head nearly touching the floor behind and before. All classes, saints and sinners, the strong as well as the weak, were thus affected. . . .
>
> The dancing exercise . . . was peculiar to the professors of religion. The subject, after jerking awhile, began to dance . . . . Sometimes the motion was quick and sometimes slow. Thus they continued to move forward and backward in the same track or alley till nature seemed exhausted, and they would fall prostrate on the floor or earth . . . .

The laughing exercise was frequent, confined solely with the religious. It was a loud, hearty laughter, but . . . it excited laughter in none else. The subject appeared rapturously solemn, and his laughter excited solemnity in saints and sinners. It is truly indescribable.[14]

Tribal societies are not immune to the flames of enthusiasm that often occur when people feel themselves possessed or seized by the sacred. Mary Douglas cites several cases in which tribal peoples experienced spirit possession and an attendant loss of conscious control. For example, the !Kung Bushmen of the Kalahari desert believe that the power to heal and drive away evil is an indication of a spirit that takes possession of their bodies during a ritual dance:

When the medicine men are curing, all of them experience varying degrees of self-induced trance, which includes a period of frenzy and a period of semi-consciousness or deep unconsciousness. They may become stiff or froth at the mouth or lie still as if in coma. Some of them habitually remain in trance for only a short time, others for hours. . . . After the curing has been going on for some time, medicine men begin to reach their state of frenzy. . . . their spasms of grunting and shrieking become more frequent and violent, their stomachs heave, they stagger and sway. They rush to the fire, trample it, pick up the coals, set fire to their hair. Fire activates the medicine in them. People hold them to keep them from falling and beat out the flames . . . they may fall into deep unconsciousness or sink down semi-conscious, eyes closed, unable to walk. . . .

The !Kung believe that at such a time the medicine man's spirit leaves his body and goes out. . . . They call this "half-death." It is a dangerous time and the man's body must be watched over and kept warm. . . . The women must sing and clap ardently while the man is in deep trance. He needs the good medicine of the music to protect him.

The curing dance draws people of a Bushman band together into concerted action as nothing else does. They stamp and clap and sing with such precision that they become like an organic being. In this close configuration—together—they face the gods.[15]

Bizarre behavior, you say, triggered only by the loneliness of the frontier or by the suggestibility of the tribal mind. Perhaps. But look a little closer at the techniques used in today's helping professions. Numerous psychotherapies, pop psychologies, and mind-expanding movements offer nirvana and more nirvana to a host of eager devotees. The path to such a peace of mind frequently begins with techniques that break down conscious control or defense mechanisms and free the feelings. Primal shrieks, nude therapy, marathon encounter groups, and the facilitated touching of each other through trust-walks or in a tightly knit circle of entwined human beings are just a few examples of the methods that are intended to help humans get in touch with what is vital and alive.

Ecstasy and Serenity

Ecstatic experiences of the sacred can be more subdued, more serene. Joy can be exhibited in solitude or in solemn rites as well as in outbursts of effervescence. Contemplative religious experience often takes the form of a feeling of bliss or peace. Meditation and prayer are the primary instruments of the contemplative life that lead to an experience of holiness. A union of the divine and the human is experienced in emptying the self of self inwardly rather than through the ecstasies of the dance or the enthusiasms of revivalism. This form of ecstasy, of transcending the self, is experienced as a serene but joyful calming of one's total being and as a peace that passes beyond all understanding.

In the Zen tradition the discipline of meditation can lead to the extinguishing of the separate, grasping, personal self. The unity of being is known in silence, in inwardness. A haiku, a form of Japanese poetry, provides a glimpse of the eloquence of silence:

> *They were silent all three*
> *the host, the guest*
> *and the white chrysanthemum.*[16]

In theistic traditions God is approached through prayer, which is both a looking inward and a reaching outward. Prayer can be a hearing act as well as a speaking act. Sören Kierkegaard suggested that the voice of God is heard in the silence of prayer:

> *In proportion as he became more and more earnest in prayer he had less and less to say, and in the end he became quite silent. He became silent—indeed, what is if possible still more expressly the opposite of speaking, he became a hearer. He had supposed that to pray is to speak; he learnt that to pray is not merely to be silent but to hear. And so it is: to pray is not to hear oneself speak, but it is to be silent, and to remain silently waiting until one hears God speak.*[17]

We should note that effervescence, spirit possession, and loss of conscious control, which can sometimes be demonic and destructive, are often as much feared as desired. Religious communities with highly developed ritual systems are less likely to give way to loss of control. Ritual, a drama of word and gesture, provides boundaries within which feelings can be expressed without a breakdown of order. From a religious perspective the pattern of ritual reflects the sacred order of the cosmos. In the Jewish tradition, for example, the observance of Sabbath is the culmination of each week, just as God's creation of peacefulness on the seventh day was the climax of creation. Judaism is relatively devoid of losses of control (spirit possession, glossolalia, trances), in part because of its rich liturgical life. Jewish philosopher Franz Rosenzweig wrote that liturgy is "the reflector which focuses the sunbeams of eternity in the small circle of the year" and that must introduce humans into the silence of togetherness—that is, in the union of God and man.[18]

All religions pronounce the name of God in their particular language.

Simone Weil
Waiting for God[19]

Different Ways of Responding to the Holy ✓

Religious experience or faith is twofold: it is an experience of the wonder and majesty of the holy, a liberating and ecstatic experience that touches total being, but it is also an interpretation of that experience. Because there are so many varieties of religious experience and different religious traditions, studying each type individually is impossible here. It is, however, possible to be familiar with typologies that group religious traditions and experiences according to characteristics they have in common. Chapter three introduced a classification of religions on the basis of whether they were distributed locally, nationally, or universally. A second typology groups religions in clusters of commonality on the basis of their conception of ultimacy.

In the following pages, the focus on the personal dimension of religion shifts from an analysis of the nature of religious experience to an examination of three different responses to the experience of ultimacy. In one type of religion and pattern of religious experience, the holy is experienced and thought of as **transcendent**—that is, as a God who is radically different from his creation. In a second type and pattern, the holy is experienced and thought of as **immanent**—that is, as inherent in things. In a third type and pattern, **mysticism,** the holy is experienced and thought of as a unity that, in a mystical union of seeker and sought, either lays aside or goes beyond transcendence and immanence.

Our relation to the holy is expressed in ceremony and gesture, words and symbolic objects. Through sacred rites and stories, humans reinforce and sustain their vision of the cosmos. In each religious tradition, words and gestures are part of a symbol system or organizing model that places human existence in an ultimate context; they not only serve as instruments through which the holy is manifested but also subtly shape the manner in which the holy is experienced and interpreted. For example, in religious traditions that stress transcendence, the sacred is believed to be wholly other than man or nature, a Holy Being who is known through divine-human encounter. The transcendent model for understanding the relationship of the divine to the cosmos is analogous to that of the artist and his or her artistic creation: as the potter molds, shapes, and brings into being a pot, so God is believed to have created the universe. Creator and creation are united by the act of creation rather than by a similarity in their respective natures.

In religious traditions that stress immanence, the holy is within things rather than beyond or above them. The immanence model is more organic. As an acorn becomes an oak tree, so the cosmos unfolds or flows from Holy Being. In an organic sense the oak's nature and structure is inherent in the acorn. As immanent, the cosmos is, in some essential way, holy. The movement from acorn to oak and from Holy Being to cosmos is a creative process rather than a creative act. The transcendent God is a personal, creative agent who is addressed in prayer and known through divine revelation, while the holy as immanent is more of an impersonal creative process that is discerned or intuitively grasped rather than divinely revealed.

Responding to the Holy as Transcendent

The holy can be experienced and thought of as a transcendent and majestic power, a something more that transcends the human. In the book of Isaiah, for example, God speaks to the prophet and tells him:

> For My thoughts are not your thoughts,
> Neither are your ways My ways, saith the Lord.
> For as the heavens are higher than the earth,
> So are My ways higher than your ways,
> And My thoughts than your thoughts.[20]

In religions of transcendence, such as Judaism, Christianity, Islam, Sikhism, and Mormonism, God is outside and radically other than human beings and nature. He is the Lord of Creation and the King of the Universe. Transcendence is the affirmation, writes Peter Berger, of a God "who is not the world, and who was not made by man, who is outside and not within ourselves, who is not a sign of human beings but of whom human beings are signs, who is symbolized and not a symbol."[21]

Models for thinking about transcendence vary. In **deism** the holy is thought of as a transcendent creator who has no ongoing personal relationship to his creation. In theistic or prophetic forms of transcendence, God is experienced as a personal being who creates, wills, knows, and is concerned with the salvation of human beings. The experience of the holy as a Thou is common to monotheism, polytheism, and tribal theisms. Real living, Jewish theologian Martin Buber believed, is "meeting" between man and nature, man and man, and man and God.[22] From a theistic perspective, all vital existence has its roots in the relationship between God and humans. The holy—the Eternal Thou, to use Buber's term—is addressed personally because it is experienced as a living presence. God is spoken to in relational terms as Our Father, or as the Mother of All Things, or as Love.

In a very traditional monotheistic formulation of transcendence, God is an all-knowing and all-powerful King of the Universe who has a vital relationship to his creation. God is the ultimate monarch who ordains what will be and who commands obedience from his subjects. The power of God is such that he needs only to say, "Let there be light," and there is light. Through his creative power, the foundations of the earth were laid. Although God demands obedience and righteousness, his justice is tempered by his grace and compassion.

In theistic religions the transcendence, the otherness of God, is more than the eye can behold; yet, paradoxically, the holy is encountered in moments of divine disclosures. The holy is transcendent, yet near. God is, in Peter Berger's words, "totally other and yet accessible in human experience."[23] In monotheistic religions God reveals himself to prophets whom he commissions to speak his words; thus, for example, the prophets Jeremiah, Isaiah, and Muhammad are said to speak the word of God. God touches human hearts through his word, through scripture. In some forms of theism, the transcendence of God is combined with the conviction that he is also immanent. For example, in one form of Hindu theism, the divine is the ground of being and is also manifested, incarnated, in Krishna; in Christianity, God is believed to have taken flesh in Christ.

A Pattern of Religious Experience in Religions of Transcendence

As a transcendent experience salvation is more an outward turning, a relationship with an objective presence, a personal God, than an inward self-examination. This is not to say that theistic traditions do not encourage introspection. The Bible urges people to search their hearts. Christianity, for example, has a long and rich contemplative tradition. Saint Augustine admonished: "Do not go abroad. Return within yourself. In the inward man dwells truth."[24] But Augustine also believed that Truth or God transcends the human mind. God is known inwardly in the soul, in the imagination, but he exists independent of the imagination and is experienced or known in a relationship.

Creature-Feeling. When confronted by such a transcendent power, humans have often experienced what Rudolf Otto characterized as creature-feeling or creature-consciousness—"the emotion of a creature, submerged and overwhelmed by its own nothingness in contrast to that which is supreme above all creatures."[25] Creature-consciousness is a feeling of inadequacy and insufficiency before the sacred. It is the perception of one's finitude, and yet it is more than the specter of mortality. It is the feeling of being absolutely dependent when faced with the overpowering presence of God. For Sarah Miles, the heroine of Graham Greene's novel *The End of the Affair*, her encounter with God exposed the cheap and artificial aspect of her existence and her longing for acceptance. She wrote in her diary, "If I am a bitch and a fake, is there nobody who will love a bitch and a fake?"[26]

In Sören Kierkegaard's analysis, the majesty, the very distance separating creature and creator, is the basis of despair. Despair is grounded in an awareness of our finitude, our dependence. And it is precisely through this despair, this consciousness of radical helplessness, that humans can become conscious of themselves before God. The man who is truly free from despair is rare, wrote Kierkegaard, and "only that man's life is wasted who lived on, so deceived by the joys of life or by its sorrows that he never became eternally and decisively conscious of himself as spirit, as self, or (what is the same thing) never became aware and in the deepest sense received an impression of the fact that there is a God, and that he, he himself, exists before this God, which gain of infinity is never attained except through despair."[27]

Self-Surrender. A second important aspect of the response to the holy experienced as transcendent is self-surrender. It is the experience of surrendering the self, of being prepared to act out the prayer, "not my will, but thine be done." Self-surrender is the giving of one's self to God. It is the attitude of total allegiance indicated by one of Simone Weil's letters to her parents: "If I had several lives I would devote one of them to you. But I have only one, and I owe it elsewhere."[28]

The surrendering of self is often preceded by a struggle to preserve one's separateness from God. C.S. Lewis observed that something in him tried to protect the temporal from being invaded by the eternal. "I came into the presence of God with a great fear lest anything should happen to me within that presence which will prove too intolerably inconvenient when I have come out again into my 'ordinary life'."[29]

Obedience, obedience to all that is true and sustaining, is one of the faces of self-surrender. In Islam, Allah is a God who commands submission. In fact, the word *Islam* and its verb form, *aslama,* means submission or surrender. In the prophetic books of the Jewish canon, the people of Israel are implored to "trust in Yahweh" and to know that God demands obedience. In an age that prizes individuality, obedience seems a relic of a more authoritarian age. Respect for authority, any authority, is problematic, and obedience is often dictated more by self-preservation than self-sur-render. Yet the ground of religious action must, in large measure, be obedience to the holy. Simone Weil managed in one of her marvelous paradoxes to illuminate what is intended by obedience to the holy: "If it were conceivable that one might be damned by obeying God and saved by disobeying him; I would nevertheless obey him."[30]

Transformed Existence and the Call to Serve. Self-surrender is usually followed by a divine imperative; it is the experience of being chosen or called to a specific task. Martin Buber wrote, "All revelation is summons and sending."[31] Obedience receives a direction, a role or mission to be accomplished. Moses is sent to Egypt to be an instrument of God's liberation of the Israelites. Muhammad is God's messenger and is ordered to recite the words that God would have him speak. A shaman is a physician of the soul because he has had an ecstatic and revelatory experience of the sacred. His power, his sacred vocation, is a gift and a call from God. Christian nuns, pastors, and priests frequently believe that they have been called to dedicate their lives to God's service.

The vision of Isaiah of Jerusalem is a good example of religious experience in traditions of transcendence because it reflects the pattern that we have indicated is typical in experiences of transcendence: a divine-human encounter, creature-feeling, self-surrender, and transformed life accompanied by a sense of direction or purpose. The Bible relates that Isaiah was called to be a prophet, a spokesman for God, in the year King Uzziah, regent of Judah, died (742 B.C.). His prophetic call was prompted by a visionary experience of God, the Holy One of Israel, in the Temple of Solomon. He saw the Lord upon a throne. Above him were six-winged seraphim, one of whom called out, "Holy, holy, holy is the Lord of hosts; the whole earth is full of his glory." The foundations of the temple shook as the words were spoken and the house was filled with smoke. In the presence of the holiness of the Lord, Isaiah felt his creatureliness and lamented, "Woe is me. For I am lost." For, in seeing God, the Lord of hosts, Isaiah knew himself as unclean and sinful. Suddenly his despair was lifted; the man of unclean lips was cleansed by the burning coals of the spirit, his guilt was taken away, and his sin forgiven. The power of God, and not that of Isaiah, produced a restored man, a prophet. The creature, helpless before the majesty of the holy, was not only accepted and transformed but was subsequently chosen or called to do God's will. To be called by God is to surrender the self—to be obedient. Isaiah, the restored man, was thus addressed by God: "Whom shall I send?"—that is, who will be obedient to my will? Isaiah responded to the call, "Here am I! Send me."[32] This numinous encounter provided the imperative for his entire prophetic life.

Seeking and Being Sought by Transcendence

Religious communities disagree as to whether the power to surrender one's self comes from God or is something humans initiate. Does the first step toward regeneration come from the divine, or can human beings prepare themselves? Christians who find Saint Paul's words normative quote the apostle: "For by grace are ye saved through faith; and that not of yourselves: it is the gift of God."[33] Regeneration is thus neither produced nor earned; it is a gift freely given. Humans are chosen, seized, or grasped by God. Simone Weil, for instance, believed that humans are sought by God and can do nothing by themselves to forge a path to God:

> There are people who try to raise their souls like a man continually taking standing jumps in the hopes that, if he jumps higher every day, a time may come when he will no longer fall but will go right up to the sky. Thus occupied he cannot look at the sky. We cannot take a single step toward heaven. It is not in our power to travel in a vertical direction. If however we look heavenward for a long time, God comes and takes us up.[34]

Here, people are addressed by God. They do not so much seek as respond to a divine presence. Jacques Durandeaux describes this sense of humans as creatures who can do nothing but wait for God's revelation:

> When man takes the initiative, his discourse on God becomes a discourse on himself; therefore a meeting with God cannot be serious unless it is God who takes the initiative. If an Other is there, standing in front of man, it is up to this other to reveal himself, to speak, and to make himself understood. God is an irruption, an unanticipated occurrence in man's life.[35]

Counter to the image of a person waiting patiently for God, is one of people who actively seek God. Even Simone Weil, who emphasized that salvation is more a waiting than an active seeking, used the metaphor of turning to God. She wrote, "We have no power to bring about salvation . . . it is desire that saves."[36] Thus, while it is not human power that saves, human longing does prompt us to turn, to be receptive to the presence of God. Sometimes this turning or drawing near God is viewed as an interior longing or innate attraction for the godhead, a desire that through God's grace moves people to seek him and prepare themselves for salvation. Prepare your hearts, the Bible commands; the prepared heart is one that in surrendering the self has turned away from sin and curruption.[37] To paraphrase Saint Augustine, we ask, we seek, we know, and this appears to come from us, but it is also a divine gift; thus even our will to turn and our longing comes from God.

In the Jewish tradition, the problem of whether humans seek God or are sought by him has not been so acute, since the human role in salvation has always been an active one. Human freedom is emphasized and the relationship between people and God is reciprocal. Humans turn to God. God seeks humans. Martin Buber wrote, "You need God in order to be—and God needs you, for the very meaning of your life."[38] Seeking or turning to God is the recognition that life is centered in the Eternal Thou; yet, paradoxically, as Buber observed, there is "no such thing as seeking God, for there is nothing in which He could not be found."[39]

The experience of the holy is, of course, not confined to the pattern reflected in Isaiah, nor is the debate whether humans are primarily active or passive in the process of salvation always a crucial problem. Each religious experience is unique, but each occurs within a religious milieu that provides a gestalt, or system of significance, for shaping and interpreting such phenomena. The pattern of Isaiah's experience of transcendence is paradigmatic for those immersed in the Judeo-Christian tradition. However, other experiences of the holy do not fit so comfortably within the formula of an encounter with transcendence.

Responding to the Holy as Immanent

In the experience of immanence, the locus of the holy is inward. The ultimate is within, in the depth of existence, rather than transcendent. Sinologist Joseph Needham elucidated something of the contrasting conceptions of transcendence and immanence: "Universal harmony comes about not by a celestial fiat of some King of Kings, but by the spontaneous cooperation of all beings in the universe brought about by their following the internal necessities of their own natures."[40]

Like the models of transcendence, models for thinking about immanence vary. In one form of Taoism, the holy is experienced as a natural process, as a movement of the Tao, rather than as a Thou addressed as a personal deity. The Tao is a cosmic process, the basis of all natural movement, rather than a personal god. In most forms of Buddhism, the sacred is an experience of self-awareness or enlightenment, although some Buddhist denominations are closer to theism. Also included among religions of immanence are all those forms of **pantheism** in which the divine is in all things or is all things. For example, one of the six orthodox schools of Indian philosophy, Advaita Vedanta, maintains that Brahman alone is ultimately real. Brahman is in all things and all that is, is Brahman. The **atman,** the human soul, is identical with Brahman; thus each human being is Brahman. The phenomenal world, the world of change and appearances, is also understood to be a manifestation of Brahman; thus all things are Brahman.

Self-Liberation and Enlightenment in Traditions of Immanence

Where the holy is experienced as transcendent, salvation is usually by a power external to human beings. The key to transformed life lies in surrender to God. Where the holy is experienced as immanent, enlightenment usually takes the form of self-liberation. In Confucianism and in most Buddhist traditions, human affairs rather than the gods are the proper concern of humankind. Salvation is not God's gift but rather is to be found in the depths of human experience. It happens, if it happens at all, because a person diligently practices the conditions leading to deliverance. The Buddha enjoined his followers to work out their own salvation. It is the task, the quest of humans. **Nirvana** is mysterious and ineffable, but Buddha was a human being who became the Enlightened One—who experienced nirvana. In Buddhism the ultimate purpose of human life is to realize Buddhahood, to experience liberation. And where can such enlightenment be found? And who can aspire to be a Buddha? Hakuin, an eighteenth-century Zen master, provided this answer:

> *Where you stand is the Land of Purity,*
> *Your person, the body of Buddha.*[41]

Religions of immanence experience the holy, the nonordinary, in the world of the ordinary. Truth is discovered in the world, in human affairs, rather than revealed from above. The Buddhist turns his gaze inward in order to be liberated from the suffering that issues from the desire to gain and permanently possess the objects of the heart's craving. Virtue—that is, the virtuous human being—is the ultimate concern of the Confucianist. The basis of virtue is found within human experience in a social and ceremonial context. Confucius taught that the essence or virtue of being fully and completely human consists in loving others.[42] The Taoist finds the holy in nature. The Tao is the unity of all things. The Taoist sage practices the virtues of kindness, simplicity, and humility and tends to sit in forgetfulness of the ways of civilization in order to attune himself to the natural flow of the Tao.

Although self-liberation is characteristic of religions of immanence, they have a passive and an active element similar to the seeking and being sought by God dilemma of religions of transcendence. In the *Tao Te Ching,* authentic life is more passive. Spontaneous, natural movement is not willed into existence; it is something that is already there. Life has its own movement. The Taoist sage orders his life after the movement of the Tao and lets things take their natural course. The emphasis is less on a quest or striving after the Tao than on simply removing the artificial barriers or, put another way, in assenting to the way of the sacred:

> *He who takes action fails.*
> *He who grasps things loses them.*
> *For this reason the sage takes no action and*
> *therefore does not fail.*
> *He grasps nothing and therefore he does not lose anything.*[43]

However, the Buddhist monk and the Confucianist sage must be energetic in their spiritual quests. Self-liberation is for them volitional and self-directed rather than passive. In Confucianism, learning has been a key building block for the preparation of virtuous people. In the *Analects,* Confucius was optimistic about the capacity of individuals to educate themselves for the better: "It is only the wisest and the most stupid who cannot be changed."[44]

The Buddhist monk must work out his own salvation. It entails a rigorous discipline. Though the actual moment of spiritual birth is described as spontaneous and inaccessible to coercion or command, it does not come to those who are uncommitted and undisciplined. The life of the historical Buddha, Siddartha Gautama, is indicative of the paradox of striving and nonstriving present in spiritual transformation. The young prince earnestly sought liberation. He initiated his spiritual pilgrimage by intentionally leaving the security that his wealth, status, and family provided. His six-year quest involved renunciation of pleasures and a severe, even health-endangering asceticism. Stymied in his efforts, he sat down at the foot of a tree vowing that "though skin, nerves, and bone shall waste away, and life-blood itself be dried up, here sit I till I attain Enlightenment."[45] According to tradition the struggle lasted forty-nine days and culminated in a spiritual enlightenment. The emphasis is on the quest, the discipline, and the vow, but the Buddhist tradition also teaches that the point of enlightenment occurred when Siddartha was no longer striving, no longer seeking, when he had died to himself; thus enlightenment in traditions of immanence, like salvation in religions of transcendence, is not something that can be forced. Curiously, then, at the point of spiritual liberation, the point in which the ego is transcended, self-salvation and self-surrender meet.

A Pattern of Religious Experience in Religions of Immanence

Experiences of the holy, whether of the transcendent or immanent type, culminate in transformed lives. But the paradigm used previously for experiences of transcendence (divine-human encounter, creature-feeling, self-surrender, and rebirth) does not fit the experience of immanence. A more appropriate pattern for religious experience of the self-salvation type would be: quest, discipline, crisis, and enlightenment.[46]

Quest. A religious pilgrimage is triggered by a conflict or disquiet. A quest for spiritual transformation implies that the seeker believes something is wrong with himself or herself and that the obstacles to liberation can be overcome. The first step toward enlightenment is therefore a commitment to seek it. The path to ultimate liberation begins with a quest and a seriousness of purpose. The quest for self-salvation involves looking inward—an exploration of inner space. The great statues of the Buddha, seated in meditation, are powerful images of this inwardness. Compare, for instance, the figure of the serene and compassionate Buddha with the tortured and tormented figure of Christ on the cross.

Meditation, Puri, India. The figure of an Indian, seated in the lotus posture, his upper body straight yet relaxed, is a reflection of the concentration that meditation requires.

Photo by Ira Kirschenbaum, Stock, Boston

Discipline. The depths of inwardness are plumbed only through discipline, at the heart of which is meditation. Through **meditation** the restless mind is stilled and insights emerge from the depths of human existence. The practice of meditation requires dedication, untiring alertness, and disciplined thought and action. Concentration is necessary. In order to facilitate meditation, care is given to the position of the body. The senses are controlled to harness distractions. Frequently a single point or object is concentrated on until the mind is emptied of all else; sometimes at this point the self disappears altogether. The process is anything but an easy one. The seeker is beset by doubts: Is it worth it? Am I making headway? Is the dharma (the doctrine) a fraud? The discipline is long and hard. As Zen master Shibayama wrote, "one has to be prepared to risk his life and even then *satori* [enlightenment] may not be accessible."[47]

Crises. Crises are an integral part of the spiritual life in both immanent and transcendent traditions. The conflict that triggers the spiritual quest can be a prelude to more intense periods of soul sickness or dark nights. During such spiritual crises, life is precarious and may seem like a single vine to which one clings in fear of falling into an abyss. The risk of losing one's way is great, and, paradoxically, those aspirants who seek liberation may also wish to hold something back.

Enlightenment. Transcendence and immanence come together at the point of spiritual transformation, for the aim of both is spiritual birth or enlightenment. Ordinary reality, the Buddhists teach, is characterized by the attitude, This is mine. I am this. This is my self. Liberation is letting go, keeping nothing back. Loss of self, C.S. Lewis maintained, is the principle that "runs through all life from top to bottom. Give up your self, and you will find your real self. Lose your life and you save it."[48] Nonpossessiveness is also the lesson of the Buddhist way: This is not mine. I am not this. This is not my self. This, then, is the pure land of liberation. Shido Bunan, a Rinzai Buddhist master, put it this way:

> *Die while alive, and be completely*
> *dead,*
> *Then do whatever you will, all is*
> *good.*[49]

Liberation, from a Buddhist perspective, is a pathless land beyond the distinction of striving and nonstriving, of self-salvation and self-surrender. It is experience of the now—of reality in its fullness. Life is one. Every thing has value—death, life, sunsets, even commonplace and monotonous things, such as washing dishes or hoeing a garden. "When the quest for salvation is laid aside," writes Sam Keen in *To a Dancing God,* "a cup of tea with my wife as the sun goes down is as graceful as anything, I can imagine. Grace surprises me in modest and hidden places."[50] Life is, in such moments, as it should be. It is neither more nor less than what it is. Nothing need be changed.

Where the movement of liberation is inward, salvation is primarily a call to humanization. Where the holy is experienced as immanent, self-liberation is an answer to the question, What does it mean to be human? Spiritual birth is always a shattering of the boundaries, a movement from the ordinary to the nonordinary. In the experience of self-salvation, the movement is from dependence to independence. Sam Keen, who has argued persuasively for a sense of the sacred as discernible in the ordinary, contrasted the Christian emphasis on self-surrender, a sense that you can't heal yourself, with the process of getting well in therapy:

> *I am responsible for my feelings, my actions and my style of life. In spite of parents, family, friends or the surrounding culture, I alone can make the decision to outgrow my dis-ease and to establish a way of life that is satisfying. There is no magic. There is no automatic dispenser of grace. There are no saviors. My final dignity is in my ability to choose my style of life.*[51]

Scriptures, teachers, rituals, organizations are guides to growth, but they can also be restraints. The Buddha stressed that "Ye must be lamps unto yourselves." The seeker must be free and must not cling to holy books and beloved teachers. For this reason, the ninth-century Zen master Hsuan-chien once wrote, "the sacred teachings [of the Buddha] are . . . only sheets of paper fit for wiping the pus from your boils."[52] Joseph Campbell takes a similar stance: to be liberated or spiritually born is to be "freed from the pedagogical devices of society, the lures and threats of myth, the local *mores,* the usual hopes of benefits and rewards. . . . In the lands of the truly 'twice-born', man is finally superior to the gods."[53] Humans are, in short, free to be fully human.

Mysticism and Mystical Experience

Some religious experiences and beliefs do not fit within the categories of transcendence and immanence. Mystics insist that the distinction separating conceptions and experiences of ultimacy as transcendent and immanent disappears in the mystical experience. Mysticism is not so much a religion as it is an experience and way of appropriating the world that is found in most religious traditions; thus there are Christian, Muslim, and Jewish mystics in religions of transcendence just as there are Buddhist, Hindu, and Taoist mystics in religions that primarily experience and think of the sacred as immanent.

Although the religious consciousness usually makes a distinction between the ordinary and the nonordinary, the sacred and the profane, the natural and the supernatural, the authentic and the inauthentic, the mystic experiences life as one. The mystical consciousness moves, as Mircea Eliade points out, toward the reduction of the sphere of the profane or even the abolishing of it altogether.[54] All life is to be hallowed. Martin Buber told the story of a disciple who was asked what was most important in his Hasidic master's life. The disciple replied, "Always just what he was engaged in at the moment."[55] The point is that all of life can be consecrated, sanctified; there is nothing in which God cannot be found. The ordinary, the profane, is simply the not-yet-hallowed.

In a sense the dialectic of religious consciousness moves in the direction of mysticism—that is, of finding the holy both within (immanence) as well as without (transcendence), or in going beyond the distinction altogether. The spiritual diary of Dag Hammarskjöld contains numerous examples of God as both an objective transcendent presence and as immanent. In one entry he wrote, we "must learn to pierce the veil of things and comprehend God within them."[56] In another, "God is wholly in you, just as, for you, He is wholly in all you meet. With this faith, in prayer descend into yourself to meet the Other, in the steadfastness of this union, see that all things stand, like yourself, alone before God."[57]

The abolition of the twofoldness of religious consciousness, the division of the sacred and the profane, is thus in the direction of the sanctification of all things. For the mystic, such a movement is unitive—a union of the divine and human. It can be a union of wills in which God's will and the individual's will become a single will, or it can be a union of natures. The thirteenth-century German mystic Meister Eckhart wrote, "The eye by which I see God is the same as the eye by which God sees me. My eye and God's eye are one and the same—one in seeing, one in knowing and one in loving."[58] In the Hindu tradition, **Brahman,** the thing unseen, which pervades every thing and is all things, abolishes twofoldness. All things are one. Some of the forms that Buddhism takes are primarily mystical. This sense of the sacred and mystical unity of all things is expressed in this Zen verse:

A long thing is the long body of Buddha
A short thing is the short body of Buddha.[59]

The mystic seeks a union experience—a loss of the self in the holy. It is an experience, the Hindu sages suggest, of being one without a second—an undifferentiated unity. In one of his sermons, Meister Eckhart compared God's unconditioned being to that of a womb:

Back in the womb from which I came, I had no god and merely was, myself, I did not will or desire anything, for I was pure being, a knower of myself by divine truth. Then I wanted myself and nothing else. And what I wanted, I was and what I was, I wanted, and thus, I existed untrammeled by god or anything else. But when I parted from my free will and received my created being, then I had a god. For before there were creatures, God was not god, but, rather he was what he was. . . .

Therefore I pray God that he may quit me of god, for his unconditioned being is above god and distinctions.[60]

In traditions of transcendence, mystics insist that God is always something more than his creation, but they also believe the divine is in some essential way like his creation. In Roman Catholicism, God is transcendent, but he is also immanent in the mystery and miracle of Holy Communion. For Quakers and many other Christians, the soul is the "still small voice of God within"—the intersection where our likeness to God meets in communion with him.

Concluding Remarks

Faith is an experience of the holy that touches the whole person, as Paul Tillich wrote, "the state of being ultimately concerned."[61] Every aspect of human consciousness participates in faith, yet faith is, in Tillich's analysis, a condition that transcends the rational (cognitive and conative) and the nonrational (affective) but does not destroy them. Faith has an ecstatic or liberating character that includes the rational and the nonrational, yet is something more than either. The ecstatic character of faith is the experience of the sacred presence—an experience of standing outside of oneself, of being grasped by the holy. From the standpoint of faith, the key that opens the door to meaningful and transformed life is a vital relationship to holiness. The Eternal Thou, to use Buber's image "is the cradle of real life"[62]—the unifying thread that gives human life its orientation.

The response of human beings to what they experience as holy is varied. One way of making sense out of this variety is to classify religions and religious experiences on the basis of whether the holy is experienced and conceived of as transcendent, a God who is wholly other than his creation; as immanent, a sacred reality that is in, rather than beyond, the world; or as a mystical unity that goes beyond the distinctions of transcendence and immanence.

Notes

1. In Max Muller, ed., *The Sacred Books of the East,* vol. V, part II (Delhi: Motilal Banarsidass, 1968), p. 9.

2. Alfred North Whitehead, *Religion in the Making* (New York: Meridian Books, 1960), p. 16.

3. William James, *Varieties of Religious Experience* (New York: Mentor Books, 1958), p. 24.

4. Joachim Wach, *Types of Religious Experience Christian and Non-Christian* (Chicago: University of Chicago Press, 1970), p. 32.

5. Ibid.

6. Paul Tillich, *Dynamics of Faith* (New York: Harper Torchbooks, 1957), p. 4.

7. John C.H. Wu, *The Golden Age of Zen* (Taiwan: National War College, 1967), pp. 66–67.

8. Job 13:15 KJV.

9. See *Kierkegaard's Concluding Unscientific Postscript,* trans. by David F. Swenson and Walter Lowrie (Princeton, N.J.: Princeton University Press, 1941), pp. 90–96.

10. Richard R. Niebuhr, *Experiential Religion* (New York: Harper & Row, 1972), pp. 44–50.

11. Paul Tillich, *The Shaking of the Foundations* (New York: Scribner's, 1948), p. 162.

12. Mohandas K. Gandhi, *The Story of My Experiments with Truth* (Boston: Beacon Press, 1957), p. 265.

13. Sam Keen, *To a Dancing God* (New York: Harper & Row, 1970), p. 77.

14. In Sydney Ahlstrom, *A Religious History of the American People* (New Haven, Conn.: Yale University Press, 1972), pp. 434–35.

15. In Mary Douglas, *Natural Symbols* (New York: Pantheon Books, 1970), pp. 77–78.

16. R.H. Blyth, *Haiku,* vol. I (Kamakura: Bunko, 1949), p. 192.

17. Sören Kierkegaard, *Christian Discourses,* trans. by Walter Lowrie (London: Oxford University Press, 1940), p. 323.

18. Franz Rosenzweig, *The Star of Redemption* (New York: Holt, Rinehart and Winston, 1971), pp. 308-09,

19. Simone Weil, *Waiting for God,* trans. by Emma Craufurd (New York: Harper & Row, 1973), p. 182. First published by G.P. Putnam's Sons in 1951.

20. Isaiah 55:8–9.

21. Peter Berger, *A Rumor of Angels* (Garden City, N.Y.: Doubleday, 1969), p. 112.

22. Martin Buber, *I and Thou* (New York: Scribner's, 1958), p. 11.

23. Berger, *A Rumor of Angels,* p. 12.

24. Augustine, *Of True Religion,* in *The Library of Christian Classics,* trans. by John H.S. Burleigh, vol. XXIX (Philadelphia: Westminster Press, 1963), p. 262.

25. Rudolf Otto, *The Idea of the Holy* (New York: Oxford University Press, 1958), p. 10.

26. Graham Greene, *The End of the Affair* (New York: Viking Press, 1961), p. 116.

27. Sören Kierkegaard, *Fear and Trembling and the Sickness unto Death,* trans. by Walter Lowrie (Princeton, N.J.: Princeton University Press, 1954), pp. 159–60.

28. Jacques Cabaud, *Simone Weil* (New York: Channel Press, 1964), p. 294.

29. C.S. Lewis "A Slip of the Tongue," *Screwtape Proposes a Toast* (New York: Macmillan, 1961), p. 121.

30. Weil, *Waiting for God,* p. 56.

31. Buber, *I and Thou,* p. 115.

32. Isaiah 6:1–8.

33. Ephesians 2:8.

34. Weil, *Waiting for God,* pp. 194–95.

35. Jacques Durandeaux, *Living Questions to Dead Gods,* trans. by William Whitman (New York: Sheed and Ward, 1968), p. 86.

36. Weil, *Waiting for God,* p. 195.

37. See Norman Pettit, *The Heart Prepared, Grace and Conversion in Puritan Spiritual Life* (New Haven, Conn.: Yale University Press, 1966).

38. Buber, *I and Thou,* p. 82.

39. Ibid., p. 80.

40. Joseph Needham, *Science and Civilization* (Cambridge: Cambridge University Press, 1956), vol. II, p. 562.

41. In Zenkai Shibayama, *A Flower Does Not Talk* (Rutland, Vt.: Charles E. Tuttle, 1970), p. 67.

42. See Analects 12:22 in *The Sayings of Confucius,* trans. by James R. Ware (New York: Mentor Books, 1955), p. 81.

43. *The Way of Lao Tzu,* trans. by Wing-tsit Chan (New York: Bobbs-Merrill, 1963), p. 214.

44. Confucius, Analects 17:3, p. 109.

45. In John Noss, *Man's Religions* (Toronto: Macmillan, 1969), p. 128.

46. See Shibayama, *A Flower Does Not Talk,* p. 39.

47. Ibid., p. 42.

48. C.S. Lewis, *Mere Christianity* (New York: Macmillan, 1952), p. 175.

49. In Zenkai Shibayama, *Zen Comments on the Mumonkan* (New York: Mentor Books, 1974), p. 114.

50. Keen, *To a Dancing God,* pp. 123–24.

51. Ibid., pp. 135–36.

52. Kenneth K.S. Ch'en, *Buddhism in China* (Princeton, N.J.: Princeton University Press, 1964), p. 358.

53. Joseph Campbell, "The Biological Function of Myth," in Frederick J. Streng et al., *Ways of Being Religious* (Englewood Cliffs, N.J.: Prentice-Hall, 1973), p. 171.

54. Mircea Eliade, *Patterns in Comparative Religion* (World, 1963), p. 459.

55. Martin Buber, *Tales of the Hasidim: The Later Masters,* vol. II (New York: Shocken Books, 1948), p. 173.

56. Dag Hammarskjöld, *Markings* (New York: Knopf, 1964), p. 143.

57. Ibid., p. 165.

58. *Meister Eckhart,* trans. by Raymond B. Blakney (New York: Harper Torchbooks, 1941), p. 206.

59. R.H. Blyth, *Zen in English Literature* (Tokyo: Hokuseido Press, 1948), p. 348.

60. *Eckhart,* pp. 228, 231.

61. Tillich, *Dynamics of Faith,* p. 4.

62. Buber, *I and Thou,* p. 9.

Chapter Eleven
Paths of Ultimate
Liberation

Consume my heart away; sick with desire
And fastened to a dying animal
It knows not what it is; and gather me
Into the artifice of eternity.

W.B. Yeats
"Sailing to Byzantium"[1]

Personal religious experience was defined in chapter ten as the experience of ultimacy. It is a complex and varied phenomenon. The purpose of this chapter is to take a closer look at a specific form of religious experience—the experience of having one's life transformed, of being spiritually born. Human beings are the only creatures who are twice-born. The physical process of human birth establishes our kinship with other animals, but it is only humans who experience life as a problem. Sickness of body is shared with all animals, but sickness of mind is uniquely human. Growing up human requires a second kind of birth, which is psychic or spiritual. In the broadest sense, this process gives birth to the individual. Ultimate liberation entails giving birth to a consciousness of the sacred or experiencing a conversion to the sacred. It is, like the process of individuation, a phenomena of growth and change.

Buddha advised us to work out our own salvation. Jesus called for a spiritual birth, "Ye must be born again." The promise of religion is authentic existence, and from a religious perspective, transfigured life is possible only when it is rooted in the ground of realness itself, the holy. Religion is thus, in part, **soteriological**—that is, it is concerned with salvation or ultimate liberation. Restored life is its message. Captives can be set free. Lives that are broken and fragmentary can be made whole.

The process of spiritual birth is illustrated by contrasting the transformational experiences of two different types of religious personalities: the troubled self and the untroubled self. Troubled selves, as a spiritual type, live through periods of intense crises before being saved or enlightened. They are battered by sufferings and afflictions that are often so great that they may despair of deliverance. To borrow Simone Weil's simile, during such dark nights, like "a being struggling on the ground like a half-crushed worm, they have no words to express what is happening to them."[2] The troubled self's soteriological pattern proceeds from crisis to restoration, from a spiritual death to a spiritual birth.

Untroubled selves are a contrasting type. Their lives are not checkered with conflicts, but are relatively smooth passages. The pattern of crisis and rebirth gives way to softer images. Crises are perceived as temporary obstacles or impediments to overcome. Spiritual weaknesses are superficial blemishes rather than symptoms of something more pervasively wrong. Untroubled selves are more nurtured than delivered, for they have little sense of self-disapproval. Their spiritual transformation is a gradual process, a pattern of steady growth rather than dramatic spiritual birth.

Two souls, alas! reside within my breast and   ## The Troubled Self
each withdraws from and repels, its brother.
                         Goethe
                         Faust[3]

The spiritual odyssey of the troubled self is fraught with conflict and suffering. The path to transformed life begins with a spiritual crisis or perhaps a series of psychic upheavals. The tension may be precipitated by physical pain, but its movement is inward to the marrow of spiritual existence. A psychic or soul sickness so uproots the whole of the individual's life that he experiences himself as broken.

The Divided Self

Of the several variations of the troubled self, one mode was identified by William James as a divided self.[4] This personality is torn asunder by an intense inner conflict. Schizophrenia is a disease symptomatic of the divided self. Discord and division are so intense that the self turns against itself and feels cut off from others and from God. The troubled self knows no peace, no unity of being. Friedrich Nietzsche, whose dislocation became so severe that he was hospitalized, described his torment in this way: "As I write this a madman is howling in the next room and I am howling with him inside of me, howling for my lost integrity, sundered from God, Man and myself, shattered in body, mind, and spirit, yearning for two-clasped hands to usher in the great miracle—the unity of my being."[5]

In theistic faiths, divided selves see themselves as pulled in one direction by their desire to do the will of God and in another by the seduction of their own inclinations. "Purity of heart is to will one thing,"[6] Kierkegaard argued, but his own personality was a battleground between the human will and the divine will. Saint Paul's experience has become, for Christians, the exemplar of the contest of wills: "For the good that I would, I do not; but the evil which I would not, that I do."[7]

The Disquieted Self

The disquieted self is another example of the spiritually troubled. The tension may be more a pervasive disquiet or uneasiness, a feeling of being unfulfilled, rather than a sharp division. In this mode, a person may have an undefined feeling that "there is something wrong with me as I am now." The protagonist of Hermann Hesse's novel *Siddhartha* was a young man who by all outward appearances had everything. He was handsome, bright, adored, yet he was unhappy. At the outset of his quest for enlightenment, Siddhartha was more restless and dissatisfied than torn. It was a disquiet, however, strong enough to prompt him to leave his father's house in a quest for self-discovery.

The Afflicted Self

Still another image of unrest is the afflicted self. This is a person uprooted and scarred to a point where the soul is nearly empty, a spiritual equivalent of death. The afflicted self is engulfed by a sea of nothingness. He is like the hired man in one of Robert Frost's poems who comes home to die. His life is empty, for he has "nothing to look backward to with pride, and nothing to look forward to with hope."[8] The afflicted self often feels so accursed, so inwardly repulsive that these feelings can, as Simone Weil noted, "prevent him from seeking a way of deliverance, sometimes even to the point of preventing him from wishing for deliverance."[9] Liberation, according to Weil, is possible for the afflicted self only where there is still an openness to the possibility of love.

> *Affliction makes God appear to be absent for a time, more absent than a dead man, more absent than light in the utter darkness of a cell. A kind of horror submerges the whole soul. During this absence there is nothing to love. What is terrible is that if, in this darkness where there is nothing to love, the soul ceases to love, God's absence becomes final. The soul has to go on loving in the emptiness, or at least to go on wanting to love. . . .*[10]

The Origin of the Troubled Self

Why do some people experience themselves as flawed and in need of deliverance? What are the roots of the troubled self? The major religious traditions, and modern psychotherapies as well, find that something in human beings stands in the way of authentic existence. Christians suggest that the individual is divided because he or she is a sinner separated from the love of God; the vision of Christianity is that our separation, our state of having fallen, can be overcome in Christ. For the Buddhist, craving, the desire to have and possess, stands in the way of ultimate liberation. In Hinduism, ignorance, the failure to see things as they truly are, binds people to the wheel of becoming and prevents them from realizing ultimate liberation. Modern psychotherapists, even though they no longer talk about sin, find it impossible to abandon the notion of the troubled self since their clients are so obviously seeking help. Gerald M. Goodman, a psychologist, observed that many therapies, including est and Scientology, seem to be saying something like this to prospective clients: "You are perfect, but with our package you can change your imperfect self-concept and distorted perception of the world."[11]

From a religious perspective humans are usually seen as flawed, as lacking something. Religion has a stake in the experience of brokenness because such crises can lead to a spiritual birth, a conversion to the holy. Not only does religion have a vital interest in alienation, some observers have even suggested that it may stimulate individuals to see themselves in that way. As Louis Dupré pointed out:

> . . . the salvation which religion promises presupposes an unsatisfactory state of being that must be remedied. Indeed, religion stands so badly in need of that preliminary feeling of alienation that one may well wonder whether it does not itself create the very condition which it wants to remedy.[12]

The origins of alienation are deep; the suggestion that the troubled self is religion's creation is facile and superficial. The unhappy consciousness is a view of man also shared by such critics of religion as Sigmund Freud and Karl Marx. Freud portrayed the self as a constant battleground between the instinctive drives of the id and the counter inhibiting demands of parents and society as assimilated in the superego. It is no wonder that the ego, the moderating or reality-principle in Freud's schema, must struggle fiercely to maintain equilibrium. Sadness and madness are endemic to humans, for the price of civilization is guilt and frustration. Freud wrote, "Every individual is virtually an enemy of civilization."[13] The ego's struggle for mastery is a precarious one, somewhat analogous to the alternation of sense and insanity described in Hamlet's statement, "I am but mad north–north-west; when the wind is southerly, I know a hawk from a handsaw."[14]

The Marxist believes that humans are flawed by institutions; estrangement and alienation are caused by the dehumanization of labor. Marx believed that profit and production were more highly valued than human beings in capitalist economies. The source and resolution of human discontent is thus socioeconomic. Chinese Marxists are acting out the Marxist ideology. The creation of the new individual in China is possible, Mao Tse-tung believed, because there is no inherent human nature. The new individual is to arise from the ashes of the old and corrupt bourgeois one. In 1958 Mao spoke of the Chinese openness to transformation:

> China's 600 million people have two remarkable peculiarities; they are, first of all, poor, and secondly blank. . . . Poor people want change, want to do things, want revolution. A clean sheet of paper has no blotches, and so the newest and most beautiful words can be written on it, the newest and most beautiful pictures can be painted on it.[15]

Freud and Marx are not alone in emphasizing the troubled character of the human condition. Existentialist philosophers trace the source of discontent and alienation to the problematic nature of human existence. Death intensifies our awareness of the preciousness of life and forces us to grapple with questions concerning the meaning of human existence. The human being is, in Nietzsche's metaphor, a bridge—a rope stretching from the givenness of birth to the future which is not yet. Humans are always unfinished. This very openness, the unfinished quality of human existence, requires invention. Each individual, the existentialist insists, must invent what he or she is to be. This results in the restless and troubled nature of the human condition, which Jean-Paul Sartre likened to a donkey who follows a carrot attached to a pole that always remains beyond reach.

Humans are troubled because the process of growing up, of becoming an individual, is a series of stressful beginnings and endings. In traditional societies the perilous passage from childhood to adult life is mediated through rites of passage. In modern societies, where the ritual process has broken down, adolescence is particularly susceptible to stress and often manifests variations of the troubled self. This period, during which a young person must invent an ego separate from that of his or her parents, is marked by a search for identity. Adolescence is an age of flying, fearfully at first, until one creates his or her own perching place. Young adults in modern societies thus frequently experience themselves as torn asunder and as standing in need of salvation.

This inventing of the self is not simply an adolescent aberration; it persists through the whole course of human life. Dante's *Divine Comedy* is one of the great stories of the pilgrimage from troubled to transformed existence. It begins with Dante, at mid-life, painfully aware that he was lost in darkness:

Midway in our life's journey, I went astray from the straight road and woke to find myself alone in a dark wood.[16]

Crisis and depression, then, are not strangers to what Carl Jung picturesquely called the "afternoon of life." The task of the afternoon is less one of identity than one of an invention of meaning. How can one savor the world, celebrate existence, when the hopes and aspirations of youth have crashed upon the reef of time? Perhaps at bottom is the disquieting realization that death is our inescapable destiny. Carl Jung learned, from his many years as a professional psychotherapist, that spiritual crises are prominent features of the afternoon of life.

Among all my patients in the second half of life—that is to say, over thirty-five—there has not been one whose problem in the last resort was not that of finding a religious outlook on life. It is safe to say that every one of them fell ill because he had lost that which the living religions of every age have given to their followers, and none of them has been really healed who did not regain his religious outlook.[17]

Not surprisingly, humans experience themselves as troubled. We are disquieted because we must invent ourselves. What should we make of ourselves? What kind of offering—to God, to others? The very movement of life from birth through adolescence and adulthood requires a series of new beginnings. To be born again is necessary in the life of the spirit because brokenness and new beginnings are inescapable features of the human story. Life is experienced as a problem because we are painfully conscious of the gaps or divisions separating the ideal and the real, the ought and the is, the expectation and the realization. The self is experienced as troubled because we know ourselves subjectively, inwardly, and often are ashamed of what we find there.

Spiritual Birth of the Troubled Self

Transformation, salvation, enlightenment, self-actualization, and ultimate liberation are rough symbols for the experience of becoming a new person. Spiritual birth is analogous to dying and being reborn. Newness is an image of the restored life. Paul, in his second letter to the Corinthians, wrote, "If any man be in Christ, he is a new creature: old things are passed away; behold, all things are become new."[18] In Hesse's novel, Siddhartha's spiritual rebirth was likened to a wonderful sleep during which he had died to the old "and on awakening he looked at the world like a new man."[19]

"Even though you die, yet shall you live"[20] is the dialectic of rebirth. It is a movement from the despair of the troubled self to a rapturous and ecstatic new being. The troubled soul is restored, lifted up, filled full through its relationship to the sacred. "To be saved is to reach the fullness of love," wrote Gustavo Gutierrez in *A Theology of Liberation*.[21] Sacral life is vital life. Amos, an eighth-century B.C. Jewish prophet, proclaimed, "Seek God and live,"[22] and the Deuteronomists sang a similar exultant refrain, "Therefore choose life that you and your descendants may live."[23] One of the Beatitudes sounds a similar note, "Blessed are they who thirst after the Holy, for they shall be filled with holiness."[24]

Spiritual birth is not merely self-improvement. We improve ourselves when we master a new skill or acquire more knowledge. If we are overweight, we can improve our health by giving greater care to our diet. Twice-borns are more transformed than improved; they stand in a different, more vital, relationship to themselves, to others, and to the holy. Theirs is an experience of joyous living and openness to others. Hesse's Siddhartha experienced a deep spiritual sleep from which he emerged as a new person. While the deeply troubled Siddhartha had grown tired and despairing of life, the new Siddhartha rose to life "full of joyous love towards everything he saw."[25]

In tribal religions the same principle applies. Transformed life comes from the sacred center. The spiritual birth that transforms an initiate into a shaman is, according to Mircea Eliade, an ecstatic experience that indicates his or her acceptance by the holy. The birth transmutes the initiate into a technician of the sacred and thus significantly alters the status of the new being vis-à-vis the holy.[26] The salient feature of salvation is thus neither moral nor intellectual improvement but rather a transforming experience of the holy.

In *Shamanism: Archaic Techniques of Ecstasy* Eliade isolated the process for the making of a shaman. It begins with a crisis, an intense suffering, usually in the form of an illness during which a symbolic death occurs. The time of crisis and danger is followed by an ecstatic spiritual birth, usually accompanied by a vision, trance, or dream, that is a form of spiritual instruction indicative of the initiate's acceptance by the spirit world. The ecstatic experience is decisive and is the moment of deliverance or resurrection. The process for the making of a shaman is roughly the same as that of the troubled self: a period of troubled existence followed by the spiritual birth of a new being.

Transformation, the making of a new person, radically changes the entire field of human perceptions. The physical conditions of life are not necessarily changed; conversion to the sacred does not alter the structure of reality. Human beings are born, suffer, and die. For those whose lives are transformed, the world remains the same yet is perceived differently. As Sam Keen says, "Nothing changes and everything changes."[27] A conversion to the sacred counters the ordinary and the transient character of human existence with the experience of authentic, transformed life.

Salvation is a change that can take place suddenly or almost imperceptibly. The untroubled self's conversion to the sacred, if it can even be called that, is gradual, more a process than a conversion. Conversely, for the troubled self the transformation is more an event than a process. It may occur in a moment and result in a sudden reversal of behavior, or it can issue from a series of conflicts and illuminations.

The time and the circumstances of one's salvation can go by almost unnoticed. The dimness of the soul may be gradually cleared, like eyes adjusting imperceptibly to the light, and be unattended by dramatic hierophanies such as being visited by an angel or hearing the voice of God. The date and time of Dag Hammarskjöld's deliverance slipped by without such a momentous occasion:

> *I don't know Who—or what—put the question, I don't know when it was put. I don't even remember answering. But at some moment I did answer Yes to Someone—or Something—and from that hour I was certain that existence is meaningful and that, therefore, my life, in self-surrender had a goal.*[28]

Salvific or transforming events can be etched graphically in the memory, as are those recounted in Saint Augustine's autobiography. Augustine's pilgrimage to self-surrender was torturous and marked by numerous conflicts and transformations. Although he lived within a Christianized world, supported by the love of his Christian mother and friends, he was not yet a Christian. He believed that becoming a Christian required such a serious break with the world that it demanded a death of his old life. Confronted by such an either/or, Augustine kept avoiding that final act of commitment, baptism. "Let me wait a little longer," he would say.[29] In a state of agitation, he found himself driven by inner turmoil and divisions to take refuge in a garden. In this tormented state, divided against himself, Augustine heard the voice of a child in a nearby house. The voice kept repeating the refrain, "Take it and read, take it and read." Augustine interpreted the words as a divine command to open his scripture and read the first passage on which his eyes should fall. The scripture, a passage from one of Saint Paul's epistles, was like a light of serenity flooding into his heart and "all the darkness of doubt vanished away."[30]

Sudden Conversions of the Troubled Self

A sudden conversion, which radically reverses the direction of one's life, is the most dramatic form of transformation. Because it is a sudden, overt, and complete turnabout, it is vividly engraved in the imagination. This quality makes it possible for those so born again to remember sharply the conditions of their rebirth. Eldridge Cleaver, former minister of information for the Black Panthers and author of *Soul on Ice,* reported such a radical reversal. In 1976 Cleaver, an exiled fugitive from California's criminal justice system and an avowed Marxist, returned to the United States and voluntarily turned himself over to legal authorities. Exiled from home and lost in a sea of conflicts, Cleaver described his conversion or decision for Christ in this way:

> *I was admiring the moon from my cell and I saw a man in the moon and it was my face. . . . Then I saw the face was not mine but some of my old heroes. . . . While I watched, the face turned to Jesus Christ and I was very much surprised. . . . I began to cry and I didn't stop. I was still crying and I got on my knees and said the Lord's Prayer. . . . It was like I could not stop crying unless I said the prayer and the Psalm and surrendered something. . . . All I had to do was surrender and go to jail.*[31]

Saint Paul's experience on the road to Damascus is also an example of a radical conversion or change of direction, although his conversion may have stemmed less from his troubled condition than from a divine initiative. Paul was a persecutor of those who followed Jesus. He witnessed with

Caravaggio, Conversion of St. Paul, *Church of Sta. Maria del Popolo, Rome. This painting depicts the dramatic conversion of St. Paul at the moment when, overcome by a divine light, he fell to the ground.*

Photo: Alinari/Editorial Photocolor Archives

approval the stoning to death of the first Christian martyr, Stephen. His life appeared to be set on its course, and he traveled the Damascus road to continue his suppression of what he must have considered a flagrant heresy. When he was near Damascus, a light shone around him and he heard a voice saying, "Why do you persecute me?" Paul said, "Who are you, Lord?" The voice answered, "I am Jesus."[32] Paul's experience resulted in a stunning reversal; the enemy of Christ became His most dedicated champion.

Sudden conversions in the Pauline fashion are prized by pentecostal and evangelical Christians. Their paramount question is, Have you been saved? They believe there are no second-generation Christians. Becoming a Christian is not like an inheritance, a birthright, but is rather a personal experience of being reborn in Christ. Not surprisingly, those who have been born again stress witnessing and testifying to their conversion.

Conversions to the Sacred as a Series of Transformations

Rather than a sudden, dramatic reversal as in Saint Paul's case, the deliverance of the troubled self is often a series of struggles, of valleys of despair and peaks of illumination. The deliverance of Al-Ghazali, a Muslim mystic, is a story of several crises and spiritual renewals. His deliverance did not entail a sudden reversal from paganism to true belief, as he was raised a Muslim and never departed from that faith. As a young man, in spite of his immersion within a Muslim family and tradition, he experienced a period of intellectual doubt. "The disease was baffling . . . at length God cured me of the malady; my being was restored to health and an even balance."[33] The restoration was, for Al-Ghazali, not the result of convincing argumentation, but the work of God who prepared his heart. As evidence of God's work he quoted from the Koran, "Whenever God wills to guide a man, He enlarges his breast for surrender."

Later in life, when Al-Ghazali was a professor in Baghdad, he was torn between his attachment to self-enhancement and total submission to God. He was, in short, a divided self torn between God's will and his own desires. One day he would resolve to give up his post and the next day abandon his resolution. He was continuously torn for six months. In July 1095 the struggle ceased to be a choice. "God caused my tongue to dry up so that I was prevented from lecturing."[34] Driven by his grief and impotence, Al-Ghazali "sought refuge with God most high as one who is driven to Him, because he is without further resources of his own."[35]

Simone Weil's poignant story is also one of an arduous and tortured path marked by several liberating experiences. She was fully convinced by her own experience that God seeks people. She was raised in a nonbelieving French family and educated, with a major in philosophy, at the Sorbonne. Not untypical of French intellectuals, she embraced Marxism and championed the working class throughout her brief life. Her religious experiences were unexpected and unintended. She did not seek God. She had never read Christian works. As she wrote later of her personal contact with God, "God in his mercy had prevented me from reading the mystics, so that it should be evident to me that I had not invented this absolutely unexpected contact."[36]

Simone Weil had several experiences through which her life was changed. In the autumn of 1938, while she was reciting George Herbert's "Love," the poem took the form of a prayer, and she felt that Christ himself had taken possession of her. Later she wrote of this experience, "in this sudden possession of me by Christ, neither my senses nor my imagination had any part; I only felt in the midst of my suffering the presence of a love, like that which one can read in the smile of a beloved face."[37] Weil described subsequent experiences in which she felt that Christ was present with her in person and that his presence was "infinitely more real, more moving, more clear than on that first occasion" when he took possession of her.[38]

No single event can awaken
within us
a stranger totally unknown
to us.
To live is to be slowly born.
        Antoine de Saint-Exupéry [39]

The Untroubled Self

Some untroubled personalities are sensitive to the holy and may see the sacred nearly everywhere, but, for the most part, they never experience an intense crisis of the spirit. Severe dislocations, with their self-destructive impulses, are unknown to them. Spiritual growth is a gradual, relatively peaceful, and nearly imperceptible process. It is a process of continuous and expansive growth in which difficulties succeed one another in time, rather than occur all at once, and thus are more manageable.

Untroubled selves find little in themselves to reject. They are optimistic and happy and do not see themselves as flawed or diseased or as sinners separated from God. They accept themselves and know that they are accepted by the sacred as well. Life is experienced not as a problem but as an opportunity for celebration. In *The Varieties of Religious Experience,* William James cited Dr. Edward Everett Hale, a Unitarian preacher and writer, as an example of such a spirit: "I always knew God loved me, and I was always grateful to him for the world he placed me in. . . . I had no idea whatever what the problem of life was. To live with all my might seemed to me easy."[40] James described the untroubled self as having "a religion of healthy-mindedness."[41] The untroubled self views the universe as a friendly rather than as a hostile home and perceives the divine as kind and merciful rather than as awesome and wholly other.

A good model for understanding the untroubled self is the experience of a person born and raised in a religious community. For children raised in religious families, nurture is often the process to spiritual maturity.

The family and the religious community are the womb that nurtures and educates the spirit. Most Jews, for example, do not choose Judaism; they are born into it. Their spirituality is more a response to their Jewishness than a preoccupation with personal salvation.

How is a person to know despair and alienation if he or she has been raised in a cocoon of love? The intent of Christian nurture, of Christian education, should be, wrote Christian theologian Horace Bushnell, that the child "grow up a Christian and never know himself to be otherwise."[42] Closely knit religious communities and sacramental religious groups provide a matrix for religious growth. A temperamentally optimistic and physically healthy person, raised in such a context, may find it difficult, even impossible, to see himself or herself as a sinner estranged from God.

Salvation in sacramental traditions is often a nurturing process in which the believer is guided safely through the new beginnings (birth, puberty, marriage, death) by a series of ritual acts. As was noted previously, in Hindu practice the second or spiritual birth is facilitated by a sacred rite rather than a private experience. Although the Catholic Church has a rich legacy of famous troubled selves who have experienced dramatic and sudden conversions, its spiritual life is most characteristically a sacramental process in which the person is born into the church through baptism and is continuously nourished through God's grace as mediated through the sacraments. The traumas of change are softened by rites that continually renew the believer's relationship to the holy. In the following statement, Bishop Fulton J. Sheen points out the relationship of regeneration to the sacraments:

> As a man must be born before he can begin to live his physical life, so he must be born to lead a Divine Life. That birth occurs in the Sacrament of Baptism. To survive, he must be nourished by Divine Life; that is done in the Sacrament of the Holy Eucharist. He must grow spiritually and assume his spiritual responsibilities; that is accomplished in the Sacrament of Confirmation. He must heal the wounds of sin; for this there is the Sacrament of Penance. He must wipe out the traces of sins at the end, to prepare for his journey to eternal life, for this there is the Sacrament of Extreme Unction.[43]

Francis W. Newman wrote, "God has two families of children on this earth, the once-born and the twice-born"[44]—the relatively untroubled and the troubled. The one cannot easily understand the other. How is the once-born, the person who does not think of himself as lost or in need of regeneration, to respond to a zealous Christian's query, Are you saved? or to the greeting, Hare Krsna, from the mouth of a joyous devotee seeking to spread the message of Krishna-consciousness? Walt Whitman is a good example of the healthy-minded person who disapproved of the tears and anguish of the twice-born.

> *I think I could turn and live with*
> * animals, they are so placid and*
> * self-contain'd,*
> *I stand and look at them long and long.*
> *They do not sweat and whine about*
> * their condition,*
> *They do not lie awake in the dark and*
> * weep for their sins.*[45]

Troubled selves are just as perplexed by their opposites. They are apt to equate the religion of healthy-mindedness and its optimism and tranquillity with a stultifying contentedness. They may feel that salvation is not to be confused with niceness, peak experiences, or even an integrated personality. C.S. Lewis wrote: "We must not suppose that even if we succeeded in making everyone nice we should save their souls. A world of nice people, content in their own niceness, looking no further, turned away from God, would be just as desperately in need of salvation as a miserable world—and might be more difficult to save."[46]

In Quest of Holiness

I am being driven forward
Into an unknown land.

Dag Hammarskjöld
Markings[47]

One of the recurrent and compelling images of spiritual or transformed life is that of pilgrimage. Frequently a spiritual pilgrimage is likened to a voyage—a crossing-over from one shore to another. In Hesse's novel, for example, Siddhartha crosses the river on those occasions when he embarks on a new mode of awareness. Vasudeva, Siddhartha's spiritual father, is a ferryman who transports souls as well as passengers from shore to shore. Similarly, Jaina saints are referred to as those who have forded the river and achieved the shore of enlightenment. In the Christian tradition the nave of the church building is a nautical derivative and suggests that the church is a ship carrying its passengers to eternal life. Catholic theologian John S. Dunne wrote, "The question 'What is God?' calls for a voyage of discovery, for a whole lifetime of discovery. As I explore the height and the depth and the breadth of life, each discovery I make about life is a discovery about God, each is a step with God, a step toward God."[48]

Flight is another symbol of the human yearning for the sacred. The expansiveness of the sky, even more than the sea, tilts the mind toward the idea of infinity and suggests that it is the abode of the timeless. In Greek mythology, Daedalus and his son, Icarus, were imprisoned in a labyrinth by King Minos. Their escape by either water or land was cut off, but the air and the sky were free. Daedalus, the inventor, made a pair of wings that they might soar upward to freedom. The soul's quest, like Daedalus' escape, often draws its images from the sky.

Like voyage and flight, ascent is also a metaphor of pilgrimage. Plato's "Allegory of the Cave" is an illuminating story of the human ascent from a state of ignorance to enlightenment.[49] Let us imagine, Plato begins, prisoners who are from childhood seated in a cave, unable to turn their heads. A fire burns behind them and casts shadows on the wall for them to see. These strange prisoners are able to see only shadows and hear only echoes. Reality is screened from them. Then, Plato continues, let us imagine that a prisoner is released and compelled suddenly to turn about and behold the fire. What would such a release be like? Would not the glare of the fire distress him? Would it not take time to adjust from the world of shadows to the reality of the fire? Suppose the prisoner is subsequently dragged out into the light of the sun. Would his eyes not again need time to adjust to the sun's brightness? The prisoner's shifts in perspective are analogous to a spiritual breakthrough—those moments in which the fog is lifted and our vision of the sacred is cleared.

What is the import of Plato's allegory? Plato compared the role of the sun in the visible world to that of what he called the Good in the invisible. As the sun gives light, the Good gives truth. As the sun is the cause of germination and growth, the Good is the source of intelligibility and order. Human life, when on the right course, is an ascent to the Good. The soul's journey is from darkness to light, from ignorance to wisdom. We are all prisoners, Plato suggests, on a pilgrimage to a higher reality, but as long as we are human we must live within the cavelike world of humankind. Though humans can have only momentary glimpses of the holy before they descend again into the shadows, they carry their vision with them.

Ascent to the sacred and descent or return to the ordinary is the dialectic of pilgrimage. In the poem "Birches," Robert Frost speaks of his own wish to swing heavenward that he might see from that perspective and yet not forfeit his place on earth.

> I'd like to get away from earth awhile
> And then come back to it and begin over.
> May no fate willfully misunderstand me
> And half grant what I wish and snatch me away
> Not to return. Earth's the right place for love:
> I don't know where it's likely to go better.
> I'd like to go by climbing a birch tree.

And climb black branches up a snow-white trunk
Toward heaven, till the tree could bear no more,
But dipped its top and set me down again.
That would be good both going and coming back.
One could do worse than be a swinger of birches.[50]

Humans may see their lives as a voyage, as a flight to the unknown, to the sacred. The pilgrimage may be likened to the flight of a bird, which alternates flying with perching in order to rest and gain a perspective. A spiritual quest is a movement, in Michael Novak's words, from "standpoint to standpoint" or from breakthrough to breakthrough.[51] Quests can also be perilous. Ships can sink in dangerous waters. High flyers can soar beyond the endurance of their craft. Daedalus' son, Icarus, became so intoxicated by the freedom of flight that he flew too close to the sun; the heat melted the glue on his wings and sent him crashing to his death in the sea. Pilgrimage is thus not simply an ascent to the sacred but also involves a descent into the world of man. Perching is as important as flying because it is during those experiences that we know the truth of Don Juan's observation in Carlos Castaneda's *The Teachings of Don Juan:* "To be man is to be condemned to that world."[52] Like Plato's prisoner we are a middle creature, rooted in the earth yet forever struggling toward the sun.

Paths Leading to Ultimate Liberation

If the spiritual life is, metaphorically speaking, a quest or a journey, then what are the paths that lead to salvation? How is the sacred to be known? Where is it found—on the mountaintop, in the recesses of the human heart, in the power and vitality of nature? Is there but a single path to salvation, or are there several yogas, many fording places, that lead to deliverance?

From one perspective, a number of yogas or paths may lead to salvation. According to Swami Vivekananda, a Hindu sage, "the ultimate goal of all mankind, the aim and end of all religions is but one—re-union with God, or, what amounts to the same, with the divinity which is every man's true nature. But while the aim is one, the method of attaining may vary with the different temperaments of men."[53] Ekai, a Zen master, made a similar point: "The great path has no gates, thousands of roads enter it."[54] Rabbi Baer of Radoshitz asked his teacher to show him a way to serve God. His teacher's answer made the point that God can be approached and served in a number of ways:

> It is impossible to tell men what way they should take. For one way to serve
> God is through learning, another through prayer, another through fasting,
> and still another through eating. Everyone should carefully observe what
> way his heart draws him to, and then choose this way with all his strength.[55]

The Yaqui sorcerer, Don Juan, came to a similar conclusion. There are a million paths, he taught; the question is whether the path that you have chosen has a heart.[56]

Each yoga, each path, involves a variety of methods or techniques for enhancing our sensitivity to the sacred. The methods are not in themselves holy, or, as Don Juan observed, "a path is only a path."[57] Study, self-denial, meditation, and prayer are some of the techniques and disciplines people employ to open themselves to the nonordinary. No single technique is essential.

Still another important point about paths deserves mention. A path is usually pointed to by someone who has already traveled it; predecessors who can be imitated and learned from are important to pilgrims. Gurus and sages, for example, are Asian guides. The initiate sits at the feet of a master and embraces his life-style in order to learn and to be guided. Saints also are models of the spiritual life. As Simone Weil wrote, "The world needs saints who have genius, just as a plague-stricken town needs doctors."[58] The life of a saint can provide a mirror of God that can be a compelling model of

A Hindu sage.

Photo by Marilyn Silverstone, Magnum Photos

sanctity. In Christ, Christians believe, they see most luminously the divine face. The Christian paradigm is thus to follow in His steps, to imitate Christ.

While there may be numerous paths for approaching the holy, perhaps three are primary: they are the yogas of knowledge, of action, and of trust. Each path must be accompanied by a commitment to travel it and therefore requires either self-discipline or obedient self-surrender. Transformed life is not for the spiritually flabby. It requires unbending intent, "for the gate is narrow and the way is hard, that leads to life, and those who find it are few."[59]

The Yoga of Knowledge

The speculative intellect is one of the approaches to the holy; it is called *jnana yoga* in Hinduism. It is the yoga of intellectual discrimination, the approaching of the sacred through a discernment of the ultimate nature of things. The Gita teaches that the "boat of knowledge" is sufficient for crossing over all evil.[60] The Hindu sage, guided by reason, cuts through *maya,* the veil of illusion and differentiation, to intuitively apprehend the sacred. The Eightfold Path of Buddhism includes the mental disciplines of alertness, mindfulness, and meditation. The Christian philosopher, knowing that he is saved through faith, nevertheless seeks understanding.

The man of knowledge is one who seeks truth and, in doing so, discovers the holy. Truth, Gandhi believed, is but a name for God: "My uniform experience has convinced me that there is no other God than Truth."[61] Truth is also an image of the sacred in the Gospel of John. Jesus is said to be "the way, the truth, and the life," and the Paraclete, the Holy Spirit, is the spirit of truth who guides us in truth. If you know the truth, the Gospel adds, "the truth shall make you free."[62]

The Yoga of Action

Right action, doing right, is one of the ways of the practical intellect. In India it is known as *karma yoga;* a Christian might associate it with good works; the Muslims know it as obedience. Right action, part of the Buddhist Eightfold Path, is reflected in concern for honest speech, appropriate conduct, and proper occupation of one's time and energy.

The *karma yogin* is more active than theoretical. The person of action seeks to do good and in doing so discovers the holy: "Not to commit any sin, to do good, and to purify one's mind: that is the teaching of the Buddhas."[63] The virtuous person, Confucius taught, practices the Golden Rule, the rule of reciprocity: "Do not do to others, what you do not wish [done to] yourself."[64] *Karma yogins* need not think explicitly of God. The person who does what is good and avoids evil knows God, Catholic philosopher Jacques Maritain wrote, "without being aware of it."[65] Good, like Truth, is also a name for the ultimate.

Duty to the will of God, obedience to goodness, is the path of the *karma yogin*. Duty is sometimes viewed as the performance of traditional obligations. The way of the sacred is known. The commandments are already given or, as in tribal religion, the ancestors have already trod the path of authenticity. For example, in traditional Hindu practice the debts to be discharged are the serious study of scriptures, the ordained sacrifices to the gods, the observance of familial rites, and the rule of hospitality. A stranger should be treated with respect, goes the Hindu rule of hospitality. "Give him a place to sit, and offer him food and drink, because we know that God can assume any form at will; for all we know, this stranger may be a God."[66]

Duty can be a powerful force for sustaining convention; morality and mores converge. It can also be an act of conscience or a sacred revelation that runs counter to traditional morality. For instance, Gandhi and Mao Tse-tung were each, in their own way, moral agents who demanded new beginnings. Hindu scriptures and centuries of practice supported India's caste system, yet Gandhi placed his own sense of right in judgment of it. In part because the morality of caste was forcefully challenged, the constitution of modern India has made civil discrimination on the basis of caste illegal. Mao, in calling for the creation of a new individual and the making of an egalitarian Chinese society, placed himself squarely in opposition to the class hierarchies and privileges of traditional China.

The person of action must strive, the Gita teaches, to perform actions without attachment "caring nothing for the fruit of the action."[67] Obedience to one's moral or sacred duty must not proceed, if it is to be either moral or sacred, from a desire to secure favors or advantages. The good must be chosen because it is right.

The Yoga of Trust

Trust is self-surrender to God. The Hindu tradition calls it *bhakti yoga*. It is the path of loving devotion. The aphorisms of Patanjali, a sage of ancient India, include the simple teaching, "As the result of devotion to God, one achieves *samadhi*"—that is, union with God.[68] The *bhakti yogin* believes that salvation is an undeserved gift of God rather than something that is earned by moral righteousness or through an apprehension of truth. In the Gita, Krishna tells Arjuna:

> *Give me your whole heart,*
> *Love and adore me,*
> *Worship me always,*
> *Bow to me only,*
> *And you shall find me.*[69]

Loving devotion can be expressed through chanting the holy name, through prayer, through ritual offering, and through service.

Trust depends on contact, or as Martin Buber put it, "a contact of my entire being with the one in whom I trust."[70] Trust grows out of a relationship, a meeting of God and humans, which serves as its basis. David, the great Jewish king, trusted in God because he saw the presence of God in his own experience and believed that the Lord had delivered him from his enemies. David praised God, saying: "The Lord is my rock, and my fortress, and my deliverer . . . in whom I take refuge . . . my shield and the horn of my salvation."[71]

Additional Yogas

There are other paths. For example, Jacques Maritain viewed the poetic or artistic experience as an approach to God. The artist seeks beauty, "the perfection of things," and discovers God because, as Maritain believed, all beauty derives from the divine beauty.[72] Beauty, like the Good and the True, is also a divine name.

Ascetic renunciation—self-denial and mortification—is another well traveled path. India's heritage abounds with stories of ascetics who have renounced the world and entered the forests or climbed the mountains to sit in solitude. Sometimes they fast and abuse their bodies almost beyond endurance. Buddha, during his quest, fasted so excessively that he was forced to seek nourishment or die. Austerities, even self-mortification, are part of the Christian story as well. Heinrich Suso, a fourteenth-century Germanic Christian, punished himself daily for twenty-two years. He wore a hair shirt with nails, which lacerated his flesh when he walked or slept, and he frequently carried a cross with exposed nails that pierced his bare back.

While Siddhartha Gautama initially was an ascetic, he eventually became the Buddha through meditation or mental discipline rather than mortification of the flesh. Buddhists and members of many other traditions, including such contemporary movements as Transcendental Meditation and Krishna Consciousness, regularly practice meditation. Meditation can be regarded as a path to ultimate liberation or as a process that is inseparable from what is sought. *Jnana yogins,* for example, usually practice meditation to cultivate an intuitive grasping of what is ultimately real, while others may insist that meditation is not merely a technique but a process that embodies or makes present the experience of self-transcendence. Meditation is a discipline for exploring inner or psychic space and can be employed to calm the mind and to lead to insight. While the practice of meditation includes approaches that incorporate chanting and others that emphasize sitting in silence, all variations require attention to the position of the body, withdrawal of the senses from disruptive external stimuli, and a slow but regular breathing that facilitates the movement from exterior to interior space.

There are, as has been noted, numerous approaches to the holy. Some have sought the sacred through mind-expanding drugs and hallucinogenics. It is a controversial and sometimes dangerous path. Sometimes the desire for altered states of consciousness, for ecstatic experience, can be little more than a form of madness. Nikos Kazantzakis's marvelous character, Zorba, confronted by a particular case of soul-sickness—in this case a preoccupation with religious subjects accompanied by a neglect of the world of man—responded in disgust: "There are seventy-seven kinds of madness, so I've heard. This one must be the seventy-eighth."[73]

Concluding Remarks

How are religious experiences to be understood? Are they genuine or illusory? From a religious perspective, trances, glossolalia, and visions are manifestations of a holy presence, but they also have parallels to psychopathological conditions. When is a trance evidence of a psychosis rather than a spiritual condition? Is it possible to distinguish between a true Messiah and a false one? Why do humans surrender their freedom to charismatic personalities and ideological straitjackets? If the goal of religious therapy is to restore the sick soul to health, why do some religious situations seem more harmful than curative?

Critics have pointed out the similarities between conversion experiences and brainwashing. For example, both involve a reversal, the death of the corrupted, inauthentic self and the birth of a new being. Brainwashing aims at a reversal of belief. The first step is to intimidate and humiliate the subject to a point of physical and mental exhaustion, a mortification of the entire being. When the spirit is broken, the subject becomes vulnerable to a substitution of an alien world view. At this point a sympathetic and friendly interrogator takes over and offers escape or liberation through the adoption of another way of seeing the world.

The similarities between brainwashing and conversions to the sacred are sometimes striking. Revival meetings have customarily employed deeply moving gospel singing, vivid sermons, testimonies, and invitations to be set free or born again to bring a distressed soul to a point of collapse and vulnerability. Separation and isolation are also techniques of those groups that offer liberating experiences and those that specialize in mind control. Modern psychotherapies sometimes employ intensive training periods, encounter marathons, in which the participants are voluntarily separated from their ordinary routines in order to break the unsuccessful structures of their lives. Although there are serious differences between prisoners held captive and subjected to brainwashing and people who voluntarily join a religious group, in some situations the techniques, pressures, and perspectives of religious groups can be coercive. Certainly the Peoples Temple is a dramatic case in which the physical and psychic isolation of the group fed its sense of separateness from the main thrust of life in the United States until it fostered a paranoia that culminated in the mass suicide of its members in Guyana.

Religious systems of significance, whatever their truth-claims, do meet human needs, including a need to belong to a supportive community and a need to discover and serve a self-transcending purpose. Nowhere is this self-transcending function more obvious than in those transformational experiences that fill with meaning a life that might otherwise be relatively empty. Ecstatic religious experiences are not less real if they are prompted by some psychological mechanism rather than by a God who is encountered.

Although religious history records many eruptions of the demonic and destructive, the dominant motif of the religious life is curative and soteriological. Religion, like modern psychotherapies, aims to set the captives free. Dying to the old and being spiritually born anew is a highly valued experience; we would all be like Zorba, seeing "everything every day as if for the first time."[74]

Humans need to dance, to be set free, to be filled with the sacred; but wild excitements and passionate outbursts, whether in revival meetings or group encounters, can turn out to be only a temporary, if intoxicating, excitement. When the high flyer comes down, he or she must attend to the day-by-day process of spiritual growth if he or she is to remain transformed. Ecstatic experiences need to be tempered by something akin to the spirit reflected in one of Sam Keen's poetic meditations:

> Surrender is a risk no sane man may take.
> Sanity never surrendered is a burden no man may carry.
>
> God, give me madness
> That does not destroy
> wisdom,
> responsibility,
> love.[75]

Notes

1. W.B. Yeats, "Sailing to Byzantium," in A.J.M. Smith, ed., *Seven Centuries of Verse, English and American,* 3rd ed. (New York: Scribner's, 1967), p. 571.

2. Simone Weil, *Waiting for God,* trans. by Emma Craufurd (New York: Harper & Row, 1973), p. 120. First published by G.P. Putnam's Sons in 1951.

3. W. von Goethe, *Faust,* trans. by Bayard Taylor (New York: Modern Library, 1950), p. 39.

4. See William James, *Varieties of Religious Experience* (New York: Mentor Books, 1958); Donald and Walter Capps, *The Religious Personality* (Belmont, Calif.:

Wadsworth, 1970); and J.B. Pratt, *The Religious Consciousness* (New York: Macmillan, 1943) for typologies of religious personality.

5. In John S. Dunne, *Time and Myth* (Garden City, N.Y.: Doubleday, 1973), p. 77.

6. Robert Bretall, ed., *A Kierkegaard Anthology* (Princeton, N.J.: Princeton University Press, 1946), p. 271.

7. Romans 7:19 (KJV).

8. *Complete Poems of Robert Frost* (New York: Holt, Rinehart and Winston, 1964), p. 52.

9. Weil, *Waiting for God,* p. 123.

10. Ibid., pp. 120–21.

11. In Ted Hulbert, "The Con in Expanded Consciousness," *UCLA Monthly* 6, no. 6 (July-August 1976): p. 1.

12. Louis Dupré, "The Wounded Self: The Religious Meaning of Mental Suffering," in *The Christian Century* (April 7, 1976), p. 329.

13. Sigmund Freud, *The Future of an Illusion* (Garden City, N.Y.: Doubleday, Anchor Books, 1964), p. 2.

14. *Hamlet,* act II, scene 2, line 396.

15. See Stuart Schram, ed., *Chairman Mao Talks to His People* (New York: Pantheon, 1974), pp. 82–83.

16. Dante Alighieri, *The Inferno,* trans. by John Ciardi (New Brunswick, N.J.: Rutgers University Press, 1954), 1:1–2, p. 28.

17. Carl Jung, *Modern Man in Search of a Soul* (New York: Harcourt, Brace & World, 1933), p. 229.

18. 2 Corinthians 5:17.

19. Hermann Hesse, *Siddhartha* (New York: New Directions, 1957), p. 92.

20. John 11:25.

21. Gustavo Gutierrez, *A Theology of Liberation,* trans. by Sister Caridad Inda and John Eagleson (New York: Orbis Books, 1973), p. 198.

22. Amos 5:6.

23. Deuteronomy 30:19.

24. Matthew 5:16.

25. Hesse, *Siddhartha,* p. 96.

26. Mircea Eliade, *Shamanism: Archaic Techniques of Ecstasy* (New York: Pantheon Books, 1964), pp. 33–34.

27. Sam Keen, *To a Dancing God* (New York: Harper & Row, 1970), p. 22.

28. Dag Hammarskjöld, *Markings* (New York: Knopf, 1964), p. 205.

29. St. Augustine, *The Confessions,* trans. by Marcus Dods (London: William Benton, 1952), Book VIII, p. 56.

30. Ibid., Book VIII, p. 61.

31. In "Decisions for Christ," *Newsweek* (October 25, 1976), p. 75. For a slightly different account, see Eldridge Cleaver's *Soul on Fire.*

32. Acts 9:5.

33. W. Montgomery Watt, *The Faith and Practice of al-Ghazali* (London: Allen and Unwin, 1970), p. 25.

34. Ibid., p. 57.

35. Ibid., pp. 57–58.

36. Weil, *Waiting for God,* p. 69.

37. Ibid.

38. Ibid., p. 72.

39. In *Sing and Pray and Shout Hurray!* compiled by Roger Ortmayer (New York: Friendship Press, 1974), p. 11.

40. In James, *Varieties of Religious Experience,* p. 79.

41. Ibid., pp. 76–111.

42. Horace Bushnell, *Christian Nurture* (New Haven, Conn.: Yale University Press, 1967), p. 4.

43. Bishop Fulton J. Sheen, *Peace of Soul* (New York: Whittlesey House, 1949), p. 262.

44. In James, *Varieties of Religious Experience,* pp. 77–78.

45. Walt Whitman, *Leaves of Grass and Selected Prose,* intro. by Sculley Bradley (New York: Rinehart, 1955), p. 51.

46. C.S. Lewis, *Mere Christianity* (New York: Macmillan, 1952), p. 167.

47. Hammarskjöld, *Markings,* p. 5.

48. John S. Dunne, *Time and Myth* (Garden City, N.Y.: Doubleday, 1973), pp. 38–39.

49. *The Republic of Plato,* trans. by F.M. Cornford (New York: Oxford University Press, 1953), pp. 227–35.

50. *Complete Poems of Robert Frost,* p. 153.

51. Michael Novak, *Ascent of the Mountain, Flight of the Dove* (New York: Harper & Row, 1971), p. 53.

52. Carlos Castaneda, *The Teachings of Don Juan* (Berkeley: University of California Press, 1968), p. 158.

53. George Williams, *The Quest for Meaning of Swami Vivekananda* (Chico, Calif.: New Horizons Press, 1974), p. 96.

54. Paul Reps, *Zen Flesh, Zen Bones* (Garden City, N.Y.: Doubleday), p. 88.

55. Martin Buber, *The Way of Man* (New York: Citadel Press, 1970), p. 15.

56. Castaneda, *Don Juan,* pp. 105–06.

57. Ibid., p. 105.

58. Weil, *Waiting for God,* p. 99.

59. Matthew 7:14.

60. *Bhagavad Gita,* trans. by Franklin Edgerton (New York: Harper Torchbooks, 1964), p. 27.

61. Mohandas K. Gandhi, *An Autobiography: The Story of My Experiments with Truth* (Boston: Beacon Press, 1957), p. 503.

62. See John 8:32, 14:6, 16:13.

63. *The Dhammapada,* in *The Sacred Books of the East,* ed. and trans. by Max Muller (Delhi: Motilal Banarsi Dass, 1968), vol. X, p. 50.

64. *The Sayings of Confucius,* trans. by James R. Ware (New York: Mentor Books, 1955), 12:2, p. 76.

65. Jacques Maritain, *Approaches to God* (New York: Macmillan, 1965), pp. 84–87.

66. In G. Morris Carstairs, *The Twice Born* (Bloomington: Indiana University Press), p. 89.

67. *Bhagavad Gita* (Edgerton), p. 14.

68. *How to Know God: The Yoga Aphorisms of Patanjali,* trans. by Swami Prabhavananda and Christopher Isherwood (New York: Mentor Books, 1969), p. 107.

69. *Bhagavad Gita,* trans. by Swami Prabhavananda and Christopher Isherwood (New York: Mentor Books, 1964), p. 129.

70. Martin Buber, *Two Types of Faith* (New York: Harper Torchbooks, 1961), p. 8.

71. 2 Samuel 22:2-3.

72. Maritain, *Approaches to God,* p. 79.

73. Nikos Kazantzakis, *Zorba the Greek* (New York: Simon and Schuster, 1966), p. 205.

74. Ibid., p. 51.

75. Keen, *To a Dancing God,* p. 119.

Chapter Twelve
Holy Communities

No man is an Iland, *intire of it selfe; every man is*
a peece of the Continent, *a part of the* maine.
John Donne
Devotion XVII[1]

We cannot be religious or even human in isolation. Our understanding of
what is involved in being human may be deepened and nourished in solitude,
perhaps even in hermitic existence, but it must begin in relationship to others
like ourselves. We are gregarious animals for whom answers to such
seemingly personal questions as Who am I? are worked out in relationship to
others. Although we sometimes like to picture ourselves as self-sufficient
and autonomous, almost every aspect of our existence is shaped by the
societal context in which we live. Language, for example, is a social
phenomenon without which we would be unable to develop our conceptual
powers, since our reasoning process depends on symbols. When children are
reared without human models to imitate (as in the few known cases of
children reared by animals) and are subsequently displaced from an animal to
a human context, they find the symbol systems and social relationships of

humans bewildering and alien. Other selves are the mirrors through which each of us is afforded a glimpse of our humanity. Even those who choose a hermitic existence are first reared in particular societies, with patterns for associating with others (family, school, role, function), and in cultures with symbol systems (language, art, music, ceremonies) that provide shared norms through which the hermit is shaped in the form of a human.

The social character of human existence has profound implications for the study of religion. A religious community is a social system and a corporate elaboration of a shared life drawn together by common symbols and concerns. The social dimension of religion is the subject of this chapter. The social aspect has already been addressed in other contexts. In chapter three, for example, the discussion of the local, national, and universal typology for classifying religion illustrated some of the ways in which social systems affect religious expression. In part II, attention was given to the social nature of sacred words and rites and the capacity of sacred rites to facilitate an experience of communitas. The social dimension of religion is explored in this chapter through a consideration of the relationship of religion and society—that is, the ways in which religion influences and is influenced by its social context—and by an examination of different types of holy communities.

Seen culturally, religion is part of the complex of prescriptions and proscriptions that guide the interaction of men in all societies.

J. Milton Yinger
The Scientific Study of Religion[2]

Religion and Society ✓

Modern scholars agree that societal values and patterns of social intercourse profoundly influence religious symbol systems—that social systems influence religion. They disagree on the extent of that influence. On one side are those who concur with sociologist Emile Durkheim and psychologist Sigmund Freud that religious symbols are projections of human associations. According to anthropologist Meyer Fortes, "Ever since Freud's bold speculations in *Totem and Taboo* and Durkheim's great work on *The Elementary Forms of the Religious Life,* anthropologists have known that the springs of religion and ritual lie in kinship and social organization."[3] Other scholars concur with anthropologist E.E. Evans-Pritchard's contention that evidence for the assertion that religious conceptions "are nothing more than a symbolic representation of the social order. . . . is totally lacking."[4] Since these interpretations have important implications for the study of religion, a good place to begin a study of the interaction of religion and society is with Durkheim's and Freud's arguments that religion is a projection of social relationships.

Haida Totem Poles in Alert Bay, British Columbia, Canada. Totems are an important feature of the religious and social life of northwest coastal Indians, such as the Haida tribe. Totems reflect the division of tribal life into clans. Each clan is associated with a particular spirit, which is at once a manifestation of the spirit world and an indication of the special relationship of such spirits to the ancestors of the clan.

Photo: The Bettman Archive, Inc.

Religion as a Projection of Societal Structures and Values

Durkheim contended that the ultimate existence to which religious expression points is not a transcendent deity, as prophetic religions claim, but the power of society itself. He believed that a concrete reality lay behind the figures of deities and the metaphors of sacred stories and dramas and that this reality was society. His conviction that deity and society are one was derived from a study of the totems of central Australian tribes like the Arunta. In Durkheim's analysis the totem, an object bearing a clan's name and an envisagement of its revered animal or plant, was a material symbol for the immaterial. It stood for the real power of the clan, a power on which each tribesman depended. As a material embodiment of the power of the clan, the totem pointed to "something greater than us, with which we enter into communion."[5] Durkheim understood this to be the shared life of a group or society.

Although Durkheim believed that religious symbols disguise the worship of human beings and society, he argued that humans are not mistaken in insisting on the importance of such symbols. Religious beliefs and practices reinforce and consecrate those things that sustain communal life and expel or purify those things that endanger group life. What people value, they preserve and reinforce; thus religion is a form of social control that validates group-enhancing patterns of behavior. Behind religious metaphors are group values and conventions that provide indispensable norms of conduct. The human mistake is one of literalism—that is, of confusing the ultimate values of a holy community with a divine plant, animal, or person.[6]

Durkheim's argument that the cosmic order is a projection of the social order is supplemented and reinforced by the work of Sigmund Freud. As was noted in chapter three, Freud believed that religion and morality have their origin in human helplessness—that is, in the precariousness and fragility of human life. For Freud, human helplessness was illustrated by the ✓ relationship of parent and child. Children, particularly infants, are radically dependent on adult care. Their helplessness is mediated, but never completely resolved, by the care and protection they receive. While parents or other adults ameliorate the helplessness of children, who or what consoles humankind? The answer to this question, Freud suggested, is that humans have mediated their helplessness, their creature-feeling, by humanizing and deifying the power of nature. Seen in this light, humans are consoled by the gods, who, in turn, are human projections rather than independent or self-existent beings. The human longing for acceptance by a heavenly Father has its prototype in the longing for an earthly father:

> When the growing individual finds that he is destined to remain a child forever, that he can never do without protection against strange superior powers, he lends those powers the features belonging to the figure of his father; he creates for himself the gods. . . . Thus his longing for a father is a motive identical with his need for protection against the consequences of his human weakness.[7]

Whatever the merit of Durkheim's and Freud's perspective, imagery drawn from social relationships, including filial ones, clearly commands a prominent place in religious expression. In primitive societies, where kinship is the primary determinant of social relationships, the holy is typically spoken of as a relative. In Black Elk Speaks, for example, the Great Spirit is personalized as the father and mother of us all, and the six directions (east, west, south, north, sky, earth) are called grandfathers. The overlapping of filial systems and religious symbols is also evident in ancestral devotion, where the honor and obedience owed to one's parents is extended from this life to the next.

Filial relationships have served as important theological metaphors in the Christian tradition. Christians, for example, understand the relationship of God to Christ as that of father and son. The filial character of Christian symbolism is also evident in Jesus' use of *father* as a metaphor for speaking about God in the parable of the prodigal son and as a mode of address in the prayer that he taught his disciples to pray ("Our Father . . ."). Just as the biblical tradition commands children to honor and obey their father and mother, it also enjoins people to love, honor, and serve their heavenly father. The conception of God as father has been a normative mode for addressing God that has only recently been seriously challenged by Christians who are critical of the distortions that result from an emphasis on the masculinity of God. They insist that the femininity of God is implicit in the doctrine that women, like men, are created in the image of God.

Filial associations are only one example of the projection of social relationships into the sphere of the sacred. Political structures influence religious expression, including conceptions of the holy. Monotheism, the belief that there is only one God, is usually paralleled in the social sphere by a strong political authority and a multileveled social system.[8] In monarchical societies God is usually thought of as an all-seeing, all-powerful monarch. For instance, in Jewish prayers God is sometimes referred to as King of the Universe, and in Christianity, Christ is the Messiah—that is, Christ the King. As noted earlier, the god-king is a frequent motif in national religions. Until the events of World War II made such a conviction almost impossible to sustain, the mikado was believed, in the religious system of Shinto, to be a god-king, a sacred presence, just as the Inca and the pharaoh were embodiments of the sacred in their respective cultures.

Rather than concur with Freud and Durkheim that religion is merely a symbolic projection of the social order, let us grant the more modest proposition that religious symbols reflect the influence of social structures, including primary structures like the family with its filial tensions. Certainly it is not surprising that family cults and ancestral reverence are most evident in those social systems where the child-parent relationship is primary. Where the social organization is based on kinship and descent, religious associations and belief systems are primarily structured and understood in terms of biological relationships. In contrast, where the organization of society is more political than biological, religious communities are more likely to be united by common ideological or spiritual concerns and commitments than on the basis of kinship.

Variations in Society and Variations in Religion

The discussion of the views of Durkheim and Freud has made clear that religion is profoundly influenced by social systems and cultural values. Because the discussion focused on the projective nature of this influence, it obscured the point that religious symbol systems, including personal experiences of ultimacy, can affect societal values and structures. For instance, the leadership and conceptions of ultimacy of such personalities as the Buddha, Jesus, and Muhammad were catalysts for change in their respective milieus and, as exemplary predecessors for the three numerically largest contemporary religious communities, their stories continue to affect human existence. Thus differences in religious symbol systems are not only reflections of variations in society; they are also indicative of variations in individuals and perhaps, as religionists insist, of variations in the ways in which the holy is manifested or revealed.

The relationship between religion and society is a complex one. The spire of a Gothic cathedral may signify the soul's longing for God, but it is also a monument to civic pride. Similarly, a Buddhist monastery is a religious center for monks who are seeking Enlightenment, but it may also double as a community school and cultural center. An analysis of the interaction of religion and society must, as J. Milton Yinger points out in *The Scientific Study of Religion,* begin with the question, What kind of a society?[9] Whether a society is small and homogeneous or large and diverse affects religion. Because some of the ways socioeconomic patterns influence religious expression have already been pointed out in the discussion of local, national, and universal religions (chapter three), only a few more examples of the interdependence of religion and society are given here.

Often the way in which a society is structured is reflected in similar patterns of religious organization. Christian traditions with an episcopal form of governance, like that of the Roman Catholic Church, reflect the organization of the Roman Empire, with its division of people and land into units of descending power and influence. Following the Roman example, Christians after the reign of Constantine (A.D. 272—337) divided the land into administrative and shepherding units from the smallest, the parish, to a collection of parishes, which constituted a diocese directed by a bishop, to an association of dioceses called a province, under the leadership of a metropolitan bishop. Gradually, and not without protest, the metropolitan bishops of Western Christendom deferred to the spiritual authority of the bishop in Rome. Like the land, people were organized, by both church and state, in a hierarchy of privilege and influence. At the pinnacle of power were king and pope, whose respective authority was, in principle, derived from God.

Sex is an important social component affecting religious practice. In patriarchal societies, for example, women generally occupy positions of inferior status and power. They usually lack educational opportunities, their roles are restricted, and their legal rights are limited. Religion in patriarchal societies reflects and reinforces the same discriminatory pattern. Women are usually precluded from performing sacred rites and denied leadership positions. In one of India's religious traditions, only a son may perform death rites for his parents; thus to die without a son is to set one's spirit dangerously adrift. On occasion, males have been given an economic value relative to females. In the Bible, for instance, the monetary value of an adult male was set at fifty shekels while that of an adult female was but thirty.[10]

Even the most personal and individual aspects of religious experience are affected by social factors. For example, Max Weber argued that socially and economically privileged classes will generally avoid the loss of self-control characteristic of effervescent religious experiences and instead will "assign to religion the primary function of legitimizing their own life pattern and situation in the world."[11] Although socioeconomic variables are important, holy communities are the primary social organizations affecting religious experience. Those who actively seek the sacred within a particular religious tradition are most likely to report experiences consistent with and intelligible within those traditions. Culture, and even contact with a religious community, do not of themselves guarantee that an individual will have an experience of the holy, but they do provide a way of legitimizing and interpreting such experiences. The ultimate experience in Zen Buddhism is known as *satori*. It is said to be a spontaneous, sudden, and momentary experience, yet it does not happen to those who have not rigorously disciplined themselves through Zen training. The experience of ultimacy in a Buddhist monastic community will assume a different pattern and receive a different interpretation than will the God the faithful Muslim obeys in making his pilgrimage to Mecca. Speaking in tongues and baptism by the Holy Spirit, both of which are numinous experiences, are much more likely to occur in pentecostal and charismatic Christian groups than in more affectively constrained Christian congregations. Dramatic adult conversion experiences are more often reported among those evangelical Christian churches that stress or require them than in Catholicism, where the emphasis is on God's grace as mediated through the sacraments.

Although the previous examples stress the influence of society on religion, we need to reiterate that religion affects society. For example, in *The Protestant Ethic and the Spirit of Capitalism,* Max Weber argued that Protestantism was one of the factors contributing to the rise of capitalism. Since the material conditions of medieval Europe and Asia were roughly comparable, Weber was puzzled why capitalism emerged first in Europe. His research led him to the conclusion that a significant variable in the rise of capitalism could be traced to differences in the religious orientations of East and West. The Judeo-Christian tradition, with its faith in a God who acts in history, produced a religious orientation, particularly in Protestantism, which Weber labeled inner-worldly asceticism. The inner-worldly ascetic seeks mastery not only over self but over all aspects of the human condition. From the Protestant perspective, this world was intended to become the Kingdom of God on earth; thus secular vocations were legitimized and Christianized, and the monastic life, with its withdrawal from the world, was devalued. For Weber the Protestant ethic called for a rational mastery over the world; whereas in Asia Buddhism had as its ideal self-mastery accompanied by worldly indifference; and Confucianism promoted a rational adaptation to, rather than transformation of, the world. The Protestant emphasis on mastery of the world was, in Weber's view, translated into the aggressive character of capitalism.[12]

Societal Values and Relationships and Ultimate Values and Relationships ✓

The point has been made that the forms religion and religious experience take are affected by their context. Differences in belief systems, ritual practices, and personal experiences of the sacred are influenced by social factors and by individual variations in temperament, talent, and openness to the nonordinary. From a religious perspective, religion is also a reaction to sacred disclosures or hierophanies; thus variations in religious expression can be explained not only by the character of human existence but by differences in the way the holy is manifested or revealed.

Seen from a religious perspective, the social nature of human existence is a twofold relationship. Just as religious expression is double-intentional in that words and gestures are employed to point beyond the ordinary to the ultimate, the religious life is double-relational. In one mode of consciousness, the individual seeks communion with the holy and in another direction seeks fellowship in a supportive community. Even the etymology of the term *religion* suggests something of its double-relational character. One of its roots, *religare,* means "to bind" in the sense of being bound to what is worshiped. A second root, *relegere,* means "to gather" in the sense of a community of faith coming together to perform its sacred rites.[13] Religion is thus a double-relational bond that binds people to what concerns them ultimately and to a community of faith.

Although holy communities are always meeting places of individuals in all the manifold relationships that such meetings imply, religionists insist that the primary relationship of individual and group life is to the ultimate. All religious experience is communal when it is a meeting place of individual and group living with the sacred. Holy communities are drawn together by a shared sense of the holy, whether it be a common seeking of a transcendent experience (nirvana) or a transcendent being (God). The Christian Church, the Muslim Ummah, the Buddhist Sangha, and the Chinese family are communities whose shared rites and symbols not only serve to foster a common life but also point beyond themselves to the ultimate and nonordinary. While an experience of holiness can take place independent of a believing community, the holy community has been, metaphorically speaking, the delivery room in which transcendent religious experiences occur, their genuineness is corroborated, their implications for living are put into practice, and their possibilities for growth are nurtured.

There is no religion which has not evoked a type of religious fellowship.

Types of Religious Groups

Joachim Wach
The Comparative Study of Religion[14]

Although the interaction of religion and society is a theme that runs throughout this chapter, the primary focus in the remaining sections is on the description and analysis of different types of religious groups. Group life is organized in some way. Every social system, including holy communities, develops structures and processes through which decisions are made, authority is acknowledged, discipline is maintained, and roles and function are differentiated. There are different types of societies (primitive, agricultural, industrial), each with different patterns for relating to others and different kinds of groups, including associations that are biological (family, clan, tribe), geographical and political (village and nation), and voluntary (clubs, fraternities, sororities, political parties).

Just as there are different types of societies, there are different types of religious groups. One method of classifying religious groups is based on whether membership is natural or voluntary. Participation and inclusion in natural religious groups is a matter of birth, lineage, or birthplace rather than personal preference or special qualifications, while membership in voluntary religious groups revolves around the priority of a transcendent religious experience and is therefore more of an ideological or spiritual association. Each type varies considerably. In the natural religious group category, Joachim Wach included all those associations whose personal and collective experience of the holy is primarily biological (family, clan, tribe), geographical (village), or national (common nationality and culture). In addition, Wach identified several types of voluntary religious groups, such as secret societies, mystery religions, and founded religions, including those groups to which the terms **church, demonination,** and **sect** apply.[15] In the following pages, attention is given to family, clan, tribe, and ancestors as examples of natural religious groups and to some of the different patterns of association operative in voluntary religious groups.

Before turning to a discussion of religious groups, we need to say something about the relationship of natural and voluntary religious groups to the local, national, and universal typology discussed in chapter three. Since the basis for classifying a religion as local, national, or universal and a group as natural or voluntary is related to whether the principle of inclusion is primarily biological, cultural, or ideological, the two typologies have much in common. Because membership in local and national religions is based on kinship and ethnic-national considerations, local and national religions are primarily natural religious groups. In contrast, since membership in universal religions is more confessional or ideological than natural, universal religions are primarily voluntary religious groups.

In spite of the similarity of the two typologies, equating them would be a mistake. Each religion, whether tribal, national, or universal, is a holy community whose primary symbols may bind together several subgroups within the larger community of faith. In this conceptualization, each religion is a group with a primary mode of inclusion, whether natural or voluntary; at the same time, each may include several subgroups, holy communities within a holy community, which operate on an opposite principle of inclusion. For example, since kinship is the major factor governing social relationships in primitive societies, a local or tribal religion can be regarded as constituting a natural religious group. However, local religions may also include voluntary associations within the tribal circle. For instance, the Zuni of New Mexico have six nonhereditary religious groups. Membership in the associations is open to those who have special spiritual blessings and powers.

The presence of holy communities within a holy community is even more characteristic of universal religions. The Christian church, for example, is a holy assembly united by faith in Christ, but it includes an almost bewildering number of distinctive churches or assemblies. Like most universal religions the church is a voluntary association, founded by a decisive personality, in which spiritual rather than natural considerations are primary. In addition, the founding of many of the churches within the church are associated with a decisive personality. Roman Catholic orders are associated with the genius of saints like Dominic, Francis, and Loyola, just as the beginnings of several different Protestant bodies are associated with reformers and prophets like Jacob Amman, John Calvin, Alexander Campbell, Jacob Hutter, Martin Luther, Menno Simons, John Wesley, and Ellen White.

Although Christian discipleship is primarily intentional and confessional rather than natural, in subgroups within the Christian tradition membership follows almost exclusively from being born and raised in a particular community. For instance, the Hutterite Brethren are a community so set apart from other Christian denominations and the secular culture that surrounds it that, while they may require a confession of faith, their primary mode of inclusion and survival of the group is birth and nurture in a Hutterite community. The Hutterites have ceased the evangelistic efforts that marked their beginnings in the sixteenth century. As a holy community they survive and even increase their number by a low rate of defection and a relatively high birthrate. Like Christianity, Buddhism is also a universal religion and intentional community; nevertheless, Buddhism is not without subgroups in which natural considerations may take precedence over spiritual ones. In Japan, for example, Shin Buddhist priests marry, and their priesthood is hereditary.

Natural Religious Groups

The distinguishing feature of natural religious groups is that their membership is natural rather than voluntary—a function of such factors as birth, marriage, birthplace, or nationality. Thus the capacity or interest of natural groups for extending their number is limited by the restrictive character of kinship as a condition of incorporation. Natural groups, therefore, are not missionary minded. In this respect they are different from voluntary religious associations, which, if they are expansive and conversionist in temper, have the potential for developing group solidarity around ideological commitments and charismatic personalities on a scale that natural affinities will not permit. Since biological regeneration is the primary way in which natural religious groups sustain themselves, such groups not surprisingly find the unmarried state objectionable and the failure to have children calamitous.

Tribal Societies as Natural Religious Groups

Although, as noted previously, there are voluntary religious associations in tribal societies, such societies can be appropriately regarded as natural religious groups. Politics, work, medicine, play, and religion are not sharply separated in tribal life. The religious dimension is part of every aspect of existence; thus it is impossible to be born and reared in a tribal community without being immersed in its religious life. Of course, not all primitives are deeply religious or never skeptical about the efficacy of their ritual ways. However, their forms of religious expression do cut across all aspects of existence and make isolation from them impossible.

Since family, clan, tribe, and ancestral lineage are the basic natural relationships operative in primitive societies, the intent here is to look at some contexts in which such relationships serve as a point of contact with the holy. Usually the religious and social life of tribal peoples takes place within a series of overlapping circles that range from the smallest family unit to the most inclusive—the tribal circle. Each extended family (father, mother, married sons, and their wives and children) may have their own totemic emblems, ancestral obligations, domestic rites, and shrines. In family worship, filial hierarchies are observed; in patrilineal descent groups, the father may function as the family priest and perform the rituals that serve as a point of contact between themselves and the sacred. In matrilineal groups, the mother and her lineage are usually more decisive in religious matters. The clan is a larger circle that unites several families in a common lineage; its religious focus is on those ancient ones or sacred beings from whom the clan is derived.

While the family is the basic unit of tribal existence, families are usually allied to other families in lineal descent groups or clans. Clan membership is based on a real or assumed kinship, which unites its members even though they may not share a common residence. The solidarity of the clan is manifested in a common name shared by all of its members and often by a common totem. Whether they are the flat wooden or stone emblems of the Arunta of Australia or the more familiar carved poles of the northwest coastal Indians of America, totems signify membership in a particular clan. The totemic design helps the clan remember its ancestors. Each clan is an extended family that recognizes kindred duties like those of cooperation, mutual aid, mourning, vengeance, and the obligation to marry outside of the clan. Where clans are operative, each one has a distinctive ritual way, including ceremonies, myths, symbols, and magical practices that belong only to them and that are taboo to other clans within the same tribal society.

Not infrequently a set of religious symbols appropriate to each of the three overlapping circles (family, clan, tribe) serves to locate the individual within each circle socially and sacrally. For example, E.E. Evans-Pritchard pointed out that among the Nuer of East Africa a close relationship exists between the order and structure of their spirit world and of their social system. The supreme spirit (Kwoth) is the most inclusive circle. He is everywhere and he is one, but Kwoth is also manifested in the particular spirits associated with specific clans, animals, totems, and fetishes. As the father of all, Kwoth is directly available to every Nuer regardless of family or clan, but, regarded as a particular spirit, he is associated exclusively with a specific lineage, family, or individual. Usually those things that affect the entire tribe are associated with Kwoth as the supreme spirit, and those things that are primarily the concern of individuals, families, or clans are associated with what Evans-Pritchard speaks of as refractions of the supreme spirit.[16]

Ancestral Spirits and Filial Piety in Natural Religious Groups

When religious symbols are grounded in natural associations, respect for and devotion to one's ancestors is likely to be a primary value, even though in only a few communities do the power and significance of ancestral spirits overshadow that of other spirits or gods. In ancestor worship the deceased are believed to continue as active members of their families, and very important people remain active, even after death, in the life of their clans and tribes. In fact, the immaterial nature of what John Mbiti, in an effort to emphasize the vital character of ancestral existence, speaks of as the living-dead,[17] makes them more powerful, more to be feared and therefore more commanding of devotion than surviving kin and more distant non-ancestral spirits. While the belief that personal existence survives death can be comforting, it can also be disconcerting. Ancestral spirits are usually benign, but sometimes the deceased are believed to undergo personality changes in which they become malevolent spirits or ghosts.

The religious life of the Tallensi of West Africa offers a good example of ancestor worship and a reminder of Freud's insistence that religious imagery is primarily a projection of filial relationships. The primary social unit of the Tallensi is the extended family composed of a father and mother, their married sons, their wives and children, and unmarried daughters. Each family is a branch of a larger unit with a common patrilineal line of descent. Each family has ancestors peculiar to it and those whom it shares in common with clan and tribe. Filial relationship and lines of descent define a person's rights and duties. The most important relationship is that of father and son. Authority is vested in the father. Only the father can perform the rituals and prayers that facilitate contact with the ancestral spirits. Married sons with children of their own have no independent religious authority until their father dies. The primary filial value is that children, regardless of age, honor and obey their parents and put their parents' wishes above their own. Naturally such an arrangement contributes to the tensions that exist between fathers and sons, in particular the eldest son, who symbolically represents all his brothers. Hostility between the generations is minimized by observing such ritual avoidances as prohibiting the eldest son from eating with his father, wearing his father's clothes, or using his bow.[18]

The importance of the father-son relationship as a primary relationship in the social system is reflected in Tallensi religious life, where obligation to one's ancestors, particularly one's father, is perpetuated on a cosmic plane. The most important filial duty that the eldest son performs is that of transforming his parents into ancestral spirits through a funeral rite. With the death of the father, the eldest surviving son may ritually approach the ancestral spirits, but his approach is through the spirit of his father.

Because the ancestral spirits have much to do with the well-being of their descendants, proper respect and devotion to them is essential. For example, each Tallensi is believed to have an ancestral guardian spirit. Early in each Tallensi's childhood, a diviner is consulted to determine the identity of the child's spirit guardian. The task of the ancestral guardian is to protect and preserve, but they can be dangerous and harmful if they are neglected. Given the importance of the ancestors, Tallensi homes, not surprisingly, include ancestral shrines that serve as places of contact between them and their descendants.

While ancestors play an important role in all tribal societies, ancestor worship and tribal religion cannot be equated. Each tribal religion is different; and generalizations are difficult. Ancestral and filial relationships are also central to the orientation of a nontribal tradition like Confucianism. Ancestral reverence and filial piety are such persistent and pervasive themes in China that they have been called China's real religion.

Before the time of Confucius, ancient China's primal religions abounded in spirits; some were associated with the sky and all its parts, and some were associated with the earth and its parts. There were good spirits and evil spirits and a high and comprehensive sky deity referred to as T'ien. But none of the spirits were more important to the conduct of life than the ancestral spirits. In ancient times, clans, composed of from 5,000 to 7,000 families bound by a common name and reverence to a common set of ancestral heroes, were more important than single families. Clan ancestors were deified spirits who were supplicated and placated in a ceremonial blend of word and gesture performed on special occasions in ancestral halls or in more modest shrines in individual homes.

The devotion to ancestors, central to China's primal religion, was incorporated into Confucianism as a natural extension of its emphasis on filial piety. As Robert Bellah points out, the family is the primary religious context in Confucianism, and its ultimate value is respect for one's parents.[19] The family is an indispensable part of a chain of being in which the order and harmony in the social and natural spheres are inseparable from the order and harmony of the family. The family is so important to the general welfare that rulers who desire order in their states must begin with the family. A Confucianist text proclaims, "When the family is regulated, the state will be in order, and when the state is in order, there will be peace throughout the world."[20]

The ordering of the Chinese family as a natural religious group and center of value is based on a system of reciprocal obligations. The primary obligations are those between father and son, husband and wife, elder brother and younger brother. The principles guiding each relationship are those of obedience and honor owed to father, husband, and elder brother and firm but benevolent guidance owed to son, wife, and younger brother. No relationship is more important than that of father and son. The obedience and respect that a son owes his father serves as a model for the obligation of subjects to their sovereign. Father and emperor rule by a Mandate of Heaven and, in a sense, the authority of the father within the family is even more absolute than that of the sovereign in the state.

The logical extension of filial piety is devotion to one's ancestors. According to the *Classic of Filial Piety,* "serving parents when alive with love and affection and when dead with grief and sorrow—this completely exhausts the basic duties of living men.''[21] Thus for Chinese who continue to adhere to what was the popular religious life of most of pre-Maoist China, devotion to parents does not cease when the parents die. The relationship is a complex ongoing process that binds the living to the dead. The process begins with elaborate burial and mourning rites designed to provide peace for the spiritual body of the deceased. Burial plans may include a study of the *I Ching* for astrological calculations of a propitious time and day for the burial. Sacrificial gifts, such as the burning of paper money and effigies, are typically part of the funeral. Cremation of the offerings is believed to transpose the offerings from the visible to the invisible. Confucianists prescribed three years of mourning for departed parents and an annual gathering of the family for sacrifices to commemorate the deceased.

Where filial and ancestral piety is a primary value, no duty is more fundamental than reproduction. Celibacy deprives ancestors of future acts of devotion; thus Confucianists have usually found the unmarried state abhorrent. Marriage is an obligation and, because the primary relationship in the Chinese family is that of father and son, the duty of a wife is to have sons. According to Mencius, one of the most influential Confucianist philosophers, ''the worst form of filial impiety is not to have sons.''[22]

Voluntary Religious Groups

Spiritual or ideological unity is the basis of fellowship in voluntary religious groups. Where the shift from natural to voluntary religious groups is most complete, natural ties, such as filial and ancestral piety, are of less value than membership in a distinctively spiritual association. The Christian church, for example, is a spiritual rather than biological family united by an experience of God through Christ. The nonbiological basis of Christian discipleship is quite evident in the New Testament. The Gospel of Mark reports one occasion in which Jesus' family, including his mother Mary, believed that Jesus was beside himself and sought to protect him from possible harm by taking him away. When Jesus was told that his mother and family were waiting for him, he turned to his disciples and said, ''Whosoever does the will of God is my brother, and sister and mother.''[23] That Jesus conceived of discipleship as a spiritual rather than a filial association is even more starkly explicit in a saying attributed to Jesus in the synoptic Gospels: ''If anyone comes to me and does not hate his own father and mother and wife and children and brothers and sisters, yea, even his own life, he cannot be my disciple.''[24]

Christianity is not alone in the elevation of spiritual ties over natural ties; Muhammad's message cuts across tribal, ethnic, and racial differences. The Ummah, the holy community of Islam, is open to all who believe that there is no God but God and Muhammad is his prophet, who accept the

Franciscan Missionaries of the Divine Motherhood, Ladywell Convent, Surrey, England. Voluntary religious groups may include smaller assemblies, such as the Franciscan Missionaries, within the larger one. The commitment of the Franciscan sisters to equality within their community is evident in the uniformity of their dress.

Photo by Eve Arnold, Magnum Photos

authority of the Koran, and who walk a common path. The Buddhist Sangha is also primarily a voluntary association. As a monastic community the Sangha is clearly a specifically religious group, since those who are accepted in it must leave behind all natural ties. A Buddhist text notes that for persons diligently working out their own salvation, "even father and mother are no hindrances."[25]

Nowhere is the breaking of natural ties more explicit than in those traditions in which celibacy (an unmarried state) and chastity (sexual abstinence) are sanctioned. In the Roman Catholic tradition, vows of chastity and celibacy are required of all priests and nuns. The nun's vows appropriate the language of marriage; although the marriage bears spiritual rather than biological fruit, Jesus is the bridegroom, the lover of her soul, to whom she is henceforth indissolubly linked. Just as a change of name occurs in a traditional marriage, the nun or sister assumes a new name that symbolizes her spiritual union.

Although celibacy and chastity are not virtues required of either clergy or laity in most Christian denominations, Roman Catholicism is not alone in sanctifying them. Shakerism, a radical form of Protestantism, demanded that everyone who shared in its common life practice sexual abstinence. The Shakers, known officially as The United Society of Believers in Christ's Second Coming, grew in the eighteenth century out of the visions and trances of Mother Ann Lee Stanley, who was regarded by herself and her followers as Christ's Second Coming. This female Christ was convinced that sexual relationships are the root of sin and insisted that in Shaker communities sexual intercourse be strictly forbidden. In their communitarian society, males and females lived in separate sections of a common dormitory. Because of the Shakers' absolute rejection of sexual reproduction, their survival shifted entirely from natural to spiritual means, including conversions, or by providing nurture for orphans. Although at their zenith the group numbered around 6,000, the Shakers no longer seek converts or raise orphans; their commitment to sexual abstinence means that when, in the near future, the last surviving members die, Shakerism will cease to be a living faith.

Chastity and celibacy are obligatory in traditions other than Christianity. As noted previously, membership in the Buddhist Sangha replaces the obligations owed to family and ancestors with those of a monastic community. Monks and nuns take a vow to abstain from sexual relationships, and those who transgress their vows may be expelled. In the Jaina tradition the highest spiritual strivers must, in addition to their obligations to practice noninjury to all forms of life, renounce sexual pleasure. The devaluation of the natural is so extreme in Jainism that the tradition venerates those whose dedication to liberation and noninjury end in their death through fasting.

Of course, the shift from natural to a specifically spiritual association is mediated by moral and spiritual sanctions that reinforce biological ties. Only relatively rare traditions, like Shakerism, so reject the natural that sexual intercourse is prohibited for priests and laity alike. Buddhist, Jain, and Christian lay persons continue to marry and raise children. In addition, filial respect is incorporated into most traditions.

Voluntary religious groups form around different centers. Some are united by devotion to a transcendent religious experience or are centered in a dedication to those who have special magico-religious powers. Other voluntary associations are open to those who share a distinctive duty and ethos, such as a society of warriors like the Templars, a religious military order initially established by Christian Crusaders in 1118 to protect pilgrims to the Holy Sepulcher. Still other groups are founded by a decisive personality. Included in this category are those groups in which the personal charisma and transcendent experience of such figures as Buddha, Father Divine, Jesus, Mani, Muhammad, Nanak, and Joseph Smith culminated in new and independent religious traditions or movements. In addition, some leaders initiate new groups that remain part of wider assemblies. Founders of assemblies within assemblies include those who, like Saint Benedict (c. 480-c. 550), founded a monastic community and formulated a monastic rule within the authority of the church and leaders like Nichiren (1222-1282) and John Wesley (1703-1791), who inspired groups that separated from other Buddhist and Christian denominations, yet remained within the circle of their respective traditions. While voluntary religious groups can vary considerably, our examination of them is limited to a discussion of founded religions.

Founded Religions ✓

Every holy community has a symbol system that unites its members in a common life and provides them with a sense of their ultimate place in the cosmos. Founded religions are symbol systems in which an extraordinary personality serves, to borrow from Wilfred Cantwell Smith, as the "master symbol" through which their followers find their lives. The cult-religion founder has an incomparable quality, which Max Weber called charisma. Charisma is, as Weber noted, "a certain quality of an individual personality by virtue of which he is set apart from ordinary men and treated as endowed with supernatural, superhuman, or at least specifically exceptional powers or qualities."[26]

In a broad sense, charisma is an extraordinary breaking-in of sacred power that is not as rare or as authoritative as Weber suggests. Although charismatic experiences are self-validating and never ordinary, spirit possession, including the gifts of the Holy Spirit sought by Pentecostal Christians, is common to many religious traditions and does not, in itself, always confer group leadership. Weber, however, uses the word in the more restrictive sense to point to a religious figure whose experience and proclamations are authoritative. When the message and the person of the charismatic personality is a new wine that cannot be contained in old wineskins, a new religious movement is born.

The set-apart quality of figures who inspire new religions is evident in the titles that they consciously assume or that are ascribed to them by their followers. Siddartha Gautama is the Buddha, the Enlightened One, who serves the Buddhist community as a master symbol of ultimate liberation. Muhammad is God's messenger—a prophet who speaks the word that God has revealed to him. His prophetic authority exceeds that of all those who prophesied before him; thus, Muhammad is the Seal of the Prophets whose divinely inspired words are the ultimate validation of the Islamic community. In the Mormon tradition, Joseph Smith, Jr.'s official title is "Seer, a Translator, a Prophet, an apostle of Jesus Christ, and Elder of the Church through the will of God the Father, and the grace of your Lord Jesus Christ." For Christians, Jesus is the Christ, God's anointed one. As the son of God, he is God incarnate and Lord and Savior.

Christians are not alone in believing in the divinity of their founder. As noted, the Shakers believe the promise of Christ's return was realized in Mother Ann Lee, and the Father Divine Peace Mission revolves around the divinity of Father Divine (c. 1878–1965) and the authoritative character of his pronouncements. Even in traditions where the founder makes no claim of divinity, glorification and veneration of the founders may lead to their deification. In some Buddhist traditions, for example, the Buddha is not only the one who has discovered the path to liberation, but he is the path.

Charismatic figures speak with authority. If they are regarded as prophets, their words are believed to be from God. The experience or path of a sage, an enlightened one, is normative for those who seek ultimate liberation. If the leader is a divine incarnation, who he or she is even more crucial to the devotee than what he or she does. Whatever their mode of validation, disciples are drawn to them. For example, the New Testament reports that Jesus walked near the shore of the Sea of Galilee and called Peter and Andrew and James and John to come with him. They dropped their fishing nets, the scriptures report, and followed him. Following his enlightenment, Buddha preached his first sermon near Benares, and those who listened became his followers. Within two months of the publication of the Book of Mormon in March of 1830, forty people accepted the genuineness of God's revelation to Joseph Smith. By 1970 the number exceeded 3 million. Sometimes the gathering of converts is a much slower process. In the first years of Muhammad's public ministry, only a few people outside his immediate family responded positively to his preaching. Whatever the case, the essence of discipleship is the willingness to walk in the footsteps of an extraordinary person.

The death of the founder has profound implications for the survival of his or her group. How can the charisma of the founder be preserved for future generations? What social system and patterns governing personal relationships are most congenial and supportive of the ultimate purpose of the founder? What did the master teach, and to whom is his or her authority passed? Can, for example, a group like the Peoples Temple survive the suicide-death of the Rev. Jim Jones and 900 of his followers at Jonestown in Guyana? Can Jones's power and vision of an integrated communitarian society survive the horror of the Jonestown tragedy?

While the survival of the Peoples Temple is problematic, spiritual renewal can come out of the ashes of defeat. The despair of the surviving members of the Peoples Temple has a parallel in the bewilderment and disorder that prevailed among Jesus' disciples after his crucifixion. The experience of a resurrected Lord, however, turned Christ's disciples from despair to exaltation and triumph, and after Christ's ascension, the presence of the Holy Spirit kept the charisma alive in the life of the church.

The death of the founder is always a turning point. If the movement is to survive, the charismatic authority of the founder must be transferred to the disciples. The bequeathing of charismatic authority can result in division and fragmentation among the disciples. Muhammad's followers, for example, divided over the issue of his successor. Their sometimes violent quarrel separated the Islamic community into two primary divisions, the Shia and the Sunnis. The death of Joseph Smith created a similar problem in the Church of Jesus Christ of Latter-Day Saints. During his ministry, Smith established an inner circle of twelve apostles. After Smith was lynched by an angry mob at Nauvoo, Illinois on June 27, 1844, leadership was transferred to Brigham Young, who became president of the Quorum of the Twelve Apostles. Dissidents who objected to Young's election and subsequent leadership withdrew to form separate Mormon churches. One group, the Reorganized Church of Jesus Christ of Latter-Day Saints, insisted that Joseph Smith had chosen his son as his successor. Smith's son became president of the Reorganized Church in 1860, and successive presidents have all been descendents of the founder.[27]

Although disciples are often divided, their task is to preserve the authority and charisma of the founder. To accomplish this end, they must develop a social structure and symbol system that provide continuity for future generations of believers. One of the first measures is the compilation and canonization of the founder's teachings, including his or her instructions regarding the formation of a holy assembly. The Muslim tradition records, for example, that the Koran was codified under the leadership of two of Muhammad's most important followers within twenty years of the Prophet's death.

A second turning point in the development of founded religions comes with the deaths of all the companions of the founder. When Christ's apostles and disciples died, the passing of the charisma fell to those who had no personal experience of the historical Jesus. Holy communities that survive this second crisis become increasingly more institutionalized. For example, out of its modest and relatively unstructured beginnings, the Christian assembly or church gradually developed into a highly structured social system. In the process the charisma of Jesus and the enthusiastic and unpredictable outpourings of the Holy Spirit were incorporated into a symbol system that provided continuity through formal channels. The routinization of charisma, as Max Weber called it, is a process whereby spiritual power is incorporated in formalized routines, doctrines, and social structures that provide a balance to the instability and unpredictable character of manifestations of the spirit. The formalization of the common life is evident in the growth and development of the Christian church. The liturgy was gradually clarified and systematized, and a concern for theological orthodoxy emerged in the form of credal and dogmatic formulations. In addition, the institutionalization of the church in the social sphere was marked by the development of a system for making decisions within the holy community, a distinction between clergy and laity, and a complex set of assumptions and practices regarding the relationship of church and state.

Religion and Conflict

Homer was wrong in saying, "Would that strife might perish from amongst gods and men." For if that were to occur, then all things would cease to exist.

Heraclitus[28]

Like all social systems, religious groups provide structures through which human interaction takes place. The structure of religious institutions shows remarkable variations. Some holy communities are highly organized with clear lines of authority, a distinct hierarchy, and an elaborate liturgy; others may have a minimum of organization, blurred lines of leadership, and a relatively informal mode of worship. Nevertheless, whenever humans eat, sleep, play, work, or worship together, they must allocate responsibilities, clarify roles, and develop processes for resolving conflicts and making corporate decisions. This section covers several aspects of the common life in holy communities. It begins with a discussion of protest and conflict resolution within voluntary religious groups and a consideration of the process by which religious protests may lead to the formation of independent religious groups or sects.

Protest in Holy Communities

Conflict is an integral part of existence. This is a truth recognized by ancients and moderns. In Greek mythology, Prometheus struggles against Zeus, and in the biblical tradition, Adam and Eve have become symbols of ultimate disobedience. In the Chinese tradition, yang and yin are the principles of opposition and complementarity. Opposition is also a major motif in modern philosophy. The conflict that Charles Darwin saw in the origin and evolution of biological life, Freud discerned in man's social and inner space. In addition, Karl Marx saw class struggle as the key to historical change.

Discord and division are not strangers to holy communities. The history of religion records many situations in which the unity of the sacred community has been buffeted by the winds of protest. Protest, reform, and fragmentation may occur in both natural and voluntary religious groups, but since voluntary groups lack the ties that provide stability for natural groups, they are more vulnerable to conflicts that culminate in the secession of the protestors. Protest may be isolated and individual, or it may be a collective act in which a group of people make their opposition known. Two forms of protest concern us here—calls for reform from within that never completely break the unity of the holy community and those situations in which the dissenters secede from the community.

Reform and Renewal in
Holy Communities

When protest remains within a holy community, it may be resolved or mediated by a decision in opposition to or in favor of the dissenters, by a compromise that offers a way out for both parties, or by ignoring the issue and hoping it will gradually go away. The Roman Catholic Church, for example, is struggling with internal opposition to its official and traditional directives regarding the use of contraceptives, ordination of women, and marriage of clergy. In addition, conflict exists over the nature of the church's response to calls for social justice for the oppressed peoples of the world and pressure to accelerate the appointment of non-Europeans to responsible positions in the hierarchy.

The creation of holy communities under the aegis of a more inclusive holy community is still another way of resolving conflicts. Perhaps the emergence of the monastic and religious orders within the broader body of the Christian church is the best example of reform from within. The forces that produced monastic communities and religious orders are complex, but they are, at least in part, a reaction and protest to corruption and imperfection in the church. As early as the third century, Christians, individually and in small groups, sought to worship God and sanctify their souls apart from the world. Eremitic monks like St. Anthony (c. 250–c. 356) sought spiritual perfection in silence and solitude, while cenobitic monks like St. Benedict lived together in self-contained and self-sufficient monastic communities. As St. Benedict conceived it, the monastery is a communitarian society whose sole purpose is to order life around the demands of the gospel. The reforming and perfectionist character of **monasticism** is evident in the high level of commitment it requires of its members, including the vow to remain sexually chaste and celibate, the embracing of holy poverty, and the willingness to be obedient to the discipline and order of monastic life.

Although the monastic orders remain part of the institutional church, they deliberately set aside the hierarchies and class distinctions that are operative in the world outside their walls. Just as Jesus' insistence that the last shall be first undermines all social hierarchies, discrimination between learned and unlettered, rich and poor, nobility and serf, master and slave, clergy and laity, are in St. Benedict's Rule to be laid aside for a common life that demands uniform clothing and exempts no able member from a life that alternates between prayer, reflection, and work. St. Benedict expected the monastic spiritual family "to make no distinction of persons in the monastery."[29] The laying aside of self, including the capacity to live unknown, continues to be a primary virtue of monastic life.

Conflict, then, can be a source of renewal and reform. The emergence of new monastic communities, religious orders, and congregations has long been a source of spiritual renewal in the Catholic Church. That such renewals continue to vitalize the church is evident in the work of the Missionaries of Charity, an order founded by Mother Teresa of Calcutta and approved by the Vatican in 1950. Sister Teresa was first a missionary nun serving as a teacher in Calcutta, but she became convinced that God wanted her to serve the poorest of the poor. Her work is a testimony to her capacity to find something lovable, something of Christ, in those with whom she comes in contact. Under Mother Teresa's leadership, the Missionaries of Charity run schools, hospitals, and relief centers in India, North and South America, Africa, and Asia.

Division and Secession

Protest can irreparably divide a holy community; this is evident both in the founding of new religions and in the internal divisions within a religion. Founded religions originate in some revelation or sense of ultimacy that leads a group to separate from existing natural or voluntary associations. When such a group claims an independent cosmic validation, it can be regarded as a distinct religion rather than as a division within a larger holy community. Christianity emerged out of what was initially a Jewish fellowship. The church's understanding of itself as a New Israel united by a new covenant in the person of Christ made remaining within the House of Israel impossible. Likewise, Buddha's dharma, with its rejection of Vedic authority and the laying aside of caste distinctions in the Sangha, led to a separation of Buddhism from Hinduism. Mormonism, with its claim to authoritative scriptures other than the Bible, is to Christianity as Christianity is to Judaism.

Religions often have internal divisions. Although Christians are united by a common scripture and a conviction that God is present to them in Christ, the Christian church is a house divided; its main divisions are Roman Catholic, Protestant, and Eastern Orthodox, which includes Greek, Romanian, Russian, and Serbian ethnic national churches. Protestantism is a thicket of separated bodies that includes, in the United States, over 300 independent groups. Internal division is not an exclusive feature of Christendom. In the United States, Judaism is separated into three broad divisions— Reform, Orthodox, and Conservative—and also embraces a Hasidic community initially founded in Europe by Baal Shem Tov (1760–1810). The Jewish community has separated over interpretations of the Torah and the observance of Mosaic law. Muslims claim that Muhammad anticipated the division of the Islamic community into seventy-three sects; Muhammad's estimate has already been exceeded in the history of Islam. Schism is not just a feature of monotheistic traditions; Buddhism is divided into three main yanas or schools (Theravada, Mahayana, and Mantrayana), and there are subdivisions within each school.

✓ The Church-Denomination-Sect Typology

Change is an essential feature of reality; even the most stable societies and enduring institutions change. Christ may be, as the New Testament proclaims, the same yesterday, today, and tomorrow, but his church has changed and his disciples have understood him quite differently. One mode of change is through renewal and reform—holy communities within a holy community. A second mode occurs when protest leads to division or secession.

One model that scholars have found useful for understanding the dynamics of change and group formation in voluntary religious groups is to distinguish between church, denomination, and sect. While this typology is primarily useful for understanding group formation within the Christian tradition, if used cautiously it can be applied to division and secession in non-Christian voluntary religious groups. Church is, of course, a term that refers to the Christian community. The Buddhist Sangha and Muslim Ummah are distinctive religious communities, but their ethos and symbols are not that of the Christian church; nevertheless, if for the purposes of this typology, church is equated with a particular type of established religious community and sect is associated with smaller, more exclusive, religious groups, then the two terms can be applied to Christian and non-Christian groups.

There are two particularly useful criteria for determining whether a specific religious group should be classified as a church, denomination, or sect. One consideration is whether membership or participation in a religious group is broad and inclusive or narrow and exclusive. A second consideration requires an assessment of the extent to which a group is committed to or alienated from society.

Church-type Group

A church is a well-established religious community. It is inclusive, universal, and deeply concerned with the total well-being of the society in which it plays a prominent role. As an inclusive group, church membership is large or constitutes a national or imperial majority that includes the committed and uncommitted, the just and the unjust, the sincere and the hypocritical. While a church is a voluntary spiritual association, its procedures for entry exclude very few from membership. No special merit is required, and children of affiliated families are easily incorporated into the body of the church. Holy baptism, for example, sacramentally incorporates infants incapable of conscious commitment into the Roman Catholic, Anglican, Lutheran, and Eastern Orthodox churches.

As a universal group the church affects the lives of those within its sphere of influence even if they are not members. This is most obviously the case when a religious group is a national or imperial church nourished and defended by the power of the state. The state or imperial church usually regards itself as uniquely legitimate and the sole mediator of salvation. When this occurs, the legal rights and religious freedom of other holy communities are likely to be constrained by the national or imperial body.

Church-type organizations are generally conservative, traditional, and highly structured. Although the heavy stake that such institutions have in a society makes them turn away from revolutionary solutions, the inner dynamics of church-type organizations, including the reform and renewal that can come from within, may allow them to serve as forces of social change rather than as mere custodians of the status quo.

Established religious groups of the church type are common to several religious traditions. In the course of Islamic history, for example, there have been several theocratic empires and national states in which the Islamic community, its law, ethos, and institutions were inclusive and universal. In a theocratic state, the secular and religious, the ecclesiastical and the civil, are not separated. In a Muslim state, Islamic law, which is believed to be given by God, provides detailed guidance and explicit instruction regarding what behavior is permitted and what is forbidden. Several twentieth-century nations have Islamic church-type national groups, including a Sunni church type supported by the Saud dynasty in Saudi Arabia. The Shia Imam, Ayatollah Ruhollah Khomeini, spearheaded a drive to establish an Islamic republic in Iran. Buddhism has also had church-type groups, including in recent times national church types in Burma, Thailand, and Tibet. In Christianity the Roman Catholic Church, prior to the Protestant Reformation, was an imperial church that dominated the life of western Europe. As a result of the Reformation, its influence in England and northern Europe was diminished by the establishment of independent national Protestant churches.

In modern industrial societies the church-type organization has, for the most part, been modified by the tendency of modern governments to separate church and state and to pass laws that protect the religious liberty of all. The formula, One king, one state, one church, which characterized Western practice for many centuries, is, for the most part, no longer operative. In the West the separation of the secular and the religious and the legitimacy and equality of all religious groups before the law have fostered an acceptance of multiple religious centers. In this century, for example, the Roman Catholic Church has gradually come to accept religious pluralism and support religious liberty. In the process it has explicitly accepted the legitimacy of other Christian bodies.

Sect-type Groups

Sects are exclusive rather than inclusive, particular rather than universal, alienated or aloof from the dominant culture rather than accommodating and congenial. As exclusive groups, sects restrict membership. Membership requires some indication of merit and does not automatically follow from some formalized and relatively perfunctory procedure. Evangelical Christian sects often require a testimony of a born-again experience and may even set aside the baptism ritual. Since sectarian groups demand a great deal from their members, they have little room for the uncommitted. The sacrificial character of sectarian demands may take the form of requiring that members give 10 percent or more of their incomes to the group, or other evidence of moral and religious commitment. Communitarian groups like the Shakers and the Peoples Temple insist that private property should become corporate property. It follows from their exclusive character that sects are small.

As particular or parochial, the sect is set apart from the mainstream of society. Sect life revolves around its peculiar sense of ultimacy. Usually sectarians are either indifferent, disenchanted, or alienated from what they see happening in the world around them. Consequently, they are seldom ecumenical or community minded. Their disaffection from what they regard as blindness, corruption, hypocrisy, or sacrilege often involves the substitution of religious status for social status[30] and is sometimes manifested in behavior that clearly separates them from others. The Hutterites, for example, live in farm colonies set apart from their neighbors and from other Christian communities. Mennonite congregations, such as the Old Order Amish, do not build churches but worship God in their homes, require plain dress, and forswear modern conveniences because such things are nonbiblical.

Like the church type, the sect is likely to regard itself as uniquely legitimate and regard outsiders as out of step. Some may develop, as the Peoples Temple in Guyana did, a paranoid conviction that outside forces intend to destroy them. The Peoples Temple acted out the sectarian principle to ''come out from among them and be ye separate'' by seeking isolation in the jungles of Guyana. The sectarian demand for total commitment and set-apart character is also evident in the Jehovah's Witnesses. Witnesses take no oaths, celebrate no birthdays, eschew Christmas, are urged to marry within the group, make no distinction between clergy and laity, and spend hours each week in proselytizing and tirelessly spreading the word that Armageddon, the final struggle between the forces of righteousness and the forces of evil, is near at hand.

A sect issues from a protest that culminates in secession from an established voluntary or natural religious group. Often, but not always, schismatics are led by a charismatic leader who has either special spiritual gifts, an authoritative religious experience, esoteric knowledge, or an uncompromising need to reform the corruption and hypocrisy that is believed to exist in the offending body. All founded religions began as sectarian movements centered on a charismatic figure.

Denomination-type Groups

Denominationalism took root in the United States, in part because no single religious body had a privileged status in colonial America. In the absence of a national church, the religious liberty and pluralism that gradually took shape provided equal status for all religious groups in the eyes of the law. Under these circumstances the established Protestant groups developed a self-understanding that rejected the Catholic and sectarian claim that there is but one true church in favor of a theology that accepted religious pluralism, supported the separation of church and state, depended on voluntary rather than state-supported subsidies for religious institutions, and recognized that no single religious group is uniquely legitimate.

Denominations are well-established voluntary groups, have a stake in society, and are concerned with the well-being of people and institutions outside their membership. Like the church-type organization, denominations are inclusive, and membership does not require a high level of commitment. They are well organized, have a keen sense of social responsibility, and seek fellowship with other congregations. The ecumenicity of denominationalism is epitomized by the words of John Wesley, the founder of Methodism:

> *I . . . refuse to be distinguished from other men by any but the common principles of Christianity. . . . I renounce and detest all other marks of distinction. But from real Christians, of whatever denomination, I earnestly desire not to be distinguished at all.*[31]

The absence of a sense of exclusive and absolute authority within denominational groups and the diffusion of authority among several independent bodies has been accompanied by a blurring of denominational lines, doctrinal unclarity, and an inability to speak with a single voice. The spread of secular culture and religious pluralism has all but eliminated the pure church-type organization. In Europe, Anglicans and Lutherans are no longer genuine national churches, and in the United States the Roman Catholic Church has absorbed much of the coloration of the main-line Protestant denominations in its willingness to accept religious pluralism and its desire to seek ecumenical dialogue. The major Protestant denominations include such groups as the Disciples of Christ, Episcopalians, Baptists of the American Baptist and Southern Baptist Conventions, Lutherans, Presbyterians, United Church of Christ, and United Methodists.

Sect Formation and Transformation

Scholars have been intrigued by the phenomenon of sect formation and the transition from sect to denomination or church. Some have insisted that the transformation of a sect, the softening of its sense of apartness, is primarily the result in changes in class. Weber argued that the form religious experience takes is affected by class or social position; in capitalist societies the upper-middle and ruling classes gravitate to those fully established churches or denominations that legitimate their social position, the lower classes have an affinity for more sectarian groups. Because those in the upper classes have more to lose, they are more likely to avoid loss of control and outbursts of enthusiasm, while those in the lower levels of the social strata, who are presumably more alienated and frustrated, prefer sectarian groups that stress personal salvation and offer more effervescent forms of religious expression.[32] Thus sects are formed and fed by those who have only a marginal stake in society—the poor, the politically impotent, the dispossessed, and the spiritually lost.

In contrast, Liston Pope argues that the denominationalizing of sects is primarily a function of size rather than class. If a group expands its membership and becomes more inclusive, it is likely to take a more accommodating attitude toward the world. Some of the indices that Pope suggests for gauging the transition from sect to denomination are a shift from poverty to wealth, from persecution to acceptance, from evangelism to religious education, from personal to institutional religion, from an unprofessional but spiritually qualified ministry to a professional clergy, and from noncooperation with other religious bodies to cooperation.[33]

The transition from sect to denomination or church is not automatic. Some sects germinate, bloom, and perish. Others, such as the Christian Church, the Muslim Ummah, and the Buddhist Sangha, develop in some cultural and historical milieus, into church-type organizations. Still others, like the Campbellites and Wesleyans, become denominations, while others, like the Old Order Amish, Hutterites, and Reformed Mennonites, survive for generations within the Christian tradition and retain their sectarian flavor. Established sects like the Amish, Hutterites, Jehovah's Witnesses, and the Salvation Army have developed structures that preserve their character from generation to generation. In addition to the established sects, others have emerged on the religious landscape more recently, such as the Children of God, the Unification Church, and the Peoples Temple.

In addition to the distinction between established and newly emergent sects, sects can be classified according to whether they are primarily evangelical, millennial, gnostic, or utopian. According to sociologist of religion Bryan R. Wilson, such classifications are valuable because the ethos of a sect may have a correlation to whether it is most likely to become a denomination or an established sect or to vanish from the religious landscape.

Evangelical sects are conversionist in orientation, make the acceptance of Christ as savior and born-again experience normative, and regard the Bible as the inerrant word of God. Numbered in this category are evangelical, pentecostal, and holiness groups. Millennial sects are preoccupied with the end of the present evil age, judgment day, and the establishment of a new heaven and a new earth. Examples of this type are Jehovah's Witnesses and the Children of God. Gnostic sects emphasize transcendental and sometimes esoteric wisdom; their founders are sages rather than evangelists or prophets. Examples of this type include Christian Science, Scientology, and the Church of Religious Science. Utopian sects seek to create a just community on earth. Like the Peoples Temple, they often form self-sufficient and self-contained communities. Many sects are mixed types; thus, for example, some evangelical groups are also millennialists. Wilson argues that evangelical sects are more likely to make the transition from sect to denomination, whereas gnostic and millennial groups are more likely to retain their sectarian character.[34]

Concluding Remarks

A holy community is a fellowship of shared concerns, beliefs, rites, and symbols. Some are primarily natural associations in which biological considerations provide the warp and woof of religious experience, while others are voluntary associations bound together by mutual spiritual concerns rather than a common ancestry. Every religious group has some system, whether simple or complex, for making decisions. Some operate on a monarchical or vertical pattern of governance in which absolute authority is centered in a single office or person, and others operate through political processes that are more democratic. In the Christian tradition, for example, the democratic process is most evident in a congregational polity; such groups determine their own priorities, frame and adopt their own bylaws, appoint their own leaders, and provide their own financial base. Mixed types involve the participation of affiliated local congregations in district, national, and international associations through a representational system that works on much the same principle as does the congressional system of the United States.

In addition to its pattern of governance, each religious group has a distinctive social structure and style of leadership. In some groups, social classes are highly stratified, and clergy and laity are sharply divided, while in others relatively little in the way of marks of status separates one worshiper from another. For example, although the caste system is illegal in modern India, the Vedic tradition of India provided a cosmic validation for a caste system that divided Indian society according to role and function. It established a sexual and religious hierarchy that discriminated against females of all castes as well as all low-caste people. Caste membership, with its privileges and responsibilities, was conferred by birth rather than by talent. All holy communities, however, have some devices, including rites of status reversal and yogas of ultimate liberation, that facilitate experiences of communitas and run counter to the hierarchical ordering of society.

Notes

1. In Helen C. White, Ruth C. Wallerstein, and Ricardo Quintana, *Seventeenth-Century Verse and Prose,* vol. I (New York: Macmillan, 1951), p. 109.

2. J. Milton Yinger, *The Scientific Study of Religion* (New York: Macmillan, 1970), p. 203.

3. *Anthropology of Folk Religion,* ed. by Charles Leslie (New York: Vintage Books, 1960), p. 47.

4. Ibid., p. 99.

5. Emile Durkheim, *The Elementary Forms of the Religious Life:* (New York: Free Press, 1965), pp. 236, 257.

6. Ibid., pp. 257-58.

7. Sigmund Freud, *The Future of an Illusion* (Garden City, N.Y.: Doubleday Anchor Books, 1964), p. 35.

8. Yinger, *Scientific Study of Religion,* p. 214.

9. Ibid.

10. Leviticus 27:1-7.

11. Max Weber, *The Sociology of Religion,* trans. by Ephraim Fischoff (Boston: Beacon Press, 1963), p. 107.

12. See Talcott Parsons' introduction to Weber, *The Sociology of Religion,* p.iii.

13. See W.C. Smith, *The Meaning and End of Religion* (New York: New American Library, 1964), ch. 2.

14. Joachim Wach, *The Comparative Study of Religion* (New York: Columbia University Press, 1958), p. 123.

15. See Joachim Wach, *The Sociology of Religion* (Chicago: University of Chicago Press, 1944).

16. See E.E. Evans-Pritchard, *Nuer Religion* (Oxford: Clarendon Press, 1956), p. 196.

17. John Mbiti, *African Religions and Philosophy* (New York: Praeger, 1969), p. 25.

18. See Meyer Fortes, "Oedipus and Job in West African Religions," in Leslie, *Anthropology of Folk Religion,* pp. 16-40.

19. Robert N. Bellah, *Beyond Belief* (New York: Harper & Row, 1970), pp. 86-88.

20. *The Wisdom of Confucius,* trans. by Lin Yutang (New York: Modern Library, 1938), p. 140.

21. In Bellah, *Beyond Belief,* p. 87.

22. In Geoffrey Parrinder, *Introduction to Asian Religions* (New York: Oxford University Press, 1976), p. 94.

23. Mark 3:35.

24. Luke 14:25–27.

25. In Wach, *The Sociology of Religion,* p. 135.

26. Max Weber, *The Theory of Social and Economic Organization* (New York: Oxford University Press, 1947), pp. 358–59.

27. Frank S. Mead, *Handbook of Denominations in the United States* (New York: Abingdon Press, 1970), p. 81.

28. In Philip Wheelwright, ed., *The Presocratics* (New York: Odyssey Press, 1966), p. 71.

29. In Victor Turner, *The Ritual Process* (Chicago: Aldine, 1968), p. 108.

30. Liston Pope, *Millhands and Preachers* (New Haven, Conn.: Yale University Press, 1942), pp. 136–38.

31. In Sydney E. Ahlstrom, *A Religious History of the American People* (New Haven, Conn.: Yale University Press, 1972), p. 381.

32. Weber, *The Sociology of Religion,* pp. 95–117.

33. Pope, *Millhands and Preachers,* pp. 30–31.

34. Bryan R. Wilson, "An Analysis of Sect Development," in William N. Newman, ed., *The Social Meaning of Religion* (Chicago: Rand McNally, 1974), pp. 269–70.

Photo: The Bettman Archive, Inc.

PART IV
BELIEF AND DISBELIEF: THE CONCEPTUAL DIMENSION OF RELIGION

You have now surveyed the conceptual, ritual, personal, and social dimensions of religion. In the process you have acquired a feel for how the human relation to the holy is symbolized and acted out in ceremony and gesture, in words and symbolic objects, and in communion and communities. Part IV, the final stage of this introductory exploration of religious phenomena, returns to the conceptual dimension of religion addressed in part II. There, the emphasis was on the symbolic nature of religious expression. The study of the conceptual dimension in part IV focuses on what is believed rather than on how it is said or performed. We will not survey a wide range of religious beliefs but will limit the discussion to problems of belief related to the questions: Does God exist? Why must we suffer? Does anything remain?

The study of religious belief and disbelief begins, in chapter thirteen, with a distinction between a philosophical and a theological study of religion and a consideration of the question, Does God exist? The chapter examines some of the traditional arguments and counterarguments for belief in God and concludes with the argument that theology, understood as a critical and systematic way of thinking and speaking about the holy, is a form of story.

Chapter fourteen continues the study of belief and disbelief by focusing on the problems that suffering and death pose for faith. Religious belief systems attempt to resolve or reconcile some of the fundamental ambiguities of human existence. No aspects of human life are more difficult to make sense of than suffering and death. Why must we suffer and die? and, Since we must, what is our destiny? are perennial concerns that religious belief systems have sought to answer. Chapter fourteen explores different responses to the questions, Why do we suffer? and Does anything remain?

Chapter fifteen returns to the question, What is religion? and suggests that the question requires a consideration of what religion is not. Conversion to the sacred is one aspect of the study of religious experience, but loss of faith is another. Three models for understanding the loss of faith are examined: loss of belief, loss of home, and loss of meaning.

One of the reasons that the modern world is increasingly difficult to make sense of is that we have so many different and conflicting models for understanding it. Although death and suffering have always been existential breaking points at which human existence and religious belief systems are most vulnerable to breakdown, in premodern societies religious beliefs were the only explanations available. In modern times, however, the capacity of religious beliefs to mediate the traumatic aspects of existence has been challenged by alternative explanations. Scientific and humanistic philosophies have made religious explanations problematic; thus the loss of faith may involve conversion to a perspective that offers more intellectually satisfying explanations. Chapter fifteen concludes with a study of humanism as an alternative to traditional religious symbol systems.

Chapter Thirteen
Belief in God

Where do we come from: Where are we going?
What is the meaning of this life? That is what
every heart is shouting, what every head is asking
as it beats on chaos.

Nikos Kazantzakis
The Saviours of God[1]

Religious belief systems are models for making sense of human existence, for replacing chaos with order. They are symbol systems that answer or, at least, mediate the perennial questions that, as Kazantzakis tells us, every heart is shouting, every head is asking. What does it mean to be human? Why are we here? Why must we suffer and die? What is the right thing to do? and What is our destiny? are typical of those questions that concern us ultimately, which religious worlds of meaning attempt to resolve.

As you have discovered, religious beliefs are quite varied. Some religious traditions primarily speak of the holy as transcendent, as a being who is wholly other than natural and contingent things, while other traditions believe that the holy is immanent rather than an independent being. Belief in God or the gods is characteristic of most religions, but they are either denied or ignored in some traditions. And while most religions agree that something survives death, they disagree on what survives. In spite of the divergence of religious beliefs, religions share a sense of ultimacy, a conviction that there is something central, a being or way of being, through which life is vitalized, by which all things are judged.

The study of belief and disbelief begins in this chapter with an introduction to philosophy and theology, two ways of seeing and speaking that insist on the rational scrutiny of religious belief. This understanding of theology is consistent with the perspective in chapter two where, in comparing and contrasting the academic and theological approaches to the study of religion, theology was depicted as a way of speaking about ultimacy that prizes clarity, consistency, and coherence, which has as its aim the nurture of the religious life.

As an introduction to problems of belief, the chapter raises the question, Does God exist? and examines some of the arguments and counterarguments for believing or disbelieving in the existence of God. The question of God's existence is an appropriate point of departure because, at least in Western religious traditions, belief in the existence of God is logically prior to the resolution of the other perennial concerns and thus has profound implication for understanding the meaning of life. The chapter concludes with the argument that, in spite of its rational character, theological discourse is, like myth and parable, a type of sacred story.

Philosophy is a battle against the bewitchment of our intelligence by means of language.
Ludwig Wittgenstein
Philosophical Investigations [2]

A Philosophical Study of Religion

Before turning to the question of the existence of God, a word needs to be said about philosophy, the philosophy of religion, and theology. Philosophers have approached their discipline in a variety of ways. Some, like Socrates, Plato, Kierkegaard, and Nietzsche, have seen philosophy as a dialogical activity. Socrates, for example, taught that the unexamined life was not worth living and believed that his mission was to engage his fellow Athenians in critical reflection. Plato preserved the dialogical character of the Socratic approach by employing dialogue as a literary device. The use of dialogue as a way of philosophizing suggests that philosophy is an interaction of people as well as an examination of ideas. It may also imply that while philosophical concerns are of monumental importance, they are never completely resolvable; thus the most appropriate way of approaching philosophy is through a format that is dynamic and open ended.

Most philosophers have shunned dialogue for more formal analysis because such a literary device, though dramatic and engaging, is imprecise. Philosophers have a preference for logically tight arguments whose conclusions can be said to be either certain or so reasonable that disagreement with them is illogical. For example, René Descartes understood the philosophical task to be the formulation of indubitable principles through rigorous formal arguments patterned after the deductive proofs of mathematics.

In opposition to the Cartesian conception of the aim of philosophy, contemporary analytic philosophers, particularly the logical empiricists, have argued that philosophy is primarily a critique of language rather than a quest for certainty. This kind of philosophy is primarily concerned with logical and linguistic analysis rather than with making statements about the world; the philosophical enterprise is to clarify the concepts used in science, logic, religion, and everyday language rather than to speculate about the ultimate nature of reality.

As noted in chapter six, philosophy of religion is the branch of philosophy that critically examines religious beliefs. Theology is closely related to the philosophy of religion in subject matter and methodology. Philosophers and theologians critically and systematically reflect on the content and implications of belief. Both examine the logical consistency of ideas and their relationship to other ideas, and both are concerned with unpacking the implications of what is believed.

While theologians and philosophers have the same critical habit of mind and deal with the same problems, theologians differ from philosophers in that they speak from within religious traditions. Theologians are philo- sophically minded—that is, they subject religious beliefs, particularly beliefs from their own traditions, to critical and systematic analysis—but they are also spokesmen, defenders, and interpreters of a community of faith. In contrast, philosophers are not obligated to harmonize or conform their work to a religious belief system. The approach taken in part IV is philosophical rather than theological in the sense that discussion of the questions, Why must we suffer? Does anything remain? and Does God exist? need not be harmonized with a particular belief system.

True and substantial wisdom principally con- **Theology**
sists of two parts, the knowledge of God and
the knowledge of ourselves.

John Calvin
Institutes of the Christian Religion [3]

Theology is a fully conscious and reflective attempt to methodical- ly or systematically examine, clarify, and explain the contents of faith. Thus theologians see as their task a reasoned explication and defense of both their received traditions and their interpretations of it. Theology, whether theist or nontheist, presumes that there is evidence for the truths of faith. Faith seeks understanding; thus the movement of theology is from religious experience to reflection. Theology does not produce faith; faith prompts theology. For Saint Anselm (c. 1033–1109) the very possibility of understanding was derived from faith: "For I do not seek to understand in order that I may believe, but I believe in order that I may understand. For also I believe this, that unless I believe, I shall not understand."[4]

Theology is rational. It is concerned with consistency and coherence, demonstration and proof, inference and evidence. As a rational activity, theology is critical. For example, in the Jewish tradition, Talmud is a compilation of critical commentary on God's revelation as contained in the Torah. Jacob Neusner, a contemporary Jewish scholar, characterizes talmudic thought as exemplifying "the perfect intellectualization of life, that is, the subjection of life to rational study. . . . what is talmudic in thinking is perpetual skepticism."[5] God is served when people respectfully honor him through intellectual acuity and honesty. Study is therefore a form of prayer in the Jewish faith. The skeptical nature of Jewish theology is reflected in an absence of credal or dogmatic statements to which the faithful must give assent.

In spite of the critical character of theology, some theologians have sought to end the debate over what is believed by appealing to what they regard as unchanging and authoritative doctrine. This has sometimes been the case in Christian theology and, in particular, in Roman Catholicism, where dogma is defined as the aspect of belief that is obligatory on the faithful. For example, in 1870, at a council in Rome, Pope Pius IX and the church hierarchy accepted and promulgated the dogma of papal infallibility as a divinely revealed truth. The dogma maintains that when the Roman pontiff speaks ex cathedra and defines doctrine in the area of faith and morals, such definitions are, by virtue of his supreme apostolic authority, infallible.

Dogma and papal infallibility notwithstanding, Christian theology, whether Protestant or Catholic, is never in fact closed. Since Pope Pius IX, popes have chosen to exercise papal infallibility sparingly, preferring to lead by moral and intellectual persuasion rather than dogmatic fiat. Further, there is continuous dialogue within Roman Catholicism as to how obligatory dogmas are to be understood and applied; thus reflective and critical inquiry as to the meaning of dogma, doctrine, or holy scripture is never complete nor settled once and for all. There is no monolithic, unchanging Christian theology; the history of doctrine is one of discontinuities, modifications, and changes as well as one of continuities. Critical doubt or talmudic thinking is always essential to vital theology.

As a rational mode of discourse, theology is an interpretation of religious experience and a clarification and defense of belief. While the interpretive and reflective character of theology indicates that it is a conscious creation, in another sense it is a response to what is given. Holy scripture, for example, is believed to be revealed. The Bible is sacred because it is the word of God, and the Vedas are first of all a hearing or disclosure of divine knowledge rather than simply human knowledge. The Koran is the word of Allah and not the private viewpoint of Muhammad. The starting point of theology is thus that which is revealed. Although theology may begin with revelation, it is primarily a fully conscious effort to interpret and draw out the meanings or implications of what is given. Even scripture, understood as God's revealed word, is a form of human communication and must be ordered and interpreted by the human mind.

Theologians disagree about the capacity of human reason to provide empirical and logical validation for what is revealed. Theologians in the Christian tradition have distinguished between revealed and natural theology: revealed theology clarifies, interprets, and defends divinely revealed truths, whereas natural theology seeks to corroborate God's revelation with evidence from human modes of discovery. Some Christian theologians have sought empirical evidence and logical proofs for the existence of God and for survival after death. Other theologians, however, vigorously assail reason as helpless and ineffectual in demonstrating the truths of faith. Martin Luther, for example, maligned reason as a whore that panders to believer and nonbeliever alike. Although those theologians who, like Luther, deny the capacity of reason to corroborate revealed truths can be antirational (critical of the claims of reason), they can never be anti-intellectual (disdainful of reasoned argument). The theologian cannot take refuge in the slogan, "I believe it because I want to believe it," but must, according to the rules of evidence and inference, provide reasons for accepting or rejecting any proposition.

In the next section the question of the existence of God is raised, and some of the traditional arguments for God's existence are presented as examples of natural theology and rational theological discourse.

Does God Exist?

If God exists then there is a power beyond all human power that is concerned with what happens to individuals and communities. If there is a God who is all powerful, all knowing, and perfectly good, then, no matter how bad things seem there is hope.

Malcolm Diamond
Contemporary Philosophy and Religious Thought[6]

Belief in God stands at the center of many major living religious traditions. For instance, Judaism, Christianity, Islam, Sikhism, Bahaism, and Mormonism share the conviction that God is the creator of the universe. As the Lord of Creation, God transcends his creation in the sense that God's creation and all of his creatures are dependent on him for their existence.

God is infinite and eternal, whereas created things are finite and transitory. In traditional monotheistic theology, God is also believed to be all-knowing (omniscient), all-powerful (omnipotent), and present everywhere in the universe (omnipresent). The radical otherness of God is moderated in monotheistic traditions by their insistence that God is a personal being, an Eternal Thou, who thinks, feels, wills, judges, forgives, hears, and speaks or makes himself known.

In the philosophical and theological traditions of the West, the existence of a powerful and absolutely good God is crucial. Westerners have tended to agree with the proposition that there can be no moral absolutes, eternal truths, or personal immortality if there is no God. The main intellectual obstacles to believing in such a deity stem from difficulties in reconciling God's goodness with the existence of evil **(theodicy)** and from the possibility that the operation of the world can be explained without reference to God. The first objection deals with the problem of whether the unsatisfactory character of human existence disproves the existence of a loving God. The second objection focuses on whether a superempirical explanation for the existence of natural things is necessary or superfluous. Since the problem of theodicy will be discussed in the next chapter, further amplification of it will be deferred in order to give first attention to those arguments that deal with whether the universe is ordered in such a way that it is intellectually defensible to conclude that God exists. Three traditional arguments for the existence of God—the cosmological, ontological, and **teleological** arguments—will be discussed.

We should note that some philosophers and theologians insist that the question, Does God exist? is not a proper one. Logical empiricists, for example, insist that in spite of the interrogative form, it is a pseudoquestion. A genuine question must, in principle, be verifiable or falsifiable in human experience. According to the logical empiricists, since no operations or experiments empirically either verify or falsify the existence of God, the question is a pseudo one. Some theologians from within religions of transcendence also agree that the question is inappropriate. They insist that arguments can never prove or disprove that God exists because God's existence is not of the same order as the existence of things.

A disinterest in such a question and disbelief in the God of monotheism is a familiar theme in nontheistic religions. Jainism, one of India's oldest faiths, rejects belief in a God of creation. Its sacred stories revolve around twenty-four great teachers or Victorious Ones who, in achieving liberation, have provided humans with a path of salvation. Many branches of Buddhism ignore the gods because they, like all other living things, are transitory and powerless to shed light on the crucial and pressing issues of existence. In Buddhist literature the Buddha is portrayed as the teacher of both gods and man. Confucius, the primary fount of Chinese humanism, likewise paid little attention to the gods. He instructed his students to devote themselves to human endeavors and to keep a respectful distance from spiritual beings. Confucius asked, "Until you are able to serve man, how can you serve spiritual beings?"[7]

The fact that nontheistic religions reject the God of theism should not imply that such religions are immune to philosophical criticism. Nirvana, Tao, and all other such transempirical constructs are open to many of the same objections that the logical empiricists have made to belief in God; namely, since they are neither verifiable not falsifiable, they are factually meaningless. Nirvana, the Buddhists insist, is ineffable; thus it lies beyond the limitations of speech. Some philosophers insist that nirvana is inexpressible because it is hopelessly contradictory. When nirvana is described as an unconditioned, uncreated, and indestructible Void, as it sometimes is in Buddhist literature, the meaning of void is stretched beyond that of mere nothingness in the direction of a ground of all being, or what is sometimes referred to by Christian mystics as the godhead. And, if nirvana is something similar to what Christians have meant by the godhead, then talk about nirvana is open to many of the same philosophical objections as the proposition, God exists.

The Cosmological Argument
for God's Existence:
St. Thomas Aquinas

The cosmological argument for God's existence attempts to account for the world by providing an ultimate reason for its existence—that is, an explanation that requires no further explanation. The cosmological argument proceeds from an observation of the movement and causal interaction of things in the natural world to the conclusion that such phenomena require, as an explanation for their existence, a self-existent being who initiates motion and the causal chain. Since things are not self-moved, motion itself must have had a beginning; thus in order to account for what we observe, we must acknowledge the existence of God.

The cosmological argument, which is in some respects indebted to the work of Aristotle, was given its most definitive formulation by St. Thomas Aquinas (c. 1224–1274). In Aquinas's view, reason can proceed from an observation of the facts of experience to a conclusion about the ultimate cause of such facts. The point of Aquinas's argument is that to account for the existence of things that we observe in the world around us,

Andrea di Bonaiuto, Triumph of St. Thomas Aquinas *(detail), Sta. Maria Novella, Spanish Chapel, Florence, Italy.*

Photo: Scala/Editorial Photocolor Archives

we must infer the existence of a necessary being who is First Mover and First Cause.

Aquinas began his proof of the existence of God with the observation that things move. According to the physics of the age of Aquinas, everything that is moved is moved by something else. A pencil, for example, will not move of itself; it must be acted upon. Although in this view, whatever moves is moved by something else, Aquinas concluded that there must be something that initially produces motion without being moved. This something, this unmoved mover, is the initiating principle of all things and is what we call God. In short, motion is impossible unless a first mover, which is in itself unmoved, is the first cause of motion.

In a second part of the argument, Aquinas inferred from the relationship of cause and effect "that there exists a first sufficient cause. This is God."[8] Just as a football game begins with a kickoff, it is necessary to conclude, if an infinite regress is to be avoided, that God is the uncaused cause and the unmoved mover, by which all things have their order and movement.

In a third part of the argument, Aquinas insisted that the existence of contingent beings—that is, things that are not self-existent and therefore might not have existed—ultimately depends on "the existence of some being having of itself its own necessity, and not receiving it from another, but rather causing in others their necessity. This all men speak of as God."[9] The supposition of this argument is that for there to be anything at all, there must have always been something rather than nothing. This something, this necessary being, is God who is the ground of all contingent things.

Serious counterarguments to the cosmological argument can be made. One objection is that the inference from cause and effect to a First Cause assumes that every effect has a cause; in concluding that there is a First Cause that stands outside the circle of causation, the argument breaks the causal chain and therefore invalidates the argument. A second objection is that the assumption that causation and motion have a beginning in time is unnecessary. Asian sages, for example, have taught that there never was a time when time was not. Accordingly, the cosmos, including its movement and causal chain, is an unbroken chain of becoming. A third counterargument is that motion, causation, and dependent things can be better explained by natural rather than ultimate explanations. When, for example, we ask why a bridge exists, we must rely on explanations that include the architectural design, the materials, and the construction process rather than seek an ultimate explanation. The universe, skeptics insist, is a brute fact and the question why anything at all should exist is ultimately unanswerable. We should also note that moving from the argument that the existence of things requires a first cause to belief in a God who is personally and caringly involved in the life of his creatures requires a gigantic intellectual leap.

The Ontological Argument
for God's Existence:
St. Anselm and Descartes

While the cosmological argument rests on inferences from experience, the ontological argument attempts to demonstrate, from an analysis of the concept of God conceived of as a Perfect Being, that God's existence cannot be rationally doubted. The ontological argument was initially developed by St. Anselm (1033–1109), a distinguished theologian and an Archbishop of Canterbury, and was subsequently elaborated by mathematician and philosopher René Descartes. The argument is a strictly formal proof of the existence of God, as is indicated by St. Anselm's account of his purpose: "I set to seek within myself whether I might discover one argument which needed nothing else than itself alone for its proof; and which by itself might suffice to show that God truly exists."[10]

St. Anselm began his argument with the proposition that God is "a being than which nothing greater can be conceived."[11] Even those who say in their hearts that there is no God understand this point—that is, they recognize that the idea of a supreme being exists in their understanding, although they may reject the idea that God exists independent of their mind. St. Anselm recognized it is one thing for an idea of something to exist in the understanding and quite another to understand that the referent of such an idea exists in reality. For instance, unicorns, gremlins, and dragons exist conceptually but have no nonconceptual existence. He insisted, however, that the idea of a perfect being, a being "than which nothing greater can be conceived, cannot exist in the understanding alone."[12] God's perfection implies existence, for to suppose that the idea of perfection exists only in the understanding contradicts the very notion of perfection. To say that God only exists in the mind is contradictory because once this assertion is examined, we discover that we can think of a still more perfect being, namely, a being that "exists both in the understanding and in reality."[13]

In a second aspect of his proof, St. Anselm argued that God's existence is uniquely necessary: "God cannot be conceived not to exist. . . . That which can be conceived not to exist is not God."[14] Every contingent being can be conceived as not existing without contradiction, but such is not the case with God. This is so because, as an infinite, supreme being, God can neither have had a beginning in time nor can he cease to exist; thus God exists "more truly than all other beings and hence in a higher degree than all others."[15]

Descartes concurred with St. Anselm's contention that existence is implicit in the idea of God's perfection. Descartes believed that perfection cannot lack existence; thus, for him, existence is an essential property or attribute of God. In the *Meditations,* he proceeded from the fact humans have an idea of a perfect being—that is, a being who is infinitely wise, powerful, and good—to an argument for the existence of such a being. I have an idea of a perfect being, Descartes began, and this idea, like all ideas, must have a cause. I am not a perfect being—that is, I am finite, imperfect, and capable of being deceived; thus the idea of a perfect being cannot have originated with me. Consequently there must exist a perfect being which caused me to possess such an idea; ergo, God exists.

While philosophers and theologians often grant that the ontological argument is ingenious and strangely attractive, they have, for the most part, insisted that it is fallacious. The first telling criticism came from Gaunilo, a French monk who was a contemporary of St. Anselm's. Gaunilo tried to expose the absurdity of the argument by pointing out that he had all sorts of unreal objects in his understanding, including the idea of a beautiful, most perfect island. If the idea of a perfect being proves the existence of such a being, does the idea of a perfect island prove that such an island exists? The problem, as Gaunilo saw it, is that the argument leads to the existence of a whole series of perfections. Although, like St. Anselm, Gaunilo believed in God, his point was that theologians are not conjurers who can, by merely conceiving a perfect being or island, bring such things into existence. In response to Gaunilo, St. Anselm made the point that because God is that which nothing greater than can be conceived, the argument applies only to the existence of such a being and cannot be logically extended to prove the existence of imaginary things.[16]

Other serious objections to the ontological argument can be made. What does it really mean, for example, to insist that existence makes the idea of a perfect being more perfect? Why is what exists both in intellect and in fact a greater perfection than something that exists only in the intellect? Certainly a real one hundred dollar bill is preferable to an imaginary one, but is it more perfect? In addition to voicing reservations about whether existence adds to our idea of perfection, philosophers have insisted that the existence, or facticity, of something cannot be deduced from an idea of it. The ontological argument may be logically valid—that is, if you grant the premise, the conclusion follows from it—but it entails an existential fallacy when it moves from a logical necessity to an existential fact. Put another way, the idea of existence may be logically part of the idea of God just as four sides belong to the idea of a square, but such an argument does not prove that there is something in the world to which the word God applies; thus it is not contradictory to deny the existence of God.

The Teleological Argument
for God's Existence:
Paley and Hume

The teleological argument is probably the most widely known and persuasive of the arguments for God's existence. It is rooted in the order or design that most of us believe present in the world. One example of this order is evident in human institutions. Each culture has a form, a logic of its own. Villages, towns, and cities are comprehensible because they have some design. Government is an alternative to anarchy. Sports have rules and well-defined playing areas. Books are possible because their authors have executed a plan. Wherever we find order in human experience, we find a mind at work, planning, designing, intending.

The order reflected in human invention, in culture, is paralleled by the order of nature. If the movement of the planets was not predictable, space travel would be impossible; the moon flights are not only a monument to human genius but a testimony to the order of nature. What is true of the stars is equally true of the earth. Our planet is a chain of interdependencies and functional adaptations. The ocean, the wind, and the earth's surface combine in a play of forces to replenish the earth with life-nourishing rain. The anatomy of man, of every species of animal, is likewise a prodigious display of proportion, intricacy, and adaptation.

Cleanthes, a figure in David Hume's (1711–1776) *Dialogues Concerning Natural Religion,* was moved by the wonder of such interdependencies:

> *Look round the world: Contemplate the whole and every part of it: You will find nothing but one great machine, subdivided into an infinite number of lesser machines . . . . All these various machines and even their most minute parts, are adjusted to each other with an accuracy, which ravages into admiration all men who have ever contemplated them.*[17]

The teleological argument maintains that the order reflected in nature, like the order present in culture, is best accounted for by attributing it to intelligent design. As Cleanthes stated, "The Author of nature is somewhat similar to the mind of man."[18]

William Paley, an eighteenth-century clergyman, used the example of a watch and watchmaker to drive this point home. If a person comes upon a watch lying in a deserted area, can he reasonably conclude that the watch is a natural feature of the environment? The watch's complex adaptation of parts rules out any such conclusion. A watch requires a watchmaker—that is, design and intelligence. If this is so for watches, Paley continued, then the order, adaptability, and interdependencies of nature, which far exceed those of the watch, must likewise be the work of intelligent design. The teleologist argues that it is impossible, or at least implausible, to conclude that the universe is the result of chance or of blind evolutionary forces; in fact, the orderly arrangement of every part of nature is the strongest proof of God's existence.

There are serious objections to the teleological argument for God's existence. In Hume's *Dialogues,* Philo undertakes a refutation of Cleanthes's defense of the argument from design. In Cleanthes's view, the design of the universe is empirical evidence that the world is the product of a creative mind. Rather than proving that God does not exist, Philo's counterarguments so seriously weaken the teleological argument that its affirmation becomes more a confession of faith than a proof.

The problem, as Philo sees it, is whether the analogy between artifacts, human creations, and natural things is legitimate. Are artifacts and natural things really so similar that both are conscious creations? Certainly we know from experience that several pieces of steel "will never arrange themselves so as to compose a watch"; neither will stone, mortar, and wood ever erect a house without an architect.[19] But, Philo asks, does the universe really bear such a close resemblance to a watch or a house? In fact, we cannot prove such a resemblance. The analogy between artifact and nature breaks down in several ways. We have, for instance, an experience of watchmakers and architects, but we can have no experience of a universe maker since the creation of the universe is without parallel in human experience. Second, is it sound reasoning to claim that the whole of reality is a conscious creation merely because one part of it, namely artifacts, are so designed? Philo argues that the examples of the watch and house merely prove the order of the human mind and not that of nature. Third, Philo points out, even if nature's design is evidence of intelligence, it is a leap of faith to assume that such an intelligence is, as monotheists believe, a single, personal deity.

Even if an order in nature is granted, serious weaknesses in the argument remain. Is it not probable, Philo suggests, that the order in nature may spring from nature itself rather than from the artifice of a designer? In fact, Philo asks, isn't it possible that use of the creator-creation model for understanding nature is seriously defective? The creator-creation model is clearly germane to the relationship of artist to art, of humans to culture, but doesn't the analogy break down when it is extended to nature?

Rather than the relationship of creator to his creation, Hume asked, isn't a process model of generation or evolution more appropriate for understanding the origin and development of natural things? In a process model, nature's order is intrinsic and needs no conscious creation to account for it; thus, for example, the movement from acorn to oak is inherent in the growth process. According to biologist Julian Huxley, living things can be better understood in this same developmental or evolutionary fashion. The direction of biological evolution, Huxley argued, needs no predication of purpose or intelligent design to account for it:

> The purpose manifested in evolution, whether in adaptation, specialization, or biological progress, is only an apparent purpose. It is just as much a product of blind forces as is the falling of a stone to earth or the ebb and flow of the tides. It is we who have read purpose into evolution, as earlier men projected will and emotion into inorganic phenomena like storm or earthquake. If we wish to work towards a purpose for the future of man, we must formulate that purpose ourselves. Purposes in life are made, not found.[20]

The Value of the Traditional Arguments

Although the cosmological, ontological, and teleological arguments were intended to be conclusive demonstrations of God's existence, counterarguments have been so forceful that most contemporary theologians no longer maintain that they are conclusive. The traditional arguments should not be dismissed altogether, for they do at least support the contention that belief in God is reasonable. If the arguments for God's existence do not provide conclusive proof, they do provide reasons for faith; in this regard they are not unlike other disciplines, such as science and history, which must support their truth-claims by evidence that is also probable and corroborative rather than certain and conclusive. The traditional arguments and other concerns of natural theology insist on the importance of critical thought in matters of faith.

In addition to serving theology's critical role, a role that can help us avoid flying off into imaginary and sometimes demonic worlds, the traditional arguments serve the religious life in other ways. For example, St. Anselm was not trying to convince himself through the ontological argument that God exists. He already believed in God; nevertheless the argument led him to a fuller understanding of God. In this sense the traditional arguments may have religious value because, even though they may not convert the disbeliever, they can function as a mode of discovery through which those who believe can come to a richer understanding of God.

Other Ways of Justifying Belief in God

If we seek for . . . a statement of what Spirit is thought to be in itself . . . Nuer do not claim to know. They say that they are merely doar, *simple people, and how can simple people know about such matters. What happens in the world is determined by Spirit and Spirit can be influenced by prayer and sacrifice. This much they know, but no more, and they say, very sensibly, that since the European is so clever, perhaps he can tell them the answer to the question he asks.*

E.E. Evans-Pritchard
Nuer Religion [21]

Faith in God is not merely a matter of empirical probabilities and logical proofs but one of feelings and will. As noted previously, some theologians have argued that appeals to evidence, whether from an observation of things in the world (motion, causation, order) or from an entirely formal argument (the idea of God requires the existence of God), are vain and that such evidence can neither prove nor disprove the truths of faith. Paul Tillich wrote, "God can be proved or again he can be refuted, by rational methods. But an idea which can be proved by means of arguments that are more or less convincing cannot give me a foundation for my existence in face of eternity . . . that which I have to prove by argument, has no immediate reality for me." [22] God, many believers insist, is known experientially rather than through arguments—that is, in divine-human encounters or in the inner life, in the soul, which, to use a Christian image, is the meeting place of God and humans. In addition to the three traditional arguments, three other approaches, which do not claim to be proofs of God's existence but which affirm or recommend belief in his existence, deserve mention.

A Pragmatic Case for Belief in God: Pascal and James

Blaise Pascal and William James are two philosophers who justified belief in God on pragmatic grounds. In their perspective, the question of God's existence cannot be resolved by an appeal to the evidence. For Pascal, a passionately committed Christian, the question was unanswerable because "if there is a God, He is infinitely incomprehensible, since having neither parts nor limits, He has no affinity to us. We are then incapable of knowing either what He is or if He is."[23] For James, the resolution of the question faltered not because of the nature of the absolute but because of the inconclusiveness of the evidence.

Although he was not a traditional theist, James justified faith in God or some higher dimension of existence. Some issues are unresolvable by an appeal to the evidence but at the same time have serious practical consequences for human happiness. Such is the case of the questions of human destiny and whether God exists. When religious resolutions to such issues do not conflict with empirical evidence, James argued, humans are justified in assenting to them. For those to whom the question of God's existence is alive—a real possibility rather than a dead issue—is forced rather than avoidable, and is momentous rather than trivial, intellectual considerations do not demand that belief be suspended until further evidence is available. Because for such people belief in God has serious consequences for their personal happiness, their passionate need to believe is sufficient justification for believing. James wrote, "On pragmatic principles, if the hypothesis of God works satisfactorily in the wider sense of the word, it is true."[24] Of course, as James and his critics have pointed out, the need to believe cannot be evidence of the truth of a belief; thus to say the hypothesis of God is true means that it is a belief that often has favorable consequences for the well-being of human beings.

Pascal is well known for having proposed a religious wager that calculated the possible consequences of believing or disbelieving in God. The wager recommended that people bet that God exists; if such a belief is true, they have everything to gain, and nothing to lose if it is false. Pascal insisted that the question of God's existence is unavoidable:

> . . . *you must wager. It is not optional.* . . . *Which will you choose then?* . . . *Let us weigh the gain and the loss in wagering that God is. Let us estimate these two chances. If you gain, you gain all; if you lose, you lose nothing. Wager, then, without hesitation that He is.*[25]

Because of the depth of his own commitment, Pascal was acutely aware that mere calculated belief in God was not enough. He believed, however, that those who made such a wager and acted as if they believed would eventually be cured of unbelief.

Faith in God as a Passionate Commitment: Unamuno and Kierkegaard

While William James merely justifies going beyond the evidence, existentialist philosophers like Miguel de Unamuno and Sören Kierkegaard insist that a leap of faith requires not only going beyond the evidence but a willingness to do violence to the evidence. For them, formal arguments and proofs lead away from God; thus, in Unamuno's words, "The road that leads us to the living God, the God of the heart, and that leads us back to Him when we have left Him, for the lifeless God of logic, is the road of faith, not of rational and mathematical conviction."[26] God, Kierkegaard believed, is known subjectively, inwardly, "because God is a subject, and therefore exists only for subjectivity in inwardness."[27] It is, to modify one of Kierkegaard's examples, as impossible to discover God in formal arguments as it is to find a San Francisco address with a road map of the United States. Faith is always a leap, a passionate commitment to God in spite of the impossibility of knowing God objectively.

In the thought of Kierkegaard and Unamuno is an element of longing to create what they do not see. "To believe in God is to long for His existence, and, further, it is to act as if He existed, it is to live by this longing and to make it the inner spring of our action."[28] In Unamuno's treatment, the person of faith is very much like Don Quixote in the musical, *Man of La Mancha.* The person of faith must see, as Don Quixote did in Dulcinea, what should be there. The danger is that in doing so we may be beguiled to substitute what our heart prefers for what our head perceives is really there. At what point can the passionate need to believe become a license for wishful thinking?

The Experience of Holiness as an Existential Presence

Primarily philosophers and theologians have busied themselves with the problem of God's existence; the faithful often simply insist that they know the sacred directly through experience rather than through arguments. Jesus, for instance, offered no arguments for God's existence. To those who are convinced that God is present in their lives, arguments often seem beside the point; thus the experience of holiness is self-authenticating. The Buddha insisted that such insoluble puzzles as whether the world is eternal or finite or

Albrecht Dürer, Praying Hands. *Prayer is a form of religious expression through which it is believed that God is existentially known.*

Photo by Harold M. Lambert, Frederic Lewis

whether a liberated person exists after death were particularly unfruitful for those who seek Enlightenment. For the Buddhist monk, nirvana is a liberating experience and not an argument. Nirvana is self-authenticating and no words can be spoken that either add to or subtract from it. For the Christian, God is present in the preaching of his word, in the sacraments, and in acts of love. Mystics of all faiths seek union with the holy. Buddhist and Taoist mystics insist that all participate in the Buddha-nature or that the Tao is the mother of all things. There is something sacred at the depth of human existence, Christian mystic Meister Eckhart believed, a divine spark in the human soul, by which humans may know God directly:

> *There is an agent in my soul which is perfectly sensitive to God. I am as sure of this as I am that I am alive: nothing is as near to me as God is. God is nearer to me than I am to myself.*[29]

The question of God's existence is, at least in the present age, an **antinomy**—that is, a question in which the affirmative arguments are so balanced by the counterarguments that the issue cannot be resolved by an appeal to the evidence. Even self-authenticating experiences of holiness, such as those of Jesus, Muhammad, and Joseph Smith, can be delusive and therefore cannot prove the existence of holy being, whether it be thought of as the self-existent God of monotheism or a process that, like the Tao, unfolds in the movement of being. Perhaps, as Buddha argued in ancient times and as the logical empiricists argue today, we should not concern ourselves with questions that cannot be answered. But is that really possible? Can we repress the desire to know what lies beyond the ordinary? Dag Hammarskjöld wrote, "God does not die on the day when we cease to believe in a personal deity, but we die on the day when our lives cease to be illumined by the steady radiance, renewed daily of wonder, the source of which is beyond all reason."[30]

Dogmatic theological statements are to be comprehended, neither as logical propositions nor as poetic utterances: They are to be taken, rather, as shaggy-dog stories: They have a point but he who tries too hard to get it will miss it.

W.H. Auden
Secondary Worlds[31]

Theology as Story

This section returns to the subject of religious language addressed initially in chapter six. There, we compared religious discourse with scientific and aesthetic ways of seeing and speaking. The treatment of religious language as story in chapter seven introduced myth and parable as two types of sacred stories. In this section, theology, a rational mode of discourse, is also regarded as story or metaphor. Although theology is a movement away from myth as an explicit story form to a more dispassionate and reasoned mode of speech, there are persuasive reasons for regarding all discourse concerning the holy (God, nirvana, Tao) as a form of story or metaphor rather than as factually descriptive.

Because theology is a rational defense of faith, it is a more direct form of discourse than either myth or parable. Myth is an evocative and ecstatic form of speech. The contents of myth are often implausible and puzzling by the standards of ordinary existence; though parables are more clearly tied to life situations, they are an art form rather than either historical narrative or systematic analysis. In spite of its direct and rational style, theology can be treated as story. Of course, in a technical sense it is not a form of story like myth and parable, but neither is it as direct or descriptive as it appears. Theology is story because the ultimate is a mystery that is always something more than words, proofs, and definitions. Theology is an imaginative, indirect form of speech because, as John Macquarrie has pointed out, "talk about God can be fully direct only if God were precisely like ourselves."[32] The task of theology, like the double-intentionality of all religious language, is to speak of reality in such a way that the ultimate is pointed to or disclosed through it.

St. Thomas Aquinas made the point that theological language is primarily imaginative and indirect. While Aquinas argued that reason could prove the existence of God, he also believed that humans could know very little, except indirectly, of God's essential nature. Since God exists in a radically different way, he can only be spoken of by **remotion** or analogy. Remotion is a form of negative speech; thus theologians can say what God is not. For instance, by the way of negation, (negative theology), God is *un*created and *un*material. In the Hindu tradition, negative theology is exemplified by *neti, neti*—that is, by the device of saying Brahman is not this, not this; thus the divine is neither male nor female, neither seen nor not seen. Since the divine, as Aquinas put it, is always more than the human intellect can comprehend, we are unable to know God's nature; "yet we are able to have some knowledge of it by knowing what it is not."[33]

Analogical theological language involves making positive comparisons between God and man. There is, Aquinas argued, some likeness between the divine and the human. Just as "the heat generated by the sun must bear some likeness to the active power of the sun," so also must the creature be in some way like its creator.[34] Those perfections that exist in humans only conditionally and imperfectly can be posited of God, in whom such perfections are absolute and unconditional; thus human beings are good, God is the highest good; human beings are powerful, God is omnipotent; human beings are knowledgeable, God is omniscient. Positive theology can say that God "is the good of every good" if it is understood that the goodness of God and that of humans is not identical. Again the theologian would remind us that it is appropriate to proclaim that God is love if we are also aware that God is infinite love and that divine and human love are neither absolutely identical nor absolutely different. Theological analogy is thus a form of indirect speech, a metaphor for speaking about the holy.

Theology is a monument to the human conviction that the ultimate is not completely discontinuous with ordinary reality—that it is not an absolutely impenetrable mystery. A massive anthropomorphism is implicit in faith in God. Humans are not alone. Absolute reality is not entirely separate from relative and dependent reality. The divine face is never totally dissimilar from the human face; thus the holy is neither completely identical with humans nor is it completely different. Theological discourse is possible because God is in some way similar to us; thus analogies can be made between human experience and the reality of God.

Remotion and analogy are examples of the double-intentionality of theological language. Theology, like all religious language, is also paradoxical—that is, it is always forced to attempt to resolve or mediate contradictions. How, for instance, is God's foreknowledge to be reconciled with human freedom? If God is omniscient, then he must have foreknowledge of the future; but if humans are free, then human choices cannot be absolutely foreseen by God. Theological discourse is inescapably paradoxical because the holy of which it speaks is a mystery that cannot be encompassed by words. "There are, indeed, things that cannot be put into words. They *make themselves manifest*. They are what is mystical," Wittgenstein wrote.[35]

If theology is double-intentional and paradoxical, then it is clearly more akin to poetry and story telling than its logical rigor suggests. W.H. Auden made the point that theological statements are like shaggy-dog stories. Such stories seem to run on and on and are in danger of losing their meaning in the process of their telling. Theological stories, like shaggy-dog stories, are open ended. They need retelling. Theology as creed, doctrine, dogma, and as systematic formulation needs constant revision and reinterpretation. As Sten H. Stenson wrote; "What, for example, is Christian dogmatic theology but a body of dogmas to the effect that all dogma is misleading and false, Christian dogma included, if we presume to think that we have more than unfathomably ambiguous or self-contradictory understanding of such symbols?"[36] If we succumb to literal-mindedness, the point of theological stories can be missed. Theological shaggy-dog stories are intended to open us to a critical and unsettling vision of holiness. If they do not produce faith, they can at least influence, modify, and nurture it.

Concluding Remarks

This chapter introduced the subject of religious belief by concentrating on the question, Does God exist? As we have noted, theologians are deeply divided as to whether the arguments that have been formulated provide reasonable and plausible grounds for belief in God. Some have insisted that the holy is ineffable and can only be known in experience. Others, such as the logical empiricists, have insisted that the question, Does God exist? is a pseudo one and that the assertion, God exists, is factually meaningless. Still others have argued that the universe is itself an unfathomable riddle. Albert Schweitzer wrote, "All thinking must renounce the attempt to explain the universe. . . . What is glorious in it is united with what is full of horror. What is full of meaning is united to what is senseless."[37]

Counter to those perspectives that are sharply critical of the worth of theological discourse is the argument that images of ultimacy, including the formal images of theology, are ways of seeing that can profoundly affect our attitudes and even shape and direct what we perceive. As philosopher John Wisdom observed, reality is more than a matter of the facts; it is organizing and interpreting facts, of seeing patterns and organizing meaningful models of reality.[38] Religious belief systems attempt, in their images of ultimate existence, to provide emotionally and intellectually satisfying models and, at least in Western thought, there has been no more compelling vision of ultimacy than the vision of God.

Notes

1. Nikos Kazantzakis, *The Saviours of God,* trans. by Kimon Friar (New York: Simon & Schuster, 1960), p. 128.

2. Ludwig Wittgenstein, *Philosophical Investigations* (New York: Macmillan, 1953), p. 47e.

3. John Calvin, *Institutes of the Christian Faith,* trans. by Henry Beveridge (Grand Rapids, Mich.: Eerdmans, 1962), Book I, ch. 1, sec. i.

4. *St. Anselm: Proslogium,* trans. by S.N. Deane (Chicago: Open Court, 1926), p. 7.

5. Jacob Neusner, *Between Time and Eternity: The Essentials of Judaism* (Encino, Calif.: Dickenson, 1975), pp. 71–73.

6. Malcolm Diamond, *Contemporary Philosophy and Religious Thought* (New York: McGraw-Hill, 1974), p. 1.

7. *The Sacred Books of Confucius,* ed. and trans. by Ch'u Chai and Winberg Chai (New Hyde Park, N.Y.: University Books, 1965), p. 10.

8. St. Thomas Aquinas, *On the Truth of the Catholic Faith Summa Contra Gentiles,* ed. and trans. by Anton Pegis (Garden City, N.Y.: Doubleday, 1955), p. 95.

9. *Basic Writings of St. Thomas Aquinas,* vol. I, ed. by Anton Pegis (New York: Random House, 1945), p. 23.

10. St. Anselm, *Proslogium,* p. 1.

11. Ibid., p. 7.

12. Ibid., p. 8.

13. Ibid.

14. Ibid.

15. Ibid., pp. 8–9.

16. Alvin Plantinga, ed., *The Ontological Argument, from St. Anselm to Contemporary Philosophers* (Garden City, N.Y.: Doubleday, Anchor Books, 1965), pp. 6–27.

17. David Hume, *Dialogues concerning Natural Religion,* ed. by Norman K. Smith (New York: Bobbs-Merrill, 1947), p. 143.

18. Ibid.

19. Ibid., p. 146.

20. Julian Huxley, *Evolution* (New York: Harper & Brothers, 1943), p. 576.

21. E.E. Evans-Pritchard, *Nuer Religion* (Oxford: Clarendon Press, 1970), pp. 315–16.

22. Paul Tillich, "The Religious Situation in Germany To-day," *Religion in Life* III, no. 2 (1934):167.

23. Blaise Pascal, *Pensées* (New York: Random House, 1941), p. 80.

24. William James, *Pragmatism and Other Essays* (New York: Washington Square Press, 1963), p. 131.

25. Pascal, *Pensées,* p. 81.

26. Miguel de Unamuno, *The Tragic Sense of Life,* trans. by J.E. Fitch (New York: Dover, 1954), p. 186.

27. Sören Kierkegaard, *Concluding Unscientific Postscript,* trans. by David F. Swenson (Princeton, N.J.: Princeton University Press, 1964), p. 178.

28. Unamuno, *Tragic Sense of Life,* pp. 184–85.

29. *Meister Eckhart,* trans. by Raymond B. Blakney (New York: Harper Torchbooks, 1941), p. 120.

30. Dag Hammarskjöld, *Markings* (New York: Knopf, 1964), p. 56.

31. W.H. Auden, *Secondary Worlds* (New York: Random House, 1968), p. 136.

32. John Macquarrie, *Principles of Christian Theology,* 2nd ed. (New York: Scribner's, 1977), pp. 126–34.

33. Aquinas, *On the Truth of the Catholic Faith,* p. 96.

34. Ibid., pp. 138–39.

35. Ludwig Wittgenstein, *Tractatus Logico-Philosophicus,* trans. by D.F. Pears and B.F. McGuinness (London: Routledge & Kegan Paul, 1966), 6:522.

36. Sten H. Stenson, *Sense and Nonsense in Religion* (Nashville, Tenn.: Abingdon Press, 1969), p. 162.

37. *The Christian Century* (Nov. 28, 1934), p. 1520.

38. John Wisdom, "Gods," in John Harrington, ed., *Issues in Christian Thought* (New York: McGraw-Hill, 1968), pp. 313–14.

Chapter Fourteen
Suffering and Death: Two Existential and Theological Breaking Points

I stand near Soberanes Creek, on the knoll over the sea, west of
* the road. I remember*
This is the very place where Arthur Barclay, a priest in revolt,
* proposed three questions to himself:*
First, is there a God and of what nature? Second, whether there's
* anything after we die but worm's meat?*
Third, how should men live? Large time-worn questions no
* doubt; yet he touched his answers, they are not unattainable;*
But presently lost them again in the glimmer of insanity.

Robinson Jeffers
"Theory of Truth"[1]

People in every culture face problems that cannot be resolved in terms of either common sense or scientific knowledge. To be human is to suffer and die and to have one's aspirations and desires subject to failure and frustration. The transitoriness of human life and the uncertainties that plague human ventures confront people with situations, as sociologist Thomas F. O'Dea put it, "in which human knowledge and social forms display a total insufficiency for providing either means of solution or 'mechanisms' for adjustment and acceptance."[2] Religious systems provide a context in which such existential breaking points as suffering and death and the "large time-worn questions" of which Robinson Jeffers's poem speaks are integrated into a larger picture of reality.

The term *breaking point* is used here in two senses. First, it refers to those life situations in which our capacity to say yes to life is threatened. The task of those who suffer is existential—to be lived through—rather than intellectual—to be explained. As Clifford Geertz observed, "the problem of suffering is, paradoxically, not how to avoid suffering, but how to make physical pain, personal loss, worldly defeat, or the helpless contemplation of others' agony something bearable, supportable, something, as we say, sufferable."[3] Second, such existential breaking points as suffering and death create serious intellectual problems for belief. Although religious belief systems provide a context in which life's breaking points are explained or mediated, belief is, paradoxically, also most vulnerable to disbelief at those points. In theistic religions, for example, suffering can turn one to God for the strength to endure, but it also raises the problem of whether undeserved suffering can be reconciled with belief in an all-powerful and absolutely good God.

Previously such ultimate concerns as Who am I? Why am I here? and Where am I going? were raised to distinguish between theological and academic questions. Two related questions are addressed here: Why do we suffer? and Does anything remain? These questions center on suffering, death, and, as Arthur Barclay, the priest in Jeffers's poem, asked, "whether there's anything after we die but worm's meat?" Such questions and the existential situations from which they arise pose acute difficulties for belief in ultimacy.

Why Must We Suffer?

I want to be there when everyone suddenly understands what it has all been for. All the religions of the world are built on this longing . . .

Fyodor Dostoevsky
The Brothers Karamazov[4]

Suffering is a common feature of existence. Sickness, hunger, the infirmities of old age, and other physical disabilities are painful. Fear of death is a cause of sorrow, as is its opposite, the longing for death. Frustrated desire is a form of suffering, as are grief, loneliness, anxiety, and despair. In addition to maladies inherent in human existence are those that issue from doing harm to others. Existence is so arranged that even when one tries, it is difficult to avoid injuring someone or something. Tarrou says in Albert Camus's novel *The Plague,* "We can't stir a finger in this world without the risk of bringing death to somebody."[5] For those whose reverence for life extends to all living things, even the most sensitive and pacifistic people daily injure living things. Our plague is that we are victim and executioner, the one who suffers and the agent of suffering. Tarrou tells his friend Dr. Rieux, "I have learned that we all have the plague, and I have lost my peace."[6]

Suffering is not just physical pain and mental anguish. It is an awareness that conditions are not as we would have them be—that suffering is contrary to what we desire, intend, or will for ourselves. The one who suffers sees the world as unsatisfactory. This judgment stems not merely from the pain but from a recognition of the existential and intellectual dilemmas of human existence. We seek certainty and must settle for that which is useful and probable. God, the book of Ecclesiastes says, has put eternity in our minds so that we ask Why? of the universe, yet our finitude makes certainty about the ultimate nature of things unobtainable. In addition, we are all victims, to a greater or lesser degree and frequency, of injustice and in such situations are painfully conscious of the gap between what ought to be and what is.

The imperfect character of existence is what Buddhists call *dukkha,* or suffering, and what Western philosophers and theologians refer to as evil. Imperfection, suffering, injustice, and moral wrongdoing is what is meant by evil. *Dukkha* results from natural causes that originate independent of human action, such as earthquakes, floods, droughts, and disease, and from human actions, including the suffering that issues from ignorance and that which comes from moral evil. Suffering is a breaking point for faith because it can crush the human spirit and jeopardize the very possibility of belief. Since religious belief systems provide an ultimate frame of reference through which human experience is made meaningful, they cannot be content merely to accept the fact of suffering without also seeking to understand its causes and to provide a yoga of deliverance through which suffering can be transcended.

We can get a sense of the problem of suffering through a comparative study of two religions in which it is a primary concern: Buddhism and Christianity. In probing Buddhist and Christian views of suffering, two questions that reflect their different conceptions are raised. Christians ask why humans must suffer and die, while Buddhists ask how liberation from *dukkha* is possible. The question of the Psalmist, "Why O Lord?" wells up through the pain and frustration that theists experience. It is a cry to the Lord of Creation for understanding. In a universe created by an all-powerful and benevolent deity, suffering must have a purpose, must have a meaning. "Teach me and I will be silent, make me understand how I have erred,"[7] Job asks of his companions and of God. Because, in the Buddhist tradition, *dukkha* is intrinsic to the structure of reality and not something willed by a creator-God, the interrogative shifts from the why of the theist, with its

William Blake, Let the Day Perish Wherein I Was Born. *(detail) The woodcut depicts Job at the point at which he is overcome by suffering and grief.*

National Gallery of Art, Washington, D.C., Rosenwald Collection

presumption of divine purpose, to what and how. From the Buddhist's perspective, speculation about the why of *dukkha* is foolish and unprofitable; it is more to the point to ask what causes it and how it can be eliminated.

A Buddhist View of Suffering

Humans ask Why? of the universe. J.B., the protagonist in Archibald MacLeish's play, says, in trying to make sense out of his grief, "What I can't bear is the blindness. If I knew why."[8] We are stalkers of meaning but perhaps, as the Buddha argued centuries ago, humans are misguided in asking Why? of the cosmos. Such a question presumes that the power in the universe is a personal being who is somehow responsible or at least aware of the purpose of suffering. Novelist Kurt Vonnegut, Jr., playfully makes a similar point in a dialogue that he imagines transpiring between God and Adam:

> *Man blinked. "What is the purpose of all this?" he asked politely.*
> *"Everything must have a purpose?" asked God.*
> *"Certainly," said man.*
> *"Then I leave it to you to think of one for all this," said God.*
> *And he went away.*[9]

In the Buddha's view, many of the questions that preoccupy human beings resolve nothing and actually create further suffering. For example, by implying that an eternal self exists, the perennial concerns of Who am I? Why am I here? and Where am I going? may cause one to misconstrue the nature of personal identity and may lead to such illusory pursuits as seeking to know whether one has or has not existed previously and whether one will or will not survive beyond this life. Such reflections do not, in the Buddha's reckoning, contribute to liberation from *dukkha*. In contrast to such speculation, the Buddha's teaching is a response to four very basic concerns: *dukkha*, its causes, its cessation, and the path leading to its cessation.

Dukkha

The truth with which Buddhism begins is the universality of suffering. The Buddha taught that all is ill or unsatisfactory. Besides the obvious and natural afflictions to which flesh is heir (disease, old age, death), there is the misery that results from immoral thoughts and actions, which range from the overt and intentional doing of harm to that which is concealed and unintended. In addition to natural and moral *dukkha*, all is ill because life is transitory. Whatsoever is impermanent, what arises and passes away, negates the possibility of permanent happiness.

The Buddha recognized that it is difficult to assimilate the fact that *dukkha* is a universal quality of existence. Awareness that things are not as they should be is often a transitory mood that disappears with the alleviation of pain and suffering, rather than a conviction that existence itself is inherently unsatisfactory. The positive aspects of existence allow us to mitigate and obscure what is unpleasant. In *The Plague,* Rambert, a youthful journalist, visits the city of Oran just as an epidemic of the plague breaks out. Quarantined in a city in which he is a stranger, Rambert tries desperately to secure an official permit to leave. "I don't belong here!" he protests.[10] Good fortune, a healthy body, and earthly delights may enable us to act, like Rambert, as if pain is something we have accidently stumbled upon and can escape. However, there comes a time for us, as it did for Rambert, when we realize that suffering or evil is not a superficial characteristic of existence. The Buddha came to such a disquieting realization when his contentment was shattered by an encounter with disease, old age, and death. Deeply troubled by suffering, the Buddha-to-be left the security of his family to discover the causes of suffering and the ways it can be overcome.

The Causes of Dukkha

From the fact of *dukkha*, the Buddha moved to an analysis of its causes. Insatiable desire or craving, which has its origin in illusory conceptions or ignorance, gives rise to suffering. Existence, in the Buddha's metaphor, is "burning with the fire of lust, with the fire of hate, with the fire of delusion."[11] Craving is reflected in a thirst for and an attachment to fame, fortune, novelty, power, ideals, beliefs, causes, pleasures of the body, and even to those who are loved. Desire is rooted in greed, in selfishness. Accordingly, writes Buddhist scholar Walpola Rahula, "all the troubles and strife in the world, from little personal quarrels in families to great wars between nations and countries arise out of this selfish 'thirst.' "[12]

Liberation from Dukkha

In the Buddhist perspective, the causes of *dukkha,* burning desire and ignorance, are overcome by cultivation of dispassionate detachment and by the wisdom that comes from an understanding of things as they ultimately are. The process in which ignorance is replaced with understanding and craving with nonattachment is known as the Noble Eightfold Path. The Eightfold Path shuns moral corruptions of speech (lying, rudeness, gossip) and promotes personal and social well-being through abstention from stealing, illicit sex, and the destruction of life. As a mental as well as moral discipline, Buddhism calls for an unbending effort to develop wholesomeness of mind through meditative exercises that stress close attention to the activities of mind and body and that intensify the powers of concentration. Mindfulness and concentration can culminate in a meditative state in which the mind is emptied of all content and is no longer aware of subject and object, good and evil, joy and sorrow. Those who understand the truth of *dukkha,* who follow and keep the Noble Eightfold Path can, in the cultivation of nonattachment, eliminate craving and realize nirvana. Nirvana is the Buddhist term for the cessation of suffering and the extinction of desire and illusion. In the ultimate, the absolute, *dukkha* is extinguished, the cycle of reincarnation is exhausted, and nothing remains to be done.

Nonattachment as a Theological Breaking Point

Just as there are philosophical objections to belief in the God of monotheism, there are intellectual dilemmas or breaking points in Buddhism. Nirvana and nonattachment are two such points. Since objections to the idea of nirvana were discussed in conjunction with the arguments against the existence of God, only a criticism of nonattachment is discussed here. Buddhism teaches that the overcoming of suffering is possible through nonattachment. In the *Dhammapada,* Buddha likened nonattachment to the severing of all ties. In another context, the liberated monk is said to neither love nor hate.

Critics of Buddhism have argued that in advocating the ideal of nonattachment, Buddhism embraces apathy as a way of responding to the world. Thus the severing of all ties is a way of mitigating psychic wounds by disengaging from emotional involvement. Nonattachment is equated with indifference. It is a justification for inaction that, in counseling the acceptance of things as they are, acquiesces to oppressive and potentially remediable social conditions.

*Daibatsu Buddha,
Kamakura, Japan. A
monumental Buddha
seated in meditation.*

Photo: Frederic Lewis

Buddhists have responded to such criticism by insisting that nonattachment should not be confused with apathy. The desire to have and to hold is a glorification of the ego that mistakenly places personal existence at the center of being. Before unbridled thirst can be overcome, the individual must learn that life cannot be controlled by acts of will. Human life is transitory, and, no matter how securely we spin our webs of possession, the outcome is unpredictable. We cannot, for example, insure that those we love will return our affection. Mature caring recognizes that when we are possessive and manipulative, we almost invariably drive those we love away from us; thus possessive love leads to sorrow. In contrast, Buddhist nonattachment is more a letting-be, a nonpossessive involvement that is compassionate, flexible, and caring. Nonattachment allows those who are loved to have room to fashion their own way of being and to work out their own salvation. When Buddhist nonattachment is understood as nonpossessiveness, it is not unlike the Christian conception of love. John Macquarrie writes, "The essence of love is precisely letting-be, and for this reason love has become, not only in Christianity but in other religions besides, the supreme symbol of divine Being."[13]

Further evidence that those who are liberated from *dukkha* are neither apathetic nor indifferent is evident in the Buddhist recognition that the annihilation of suffering does not eliminate pain or preclude the possibility of enduring pain for the well-being of others. Enlightened ones, Buddhas, experience physical pain and death. What they have destroyed is the anguish that stems from the desire to exist in a world in which self-gratification is assumed to be the highest good. Pain that results from a genuine caring rather than a masochistic thirst is honored by Buddhists. The Buddha is the compassionate one who taught those who follow the Buddhist path to cultivate love without limit toward all existence. In the *Dhammapada*, Buddha teaches his followers to "conquer anger by love, evil by good; conquer the miser with liberality, and the liar with truth."[14] A tradition with such a concerned founder would naturally gravitate to what is known as the Bodhisattva ideal—namely, the approval and veneration of those Buddhas who have embraced and endured pain out of a compassionate regard for others. The Buddhist willingness to serve and even suffer for others leads naturally to a consideration of the Christian concept of redemptive suffering and of Christ, the man for others.

A Christian View of Suffering

In attacking the problem of suffering, Buddhism begins with the fact of *dukkha,* diagnoses its causes, and prescribes an antidote. The problem and its resolution is entirely a human matter. In Christianity the difficulty that suffering poses for the human spirit leads from the existential character of human affliction to God, the Lord of Creation. Theodicy, the difficulty of reconciling the existence of evil with belief in a God who is all-powerful, all-knowing, and absolutely good, has been from ancient times the most imposing problem that Christians and other monotheists face. The dilemma or breaking point that theodicy raises for theism is stated quite succinctly by John Hick: "If God is perfectly good, He must want to abolish evil; if He is unlimitedly powerful, He must be able to abolish all evil: but evil exists; therefore either God is not perfectly good or He is not unlimitedly powerful."[15]

Christian Views on the Genesis of Evil

While there is no single Christian explanation of the origin of evil, the dominant Christian perspective has attempted to absolve God of the responsibility for evil by insisting that Adam and Eve were responsible for the loss of paradise. In this interpretation, suffering and death are the consequence of sin—that is, of human being's willful turning from God. Essential to the argument that makes human beings rather than God culpable for the origin of evil is the belief that God created us free. In choosing to disobey God, Adam and Eve forfeited their place in the Garden of Eden not only for themselves, but for all human beings. The result of this original sin is that suffering, death, and a will that corrupts the goodness of God's creation are universal features of fallen existence.

In a more cosmic version of the Fall, the sin of Adam and Eve was preceded by a heavenly rebellion in which angels led by Satan revolted against God and his loyal subjects. Cast from his heavenly abode, Satan, in the form of a serpent, tempted Adam and Eve to sin. In one apocalyptic interpretation of this myth, the present age is so under the dominion of Satan that it is no longer redeemable. Seen in this light, there is an answer to the prophet Jeremiah's perplexing question, "Why does the way of the wicked prosper? Why do all who are treacherous thrive?"[16] In this view, the righteous suffer because Satan and his dominions have corrupted God's creation. The apocalyptic message is that God hears the cries of the righteous and will one day break Satan's rule. When that day comes, suffering, death, and all that is evil will be overcome and God will establish "a new heaven and a new earth."[17]

The Meaning of Suffering in Christian Theology

While Christian theology has explained the origin of evil by insisting that it is the consequence of a misuse by human beings and angels of their God-given freedom, the intellectual dilemma that suffering poses for Christian theism is not resolved by such an explanation. Although evil originates in a willful corruption of God's creation, if God is all-powerful he must at least permit evil to exist; thus, the question arises as to the purpose and meaning of suffering in a world created by an absolutely good God. Traditionally, Christians and other monotheists have responded to this question in several ways. Suffering has been seen as punishment for sin, as a test of faith, and as a teacher.

The contention that suffering is punishment for sin is one of the ways in which the theist has reconciled belief in the justness of God with the unsatisfactory character of human existence. It is the explanation that Job's friends (Eliphaz, Bildad, and Zophar) used to rationalize Job's misfortunes. Job's companions believed that God is just, that he neither perverts justice nor allows the innocent to perish. And if God is just, then undeserved suffering is unthinkable. Job's three friends believed that in a just world the good are rewarded by good and the evil by evil; thus Job's suffering was evidence of his guilt. Convinced that his suffering was undeserved, Job rejected the assessment of his comforters as inadequate to account for those life situations in which the wicked prosper and the blameless suffer.

Christian theology has attempted to resolve the problem of Job and his comforters—that is, the problem of reconciling God's justice with the suffering of the righteous—by insisting that none are innocent, save God. J.B. exclaims in MacLeish's play, "We have no choice but to be guilty. God is unthinkable if we are innocent."[18] Humans are the creatures who, in desiring to be God, have corrupted human existence and, even if the Fall was facilitated by Satan's lies, they are responsible for evil. And yet, Christian theology has never stopped at a concept of divine justice that is entirely punitive. The heart of Christian faith lies in the message that the unity of God and humankind that existed in the Garden is again possible for those who have faith, because Christ atoned for the sin of the primeval couple and redeemed those who believe in him. The good news is that salvation and the forgiveness of sin is possible. The ancient crime of Adam and Eve, which is somehow that of all people, is remediable. Suffering is punishment for sin, but it also serves a larger redemptive purpose. St. Augustine believed that "God judged it better to bring good out of evil than to suffer no evil to exist."[19] Thus, suffering is part of God's plan of salvation not only in the person of Christ, who is the perfect sacrifice and redeemer, but in the sense that God is working to bring good out of human suffering.

Some Christians also believe that suffering is a test of faith. God, in this view, seeks spiritual athletes. Straight is the way and narrow is the gate that leads to God's heavenly kingdom. Suffering is God's instrument for culling out the spiritually flabby. While the notion that suffering is a test of faithfulness often surfaces when Christians talk about the purposes of suffering, it is vulnerable to serious objections. For instance, squaring such a view with Jesus' love and compassion for sinners is almost impossible. In fact, many of Jesus' parables reverse the expectations of conventional piety as to who will enter the Kingdom of God. A second objection follows from the problem of reconciling God's goodness and power with evil. If God knows in advance how his tests will turn out, then he must be aware of those conditions in which suffering is so devastating and overwhelming that it is impossible to even speak sensibly of passing such tests. If God is good, he does not want his creatures to be so afflicted, and if he is omnipotent, he is capable of abolishing conditions that make a mockery of the concept of suffering as a test. How, for example, can the Nazi's execution of millions of Jews be justified either as a test of faith or as a punishment for sin?

Although many Christians reject the idea that God countenances suffering in order to test faith, they often affirm that suffering is a teacher. In this view, suffering is redemptive when it turns a person to God. Sometimes material and physical well-being produces a feeling of self-sufficiency that edges God out of one's life altogether, but desperation has a way of forcing people to reach out for a supportive community and a caring cosmos. As a teacher, suffering can help people to see God—that is, to see what was already there, which self-sufficiency obscured. It can also make us more sensitive and compassionate to the frustration and sorrow of our fellow human beings. Suffering thus can teach us to love God and to love others.

Suffering teaches—that is, it is somehow in the nature of things that wisdom comes from suffering. Buddhists and Christians can agree with this conclusion; however, the Buddhist does not concur that suffering is compatible with faith in the God of theism. The pain and anguish of existence was for the Buddha, as it is for many nontheists, an insurmountable stumbling block to belief in the existence of a God who is unlimited in power and goodness. Suffering, Dr. Rieux says in *The Plague,* taught him that God does not exist.[20] For Christians and other monotheists, human suffering presses beyond the questions of its origin and meaning to whether the existence of evil can be reconciled with belief in God.

Theodicy as a Theological Breaking Point

The question, Does God exist? has been raised in another context. Here the question shifts from arguments that infer God's existence from the evidence of nature to theodicy—that is, the problem of whether the existence of suffering and evil makes belief in an absolutely good and powerful God virtually impossible to defend rationally. As noted in the preceding section, the traditional answer of Christian theism has been to defend God's innocence and goodness by finding humans guilty. "What is man's crime?" Camus asks in *The Plague;*[21] Christian theologians have argued that our misuse of our God-given freedom is the primal crime. God did not originally intend that we suffer and die; suffering is punishment for sin, for choosing wrongly.

In spite of the argument that suffering is a consequence of a corruption of human freedom, Christian theology has not been successful in shifting the burden of responsibility for the origin of evil and suffering from God to humans. If God created the cosmos from nothing, as Christian theology affirms, then it follows that, from its inception, creation contained the possibility of evil. And if God knew in advance what would transpire in the Garden of Eden and was powerful enough to have created an obedient Adam and Eve, then he not only permitted their rebellion but is the ultimate cause of evil since it stems from the very nature of his creation.

In the 1950s, Antony Flew shifted the philosophical objections of the logical empiricists from the statement, God exists, which they argued was neither a necessary truth nor an empirically verifiable one, to the meaningfulness of the statement, God loves us as a father loves his children. In an essay entitled "Theology and Falsification," Flew asked theists what would have to occur for them to say morally and logically that "God does not love us or even God does not exist?"[22] For many Jews, it was the Holocaust, an evil so excessive and undeserved that it could not be rationalized, that opened their eyes to a world without God. Should God be praised because he permitted thousands to be burned in Nazi death camps? In the light of the Holocaust, what can it possibly mean to say that God loves us, that God is merciful?

If, because of the sheer number of victims, the evil of the Holocaust is impossible to comprehend, then what of the suffering of a single child? In Dostoevsky's novel, Ivan Karamazov says, "I meant to speak of the suffering of mankind generally but we had better confine ourselves to the sufferings of the children."[23] Ivan continues his plunge into the problem of theodicy by speaking of the senseless and undeserved brutalizing of a child. It is, of course, a daily occurrence. A 1978 news item, for example, reported that a two-year-old died from injuries resulting from rape. Can such suffering be deserved? What can it possibly teach? In *The Brothers Karamazov,* Ivan asks his brother Aloysha to imagine that he was "creating a fabric of human destiny with the object of making men happy in the end." If in achieving such a worthy goal, Ivan continued, " 'it was essential and inevitable to torture to death only one tiny creature . . . would you consent to be the architect on those conditions? Tell me, and tell the truth.' 'No, I wouldn't consent,' said Aloysha softly."[24]

Like Dostoevsky, philosopher Antony Flew takes up the suffering of children in order to discredit the claim that humans are loved by God. Flew writes of a child dying of cancer and contrasts the frantic effort of the child's earthly father to help, with the lack of a sign of concern from the child's heavenly father. He concludes that the belief that God loves us as a parent loves his or her children has been and continues to be repeatedly falsified by the suffering and evil that innocent victims endure.[25]

Can Christian theism survive such devastating objections? Is the claim that God is love compatible with whatever may happen, no matter how gross or barbarous? The response that evil is punishment for sin appears, in the light of those human situations in which suffering is excessive or undeserved, to be an indefensible effort to preserve God's innocence. While continuing to argue that all humans are in some basic way sinful, Christian theology, in insisting that God brings good out of evil, has not been content with the formula that suffering is evidence of sin.

Theologian John Hick has articulated what he believes is a more rationally defensible Christian theodicy. It is a theodicy that Hick traces back in the early church to Irenaeus (c. 130–c. 202), Bishop of Lyons, and more recently to the work of Protestant theologian Friedrich Schleiermacher (1768–1834). Hick argues that the dominant Christian theodicy, which stems from St. Paul and St. Augustine, is based on a misconception of the purpose of God's creation. In creating humans in his image, Hick asks, did God aim at the creation of happy beings or moral ones? If God's ultimate purpose is the happiness of his creatures, then an idyllic Garden of Eden is the rational consequence, and man's fall from grace is the ultimate evil. However, if God intended to create moral beings—that is, men and women who are free to choose to turn to or from God, and who must, in an autonomous pilgrimage of the spirit, work out the implications of being created in God's likeness—then perhaps a world in which suffering and evil are illuminated by their opposites, is best suited to such a divine purpose.[26] If life is a process through which we take on the likeness of Christ, then happiness is not the ultimate good and suffering is not the ultimate evil. The Irenaean theodicy that Hick defends does not eliminate the problem of reconciling the existence of evil with a God of love, but it does offer a more intelligible way of understanding how God allows evil to exist in order to bring good out of it.

More than any carefully reasoned theodicy, it is the figure of Jesus the Christ, the God-man who suffered and died that humans might know resurrected life, that enables Christians to endure and transcend suffering. At the heart of the Christian message is a God who identifies himself so thoroughly with his creatures that he takes flesh in Christ and suffers as we do. The seated Buddha is an image of one who is happy, serene, compassionate, and undisturbed by woe or passion. Counter to this image is that of the crucified one, the man of sorrows who is acquainted with grief and despair, a figure of a God who loves his creatures so much that he makes their fate his own. In one of Dorothy Sayers's plays, one of the magi describes what it means for him to believe that God is not indifferent, that God also suffers:

> *I do not mind being ignorant and unhappy—*
> *All I ask is the assurance that I am not alone,*
> *Some courage, some comfort against this burden of fear and pain.*
>
> *. . .*
>
> *If He is beside me, bearing the weight of His own creation,*
> *If I may hear His voice among the voices of the vanquished,*
> *If I may feel His hand touch mine in the darkness,*
> *If I may look upon the hidden face of God*
> *And read in the eyes of God*
> *That He is acquainted with grief.[27]*

Does Anything Remain?

I don't know why it is, but it doesn't seem to me that I shall ever cease to live on earth. I can't imagine with the farthest stretch of my imagination my own death scene.

Emily Dickinson[28]

This Me—that walks and works—must die,
Some fair or stormy day.

Emily Dickinson[29]

Like suffering, death is an existential and theological breaking point that religious belief systems attempt to provide a way of understanding and accepting. The question this section addresses, Does anything remain? begins with the problem that death raises for human existence and concludes with those religious beliefs that see death as a liminal stage leading to another way of being.

Death is difficult to speak of. Like religion and politics, it is a subject in poor taste. Usually we do all we can either to avoid mentioning it altogether or, if unavoidable, to disguise it. Death can be set aside by refusing to think about it and by attending to the rewards and routines of living. In youth we are often so intoxicated by life's power that death retreats before youth's seeming immortality, and in life's mid-passage, a heavy round of routine seems to shield us from it. And perchance if death cannot be avoided, its finality can be disguised. Dead pets are but asleep; deceased friends have either passed away or been taken from us, much like those who have changed residence or been unavoidably detained. Frequently it is debated whether the terminally ill should be told of their condition. Hospitals, homes for the aged, and funeral homes screen dying and death from us. And if we do come in direct contact with death, we may do all we can to deny it. If, for example, six persons are chosen for a dangerous mission from which only one or two are likely to survive, something in each of them allows them to believe that it is he or she who will safely return. Likewise, if a friend or family member is dying, we may avoid talking about it with them and even remark how well they look and assure them that they will soon be as good as new. We are gratified that the corpse of a loved one looks so natural, so lifelike. And, like the character in Leo Tolstoy's novel *The Death of Ivan Ilych,* who comes to pay his last respects to the deceased and his family, we say, if only unconsciously, "It is he who is dead and not I."[30]

The human need to repress an awareness of the precariousness of human existence, Buddha suggested in a parable, is like the man who was pursued by a tiger. The man's flight brought him to a cliff, where his life was spared by swinging over the cliff's edge on a vine. Sustained only by the vine, the frightened man looked below for an avenue of escape, only to be greeted by still another tiger waiting to eat him. Two mice began gnawing away on the vine, but the man's attention was drawn away from the certain death that surrounded him by a luscious strawberry he saw near by. "Grasping the vine with one hand, he plucked the strawberry with the other. How sweet it tasted!"[31]

Death in the abstract is not unacceptable. We know, at least intellectually, that all people die and, like Ivan Ilych, we may never have had trouble accepting it. In his logic lessons, Ivan Ilych had learned the syllogism, "Caius is a man, men are mortal, therefore Caius is mortal"; the reasonableness of it "had always seemed to him correct as it applied to Caius, but certainly not as it applied to himself."[32] Similarly, it is our own death that seems unfair and incomprehensible. The English poet and preacher, John Donne, wrote of a monastery bell that was tolled when any of the house was sick to death. The ringing of the bell always set the people to wondering who was dying. There comes a time, however, when death is so real that we can no longer deceive ourselves into believing that the ringing of the bell is only for Caius. "And therefore never send to know for whom the *bell* tolls; it tolls for *thee*."[33]

Since dying is inescapably personal, something no one else can do for you, why not think about your death. Do you ever wonder how one goes about dying? You can take swimming lessons and learn to correct mistakes and perfect your strokes. But death is not something we live through and can do over again. What lessons are there for dying? Nietzsche's Zarathustra taught that we should "die at the right time!" but most of us seem to die either too late or too early.[34] I am anxious, even a little afraid of dying. Are you? Imagine you have but six months to live. What would you do with your death, with your life? How would you say goodbye?

Death as the Fear of Nothingness

The fear of death is at root a fear of nonbeing, of nothingness. We are not timeless, and death is the mark of our finitude and powerlessness; thus our fear of death is an anxiety about the end and the possibility that life ends in nothingness. This anxiety, this fear of thanatos, belongs to human existence and is therefore neither necessarily neurotic nor abnormal.

Fear of death is often expressed in feelings of rejection, resentment, and rage. For several years, the work of Dr. Elisabeth Kubler-Ross, as psychiatrist and doctor, has been with those who are dying. In listening to them, she has identified some of the stages that dying patients usually go through. When patients are told that they are terminally ill, their initial reaction is usually one of denying or rejecting such a verdict. Kubler-Ross calls it the "no-not-me" stage.[35] In this stage, the patient goes from physician to physician seeking a more favorable prognosis. The rejection of nonbeing is so powerful that some moderns hope, even demand, that a technological breakthrough will defeat death through a feat of medical engineering. They see death's sting as an unacceptable injustice that can be rejected and overcome through science and technology.

Rejection is followed by rage and resentment, or what Kubler-Ross calls the "why me?" stage.[36] If all human inventiveness ends as worm's meat and fertilizer, then what does life mean? In the "why me?" stage, the afflicted person's anger is directed at God and at all those whose health is only a reaffirmation of his or her affliction. The fear of death that haunts us and makes us avert our eyes from the dying is reciprocated by the dying person's anger at a world in which God appears to be absent and in which the healthy can be so cruel. In the "why me?" stage, the rage of the terminally ill is symptomatic of their powerlessness. The stage of rejection and rage is sometimes followed by one of resignation. Resignation is not the same as acceptance or liberation. It is neither a peaceful acceptance nor a liberating letting-go of our fear of nothingness. Resignation is recognition that nothing can be done, that death is inevitable.

Death, Acceptance, and Liberation

To be religious involves not only a way of living but a way of dying. The practice of philosophy, Socrates taught, is a preparation for dying. Zen also is a preparation for dying. A young physician once asked his friend what Zen was. His friend replied, "I cannot tell you what it is but one thing is certain. If you understand Zen, you will not be afraid to die."[37] The courage to live requires the courage to face nonbeing.

The Gilgamesh epic, a story from ancient Sumer, raises some of the deepest questions about life and death and illustrates the stages of rejection, rage, and acceptance. In the beginning of the epic poem, Gilgamesh, the King of Uruk, was carefree and extroverted. He had not yet looked at death—that is, he knew of death only intellectually. Though he was king, or perhaps because he was king, Gilgamesh felt alone and longed for companionship. In Enkidu, a wild, shaggy-haired man from the steppes, Gilgamesh found a friend who filled his loneliness. After many adventures and great deeds, including the slaying of a monster, the brash insulting of the goddess Ishtar, and the killing of the Bull of Heaven valued by the gods, the death of Gilgamesh or Enkidu was demanded by the heavenly council. When Enkidu fell ill, Gilgamesh sought desperately to save his friend's life. In anguish, Gilgamesh cried out for help and knew tears for the first time. But Enkidu perceived that he was to die and that Gilgamesh would be left alone in a world where, in the loss of the beloved, nothing seems to live.

When Enkidu died, Gilgamesh initially refused to accept his death and insisted that he was only asleep. In a desperate act of rejection,

Gilgamesh dressed Enkidu like a bride, but it was no use. Enkidu was dead. Alone in the desert of his heart, Gilgamesh's sorrow turned him inward. Fearing death, he fled to the desert. There on the steppes, dressed in animal skin and with long unkempt hair, Gilgamesh began a pilgrimage in quest of immortality. His travels led him to Utnapishtim, the one who had survived the flood and death itself, and who knew the secret of everlasting life. Utnapishtim told him that immortality is for the gods alone, and that to be human is to die. Gilgamesh's quest for immortality, his desire to conquer death, ended in his courageous acceptance of mortality; thus he resolutely returned to Uruk, put on the garments of civilization, and accepted mortal life.

If the bell tolls for each of us, then little is to be gained and perhaps much to be lost by not facing death more directly. If religion is entwined with the telling of stories, then death is that which brings our stories, as we know them, to an end. Our concreteness becomes a memory and our artifacts but a trace of our being. And yet death is more than an unperceivable limit we cannot reach beyond, because death influences life in profound ways. In fact, the acceptance of death is the first step in facing life.

Our mortality gives life its urgency. Because life is transitory, the preciousness of the moment comes into focus, and we are able to say with Albert Camus, "If I still feel a grain of anxiety, it is at the thought of this unseizable moment slipping through my fingers like a ball of quicksilver."[38] Tolstoy's story of Ivan Ilych is a story not only of Ilych's agonizing end, but one of how Ilych, in insulating his life from the reality of death, never appreciated the gift of life. As the end drew near, Ilych saw that his life was "a terrible and huge deception which had hidden both life and death."[39] He had squandered his life and now it was too late. Consciousness of death can strip us to the bare essentials so that what matters most stands out in bold relief. In *Zorba the Greek,* Zorba met a ninety-year-old man who was busy planting an olive tree. In explaining why, at his age, he was planting such a slow-growing tree, the old man said, "My son, I carry on as if I should never die!" And Zorba, finding holiness in the moment rather than in timelessness, replied, " 'And I carry on as if I was going to die any minute.' "[40]

Liberation comes, the Buddha taught, only when we are able to let go of all that we have seized and would possess. We can be so consumed by our desire to hold on to life that we fail to live. We settle for quantity rather than quality. Graceful living, transfigured life, is not calculated in years but in a way of being. From a religious perspective, when we lose ourselves in living, in Holy Being, or as a Buddhist might prefer in No-Thing, we are freed from the tyranny of life and death. Shoun, a Soto Zen master, told his disciples that he was going to die at noon, and for the occasion he wrote this poem:

For fifty-six years I lived as best I could,
Making my way in this world.
Now the rain has ended, the clouds are clearing,
The blue sky has a full moon.[41]

Death is natural, inevitable and, for those like Shoun who accept it, even joyful and peaceful.

Life beyond Death

Life after death is one of the most ancient and persistent hopes of humankind, yet it is such an uncharted country that belief in immortality may be a testimony to the power of wishful thinking. Is death a threshold to be crossed over, a door that leads to other worlds, or is it a door that brings our world to its end? Ludwig Wittgenstein wrote that "at death the world does not alter, but comes to an end. Death is not an event of life."[42] Death is, he believed, the limit beyond which there is no world, and since our death is not an event in our life, like a birthday celebration, we do not experience our own death.

In spite of the ambiguities and uncertainties of life after death, the feeling persists that something survives beyond our world. Perhaps this is so because the fear of nothingness, of our powerlessness before death is so fundamental. Woody Allen, whose humor is so obsessed with death and immortality, puts it this way: "Eternal nothingness is O.K. if you're dressed for it."[43] The problem, of course, is that most of us are not ready for it and, in spite of our doubts about survival after death, find ourselves wanting to believe. Allen tells us, "I don't want to achieve immortality through my work, I want to achieve it through not dying."[44] Part of the appeal of Allen's dark humor is the manner in which his jokes juxtapose our doubts and our hopes of immortality: "I do not believe in an afterlife, although I am bringing a change of underwear."[45]

In the *Symposium,* Plato argued that much of what humans do is prompted by a love or desire for immortality—that is, that which is eternally Good, True, and Beautiful. In his view, even human procreation and the quest for fame are motivated by a longing for the eternal. The religious consciousness has generally agreed with Plato and insisted that, in spite of the transitoriness of human existence, something does remain, something does survive the sting of death. John S. Dunne, a contemporary theologian, writes, "Death itself is one of the adventures of the spirit, a voyage with the unknown into the unknown, a voyage with the unknown God and to the unknown God."[46] Death is, in Dunne's view, something lived through, an event of life that we do experience.

Although life after death is an unknown and uncharted country, people have an almost bewildering number of beliefs about it. They speculate about whether such an existence is personal or impersonal. They disagree about whether what survives is repeatedly reborn or whether each individual lives only once, and whether there are many worlds or only two, this world and the next. And they question whether what survives is material or immaterial. While no exhaustive treatment of these problems is possible, some of the options will be examined.

Belief in the Survival of Individuality

The belief that something personal survives death is found in many religions. In India's oldest scripture, the Rigveda, humans aspired for a long and full life here on earth followed by a heavenly existence in fellowship with the gods. They believed that the cremation fire of the death rites carried the soul to its heavenly bliss where it survived without end. In classical Hinduism this view of survival was gradually replaced by that of **reincarnation**—that is, the transmigration of souls from one body to another. In reincarnation the eternal soul may go through multiple transmigrations in which it repeats the cycle of birth to death, only to be reborn.

The Katzie Indians of British Columbia believe that at death the body perishes and the soul returns to He Who Dwells Above. The Katzie also believe that other elements of personal existence survive. In their view, each person has a vitality that pervades the whole body and which at death merges with their reflection to produce an invisible shade or ghost that roams their homeland. Such shades are feared by surviving relatives. While the Katzie do not embrace reincarnation for all, they believe that unstinting mourning of a dead relative might move the divine to return a soul in the body of a newborn.[47]

Religions that stress God's transcendence often affirm the survival of personal being. Certainly this is true of Christianity and Islam and, to a lesser degree, of Judaism. We should note, however, that belief in personal immortality is not always a feature of religions of transcendence. For example, the Sadducees, an important Jewish party in the days of Jesus, rejected belief in the survival of the individual because such a belief was not evident in the books of Moses. In its most popular form, the survival of individual existence has been associated with heaven and hell. Individuals have been visualized as dwelling in God's celestial kingdom from everlasting to everlasting, or, as Dante suggests in his *Inferno,* longing for a second death in hell.

While Christians agree that eternal life is fundamentally personal, they may differ as to whether what survives is an immaterial soul or a resurrected body. From one Christian perspective, the biblical message primarily supports a belief in the **resurrection of the body.** Life everlasting is a miraculous gift of God rather than an automatic function of some spiritual or karmic law. Belief in the resurrection of the body is an expectation that God has promised, in some future act, to raise the whole person to life everlasting. The survival of the whole psychophysical organism provides a basis for identifying and maintaining personal relationships, including friendships and families, in the afterlife. Given this conception, it is not surprising, for example, that Dante, on his descent through the circles of hell and his ascent through purgatory to the celestial city, recognized those who had died. The corporeal and personal nature of the afterlife is even more emphatic in Mormonism, where a baptism of the departed is practiced and where God is believed to have a body. We should note that many Christians, in keeping with St. Paul's letter to the Corinthians, think of the promise of resurrected life as a gift of a spiritual body that, though shed of its worldly limitations, will still be identifiable.

Belief in the **immortality of the soul** offers an alternative model for understanding personal survival. In this conception, which in its Western derivations is indebted to Plato, what survives death is an immaterial soul. In the doctrine of the resurrection of the body, the body, even if it is thought of as a creation of a new order of being, is essential to personal existence; thus to be human in this life or the next is to have a body. In contrast the concept of the immortality of the soul is derived from a dualistic understanding of the nature of human beings. In Plato's philosophy, body and soul are the two primary dimensions of human existence. Since the body is phenomenal and transitory, it perishes. However, Plato argued, the human soul is eternal, uncreated, and indestructible. At death, the soul is liberated from its imprisonment in the body. Although the immortality of the soul and the resurrection of the body are based on two divergent views of human nature, they have sometimes been merged in Christian practice.

In still another Christian perspective, the question of survival after death, with its characteristic desire for an endless prolongation of life, is subordinated to a concern with a way of being. This approach emphasizes the fullness of life, the touch of eternity in time, rather than speculation as to whether what survives is a disembodied soul or a whole person, or whether such artifices of eternity as heaven and hell are places of eternal reward and punishment. In this view, eternal life is life with God. It begins in saying Yes to Holy Being. Hell, like heaven, is less a place of being than a way of being— a choosing to live without God; hell is living without hope or love. "Fathers and teachers, I ponder, 'What is hell?'" Father Zosima asks rhetorically in Fyodor Dostoevsky's *The Brothers Karamazov* and answers, "I maintain that it is the suffering of being unable to love."[48]

The Absence or Rejection of Belief
in Personal Immortality

Belief in the survival of individual existence in an afterlife that is without end is so ingrained in the Christian perspective, that it is often surprising to find that such a view is not universally shared. Because it is not, we should look at some of the religious traditions that either lack or reject belief in personal immortality. In several faiths the hope of eternal life is absent. Certainly the peoples of ancient Mesopotamia, like Gilgamesh, accepted the harsh reality that only the gods are immortal. The Olympian faith of the Greeks shared this view. In the poetry of Homer and Hesiod, Zeus ruled all the immortals while the days of humans were few and filled with trouble. Odysseus, the human hero of Homer's *Iliad,* was an expert in adversity who courageously endured the challenges and troubles that came his way. Man's taste of immortality was in what he did with his life, in his deeds; thus Odysseus, Achilles, and Hector lived in the repetition of their stories. Like the Mesopotamians and the Greeks, the patriarchs and prophets of ancient Israel did not expect to be rewarded or punished in an afterlife. Their faith was centered in the keeping of God's covenant. Obedience to God was believed to be rewarded by a long and fruitful life and by the survival and establishment of God's chosen people.

While the faiths of ancient Mesopotamia, Greece, and Israel lacked a conception of personal immortality, others, particularly in Asia, explicitly reject such a belief. Although Buddhist and Hindu views of what survives death vary considerably, both normally seek liberation from individuality and find personal immortality neither desirable nor defensible. In one Hindu perspective, the human soul or *atman* is an eternal unchanging reality without beginning or end. The soul is of the same nature as Brahman—that is, eternal, perfect Being; thus *atman* is Brahman. Brahman is the underlying basis of the phenomenal world, the world of appearance and change. Human existence is at once part of the wheel of appearance and the unperishable Brahman. The love of life and ignorance of true being keep humans slaves of the world of becoming; thus the soul transmigrates from one body to another and experiences numerous births. The ultimate goal, the Upanishads teach, is liberation from the cycle of reincarnation. Liberation is a release from the particularity of individual existence, with its suffering, pain, and ignorance, through a union with Brahman. As many tributaries flow into the sacred Ganges and become one great river, so also the human soul sheds its separateness, becomes one without a second, in Brahman.

Buddhists are even more emphatic in their repudiation of the survival beyond death of a permanent self or *atman.* In fact, Buddhist dharma or doctrine denies the notion of the existence of a substantial self in this world or any other. Theravada Buddhists believe that *the self* is but a general term for an aggregate of things (sensations, body, conceptions, impulses, consciousness), like the word *college* is a notation for those things associated with a college (books, students, teachers, laboratories). Just as a college does not exist independent of its components, the self has no substantial existence of its own.

Although Buddhists reject the idea of a permanent, unchanging self, they do affirm a belief in rebirth or reincarnation that, of course, raises the problem of what survives. Buddhists and Hindus agree that the chain of becoming and rebirth is governed by karma—that is, the perpetual flux of the phenomenal world is causally determined. What people sow, they reap; thus rebirth is a consequence of what people do. Hateful and injurious acts produce more of the same, while noninjurious and compassionate acts shape and give birth to a noninjurious and compassionate world.

While Buddhist answers to the question of what survives death are subtle and varied, the matter can be illuminated by looking more closely at their understanding of rebirth and nirvana. Buddhists believe in many worlds, multiple heavens and hells, besides this one. Life in these worlds is conditioned by karma. Some acts produce immediate karmic effects, while the effects of other acts take longer to mature and are manifested in subsequent births. Although there is no substantial self that periodically dies and is reborn, a karmic continuity to life connects this life and this world to other lives and other worlds. Karmic causation applies to personal and social existence, not only in this life but in all subsequent rebirths.

Just as the Hindu sage ultimately seeks liberation from the wheel of rebirth, Buddhists believe that the suffering inherent in existence is eliminated in the achievement of nirvana. In one sense, nirvana is the blowing out or extinguishing of phenomenal and personal existence by the cessation of desire. There would be no world of appearances, no alienation, Buddhists teach, if desire and ignorance were overcome. Nirvana is sometimes described as no-thing, but it is not mere nothingness. It is an indescribable Void that cannot be spoken of in the same way that things in the phenomenal world are spoken of; thus it follows that nirvana is ineffable. Nirvana, a way of being in which craving and ignorance is overcome, is possible in this life. When an enlightened one dies, the rebirth and the suffering that is part of existence is ended. Where, then, does an enlightened one go after death, and where is the place of nirvana? To ask these questions, the Buddha taught, is to fall into the trap of applying the categories of ordinary existence to nirvana; thus the Buddha rejected such questions as uninstructive and unprofitable.

Survival after Death

While the human desire for personal survival is a persistent hope, what is the evidence for it? The faithful often quote their scriptures as validation of their belief: So Muhammad believed, so I believe. The empirical evidence is another matter, which depends primarily on investigations of mediums who maintain that they have made contact with those who have passed over from this life to the next, on the testimony of those who claim to have remembered previous lives, and, more recently, on reports of out-of-body experiences.

Several current studies are attempting to provide observable facts and scientific evidence for the survival of personal existence after death. Dr. Raymond A. Moody, in *Life after Life,* compiled several case histories of people who "died," were revived, and who related what is described as an out-of-body experience. It is an experience of leaving one's body while maintaining a consciousness independent of the body. Some individuals even report that in the interim between their "death"—some were actually pronounced dead—and their subsequent revival, they traveled invisibly to other places. Dr. Elisabeth Kubler-Ross's work with the terminally ill has brought her into contact with those who report similar experiences, including a sense of floating outside one's body, a feeling of peace, and a contact with a spiritual guide who facilitates the newly dead one's transition to a different form of being. Moody and Kubler-Ross believe that their work provides evidence of life after death.

Wayne Suttles reported a Katzie story of what must have been an out-of-body experience. After an old man died, his body was wrapped in goat's wool blankets and placed, as was the custom, on a high platform. His widow visited his resting place each day. On the third day, she saw the blankets move and, in terror, she fled to her village. Strengthened in her resolve by accompanying relatives, she returned, only to find that the blankets still moved. After his body had been unwrapped, the old man sat up and asked to be taken home. Secure in his own home, the old man, who was subsequently known as He Who Came Back to Life, spoke of his experiences:

> I shall now tell you what I have seen, so that you may tell other people later. He Who Dwells Above is truly holy; He takes us from this earth, back to Himself. I cannot describe to you how beautiful is the place in which He dwells, for nothing on earth can be compared with it.[49]

In addition to the reports of out-of-body experiences, evidence comes from mediums. From very early times, people have claimed to have made contact with those who have died. The medium serves as a conduit of communication with the souls, or astral bodies, of those who have departed. Communication between this world and the spheres of the departed is often facilitated by séance, table-tapping, and use of the Ouija board. While the opportunity for deception is great, what is puzzling and requires serious consideration is the capacity of some mediums to supply information of an intimate and nonpublic nature about the deceased.

Those who believe in reincarnation are reinforced by those who report recollections of prior lives. Some Buddhists believe in the possibility of remembering past lives, through a kind of recapitulation of one's karmic field by means of meditation. The Buddha, for instance, reported an awareness of previous lives and previous worlds. In more recent times, a number of such reports have occasioned research. In several cases the life that was recollected was fairly recent and occurred in a place that has remained relatively unchanged. When this was the case, a correlation between the remembered life and the historical-geographical scenario was possible. Sometimes the two were remarkably similar. The reincarnationist argues that the transmigration of the soul from one body to another is the most plausible way to account for the similarities.

We should emphasize that stories like that of He Who Came Back to Life and studies like those of Dr. Moody and Dr. Kubler-Ross do not prove that survival after death is a reality; such reports may be hallucinatory and illusory. Perhaps out-of-body experiences are evidence of the mind's unwillingness to accept death and thus are a last desperate effort to pretend that death is not real. Likewise, the sometimes remarkable information that a medium gains from a séance may reflect telepathic mind-reading powers rather than contact with the dead. Although survival after death is becoming an area for scientific research as well as an article of faith, it still remains a mystery.

Concluding Remarks

Religious belief systems provide an ultimate frame of reference through which human existence is given meaning in spite of the fact that we must suffer and die. As existential and theological breaking points, the questions, Why must we suffer? and Does anything remain? are not problems to be solved as one might arrive at a sum of numbers. The reconciliation of evil, for example, with an all-powerful and loving God eludes once-and-for-all solutions. In a sense the religions of the world offer images and paths of deliverance through which suffering and death are not so much explained away as given meaning, not so much simply endured as transcended. If suffering is redemptive, as Christians believe, or is an indispensable prelude to Enlightenment, as the Buddhists recognize, then perhaps it is possible to accept the words of the Katzie god, He Who Dwells Above:

> *You shall have joy in the world, but you shall also have sorrow. Both joy and sorrow are sacred.*[50]

Notes

1. *The Selected Poetry of Robinson Jeffers* (New York: Random House, 1938), p. 615.

2. Thomas O'Dea, *The Sociology of Religion* (Englewood Cliffs, N.J.: Prentice-Hall, 1966), p. 5.

3. Clifford Geertz, "Religion as a Cultural System," in Michael Banton, ed., *Anthropological Approaches to the Study of Religion* (London: Tavistock, 1966), p. 19.

4. Fyodor Dostoevsky, *The Brothers Karamazov,* trans. by Constance Garnett (Chicago: William Benton, 1952), p. 126.

5. Albert Camus, *The Plague* (New York: Modern Library, 1948), p. 228.

6. Ibid.

7. Job 6:24.

8. Archibald MacLeish, *J.B.* (Boston: Houghton Mifflin, 1958), p. 108.

9. Kurt Vonnegut, Jr., *Cat's Cradle* (New York: Dell, 1965), p. 177.

10. Camus, *The Plague,* pp. 77–79.

11. Walpola Rahula, *What the Buddha Taught* (New York: Grove Press, 1974), p. 95.

12. Ibid., p. 30.

13. John Macquarrie, *Principles of Christian Theology,* 2nd ed. (New York: Scribner's, 1977), p. 144.

14. Rahula, *What the Buddha Taught,* p. 132.

15. John Hick, *Evil and the God of Love* (New York: Harper & Row, 1978), p. 5.

16. Jeremiah 12:1.

17. Revelation 21:1.

18. MacLeish, *J.B.,* p. 111.

19. In Hick, *Evil and the God of Love,* p. 176.

20. Camus, *The Plague,* pp. 116–18.

21. Ibid., p. 92.

22. Antony Flew and Alasdair MacIntyre, eds., *New Essays in Philosophical Theology* (New York: Macmillan, 1955), pp. 98–99.

23. Dostoevsky, *The Brothers Karamazov,* p. 122.

24. Ibid., p. 127.

25. Flew, *New Essays,* pp. 97–99.

26. See Hick, *Evil and the God of Love,* pp. 253–58.

27. Dorothy Sayers, *Four Sacred Plays* (London: Gollancz, 1948), p. 227.

28. *The Letters of Emily Dickinson,* ed. by Thomas H. Johnson (Cambridge, Mass.: The Belknap Press of Harvard University Press, 1958).

29. *The Poems of Emily Dickinson,* ed. by Thomas H. Johnson (Cambridge, Mass.:

The Belknap Press of Harvard University Press, 1955).

30. Leo Tolstoy, *The Death of Ivan Ilych* (New York: New American Library, 1960), p. 96.

31. Paul Reps, *Zen Flesh, Zen Bones* (Garden City, N.Y.: Doubleday), pp. 22–23.

32. Tolstoy, *Death of Ivan Ilych,* p. 131.

33. *The Complete Poetry and Selected Prose of John Donne,* intro. by R.S. Hillyer (New York: Modern Library, 1941), p. 332.

34. *The Portable Nietzsche,* trans. and ed. by Walter Kaufmann (New York: Viking Press, 1968), p. 183.

35. Elisabeth Kubler-Ross, *On Death and Dying* (New York: Macmillan, 1969), p. 38.

36. Ibid., p. 50.

37. Reps, *Zen Flesh, Zen Bones,* p. 21.

38. Albert Camus, *Notebooks 1935-1942,* trans. by Philip Thody (New York: Knopf, 1963), p. 9.

39. Tolstoy, *Death of Ivan Ilych,* p. 152.

40. Nikos Kazantzakis, *Zorba the Greek* (New York: Simon and Schuster, 1966), p. 35.

41. Reps, *Zen Flesh, Zen Bones,* pp. 19–20.

42. Ludwig Wittgenstein, *Tractatus Logio-Philosophicus,* trans. by D.F. Pears and B.F. McGuinness (New York: Humanities Press, 1963), p. 147.

43. Woody Allen, *Getting Even* (New York: Warner, 1972), p. 31.

44. In John Dart, "The Devious Approach to Theology," *Los Angeles Times* (Oct. 4, 1975), p. 19.

45. Allen, *Getting Even,* p. 90.

46. John S. Dunne, *Time and Myth* (Garden City, N.Y.: Doubleday, 1973), p. 39.

47. Wayne Suttles, *Katzie Ethnographic Notes: The Faith of a Coast Salish Indian* (Victoria, B.C.: British Columbia Provincial Museum, 1955), p. 36.

48. Dostoevsky, *The Brothers Karamazov,* p. 169.

49. Suttles, *Katzie Ethnographic Notes,* p. 40.

50. Ibid., p. 71.

Chapter Fifteen
Closing the Circle

•

The wheel is come full circle.

William Shakespeare
King Lear [1]

Max Weber once observed that religion cannot be defined at the beginning of a study: "Definition can be attempted, if at all, only at the conclusion of the study."[2] Nonetheless, this text began with the problem of definition and, in spite of the limitations of all definitions, posited that religion can be fruitfully defined as a seeking or responding to what is experienced as holy. However, Weber's insistence that the formulation of a definition be put off until the study is completed has some virtue. Certainly a clearer and broader conception of religion should emerge at the end of a systematic study than at the beginning. We can now bring the wheel full circle by returning to the question with which the text began, What is religion?

Up to this point the question of what religion is has been illuminated by a study of its primary forms or dimensions. We have explored symbols, sacred rites and stories, religious experience, holy communities, and existential and theological breaking points in order to achieve a broader and deeper understanding of religion. If, for example, we agree with Robert Bellah's definition that religion is "a set of symbolic forms and acts that relate man to the ultimate conditions of his existence,"[3] then the study of the conceptual, ritual, personal, and social dimensions of religion should provide a context for unpacking some of the implications of Bellah's definition.

Another valuable way of enlarging our understanding is to shift the question from what religion is to what it is not. Can a person or a people be nonreligious? Do you recall the observation in chapter one that religion is as characteristic of human existence as language? This may have been true of archaic and prescientific cultures, but is it true today? In communist China, for instance, the Buddhist temples and Christian churches, which were so in evidence in pre-Maoist China, have all but ceased to function as places of worship. The buildings have been converted to other purposes; cultural treasures have become museums—monuments to dead Pans. The Buddhist monasteries have been closed down, and the monks have returned to secular lives. Are modern Chinese a nonreligious people—a people who have banished the gods and who have broken the power of the monks and priests?

One way of distinguishing between the religious and the nonreligious is to examine contexts in which people stand outside the traditional ways of being religious. What, for example, does it mean to be religious in a tribal society? Are the categories for distinguishing between what is religious and nonreligious in a monotheistic faith like Christianity applicable to the tribal experience? The study of conditions in which faith is lost, rejected, or ignored sheds light on what religion is and supplements the understanding of it derived from a familiarity with the forms it takes. While there may be several senses in which humans have either experienced a loss of faith or have been judged by others to be nonreligious only three are examined in detail: loss of belief, loss of home, loss of meaning. Although the imagery of loss of faith implies that faith was at some point part of one's way of being, loss is used here as a metaphor for those who have always stood outside the circle of a believing community as well as for those who have turned away from one.

Loss of Belief

As with faith, so the loss of faith is often equally a flood of grace, a sudden light. Reason counts for nothing: the smallest thing is enough—a word, silence, the sound of bells. A man walks, dreams, expects nothing. Suddenly the world crumbles away. All about him is ruins. He is alone. He no longer believes.

Romain Rolland
John Christopher: Storm and Stress[4]

Largely because of the influence of Christianity, one of Western civilization's conventional ways of distinguishing between the religious and the nonreligious centers on what is believed. Where belief in God who is the creator of all living things is the test of religiosity, **atheists** and **agnostics** who do not share this belief are considered nonreligious. Unbelief is, of course, as complicated as belief. In a broad sense, all who stand outside a particular community of faith are nonbelievers, even though they may have theological or ideological commitments of their own. In contexts where belief is the key to faith, disbelief is its counterpoint. The discussion of a loss of belief—including both disbelief, the positive rejection of religious worlds of meaning, and unbelief, the withholding of assent or indifference to the claims of faith—concentrates on those forms of nonbelief that have proved disquieting to Christianity and other monotheistic religions.[5]

Although in Christian theology faith is a complex word symbolizing a total human response to what is experienced as holy, in practice it is sometimes used as a synonym for belief. One consequence of this reduction of faith to belief is the tendency to identify what is Christian with correct belief (orthodoxy) rather than with correct practice (orthopraxis). Since the test of Christian faith has often been correct belief, creed and dogma have sometimes served not only as communal declarations of faith but as tools to separate believers from nonbelievers. Those outside the circle of Christian orthodoxy have fallen into four primary categories: pagans, heretics, agnostics, and atheists.

Pagans and Heretics

From a traditional Christian perspective, pagans are either ignorant of the one true God—that is, they are polytheists or animists who have not yet heard God's word, or who, in spite of having heard the gospel, persist in following the religious ways of their ancestors. Heretics are another matter. They do not walk in the darkness of superstition, nor can ignorance of the Gospel serve as their defense. Unlike the pagan, the heretic has lived within the circle of Christian faith but has broken with the faithful because of irreconcilable differences. Insiders consider heretics to be more reprehensible than pagans because they have rejected a shared body of beliefs and practices. Heresy trials have always been rancorous, and conviction has carried severe penalties ranging from loss of position and expulsion to execution.

Christians have an unenviable history of intolerance and persecution of disbelievers, but other monotheistic faiths have exhibited similar behavior. Muslims have been particularly harsh on those Muslims who transgress the limits of orthodoxy and, like Christians, both Muslims and Jews have been implacable enemies of paganism. For example, the Hebrew conquest of the promised land was a protracted struggle between the Hebrews, who believed that obedience to Yahweh demanded a ruthless suppression of paganism, and the Canaanites, who worshiped many gods (baals). While Hebrew scriptures record many clashes between those who trusted in

Yahweh and the pagan Canaanites, one example will suffice to illustrate the intensity of the conflict. In a dramatic scene on Mt. Carmel, the Hebrew prophet Elijah challenged 450 prophets of Baal to a contest pitting the power of Yahweh against that of Baal. The contest called for two bulls to be cut in pieces and laid in separate places; the prophets were to call upon their respective deities to consume the offering by fire. Elijah said to the prophets of Baal, "And you call on the name of your god and I will call on the name of the Lord; and the God who answers by fire, he is God."[6] The prophets of Baal beseeched their god to answer them from morning until noon, but there was no answer. When Elijah prepared his offering the Lord consumed it by fire, and when the people saw it they proclaimed, "The Lord, he is God; the Lord, he is God."[7] As a postlude to Yahweh's triumph, Elijah directed the Hebrew people to seize and slay the 450 prophets of Baal.

Although Judaism is no longer locked in mortal combat with paganism, the aggressive missionary character of Christianity and Islam raises the question of whether they are so inherently expansive and exclusive that they must remain inhospitable to alternative ways of appropriating the world. Certainly the persecution of heretics and outsiders on religious grounds continues to be part of modern life. Division between Protestant and Catholic Christians is one ingredient in the violence in Ireland, and conflicts between Muslims and Christians erupted during the 1970s in Chad, Lebanon, Uganda, and the Philippines. While Christianity and Islam will probably never lose their missionary character, the sensitivity of many twentieth-century Christians and Muslims to other ways of being religious has moderated their zealousness. We should also note that the dogmatic and sometimes fanatical defense of orthodoxy is not limited to religious groups. It has become a feature of communist regimes, which, in the name of ideological correctness, suppress domestic dissent and, at the same time, support revolution as a means of liberating noncommunist peoples.

Atheists and Agnostics

Although paganism and heresy have been offensive to Christian orthodoxy, the distance separating them is bridged, in part, by a shared belief in the supernatural. Pagan, heretic, and Christian have differed, often in collisions of devastating proportions, but the disbeliever, in rejecting belief in God altogether, represents a more radical alternative to orthodoxy. If belief in deity is the criterion for separating the religious from the non-religious, then the atheist, who rejects such a belief, and the agnostic, who suspends belief because the evidence for or against God's existence is inconclusive, are nonreligious. While the atheist finds persuasive and compelling reasons for disbelieving in God, the agnostic argues that the evidence supports neither belief nor disbelief. Perhaps there is no more succinct statement of agnosticism than that made in the fifth century B.C. by Protagoras of Abdera:

> As for the Gods, I have no way of knowing either that they exist or that they do not exist; nor, if they exist, of what form they are. For the obstacles to that sort of knowledge are many, including the obscurity of the matter and the brevity of human life.[8]

One scenario for a loss of belief is that of a young person who goes off to college a believer and returns home a nonbeliever. The student's intellectual environment can be intoxicating and liberating, a time of experimentation and quest for identity. The life of the mind is critical and entails an exposure to alternative ways of believing and doing. It is difficult for college students to be so insulated from the world that their faith remains oblivious to criticism; thus the pilgrimage to self-discovery is sometimes a movement away from the faith of their parents to that of their teachers. In some cases, traditional belief systems are displaced by an ideological shift to atheism or agnosticism, although conversion from one religious community to another is more common.

James Joyce's *A Portrait of the Artist as a Young Man* is the story of Stephen Dedalus's journey from belief to unbelief. Dedalus was raised in an Irish Catholic family and was educated in Catholic schools. As a young man he practiced a spiritual regimen so vigorous that his priest-mentors asked him to consider the priesthood; and yet a yearning that came from deep within his being led him to a life outside the church. Dedalus told his closest mentor and friend, "I will not serve that in which I no longer believe, whether it call itself my home, my fatherland, or my church: and I will try to express myself in some mode of life or art as freely as I can and as wholly as I can, using for my defence the only arms I allow myself to use—silence, exile, and cunning."[9] Irreconcilable doubts about the Eucharist, the Blessed Virgin, and the person of Christ, left Stephen Dedalus capable of neither belief nor disbelief. Is it possible, Dedalus and his friend wondered, that Jesus himself was not what he pretended to be, "that he was himself a conscious hypocrite?"[10]

In contrast to agnostics like Dedalus, atheists have found belief in God to be an intellectual dead letter. They argue that belief in God is, in the light of what moderns know about the natural world, neither supported by the evidence nor any longer intelligible. Humans have a credibility point, the atheist might suggest, beyond which beliefs become so preposterous that assent is impossible. The credibility point is relative to each believer. For some Christians, the Devil is a malicious and cunning personal being who seeks to enslave human souls, while for other Christians, the Devil is a product of the imagination left over from an earlier period in church history.

And yet Christians who no longer take Satan seriously and who may use the term merely as a metaphor for destructive inner impulses confess that they believe God took flesh in Jesus the Christ and that through Christ's crucifixion and resurrection the power of death was broken.

The atheist might respond to such a profession of faith that, in the light of the incredible vastness of the cosmos, an act of unparalleled credulity and provinciality is required to believe that the life of a Galilean carpenter was so momentous that human salvation is dependent on believing in him. There are many solar systems besides our own and, at some point in their evolution, many of them must have been suited to support consciousness. If the earth is but a speck in the universe, one star among millions, then how can the events that transpired in either Jerusalem or Mecca have the significance that is claimed for them?

A loss of belief can involve a wrenching of one's whole being, as it did for Stephen Dedalus, but it can also be a turning point leading to a more viable and emotionally satisfying belief system; thus in rejecting or withholding assent in the God of theism, the atheist and agnostic may be committed to a symbol system that lies outside of theism. In fact, Protestant theologian Paul Tillich was critical of the tendency in Christianity to understand religiosity in terms of belief and suggested that Christians stand in need of a revised definition of atheism. For Tillich the experience of life as empty, senseless, and shallow is more indicative of a loss of faith, of what it means to be nonreligious, than is atheism or agnosticism. Since, in Tillich's theology, God symbolizes the infinite, inexhaustible depth and ground of all being, Christians should join atheists in rejecting images of God that conceive of him as a superperson who dwells in the sky. If God is depth, the atheist, as Tillich would have us understand him, is one who lives on the surface of being and never drinks deeply from life rather than one who rejects the God of traditional theism.

> For if you know that God means depth, you know much about Him. You cannot then call yourself an atheist or unbeliever. For you cannot think or say: Life has no depth! Life itself is shallow. Being itself is surface only. If you could say this in complete seriousness, you would be an atheist; but otherwise you are not. He who knows about depth knows about God.[11]

Unlike Christianity, where a profession of belief is of great import, most religious traditions distinguish the religious from the nonreligious by an emphasis on what is done rather than on what is believed. In tribal cultures, for instance, the use of creed or dogma as a body of beliefs to separate disbelievers from the faithful is absent altogether; thus distinctions that suggest ideological dissent, such as atheism, agnosticism, heresy, and paganism, are not applicable to the tribal religious experience. Although tribal peoples have rich storehouses of beliefs and may voice skepticism, their understanding of religiosity is more a matter of correct or customary practice than of right belief.

For those who are from religious communities that make what is believed central to faith, the absence of such an emphasis is sometimes difficult to assimilate. However, not only tribal religions lack such a feature. In India, for example, it is almost impossible to isolate any ideological principle that can serve to unite all those movements and philosophies that are loosely housed under the rubric of Hinduism, unless it is the acceptance of the inspired character of the Vedas. But even this parameter is so nonrestrictive that it can be made to embrace Hindu philosophies that are incredibly diverse, as well as the bewildering collage of theistic and polytheistic cults that constitute popular Hinduism. Even in a monotheistic faith like Judaism, orthopraxis—that is, identification with a Jewish way of living and being—rather than orthodoxy makes one Jewish. It is difficult, if not impossible, to suggest a proposition respecting either the nature and character of God or the authority of the Torah to which all Jews must give assent.

Loss of Home

We are vanishing from the earth, yet I cannot think we are useless or Usen would not have created us. He created all tribes of men and certainly had a righteous purpose in creating each. For each tribe of men Usen created, He also made a home. . . . When Usen created Apaches He also created their home in the West.

Geronimo
His Own Story[12]

Home is always a place and, by extension, is related to sacred places and holy lands. In traditional societies, families and peoples have been rooted in a homeland through a relationship that acknowledges a kinship between human existence and the land; the land is the place of the fathers and the earth is a mother who nourishes and sustains. This is especially true of tribal societies whose people have remained in the land of their ancestors; such people remain close to the sacred center and to those specific places in space where the sacred has been manifested.

Loss of home has profound implications for religion. When a people are separated from their sacred places and holy lands, they can become like persons who have lost their compass and can no longer find their way. Two different conditions in which a loss of home is experienced are germane to locating a sense of what it is to be nonreligious. One condition is that of the disinherited; this is a situation in which a person or a group of persons are expelled from the community of faith. Such persons may actually continue to live within their home or tribal land but be forced to exist outside their tribe or spiritual community. A second type of loss of home is that of the dispossessed; the dispossessed are those who are forced to flee their homelands because of war, political repression, racial strife, religious persecution, or natural calamity.

The Disinherited

Because the discussion of the loss of belief concentrated primarily on what it means to be nonreligious from a particular Christian perspective, examples of the loss of home are drawn chiefly from tribal faiths. It is often observed that tribal societies have no nonreligious persons. This is so for a number of reasons. First, tribal societies are small, and religion permeates the whole of tribal life so thoroughly that the modern distinction between the sacred and the secular does not readily apply to it. Second, to be a member of a tribe is to participate in its ritual life, to conform to its customary way of doing things, and to share in its understanding of the world. Characteristically, folk religions have no creeds and seek no converts. Salvation or transformation takes place through sacred rites and power visions. This form of religion is more danced and sung than preached.

As noted previously, kinship is a principal feature of tribal life—a kinship that not only unites family, clan, and tribe, but unites people through ancestral ties with the land, animals, plants, and the spirit world. To live well is to live as the sacred power of the world lives and moves for, as the Lakota Sioux Black Elk taught, it is "the life of things."[13] Because kinship is the dominant force in tribal social organization, learning is more imitative than experimental or innovative. Ancestral wisdom shows tribal people how to live; thus their responses to the ultimate situations and ultimate concerns that life poses are resolved primarily through the repetition of sacred rites and sacred stories.

In such a religious milieu, the person who is disinherited or expelled from the life of the tribe can be said to be nonreligious. Life outside the clan is a naked and vulnerable existence—an existence without the protection and meaning that ritual patterns and a supportive community provide. In tribal religions, expulsion results primarily from serious breaches in acceptable practice; thus the disinherited are more antisocial than ideologically unsound. In fact, the disinherited may continue to believe in the spirit world, may even be preoccupied with it, yet because they are excluded from communal life, they are in a tribal context, nonreligious.

Disinheritance is not unknown in modern world religions. Within the Roman Catholic tradition, excommunication, which in its most serious form excludes one from participation in the sacraments, is a form of loss of home. In addition, some Christian sects practice shunning—that is, members of the group refuse to have any social contact with those who are expelled.

The Dispossessed

The present age is one of an unprecedented dislocation of people from their homelands. The United States Committee for Refugees estimated that in 1978 more than 13 million refugees were scattered over the world. Some of the dispossessed are a legacy of the United States' involvement in Southeast Asia and the dislocation that has resulted from the establishment of communist governments in Cambodia and South Vietnam. Refugees are one of the central issues in the Middle East, where the Palestinian Liberation Organization is a would-be nation of dispossessed Arabs. In Africa, civil

Vietnamese Boat People. The loss of home can be a time of a loss of faith.

Photo by Jean-Pierre Laffont, Sygma

wars, tribal conflicts, natural disasters, and struggles to establish black majority rule in Rhodesia (Zimbabwe) and the Union of South Africa have left over 3 million uprooted.

Although the dispossessed are not necessarily without faith, such upheavals can have a very serious effect on both religious communities and personal religious experience. Refugees are always torn between preservation of their ancestral ways and assimilation to their new environment. How difficult it must be for Vietnamese, for example, to endure the ignominy of learning to speak all over again and to adjust to a land that observes no Vietnamese customs or festival days. How does one continue to walk in a sacred manner when the path has been obscured by alien footsteps? A loss of home, therefore, involves a loss of identity. It is an uprootedness that leaves one without parameters and guideposts.

The contact of tribal peoples with civilization has been devastating. They have been uprooted, herded onto reservations, sometimes enslaved, and always shaped into the image of their conquerors. Their choice often has been to assimilate or to die. "Yes—we know that when you come, we die,"[14] Chiparopai, a Yuma Indian, said of the white man. In some cases, entire communities of faith have disappeared from the earth. Certainly this was the case of the Yahi Indians of California, whose last survivor, Ishi, died in 1916. Likewise, the African slave trade destroyed kinship patterns and made the preservation of tribal ways impossible for those who were sold into slavery. Languages, names, and customs were left behind or buried deep in the African's unconscious, only to surface now and again in Christianized form.

American Indians have been subjected to many of the same stresses as the uprooted Africans, and though they have not been enslaved, the result has been just as appalling. Those who survived the westward expansion were corralled on reservations, sometimes far from their ancestral homes. Because they were pressured to walk in the way of the whites—to speak their tongue, to wear their clothes, and to pray to their God—it is no wonder that the Indian way was almost extinguished. The eclipse of the way of the American Indian is a theme in Black Elk's autobiography. Born in a time before the white man had seriously disrupted the Sioux, he lived to see the death of the Sioux nation and the near extinction of their way of life. In his autobiography, Black Elk used the image of a broken center to capture the desolation of his people: "There is no center any longer, and the sacred tree is dead."[15] The tribal unity that marked the Indian way was broken, and the tree of life that stood, in the vision of his youth, at the center of tribal life was lifeless. With the breaking of the sacred center, the Sioux were left to follow their little visions and to obey their private rules.

Loss of home feeds the destruction of religious ways of appropriating the world. Sometimes the strain is so great that a people's vision grows dim and all that is left is a longing for lost roots. In some cases, like that of the Yahi, entire religious worlds of meaning have vanished.

Of course, the loss of home is not exclusively a story of the loss of faith. It can be an occasion for strengthening and revitalizing faith or converting to a new faith. The dispossessed may find, in the jumble of their lives, a new order that is as promising as the one left behind. The United States is, after all, a nation of refugees who have, on the balance, found hope rather than wretchedness.

Sometimes the old center can be preserved. For instance, the forced exile of the Jews from the Holy Land by the Babylonians in the sixth century B.C. did not destroy the Jewish faith, although it was severely tested. Like the exiled Jews, Black Elk, Chief Seattle, and Ishi kept the faith even though their sacred lands had been invaded. Perhaps the tribal faiths of African and native Americans will bloom again in the stirrings of the spirit that today animates black and red liberation movements, and Black Elk's prayer, "O make my people live!"[16] will be answered.

There is nothing worse in life than life itself.
    Carolina Maria de Jesus
        Child of the Dark[17]

Loss of Meaning

A third sense of what it is to be nonreligious can, for the lack of a better label, be called the loss of meaning. The loss of meaning—the experience of life as flat and empty—is primarily an ontological sickness—that is, a sickness of being. It manifests itself in two very different circumstances. One situation is that of a person who, in the midst of material plenty and well-being, is nauseated by life. The second circumstance is that of a person so afflicted by poverty and hunger, or by some other form of oppression, that life itself is a painful, joyless darkness. One is the soul-sickness of the affluent, while the other stems from a poverty or violence so oppressive that it impoverishes the spirit as well.

The Broken Center and the Death of God

The loss of meaning is in one sense the loss of a center—that is, the absence of an image by which humans can grope for authentic existence. It is a judgment not merely that life is no good but that it has no meaning, that it is absurd. Those who are so afflicted have plunged deep into the recesses of their souls only to experience the horror of an impenetrable darkness at the center of their beings. In one of his short stories, Ernest Hemingway transposed the joy and praise of the Ave Maria into a litany of such emptiness: "Hail Nothing, full of nothing, nothing is with thee."[18]

The death of God, like the image of the broken center, is a metaphor for a loss of meaning; at least in Western civilization, to proclaim that God is dead is to profess that life can have no transcendent meaning. In a piece entitled "The Madman," Friedrich Nietzsche wrote of a madman who rushed into a sunlit marketplace with a lighted lantern, in search of God. " 'Where is God gone?' he asked and then, in answer to his own question, he exclaimed, 'I mean to tell you! We have killed him—you and I! We are his murderers! But how have we done it? How were we able to drink up the sea? . . . God is dead! God remains dead! And we have killed him!' "[19] Sometimes our intellects refuse to give assent to such a requiem, and we keep repeating the prayers and acting out the liturgy; in the secret chambers of the heart, Nietzsche insisted, humans know that the madman's words are true.

Moderns live in an age in which its poets, philosophers, and even its theologians have spoken of God's death or of his hiddenness. In one perspective, it is an age of a twilight of the gods, a time in which the traditional centers of value can no longer serve as maps for making sense out of human experience. For some, the death of God is liberating, a call to celebrate human life rather than an occasion for sorrow and longing; but for others, when their faith in God died, hope died as well. In *Conversation at Midnight,* Edna St. Vincent Millay, in firm, crystal strokes, re-creates the forlorn longing that haunts the hearts of those for whom the death of God has resulted in an emptiness at the center of their being:

> *Man has never been the same since God died,*
> *He has taken it very hard.*
>
> *Why, you'd think it was only yesterday,*
> *The way he takes it.*
>
> *Not that he says much, but he laughs much louder than he used to.*
> *And he can't bear to be left alone even for a moment.*
> *And he can't sit still . . . .*
>
> *He gets along pretty well as long as it's daylight:*
> *He works very hard,*
> *And he amuses himself very hard with the many cunning amusements*
> *This clever age affords.*
> *But it's no use; the moment it begins to get dark,*
> *As soon as it's night*
> *He goes out and howls over the grave of God.*[20]

Descent into Hell

If it is possible to avoid thinking of hell as a geographic location, it is a particularly fruitful image of meaninglessness. In Dante's *Inferno,* cut in the Gate of Hell are the words, "ABANDON ALL HOPE YE WHO ENTER HERE"; thus hell is a condition of hopelessness, a soul-sickness in which the afflicted can neither die nor live. What cold winds can make the flame of faith in God flicker and die out? What circumstances can result in an experience of nothingness, in the judgment that life is empty and absurd? The horror of hell, the abyss of meaninglessness, has several faces, including those of murder, violence, hunger, poverty, and despair, that can destroy faith.

The Horror of Murder and Violence

Out of the Nazi death camps and the violence of the Second World War came a voice, more numb than mad, asking in a hushed whisper rather than a crazed shout, Where is God? In his autobiography, Elie Wiesel, who survived the unspeakable suffering of the death camps in which his family perished, tells of a Polish rabbi who, in the dark, hopeless world of the prison camps that the Nazis had constructed for the forced labor and ultimate liquidation of the Jews, was driven to despair, to a loss of faith. The rabbi asked, "Where is the divine Mercy? Where is God? How can I believe, how could anyone believe, in this merciful God?"[21]

The death camps were not alone in obscuring the light. German soldiers experienced a similar emptiness. *Last Letters from Stalingrad* is a poignant collection of letters from German soldiers facing death in the Battle of Stalingrad. Cut off from any course of retreat by Russian forces and left by the German high command to perish or surrender, the soldiers were afforded, in January of 1943, what was to be their last chance to send letters home. One letter from a son facing death, to his father, a Christian pastor, illuminates the way in which senseless suffering and violence can result in a loss of meaning.

> In Stalingrad, to put the question of God's existence means to deny it. I must tell you this, father, and . . . . I regret my words doubly, because they will be my last. . . . You are a pastor, father, and in one's last letter one says only what is true or what one believes might be true. I have searched for God in every crater, in every destroyed house, on every corner, in every friend, in my fox hole, and in the sky. God did not show himself, even though my heart cried for him.
>
> The houses were destroyed, the men as brave or as cowardly as myself, on earth there was hunger and murder, from the sky came bombs and fire, only God was not there. . . . And if there should be a God, he is only with you in the hymnals and the prayers, in the pious sayings of the priests and pastors, in the ringing of the bells and the fragrance of the incense, but not in Stalingrad.[22]

God is not the only casualty of murder and violence. In the face of the incomprehensible genocide of the Holocaust, the barbarism of Stalin's repression of his own people, and the aimless violence that marks much of contemporary life, belief in either the existence of God or the goodness of humanity is difficult to sustain. The death camps are both a reminder of God's silence and a stark portrait of human betrayal and degradation. While God did nothing to stop the slaughter of the innocent, humans were the instruments of death and destruction. In the experience of senseless violence, the death of God is, not surprisingly, accompanied by a loss of faith in humankind. It is an experience of brokenness in which the sense of ultimacy dies in the very center of one's being and only the heart of darkness remains. Of this incomprehensible night, this interminable darkness, Wiesel wrote:

> Never shall I forget that night, the first night in camp, which has turned my life into one long night, seven times cursed and seven times sealed. Never shall I forget that smoke. Never shall I forget the little faces of the children, whose bodies I saw turned into wreaths of smoke beneath a silent blue sky. Never shall I forget those flames which consumed my Faith forever. Never shall I forget that nocturnal silence which deprived me, for all eternity, of the desire to live. Never shall I forget those moments which murdered my God and my soul and turned my dreams to dust. Never shall I forget these things, even if I am condemned to live as long as God Himself. Never.[23]

The Horror of Hunger and Poverty

Hunger, like war, has been an altar on which God has been slain and our humanity laid aside as useless appendages in the struggle for survival. Of the 4 billion people on this planet, millions are refugees and, by one estimate, at least half of the world's burgeoning population is undernourished. For those who are hungry and poorly clothed, life is unrelentless misery, an existence that has poverty and the constant dull ache of hunger as its companions. Such a life is hell, or as Carolina de Jesus characterized the Brazilian slum where she lived, a "branch of Hell, if not Hell itself."[24]

In *The Mountain People,* Colin Turnbull chronicled the spiritual and physical destruction of the Iks, an African tribal people of northern Uganda. The Iks have been so plagued by years of drought and famine that they have shed their humanity thoroughly enough to become, in Turnbull's words, a "loveless people." When Turnbull made his study, the Iks had almost entirely abandoned their traditional ways, and their sense of the spirit world was so obscured that their sacred rites and stories had nearly vanished. Each person was reduced to looking out for him- or herself. Turnbull wrote, "They were, each one, simply alone and seemingly content to be alone."[25] Parents abandoned their young and the old were left to die. Cruelty replaced love. Enveloped in misery, the Iks "had lost all trust in the world, lost all love and all hope." They merely "accepted life's brutality and cruelty because it was empty of all else."[26] How remarkably similar is Turnbull's description of this loveless people, the Iks, to Elie Wiesel's characterization of his experience in the concentration camps: "Here, every man has to fight for himself and not think of anyone else. Even of his father. Here, there are no fathers, no brothers, no friends. Everyone lives and dies for himself alone."[27] In such a darkness, how is faith in either God or man possible?

The Horror of Despair and Nothingness

Violence, murder, hunger, and poverty are faces of hell. They are conditions in which deprivation and suffering may be so unbearable that belief, even one's humanity, may shrivel and die. But a loss of meaning is also possible in the midst of plenty; the affluent are also susceptible to feelings of despair—that is, the feeling that nothing matters, that they have nothing to live for. Perhaps the horror of despair is at heart a fear of nonbeing—a terror of an ultimate nothingness. Albert Camus wrote in *The Myth of Sisyphus,* "There is but one truly serious philosophical problem, and that is suicide."[28] The question Camus raises is whether it makes sense to go on living if God and the values grounded in his authority are illusory. The nihilist assures us that life is absurd—a ludicrous drama of a being condemned by some quirk of nature to seek meaning in a pointless cosmos.

The despair of those who are affluent, yet spiritually impoverished, takes several forms. It can be manifested in a pervasive, unshakable boredom, a kind of voracious appetite for titillation that flits from novelty to novelty but is never satisfied. For those who are bored, nothing matters. Life is a tedious waiting, and nothing happens to relieve the boredom.

Despair can also manifest itself in an emotional numbness and isolation that effectively insulates the self from being able to experience love or compassion. Meursault, in Camus's *The Stranger,* is such a person. He is in the world yet impervious to it. When his mother dies, he feels no grief. He has no friends, no passions, no hopes, no loves. He is passive and indifferent. On trial for his life, he cannot even get involved in his own defense. Life is, for Meursault, something to be observed without interest or passion.

We need a theme? then let that be our theme:
that we, poor grovellers between faith and doubt,
the sun and north star lost, and compass out,
the heart's weak engine all but stopped, the time
timeless in this chaos of our wills—
that we must ask a theme, something to think,
something to say, between dawn and dark,
something to hold to, something to love.

Conrad Aiken
"Time in the Rock"[29]

Religion and the Growth of Secularism

Although assessing how many moderns have experienced a loss of faith is impossible, experience of one or more of the losses of faith is apparently not uncommon. Probably the number of shifts from one religion to another or from one ideology to another is greater than at any time in the past. In fact, Robert Jay Lifton has suggested that moderns, like the Greek god Proteus, are capable of quickly abandoning one belief for another. Thus a modern may be involved in Transcendental Meditation, Scientology, Zen, Marxism, and some Christian movement alternately or all at once.[30] Besides shifts in belief, alarming numbers of people are physically dispossessed, and even greater numbers have been cut off from either their roots in the land or a meaningful heritage. Whether from conditions of subsistence living or rootlessness, the loss of meaning is very much a feature of modern life. While the majority of people in affluent societies may not live "lives of quiet desperation," the number of people who are either suicides or drug or alcohol addicts, or who otherwise experience life as empty and boring, is sizable.

The recognition that some moderns have experienced a loss of faith is not intended to suggest that moderns are nonreligious. Humans continue to seek and find "something to hold to, something to love." Universal religions, for instance, continue to be an important ingredient of contemporary life. Worldwide, one of every four people is associated with one of the divisions of Christendom. Judaism is vigorous in the United States and Israel. Islam numbers over 700 million adherents. Buddhism is flourishing in Japan and has, for the first time, taken hold in the United States among non-Asian Americans. The vitality of contemporary religion is evidenced in the spectacular growth of two Buddhist sects, Rissho Koseikai and Soka Gakkai (Nichiren Shōshū) in post–World War II Japan, and in the steady, worldwide expansion of the Church of Jesus Christ of Latter-Day Saints.

Although membership in traditional religions remains strong, a significant segment of the people who live in industrialized countries seems either to no longer feel a need for association with a religious group or to have rejected traditional belief systems altogether. In the nation of Israel, for instance, Jews who practice their faith are in the minority, although they continue to have considerable influence on Israeli politics and law. Chinese Marxists have moved away from Confucianism and Buddhism and have endangered, through conquest, the survival of Buddhism in Tibet. The triumph of indigenous communist movements in Southeast Asia has serious implications for the continuation of Buddhism in Laos, Cambodia, and Vietnam. In the Union of Soviet Socialist Republics, communist party membership, with its promise of economic and social advantage, is more overtly prized than is association with the Russian Orthodox Church, even though the Orthodox Church claims an active membership of over 60 million. If church attendance is a barometer of religiosity, European countries are only marginally Christian.

The shift away from traditional or inherited centers of meaning is evidenced in the rise of secularism. All scientific and technological societies have become increasingly secular—that is, they have moved, as Peter Berger points out, in the direction of separating the educational, economic, legal, and political sections of society "from the domination of religious instruments and symbols."[31] This is especially obvious in historically Christian countries. For instance, in spite of opposition from the Roman Catholic hierarchy, Italians recently passed legislation legalizing abortion, and in the 1970s their opposition to communism was not sufficient to keep the electorate in Rome from electing a communist mayor.

In the second half of the twentieth century, the trend in the United States is so unmistakenly secular that an overt and civilly sanctioned Christian presence in the public schools and in other areas of public life is disappearing. Belief in God is so on the boundary of public life that an interjection of "God talk" in public discourse is an inexcusable breach of etiquette. As Peter Berger puts it, "Transcendence has been declared 'inoperative' by the major agencies that 'officially' define reality."[32]

Theism is not alone in feeling the effects of secularism. In China, Buddhism and Confucianism no longer influence public life. Although the constitution of communist China provides freedom of religion, the Maoist reorganization of Chinese society, with its hostility to monastic communities, threatens the very existence of Buddhism's emphasis on the exploration of a person's inner space. Even Confucius, who stressed social virtues, has been vitriolically attacked by the Maoists as an enemy of the new China. The decline in influence of the traditional religions in modern societies was characterized by Christian historian Martin E. Marty in this fashion: "Ours is the first attempt in recorded history to build a culture upon the premise that it is not important for the workings of man and society whether or not God is present."[33]

The spread of secularism and the scientific way of seeing makes it more difficult for people to sustain religious symbols and to continue to believe that they work. Clifford Geertz notes in his study of religious change in modern Morocco and Indonesia that even the humblest peasants today know that there are alternative ways of understanding the world including scientific ones. Geertz asks, "How do men of religious sensibility react when the machinery of faith begins to wear out?"[34] People respond quite differently. Those whose symbol system is threatened but not destroyed by the challenge of modernity may respond by reforming and restructuring their beliefs, while others may overcome such tensions by rejecting the secular and scientific and passionately clinging to their traditional religious beliefs. When faith is lost, some may convert to a different religious belief system, or turn inward, or clothe their loss of faith in cynicism and skepticism. Others, as

Geertz suggests, may turn their capacity for commitment to secular activities, including political ones, and may embrace philosophies that explicitly reject the traditional religions.

The next section examines those world-organizing models that have rejected traditional religion. The study of disbelief offers still another frame through which an understanding of what religion is can be brought into focus. Of the philosophical alternatives to religion, only humanism is addressed.

Man is the measure of all things: of things that are, that they are, of things that are not, that they are not.

Protagoras
"Fragments"[35]

Humanism: An Alternative to Religious Belief Systems

Although **humanism** is an important contemporary philosophy, it was given birth in ancient times. In the West, it was nourished by the philosophies of Protagoras and Socrates and, in the East, by the teachings of Confucius and Buddha. The humanism of ancient Greece survived the breakup of the Roman Empire and the otherworldly character of much of medieval Christian thought by fusing Greek and Christian perspectives to form, during the Renaissance, a Christian humanism. Christian humanists turned their attention from heaven to a study of God's creation and a delight in the world of man. In this century, Christian humanism continues, through a union of Marxist-Socialist commitments and Christian theology, to play a significant role in contemporary liberation movements.

Although Christian humanism is still a potent force, the following discussion is limited to the secular humanistic philosophies that provide an alternative to the more traditional religions. While there are several varieties of humanism, including atheistic **existentialism,** Marxism, and a liberal humanist movement within Anglo-American philosophy, the primary focus of the discussion is on those beliefs and attitudes that such humanists share. Despite the very real areas of disagreement, existentialists, Marxists, and Anglo-American humanists share a philosophy that is atheistic, human-centered, and this-worldly.

Atheism

Humanism can be considered a negative philosophy, since it begins with an explicit rejection of belief in God. For the atheistic humanist, belief in the God of theism—that is, faith in a God who directs human destiny, who hears and responds to prayer, and who loves and cares for his creation—is unwarranted by either the test of scientific evidence or a rational analysis of human experience.

Chairman Mao Is Honored. Under the leadership of Comrade Mao, the traditional religions have been replaced or eclipsed in China's public life by a Marxist-humanist belief system.

Photo: The Bettman Archive, Inc.

In 1973 *The Humanist,* a publication of the American Humanist Association and the American Ethical Union, published a proclamation of humanist principles. The proclamation, entitled "The Humanist Manifesto II," revised and updated a manifesto issued in 1933. Both proclamations reject the God of theism. The Manifesto of 1933 begins with an affirmation that the universe is self-existing and thus needs no creator to account for it; Manifesto II characterizes belief in the God of theism as "an unproved and outmoded faith." Rational people, the Manifesto insists, have concluded that belief in the existence of God is unsupported by the evidence and have rejected personal immortality as a false hope. Manifesto II states: "We find insufficient evidence for belief in the existence of a supernatural; it is either meaningless or irrelevant to the question of the survival and fulfillment of the human race. As nontheists we begin with humans not God, nature not deity."[36]

Atheism has profound implications. If God does not exist, then humans are part of a natural evolutionary process that is more an interaction of forces than a creative act. Such a universe can have no essential meaning or ultimate purpose because, as atheistic existentialist Jean-Paul Sartre put it, "there is no infinite and perfect consciousness to think it."[37] Without God there can be no human destiny, no absolute truths or absolute values. Humans are free, the humanist insists, and finally responsible for themselves and the character of the societies in which they live. Humanist Manifesto II proclaims, "No deity will save us; we must save ourselves."[38] This pronouncement is not unlike one iterated centuries ago by the Buddha: "All conditioned things are impermanent. Work out your salvation with diligence."[39]

Humanists have responded to the "death of God" quite differently. For Sartre, life without God is a forlorn existence, since it means that humans are alone in the universe and must face life without the consolation that comes from believing in eternal values, heavenly rewards, and a cosmic plan of salvation. In a world without God, a world that is ultimately meaningless and indifferent, humans are, to use Sartre's dramatic statement, "condemned to be free." It is a dreadful freedom; while humans are responsible for their choices, they can never know whether they have chosen correctly since human choices have no cosmic validation.

While atheistic existentialists analyze human existence through such categories as alienation, despair, and forlornness, other humanists are much more cheerful. Anglo-American humanists, for instance, are usually not distressed by a world in which God is absent. In their typically practical and matter-of-fact tone, they conclude that since belief in God is neither reasonable nor scientific, the creeds and institutions that perpetuate it should be set aside as both intellectually dishonest and an impediment to the fulfillment of human potential. Traditional theism, the humanist argues, fosters dependence, fear, and irrationality rather than independence, courage, and rationality. The Anglo-American humanist is inclined to accept the consequences of atheism with an attitude that suggests, "Very well, if there is no God, then let's get on with the business of living and make the best of it."

We should note that, in spite of the active presence of the American Humanist Association, atheism has never been widespread in the United States. Public surveys of religious beliefs indicate that Americans, usually at a rate of 90 percent or higher, affirm that they believe in God. However, the conviction that God does not exist or that he is irrelevant has found a responsive ear within one of America's traditional religious communities; a group of Jewish rabbis are building congregations around the tenets of Judaic humanism. Rabbi Sherwin Wine, one of the prime movers of the Society for Humanistic Judaism, put it this way: "Whether there is or isn't a God makes no difference since He can't affect human lives." Therefore, Wine concludes, "we must turn to available powers to solve our problems and the only powers we know are human powers."[40]

Human-Centeredness

While disbelief in God and other transempirical conceptions, such as nirvana, is an important feature, humanism is not merely a negative philosophy. At the core of humanism is an affirmation of human values and a vision of hope for the future of mankind. Nietzsche pronounced the death of God not merely to shock or destroy but to set humans free. If, as the humanist contends, belief in the God of theism is no longer intellectually defensible and much of what religions of transcendence teach is mistaken, then humans and the natural world of which they are a part can be lifted up and celebrated as that which concerns us ultimately. Nietzsche's madman exclaimed, "Shall we not ourselves have to become Gods in order to be worthy of such a momentous murder?"[41]

Since, from the humanist perspective, the universe as understood by science provides little evidence of cosmically sanctioned values, humans must in their choices create the conditions that enhance the fulfillment of human potential and make the good life possible. A world without either absolute moral values or absolute truths should not, the humanist insists, reduce us to despair. If values are relative to a context, they are nevertheless real rather than imagined and can be judged by human reason in the light of experience. For the humanist, the human being is the primary value; institutions and practices must be judged by whether they liberate or enslave, nurture or repress, enhance or endanger the fulfillment of human life, individually and collectively.

Humanism celebrates human life. The Manifesto of 1933 commended as the end toward which human life should aspire the "complete realization of human personality . . . in the here and now."[42] The Manifesto of 1973 reaffirmed the principle: *"The preciousness and dignity of the individual person* is a central humanist value. Individuals should be encouraged to realize their own creative talents and desires. We reject all religious, ideological or moral codes that denigrate the individual, suppress freedom, dull intellect, dehumanize personality."[43] The liberal and optimistic tenor of Anglo-American humanism envisions humanity liberated from the tyranny of the gods, informed by both a love and scientific investigation of nature, and succored by a supportive community.

This-Worldliness

Two meanings of secularism are germane to a discussion of humanism. As was noted, secularism is the separation of the major institutions of public life from the sanction of religious symbols and practices. In this sense, secularity is a characteristic of modern life for both humanists who promote such a disassociation and religionists who may embrace or lament it. A second meaning of secularism is characteristic of all humanism, whether ancient or modern. In this second and older usage, secularism means this-worldly. Humanism is secular in both senses; it is this-worldly rather than other-worldly and also seeks the removal of religious considerations from public life.

Humanists look to man rather than the gods, to this world rather than the next. They believe that the natural world is, in the words of poet Wallace Stevens, "all of paradise that we shall know."[44] The Kingdom of God that is the focal point of Jesus' preaching is transformed by the humanist into a vision of the kingdom of man. Marxists, for instance, envision as a utopian end a classless society in which people are rewarded according to their needs rather than by their contributions. According to Karl Marx, before this communist utopia can be achieved, the forces that alienate humans from themselves and deny them a sense of community and personal worth must be overcome. The other-worldliness of theism blinds people to the actual character of their existence and is a source of alienation, since it substitutes an illusory heavenly reward for justice in this world. Karl Marx wrote, "The abolition of religion as the illusory happiness of men, is a demand for their real happiness. The call to abandon their illusions about their condition is a call to abandon a condition which requires illusions."[45] Of course, the Marxist acknowledges that religion is not the only source of alienation; thus the unmasking of religion is followed by a critique of political-economic systems and, in particular, of the inequalities that mark distribution and ownership of goods in capitalist societies.

Like Marxists, other humanists are concerned with this world, although they are likely to be sharply critical of the tendency of communists to sacrifice the present generation for a utopian future. Albert Camus, for one, turned away from Marxism because of its willingness, in practice, to suppress human liberty and sacrifice people on the altar of such abstractions as the classless society, the rule of the proletariat, and the withering-away of the state. Anglo-American humanists are also usually critical of the deterministic and collectivist character of Marxism; they juxtapose to the Marxist state a world community founded on a deep and abiding respect for human life and committed to democratic principles, libertarianism, racial and sexual equality, a more equitable distribution of food, education, medical care, and wealth, and reasonable rather than violent resolutions of conflicts.

The this-worldly character of humanism, with its commitment to the value of human existence and concern for the quality of community life, gives it a lived-through quality not unlike that of the traditional religions. In a sense, contemporary humanism, especially when it takes on the ideological character of Marxism, is a way of life as well as a way of interpreting the world. The humanist is often a social activist committed to the building of a society in which the conditions for the good life are optimally present. British humanist Bertrand Russell's dedication to the cause of peace and justice is well known. And, of course, communists, imbued with Karl Marx's conviction that merely interpreting the world is insufficient and that it must be changed, have been the major missionary and revolutionary force in the twentieth century. The fact that approximately half of the world's population live under communist governments is indicative of the success of Marxist liberation movements.

Concluding Remarks

In this concluding chapter, the implications of what religion is are brought into sharper relief by looking at different senses in which humans have been considered nonreligious and by examining humanism, a philosophy that rejects the traditional religious worlds of significance. As indicated by the discussion of the loss of faith, the implications of being religious or nonreligious can be understood in different ways. Christianity, for example, has conventionally separated the religious from the nonreligious by insisting that profession of faith in Christ and assent to a body of beliefs is necessary. Although atheists and agnostics may have deeply held commitments, they are seen as nonreligious because they do not believe in the God of Christian theism.

Since this conceptual model is not applicable to most of the world's religions, loss of home was suggested as a more defensible way of getting at the meaning of being nonreligious in tribal societies. Perhaps loss of meaning is a soul-sickness of greater gravity than either loss of belief, which may be mitigated by a commitment to another belief system, or loss of home, which can be endured by the disinherited and dispossessed when hope is not destroyed and there is someone with whom to share their loss. The loss of meaning is a condition in which hope and love have so shriveled and died that faith is no longer possible.

Now that you are familiar with humanism and three conceptions of what is implied by being nonreligious, how would you answer the questions, Are humanists religious? and Is humanism a religion? Such questions return to the issue raised in chapter one of whether religion should be defined by what is believed (substantively) or by what it does (functionally). If religion is understood functionally as a meaning-giving activity, we can think of humanism as a religion and humanists as religious. Humans are driven toward meaning. We are condemned, as it were, by some inner compulsion to discern in the breaking points of human existence a meaningful cosmos. In spite of their rejection of the traditional religions, humanists are, in this view, religious insomuch as they have been able to create for themselves lives that do not lack significance and commitment. When religion is equated with meaning-giving, only those who have said No to life are nonreligious.

A functionalist approach that understands religion as a meaning-giving drive has much to recommend it. It embraces not only theistic religions, but includes Jainism, Buddhism, and Confucianism, which reject the God of theism. It is also able to include other world-organizing models, including humanism, under the umbrella of religion. Even the movement within Judaism toward an atheistic humanism is, in the functionalist view, primarily a shift of emphasis rather than a loss of faith, since it continues to provide a meaningful way of understanding human existence.

Although such a functionalist approach is attractive, this book has opted for a substantive or essentialist approach that understands religion more in terms of what is believed, though it does not neglect what religion does. In this perspective, religion is a seeking and responding to what is experienced as holy or sacred. In order to avoid equating the holy with the God of theism, the holy has been conceptualized in such an open-ended way that it can point to a superempirical reality that transcends the ordinary and lies beyond the empirical and analytic modes of knowing, regardless of whether the holy is addressed as a personal being or thought of as an impersonal power. The sacred and religious are distinguished from the secular and profane in experience by a manifestation of the sacred—that is, an experience of ultimacy. No acts, things, or conditions are inherently religious, and yet potentially all acts, things, or conditions are hierophanies of the sacred. As ultimate, the holy is the unconditioned presupposition of existence. Langdon Gilkey writes, "The ultimate or unconditional element in experience is not so much the seen but the basis of seeing; not what is known as an object so much as the basis of knowing; not an object of value but the ground of valuing; not the thing before us, but the source of things."[46] As nonordinary, the holy is mysterious and ineffable, yet is known in experience, in the depths of existence. For monotheists, the holy is a mysterious and powerful God of creation, a Wholly Other, whose glory and majesty is fascinating and terrifying and to whom the appropriate human response is faith. For nontheists, who seek the holy in inwardness, talk about God may miss the mark; yet the Buddhist, for example, seeks in the attainment of nirvana that which is ultimately deathless, which transcends the transitory and sorrowful character of ordinary existence.

From such an essentialist perspective, humanism is not a religion, nor are humanists religious, even though their lives may be on the whole as meaningful, moral, and happy as those of religionists. The world as experienced by humanists and by religionists does not differ in detail. They do not disagree about the natural and created things of the world. The experience of pain and pleasure, joy and sorrow, moral outrage, and moral weakness are common to each. Their worlds are the same, but the religionist sees in it something more, which makes everything different, while the humanist insists that there is nothing more to life than life itself.

The contention that humanism is not a religion is a judgment with which humanists are likely to concur, although some humanists think of themselves as religious in the sense that they are committed to a functionally meaningful belief system. Most humanists, however, would like to set aside the question of whether what is believed is emotionally and intellectually satisfying and consider instead the nature of what is believed. From the humanist perspective, religion is inseparable from belief in a transempirical reality, and it is such a belief that they reject. Karl Marx called for the abolition of religion and would have been appalled by definitions that would include his philosophy within the circle of religion.

What is the truth of the matter? Is there something more, as religionists affirm, or is there nothing more, as humanists argue? As the beloved priest in Miguel de Unamuno's story, *Saint Emmanuel, the Good Martyr,* believed, the truth is so unbearable that most people could not live with it. Religion is an opiate, the atheist priest acknowledged, but it is one that lets humans "console themselves for having been born" and lets them "live as happily as possible in the illusion that all this has a purpose."[47]

Counter to this vision of cosmic loneliness is the conviction that something more exists, that humans are not alone, that the breaking points of human existence are thresholds leading to transformed life. Religionists do not make light of the unsatisfactory character of existence or flee from it through infantile fantasies. They may even agree with humanists that all statements about the holy are lies and all institutions, including religious ones, are suspect, but they would also insist that they are "lies" that clothe the truth and structures that point a way to transfigured life.

Notes

1. *King Lear,* act V, scene 3, line 176.
2. Max Weber, *The Sociology of Religion* (Boston: Beacon Press, 1963), p. 1.
3. Robert Bellah, *Beyond Belief* (New York: Harper & Row, 1970), p. 21.
4. Romain Rolland, *John Christopher: Storm and Stress,* vol. II, trans. by Gilbert Cannan (London: William Heinemann, 1911), pp. 27–28.
5. See Martin E. Marty, *Varieties of Unbelief* (New York: Anchor Books, 1966).
6. 1 Kings 18:24.
7. 1 Kings 18:39.
8. Philip Wheelwright, *The Presocratics* (New York: Odyssey Press, 1966), p. 240.

9. James Joyce, *A Portrait of the Artist as a Young Man* (Middlesex, England: Penguin Books, 1968), p. 247.

10. Ibid., p. 242.

11. Paul Tillich, *The Shaking of the Foundations* (New York: Scribner's, 1948), p. 57.

12. Geronimo, *His Own Story,* ed. by S.M. Barrett (New York: Ballentine, 1971), p. 67.

13. John G. Niehardt, *Black Elk Speaks: Being the Life Story of a Holy Man of the Oglala Sioux* (New York: Pocket Books, 1972), p. 232.

14. *Touch the Earth,* compiled by T.C. McLuhan (New York: Pocket Books, 1972), p. 113.

15. Niehardt, *Black Elk Speaks,* p. 230.

16. Ibid., p. 234.

17. Carolina Maria de Jesus, *Child of the Dark* (New York: New American Library, 1962), p. 140.

18. Ernest Hemingway, "A Clean Well Lighted Place," in *The Short Stories of Ernest Hemingway* (New York: Scribner's, 1953), p. 383.

19. F.W. Nietzsche, "Joyful Wisdom," in *The Complete Works of Friedrich Nietzsche,* vol. x, Oscar Levy, ed. (New York: Russell & Russell, 1964), p. 168.

20. Edna St. Vincent Millay, *Conversation at Midnight* (New York: Harper & Brothers, 1937), pp. 94–95.

21. Elie Wiesel, *Night* (New York: Avon Books, 1969), p. 87.

22. *Last Letters from Stalingrad,* trans. by Franz Schneider and Charles Gullans (New York: New American Library, 1965), pp. 65–66.

23. Wiesel, *Night,* p. 44.

24. de Jesus, *Child of the Dark,* p. 140.

25. Colin Turnbull, *The Mountain People* (New York: Simon and Schuster, 1972), p. 238.

26. Ibid., p. 264.

27. Wiesel, *Night,* p. 122.

28. Albert Camus, *The Myth of Sisyphus,* trans. by Justin O'Brien (New York: Vintage Books, 1955), p. 3.

29. Conrad Aiken, *Collected Poems* (New York: Oxford University Press, 1953), p. 666.

30. Robert Jay Lifton, "Protean Man," in Norbert O. Schedler, ed., *Philosophy of Religion* (New York: Macmillan, 1974).

31. Peter Berger, *The Sacred Canopy* (Garden City, N.Y.: Doubleday, 1969), p. 107.

32. Peter Berger, "Cakes for the Queen of Heaven," *The Christian Century* (Dec. 25, 1974), p. 1220.

33. Martin E. Marty, *Varieties of Unbelief* (New York: Holt, Rinehart and Winston, 1964), p. 58.

34. Clifford Geertz, *Islam Observed* (New Haven, Conn.: Yale University Press, 1968), pp. 3, 103.

35. In Wheelwright, *The Presocratics,* p. 239.

36. Humanist Manifesto II, *The Humanist* (Sept./Oct. 1973), p. 5.

37. Jean-Paul Sartre, *Existentialism and Human Emotions* (New York: Philosophical Library, 1957), p. 15.

38. Humanist Manifesto II, p. 6.

39. Edward Conze, *Buddhism: Its Essence and Development* (New York: Harper Torchbooks, 1959), p. 16.

40. "Jewish Sect Rejects God, Turns to Man," *Los Angeles Times* (March 11, 1978), Part I, p. 23.

41. Nietzsche, "Joyful Wisdom," p. 168.

42. Humanist Manifesto of 1933, reprinted in *The Humanist* (Jan./Feb. 1973), p. 14.

43. Humanist Manifesto II, p. 6.

44. Wallace Stevens, "Sunday Morning," in *The Oxford Book of American Verse* (New York: Oxford University Press, 1950), p. 635.

45. Karl Marx, *Early Writings* (London: C.A. Watts, 1963), p. 43.

46. Langdon Gilkey, *Naming the Whirlwind* (Indianapolis, Ind.: Bobbs-Merrill, 1969), p. 296.

47. Miguel de Unamuno, *Saint Emmanuel, the Good Martyr* (Chicago: Henry Regnery, 1970), pp. 246–47.

Glossary

agnosticism the suspension of belief in the existence of God and other transempirical phenomena, such as the Tao and life after death, because the evidence for belief or disbelief is inconclusive.

ancestral devotion a reverence for ancestral spirits through acts of remembrance. Their much-feared capacity to do harm to the living is placated by magico-religious practices. Devotion to ancestral spirits assumes that the spirits of one's ancestors survive death and continue to have an important relationship to the living.

animism a sense that the world is filled with personal spirits. Animals, plants, and other natural phenomena, such as sun, moon, rivers, mountains, and fire, are spirit beings endowed with qualities of the human spirit—thinking, intending, feeling, hearing.

anthropomorphism a humanizing of the cosmos by regarding God or the gods and natural phenomena as having human qualities. In Genesis, for example, God walks, as humans might, in the Garden of Eden during the cool of the day.

antinomy arguments or principles opposed to each other. The arguments and counterarguments for the existence of God are what Immanuel Kant regarded as an antinomy—a problem in which the contradicting arguments cancel each other out and make it impossible, on the basis of the evidence, to resolve the problem.

atheism   the rejection of belief in God.

atman   a Hindu term for the human soul or the imperishable aspect of living things.

Brahman   in the Upanishads, Brahman is the Hindu term for the ultimate ground of existence. Brahman is the basis of all things, is in all things, is all things.

church   in one sense, the Christian community, the body of Christ, conceived as a fellowship of those who share common concerns and traditions. In a second sense, can refer to a type of religious organization that is well established, inclusive in membership, concerned with the well-being of the entire society, and that understands itself as the only legitimate custodian of truth.

communitas   an experience of community, of a common humanity. Communitas is facilitated through those moments in the ritual process that remove distinctions separating humans according to class, role, and privilege.

cosmology   the aspect of metaphysics that is concerned with the nature and structure of the universe. The cosmological argument for the existence of God concludes that the most plausible explanation for the origin of the universe is God.

deism   belief in a deity who created the cosmos and laws operative in it but who neither responds to prayer nor miraculously suspends the laws of nature.

denomination   a type of religious organization that is well established, concerned with the general well-being of society, and inclusive in membership but that also recognizes the legitimacy of other religious organizations and accepts religious pluralism.

double-intentional   the use of symbols in such a way that they point not only to things in ordinary experience but to that which is nonordinary or holy. For example, Jesus' parable of the prodigal son speaks of the relationship of a father and his sons in such a way that the story points beyond itself to a second level of intentionality, that of the relationship of God and humankind.

empathy   the capacity to place oneself vicariously in the world of someone else. Historical and phenomenological empathy or sympathy as it relates to the study of religious phenomena is the capacity to see the world through the eyes of the believer.

empirical   refers to knowledge acquired from the senses. In respect to the scientific way of knowing, it indicates an insistence on empirical validation for scientific truth-claims.

epistemology the branch of philosophy concerned with problems of knowledge, including the sources and limitations of human knowledge.

eschatology religious or mythological beliefs about last things or ultimate ends. It includes beliefs about human destiny and future expectations, such as the longing for the return of the eternal and the ultimate reconciliation of the divine and the human.

eternal without beginning or end, everlasting.

exegesis drawing out or explaining the meaning of a text; in religious studies, a sacred text.

existentialism a contemporary philosophy that insists that there is no essential human nature. As a consequence, humans are free to create themselves.

faith a synonym for religious experience understood as a condition of being totally affected by an experience of the holy.

fetish an object believed to contain a nonordinary or magical power that can be manipulated or used by those who have mastery over such power objects.

functionalism an approach that understands and defines religious phenomena in terms of the human needs they meet and the functions they perform.

gifts of the Holy Spirit the presence of the Holy Spirit, manifested or signaled by such gifts as speaking in tongues, healing, miracles, prophecy, and wisdom.

henotheism a loyalty and devotion to one god that does not deny the existence of other gods. For example, a Hindu may be exclusively devoted to Vishnu yet acknowledge the existence of Shiva, Kali, and other Hindu deities.

hermeneutics the science of interpretation that is concerned not only with drawing out the meaning of a text **(exegesis)** but with the formulation and criticism of the methodologies operative in the interpretative process.

heuristic employing words and gestures as a mode of discovery. Religious symbol systems are heuristic in the sense that they are human inventions that serve as vehicles for discovering what is ultimate.

hierophany things, events, or conditions in which the sacred manifests itself.

holy the primary focus of religion and religious experience. Understood in this text as that which is ultimate (nothing greater) and nonordinary (a mysterious incomparable power).

humanism a philosophy that focuses on human existence as the primary value. Humanism is atheistic, human centered, and this-worldly or secular.

icon an image through which the holy is made present. In Eastern Christendom, sacred paintings or icons are windows or transparencies through which the holy is seen.

iconoclasm a perspective that judges the reverence or respect shown to icons or images to be idolatrous and at odds with the commandment prohibiting the making of graven images.

immanent dwelling within. In religion, the conviction that the holy is not only present everywhere (omnipresent) but permeates or is inherent in things.

immortality of the soul the belief that an imperishable soul survives the death of the body. In this perspective the soul is regarded as the real or true self and the body as the phenomenal or transitory aspect of sentient existence.

koan difficult or hard-to-penetrate problems, such as "Does a dog have the Buddha nature?" Koans are employed by Zen masters to break down their students' reliance on conventional problem solving by forcing them to be open to intuitive or more direct ways of knowing.

liminal a stage in the ritual process in which the participants cross over from one way of being to another.

magic the mastery and manipulation of supernatural power by those who know the magical or occult arts. Magical power can be employed malevolently (sorcery and witchcraft) or benevolently (healing or exorcism).

mana a tribal religious conception of the permeation of all things by a sacred force or power. Mana is both feared and desired as a force enabling humans to perform incredible feats.

mandala a sacred image, diagram, or scroll that devotees may fix their eyes on while chanting and meditating.

mantra a sacred sound, prayer, or verse.

Marxism a humanistic philosophy that argues that history is a chronicle of class struggle. It insists that class divisions and other forms of human alienation have their basis in the private ownership of the means of production; thus it calls for an abolition of private property as the first step to a classless and nonalienating society.

meditation a discipline for exploring psychic or inner space that also requires attention to the body (breathing, postures, physical exercises). Meditation can lead to self-discovery, insights, physical and mental alertness, and enlightenment.

metaphysics the branch of philosophy that is concerned with what is ultimately real. A search for first principles that serve as conceptual handles for understanding reality.

miracle a wondrous or amazing event that is performed by a divine agent, an event in which the sacred manifests itself. In modern thought, miracles are often defined as extraordinary events or phenomena that suspend the natural or normal order of things, such as walking on water, raising the dead, and the parting of the Red Sea.

monasticism a mode of life of voluntary religious groups, which are organized communally and exist separately from the dominant social structures. The monastic life involves the taking of vows, the sharing of a common residence, dress, and diet, and the minimizing of marks of status in order to concentrate on the demands of the religious life.

mondo question and answer. A Buddhist story-form that preserves particularly illuminating responses to puzzling questions.

monism in metaphysics, the viewpoint that all things are a form of one irreducible and indivisible substance; for example, the philosophy that all that is, is mental or spiritual.

monotheism belief that there is only one God, who is the creator and sustainer of all things.

mudra ritual gesture, particularly with the hands and fingers; thus, in Buddhist art, the positions of the Buddha's fingers are symbolic.

mysticism the belief that, in spite of the bewildering variety of things in this world, reality is ultimately one. Mystics insist that direct confirmation of the oneness of reality is possible through a unitive experience—an experience of dying to the ego-self and becoming one with the ultimate.

myth a type of sacred story that has as its subject either the primeval or cosmic time of origins or the end of historical time.

nirvana in Buddhism, a transformed state of consciousness, rather than a place or a thing, in which the enlightened one is liberated from grasping and overcomes suffering.

noetic related to the mind and to knowing or understanding.

numinous the nonrational or nonordinary quality of the sacred.

ontology the aspect of metaphysics that is concerned with being, including the existence of an ultimate being, or God.

orthodoxy correct or right beliefs.

orthopraxis correct or right actions.

pantheism the conception that the holy or divine is immanent in all things or is all things.

paradox a form of expression and a way of illuminating truth that unites or holds in creative tension mutually exclusive or apparently incompatible assertions. Religious language is paradoxical when it says that those who would find themselves must first lose themselves; or that those who know, do not say and those who say, do not know.

phenomenology   a philosophical perspective that sets aside what it regards as an unresolvable debate over what things are in themselves in favor of concentrating on a description and analysis of the world as it is known in experience. In religious studies, phenomenology is concerned with reporting as faithfully as possible the world as experienced by the believer.

polytheism   belief and worship of many, or at least more than one, gods.

prayer   a vocal or mental address in which communion with a personal divine being is sought or invoked. Prayer may be private or public, formal or informal. The primary themes of prayer are petition, penitence or confession, praise or adoration, and thanksgiving.

psychism   a mental state or condition.

reincarnation   rebirth of the individual soul in a subsequent life form. In Asian religious traditions, the multiple life-death-rebirth cycle is governed by the law of Karma, or deeds.

remotion   the aspect of Christian theology that speaks about God by saying what God is not. Since God cannot be encompassed by human formulations and definitions, one way of speaking about him is by remotion or negation.

resurrection of the body   the belief that personal survival after death is a gift of God, which takes the form of resurrected life—a resurrection of a whole, embodied self.

rites of passage   rituals that mark the major turning points in the human life cycle: birth, adulthood, marriage, death.

ritual   the established form of sacred rites; a repetitive, performative, and social form of doing intended to commemorate sacred occasions or to invoke a sacred presence.

sacrament   gestures and words through which the sacred is manifested; presentational symbols or rites.

sects   religious groups that protest and ultimately separate from a parent religious group. Sects generally regard themselves as exclusive custodians of truth, demand sacrifice and uniformity among their members, see themselves as set apart and having little at stake in the larger society.

secularism   the tendency in scientific and technological societies to conduct public life independent of religious institutions and symbols.

soteriological   concerned with those religious experiences in which humans experience themselves as saved, transformed, or enlightened, including patterns of spiritual birth and growth, conversion experiences, and paths that lead to ultimate liberation.

spirit possession   belief that spirit beings, such as demons or the Holy Spirit, can enter and take possession of corporeal beings. When spirit possession is dangerous or malevolent, folk doctors may restore the victim to health by exorcising the offending spirit.

substantive   an approach that seeks to define religion or religious phenomena in terms of its essential nature rather than by what it does.

taboo   something forbidden or marked off as sacred and dangerous.

teleology   a concern with the design, purpose, and ultimate end of the cosmos.

theism   belief in gods or God as personal being(s).

theodicy   the area of theology that attempts to reconcile the goodness of God with the existence of evil.

theology   a reasoned defense and critical explication of religious beliefs from within the circle of faith.

totemism   regarding an animal or plant as a member, benefactor, and perhaps an ancestor of a family, clan, or tribe.

transcendent   going beyond or surpassing the ordinary. The idea of the holy as ultimate and nonordinary is an example of what is meant by a transcendent or transempirical reality; the holy transcends the limits of human knowledge and speech. The concept of transcendence can also be used to distinguish between religions of transcendence, which have as their ultimate focus a creator God who is radically different from his creation, and religions of immanence, in which the ultimate is within rather than outside of things.

transempirical   something that lies beyond or transcends the senses. (See **transcendent**.)

ultimate   that which is primary, complete, perfect, and unconditional. The eternal and enduring ground of all things.

witchcraft   the doing of evil by exercising an inherent and malevolent magical power.

yantra   instrument through which the holy is manifested.

Selected Resources

Bibliography

A list of books relevant to the material covered is broken down by chapter. Valuable bibliographic references are also included in the chapter notes. Most of the references for chapter one are introductory texts that discuss the primary forms of religious expression; while these texts are listed under chapter one, they also contain materials germane to other chapters.

Chapter One: What Is Religion?

Ellwood, Robert S., Jr. *Introducing Religion from Inside and Outside.* Englewood Cliffs, N.J.: Prentice-Hall, 1978. Examines the sociological, psychological, symbolic, ritual, and conceptual forms of religious expression from the perspective that religious activity is an exploration in self-discovery.

King, Winston, L. *Introduction to Religion: A Phenomenological Approach,* 2nd ed. New York: Harper & Row, 1968. Defines religion as a quest for and response to ultimacy. Discusses different manifestations of the sacred, including sacred space, time, revelation, community, and act.

Kristensen, W. Brede. *The Meaning of Religion: Lectures in the Phenomenology of Religion.* The Hague: Martinus Nijhoff, 1960. Includes an excellent discussion of the phenomenology of religion, as well as different conceptions of the holy, life cycle rites, sacraments, sacrifice, prayer, sacred places, sacred times, and sacred images.

Novak, Michael. *Ascent of the Mountain, Flight of the Dove.* New York: Harper & Row, 1971. An invitation to religious studies that discusses what religion is and is not, the interaction of religion and society, and different patterns of religious organization. It is also valuable as an introduction to the autobiographical and story character of religion.

Smith, Wilfred Cantwell. *The Meaning and End of Religion.* New York: New American Library, 1964. A profound and provocative history of the term religion that argues the question, What is religion? is not a fruitful one. Smith argues that it is more beneficial to think of the religious life as a dialectic between personal faith and the cumulative tradition of a religious community.

Streng, Frederick J. *Understanding Religious Life,* 2nd ed. Encino, Calif.: Dickenson, 1976. Defines religion as a means to ultimate transformation. Discusses theism, sacramentalism, dharma (cosmic law), and mysticism as four traditional ways of being religious.

van der Leeuw, Gerardus. *Religion in Essence and Manifestation,* 2 vols. Trans. by J.E. Turner. New York: Harper & Row, 1963. A classic phenomenological study of religion. Begins with an analysis of sacred power and discusses different types of sacred persons, holy communities, ritual action, and transformational experiences.

Wach, Joachim. *The Sociology of Religion.* Chicago: University of Chicago Press, 1962. A good introduction to the nature of religious experience and the relationship of religion and society, including the distinction between natural and voluntary religious groups and different types of religious authority and leadership.

Chapter Two: The Study of Religion

Berger, Peter L. *A Rumor of Angels.* Garden City, N.Y.: Doubleday, 1969. Helpful for understanding the distinction between the academic and theological approaches to the study of religion. It is also extremely fruitful for autobiographical reflection regarding what Berger calls "signals of transcendence"—that is, experiences that point beyond themselves to the holy. Includes a discussion of the death or eclipse of God, a subject addressed in the final chapter of *Exploring Religion.*

Dunne, John S. *Time and Myth.* Garden City, N.Y.: Doubleday, 1973. A fascinating treatment of human life as a story or myth and of such theological concerns as, Who am I? Why am I here? and Where am I going?

Harvey, Van. *The Historian and the Believer.* New York: Macmillan, 1966. Provides a richer and more substantive context for understanding the different perspectives and purposes of the believer and the historian.

Keen, Sam. *To a Dancing God.* New York: Harper & Row, 1970. A delightful exercise in religion as autobiography and story. If you are interested in exploring your story for evidence of the holy through regular entries in a journal, this book is a valuable resource.

Yinger, Milton J. *The Scientific Study of Religion.* New York: Macmillan, 1970. A solid introduction to a scientific study of religion. Contains a wide range of material related to this text, including the distinction between functional and substantive definitions, the relationship of religion, science, and magic, types of religious organization, and varieties of religious experience.

Chapter Three: Religion and Magic

Bellah, Robert. *Beyond Belief.* New York: Harper & Row, 1970. Includes several important essays. The essay "Religious Evolution" contains Bellah's typology of the historical development of religion.

de Vries, Jan. *The Study of Religion: A Historical Approach.* New York: Harcourt Brace Jovanovich, 1967. A history of different interpretations of religion, including different theories of the origin and evolution of religion. Also examines magic, sacrifice, and myth.

Eliade, Mircea. *The Quest: History and Meaning in Religion.* Chicago: University of Chicago Press, 1969. Reflections on the history of religions and the quest for the origins of religion.

Freud, Sigmund. *The Future of an Illusion.* Garden City, N.Y.: Doubleday, 1964. A provocative piece that argues that religion grows out of man's helplessness.

Lessa, William and Evon Vogt, eds. *Reader in Comparative Religion,* 3rd ed. New York: Harper & Row, 1972. Valuable collection of essays on subjects directly applicable to this text, including different views on the origin and development of religion, the function of religion, myth, ritual, mana, taboo, totemism, magic, witchcraft, death, ancestor worship, and shamanism.

Middleton, John, ed. *Magic, Witchcraft and Curing.* Austin: University of Texas Press, 1976. A collection of essays helpful for understanding magic, spells, sorcery, witchcraft, shamanism, and divination.

Russell, Jeffrey B. *Witchcraft in the Middle Ages.* Ithaca, N.Y.: Cornell University Press, 1972. In addition to providing a historical study of Western witchcraft, with its satanic orientation, it includes an excellent introductory chapter to magic and witchcraft.

Chapter Four: The Holy

Buber, Martin. *I and Thou.* New York: Scribner's, 1958. The discussion of the "Eternal Thou" is related to the idea of the holy. In addition, Buber's conception of two types of relationships, I-Thou and I-It, is related to the discussion of religious experience in part III of this text.

Durkheim, Emile. *The Elementary Forms of the Religious Life.* New York: Free Press, 1969. Argues that the distinctive characteristic of religious thought is the division of reality into the domains of the sacred and the profane. Includes discussions of animism, mana, totemism, ritual, and the social character of religion.

Eliade, Mircea. *The Sacred and the Profane.* Trans. by Willard Trask. New York: Harcourt Brace Jovanovich, 1959. A primary source for understanding Eliade's conception of the sacred and what he means by a hierophany. Includes a discussion of sacred space, sacred time, and myth.

Lienhardt, Godfrey. *Divinity and Experience.* London: Oxford University Press, 1961. One way of understanding the holy is to examine the conceptions and experiences of a particular people. Lienhardt's work provides an analysis of what the Dinka of the Western Sudan call Divinity.

Otto, Rudolf. *The Idea of the Holy.* Trans. by John W. Harvey. New York: Oxford University Press, 1958. Argues that the holy regarded as a "Mysterium Tremendum"—that is, a majestic and ineffable Being—is the primary religious category. In addition to his analysis of the idea of the holy, Otto discusses human responses to experiences of the holy in terms of what he calls "creature-feeling."

Macquarrie, John. *Principles of Christian Theology,* 2nd ed. New York: Scribner's, 1977. While this book covers the broad range of Christian theology, including the person and work of Jesus the Christ, there are several subjects related to this text, including an analysis of Holy Being, a discussion of theology and its relationships to other disciplines, a typology of different forms of religion, and a discussion of rites as sacraments.

Tillich, Paul. *The Shaking of the Foundations.* New York: Scribner's, 1948. A collection of sermons, including "The Depth of Existence" and "The Experience of the Holy," that can further clarify what is meant by ultimacy and holiness.

Wach, Joachim. *Types of Religious Experience, Christian and Non-Christian.* London: Routledge & Kegan Paul, 1951. The concluding chapter provides an analysis of the idea of the holy. The book also includes a discussion of the distinction between church-, denomination-, and sect-type religious groups.

Chapter Five: The Symbolic Process

Campbell, Joseph. *The Mythic Image.* Princeton, N.J.: Princeton University Press, 1974. A superbly illustrated study of religious symbolism and mythic themes from a Jungian perspective.

Firth, Raymond. *Symbols: Public and Private.* Ithaca, N.Y.: Cornell University Press, 1973. An anthropological study that begins with a definition of symbols and discusses artistic and religious symbolism, symbols in rites of passage, symbols of greeting and parting, the symbolism of flags, and such Christian symbols as the Sacred Heart and images of Christ. Also valuable for studying ritual.

Jung, Carl G. *Psyche and Symbol.* Garden City, N.Y.: Doubleday, 1958. Includes material relevant to the discussion of presentational symbols, particularly in relation to Holy Communion.

Langer, Susanne K. *Philosophy in a New Key.* New York: Mentor Books, 1964. A seminal work for understanding the symbolic process, signs, representational and presentational symbols, and the symbolic character of art, sacrament, and myth.

May, Rollo, ed. *Symbolism in Religion and Literature.* New York: Braziller, 1961. Includes essays by Erich Kahler on the nature of the symbol and by Paul Tillich on religious symbolism.

Moore, Albert C. *Iconography of Religions.* Philadelphia: Fortress Press, 1977. An introduction to religion through art. Begins with a discussion of images and icons as representational and presentational symbols and then introduces several different religious traditions through their symbolism.

Ross, Ralph. *Symbols and Civilization.* New York: Harcourt Brace Jovanovich, 1962. A clear and easy-to-read introduction to symbols in science, morals, religion, and art, which stresses the representational nature of symbolism.

Chapter Six: Three Ways
of Seeing and Speaking

Alston, William. *Philosophy of Language.* Englewood Cliffs, N.J.: Prentice-Hall, 1966. An excellent introduction to symbols, signs, icons, metaphor, and different uses of language.

Crossan, John Dominic. *Raid on the Articulate.* New York: Harper & Row, 1976. A stimulating introduction to language and to the use of comedy, paradox, and parable as ways of speaking about the holy.

Ferré, Frederick. *Basic Modern Philosophy of Religion.* New York: Scribner's, 1967. Includes chapters on religious language and its relationship to other types of discourse. Also discusses the arguments for the existence of God.

Gilkey, Langdon. *Naming the Whirlwind: The Renewal of God-Language.* Indianapolis, Ind.: Bobbs-Merrill, 1969. A valuable resource for a study of religious language, hermeneutics, and symbolism, including the multivalent and double-intentional character of religious discourse.

Hepburn, Ronald. *Christianity and Paradox.* New York: Pegasus, 1966. An important work for understanding the nature, limitations, and functions of religious language.

Rudner, Richard. *Philosophy of Social Science.* Englewood Cliffs, N.J.: Prentice-Hall, 1966. An introduction to scientific ways of seeing and speaking.

Stahmer, Harold. *Speak That I May See Thee: The Religious Significance of Language.* New York: Macmillan, 1968. An introduction to religious language through a discussion of the ideas of Johann Hamann, Eugen Rosenstock-Huessy, Franz Rosenzweig, and Martin Buber.

Stenson, Sten H. *Sense and Nonsense in Religion.* Nashville, Tenn.: Abingdon Press, 1969. An introduction to the mythopoeic character of religious language that includes an interpretation of myth, metaphor, parable, and pun as well as a discussion of the truth-value of religious statements.

van der Leeuw, Gerardus. *Sacred and Profane Beauty: The Holy in Art.* London: Weidenfeld and Nicholson, 1963. An excellent source for thinking about the relationship of religious and artistic modes of expression. Discusses sacred and profane dance, drama, poetry, pictorial arts, architecture, and music. Van der Leeuw begins with a discussion of ultimacy and holiness; his analysis has influenced my interpretation of the holy as ultimate and nonordinary.

Chapter Seven: Religious Language
as Story

Ayers, Robert A. "Religious Discourse and Myth." In Robert A. Ayers, ed., *Religious Language and Knowledge.* Atlanta: University of Georgia Press, 1972. A good discussion of myth, including the argument that all religious discourse contains mythic elements even when it is not an explicit story form.

Campbell, Joseph. *Myths Men Live By.* New York: Viking Press, 1972. Regards myths not merely as a collection of primitive stories but as a reflection of an ongoing human need for an emotionally and intellectually satisfying understanding of our place in the cosmos.

————. *The Hero with a Thousand Faces*. Princeton, N.J.: Princeton University Press, 1968. A psychoanalytic analysis of the hero as a mythic figure and of the relationship of such figures to our psychic needs.

Jeremias, Joachim. *The Parables of Jesus*. New York: Scribner's, 1970. Interprets the parables of Jesus and sheds light on the nature of parables.

Kirk, G.S. *Myth: Its Meaning and Function in Ancient and Other Cultures*. Berkeley: University of California Press, 1970. A scholarly introduction to myth, ritual, and folktale, including different approaches to the interpretation of myth.

Long, Charles H. *Alpha: The Myths of Creation*. New York: Braziller, 1963. A good resource for a study of origin myths.

Malinowski, Bronislaw. *Myth in Primitive Psychology*. Westport, Conn.: Negro University Press, 1971. Distinguishes between folktale, legend, and myth and argues that the context in which the myth is spoken is the key to its interpretation.

Otto, Walter F. *Dionysus: Myth and Cult*. Bloomington: Indiana University Press, 1965. Interprets myth and its relationship to holy communities with a primary focus on the myths associated with Dionysus.

Reps, Paul, ed. *Zen Flesh, Zen Bones*. Garden City, N.Y.: Doubleday, Anchor Books. A delightful collection of Zen stories.

Ricoeur, Paul *The Symbolism of Evil*. New York: Harper & Row, 1967. An analysis of symbolism and myth, particularly those myths that speak of the beginning and end of evil.

Wiggins, James B., ed. *Religion as Story*. New York: Harper & Row, 1975. Valuable for understanding religion as a form of story or metaphor.

Chapter Eight: Holy Rites

Douglas, Mary. *Natural Symbols*. New York: Pantheon Books, 1970. A good resource for a study of the functions and characteristics of ritual, symbolism, and antiritualism.

Fingarette, Herbert. *Confucius: The Secular as Sacred*. New York: Harper Torchbooks, 1972. A profound discussion of the character and value of ritual in the context of Confucianism.

Kluckhohn, Clyde. "Myths and Rituals: A General Theory." In Robert A. Georges, ed., *Studies in Mythology*. Homewood, Ill.: Dorsey Press, 1968. An important interpretation of myth and ritual.

LaFontaine, J.S., ed. *The Interpretation of Ritual*. London: Tavistock, 1972. Collection of essays that illustrate some of the general features of rituals and different types of rituals.

Nagendra, S.P. *The Concept of Ritual in Modern Sociological Theory*. New Delhi: Academic Journals of India, 1971. Introduces some of the primary models for understanding ritual, including those of Langer, Durkheim, Radcliffe-Brown, Freud, and Jung.

Underhill, Evelyn. *Worship.* New York: Harper Torchbooks, 1957. A very readable introduction to the forms of worship, including sacred rites and prayer. Includes a good discussion of the sacramental perspective and of symbolism.

Chapter Nine: Patterns and Types of Holy Rites

Bettelheim, Bruno. *Symbolic Wounds: Puberty Rites and the Envious Male.* New York: Collier Books, 1968. An interpretation of the wounds and pains that often accompany initiation rites, which argues that the wounding of adolescent males is a form of vaginal envy.

Cox, Harvey. *Feast of Fools: A Theological Essay on Festivity and Fantasy.* Cambridge, Mass.: Harvard University Press, 1969. A valuable resource for a discussion of parallels between sacred rite, drama, and play.

Eliade, Mircea. *Rites and Symbols of Initiation: The Mysteries of Birth and Rebirth.* New York: Harper & Row, 1973. An introduction to ritual and symbol through a focus on the transformational character of initiation rites.

Gaster, Theodor H. *Thespis: Ritual, Myth, and Drama in the Ancient Near East.* New York: Harper Torchbooks, 1966. A comparative analysis of biblical stories or myths with Near Eastern myths that have similar motifs.

Huizinga, Johan. *Homo Ludens: A Study of the Play Element in Culture.* Boston: Beacon Press, 1950. A good resource for an analogy between rite and drama.

Turner, Victor. *The Ritual Process: Structure and Anti-Structure.* Chicago: Aldine, 1968. In addition to discussing the symbolism of ritual and different types of rites, contains an intriguing model for understanding the ritual process.

van Gennep, Arnold. *The Rites of Passage.* Trans. by Monika B. Vizedom and Gabrielle L. Caffee. Chicago: University of Chicago Press, 1960. The classic study of those rites that mark key transition points in the life-process.

Chapter Ten: Patterns of Religious Experience

Allport, Gordon. *The Individual and His Religion.* New York: Macmillan, 1950. An easy-to-read introduction to the stages and patterns of religious development.

Eliade, Mircea. *Shamanism: Archaic Techniques of Ecstasy.* New York: Pantheon Books, 1964. Identifies a pattern in the transformational experiences of the shaman and provides a feeling for the role of the shaman.

James, William. *The Varieties of Religious Experience.* New York: Mentor Books, 1958. A classic that never seems out of date. Includes a discussion of what James calls sick souls and well souls, the religion of the healthy-minded, conversion experiences, mysticism and mystical experiences, and the psychopathological character of some religious experiences.

Niebuhr, Richard R. *Experiential Religion.* New York: Harper & Row, 1972. Valuable for a discussion of religious experience and the cognitive, conative, and emotional aspects of faith.

Pratt, J.B. *The Religious Consciousness.* New York: Macmillan, 1943. Covers a wide range of subjects: ritual, prayer, mystical experience, different patterns of religious growth and change, including the experiences of once-borns and twice-borns.

Shibiyama, Zenkai. *A Flower Does Not Talk: Zen Essays.* Rutland, Vt.: Charles E. Tuttle, 1970. In addition to being a very good introduction to Zen and to religious language, includes a discussion of transformational experiences in the Zen tradition.

Suzuki, D.T. *Mysticism: Christian and Buddhist.* New York: Collier Books, 1962. In addition to arguing that the ultimate focus of Christian mysticism and Zen have much in common, Zuzuki distinguishes between those who work out their own salvation and those who believe salvation is a divine gift.

Tillich, Paul. *The Dynamics of Faith.* New York: Harper Torchbooks, 1957. A stimulating discussion of faith understood as a response to what humans experience as ultimate. Distinguishes between what faith is and what it is not and makes a case for the close relationship of faith and doubt.

Wach, Joachim. *Types of Religious Experience, Christian and Non-Christian.* London: Routledge & Kegan Paul, 1951. The chapter "Universals in Religion" includes an excellent definition and discussion of the nature of religious experience.

Chapter Eleven: Paths of Ultimate Liberation

Capps, Donald and Walter H. Capps. *The Religious Personality.* Belmont,Calif.: Wadsworth, 1970. Identifies four distinct types of religious personality and varieties of religious experience, including the Resigned Self, the Chastised Self, the Fraternal Self, and the Aesthetic Self.

Clark, Walter H. *The Psychology of Religion.* New York: Macmillan, 1958. A standard introduction to the psychology of religion that includes a consideration of divided selves, conversion experiences, and stages of religious development in relationship to biological development (childhood, adolescence, etc.).

Clark, W., H. Maloney, et al. *Religious Experience.* Springfield, Ill.: Charles C. Thomas, 1973. Includes a discussion of personal experiences of the sacred, such ecstatic experiences as glossolalia, conversion experiences, and the effects of such experiences on behavior.

Jung, Carl. *Modern Man in Search of a Soul.* New York: Harcourt, Brace & World, 1933. A good resource for understanding the relationship of psychological needs, personal well-being, and religious experience.

Maritain, Jacques. *Approaches to God.* New York: Macmillan, 1965. Discusses some of the practical and speculative paths that lead to God.

Maslow, Abraham S. *Religions, Values, and Peak Experiences.* Columbus: Ohio State University Press, 1964. A good resource for a discussion of the naturalness of religious experience and its relationship to creative, self-fulfilling experiences.

Suzuki, D.T. *The Training of a Zen Buddhist Monk.* New York: University Books, 1959. Describes the monastic life of Zen monks from the point of their joining the monastic fellowship.

Tart, Charles. *States of Consciousness.* New York: E.P. Dutton, 1975. Examines different states of consciousness, including the mystical and parapsychological.

Chapter Twelve: Holy Communities

Hill, Michael. *A Sociology of Religion.* New York: Basic Books, 1973. A survey of different models for distinguishing between church-, denomination-, sect-, and cult-type religious groups. Also includes a discussion of charisma.

Kitagawa, Joseph M. *Religions of the East.* Philadelphia: Westminster Press, 1974. An introduction to Asian religious traditions that concentrates on their communal aspect.

O'Dea, Thomas F. *The Sociology of Religion.* Englewood Cliffs, N.J.: Prentice-Hall, 1966. Contains material relevant to much of this text, including a discussion of the sacred, religious experience, the institutionalization of religion, religion and social stratification, religion and conflict, church and sect.

Pope, Liston. *Millhands and Preachers.* New Haven, Conn.: Yale University Press, 1965. An important work on the relationship of class to membership in church-, demonination-, or sect-type religious groups, which concludes that the transition from sect to denomination is more a function of size than of class.

Weber, Max. *The Sociology of Religion.* Trans. by Ephraim Bischoff. Boston: Beacon Press, 1963. An older but seminal work that includes Weber's discussion of charisma and social change, the routinization of charisma as a way of understanding the movement from sect to church, and a discussion of soteriological themes.

Wilson, Bryan R. *Religious Sects.* London: Weidenfeld and Nicholson, 1970. Distinguishes between ongoing or second-generational sects and newly emerging ones and develops a typology that identifies seven different kinds of sects on the basis of their response to the world.

Yinger, J. Milton. *The Scientific Study of Religion.* New York: Macmillan, 1970. A comprehensive work that discusses ways that religion affects and is affected by society, provides a church-sect typology, deals with the problem of schism among religious groups, and examines the relationship of religion to patterns of social stratification.

Chapter Thirteen: Belief in God

Diamond, Malcolm L. *Contemporary Philosophy and Religious Thought.* New York: McGraw-Hill, 1974. An excellent introduction to problems in the theological traditions of the West, including the question of the existence of God and theodicy. Makes a distinction between philosophical and theological discourse and discusses the theologies of Rudolf Otto, Martin Buber, William James, Sören Kierkegaard, Rudolf Bultmann, and Paul Tillich.

Hick, John. *Philosophy of Religion,* 2nd ed. Englewood Cliffs, N.J.: Prentice-Hall, 1973. A solid introduction to the philosophy of religion. Includes grounds for belief and disbelief in the existence of the God of theism, the question of human destiny, a discussion of religious language, and the quest for verifiability of religious statements.

Hume, David. *Dialogues Concerning Natural Religion.* New York: Bobbs-Merrill, 1947. A classic philosophical dialogue that probes arguments and counterarguments for the existence of God, with an emphasis on the teleological argument.

Plantinga, Alvin, ed. *The Ontological Argument from St. Anselm to Contemporary Philosophers.* Garden City, N.Y.: Doubleday, Anchor Books, 1965. Includes a valuable introductory essay on the ontological argument written by Richard Taylor, as well as primary selections from St. Anselm and more recent defenders of the argument.

Smart, Ninian. *Philosophy of Religion.* New York: Oxford University Press, 1979. A very readable introduction to the philosophy of religion that attempts to treat the problems of suffering, evil, and human destiny from the vantage point of both Western and non-Western religious traditions.

Streng, Frederick J., ed. *The Religious Life of Man.* Encino, Calif.: Dickenson. A valuable, multivolumed series for the study of the beliefs of several different religious traditions that includes: Cragg, Kenneth, *The House of Islam;* Earhart, Byron, *Japanese Religion;* Hopkins, Thomas, *The Hindu Religious Tradition;* Neusner, Jacob, *The Way of Torah;* Robinson, Richard, *The Buddhist Religion;* Thompson, Lawrence, *Chinese Religion.*

Chapter Fourteen: Suffering and Death: Two Existential and Theological Breaking Points

Becker, Ernest. *The Denial of Death.* Glencoe, Ill.: Free Press, 1974. A probing of ways humans deal with death.

Bowker, John. *Problems of Suffering in Religions of the World.* London: Cambridge University Press, 1970. A comparative treatment of the problem of human suffering as it is understood by the major religious traditions.

Brandon, S.G.F. *The Judgment of the Dead: The Idea of Life after Death in the Major Religions.* New York: Scribner's, 1967. A comparative study of beliefs about survival after death.

Hick, John. *Evil and the God of Love,* rev. ed. New York: Harper & Row, 1978. A treatment of the problem of theodicy from within the Christian tradition that argues suffering and evil are indispensable features of a moral universe.

——. *Death and Eternal Life.* New York: Harper & Row, 1977. Examines the primary responses to the question of what happens to us when we die.

Penelhum, Terence. *Immortality.* Belmont, Calif.: Wadsworth, 1973. Distinguishes between the immortality of the soul and the resurrection of the body. Evaluates the evidence for life after death.

Plato. *The Phaedo.* Trans. by F.J. Church. New York: Bobbs-Merrill, 1951. A classic philosophical defense of the immortality of the soul.

Chapter Fifteen: Closing the Circle

Bellah, Robert N. *Beyond Belief: Essays on Religion in a Post-Traditional World.* New York: Harper & Row, 1970. Helpful for understanding the secular character of modern life.

Berger, Peter L. *A Rumor of Angels.* Garden City, N.Y.: Doubleday, 1969. Has much to say about the affect of secularism on religious beliefs, the "death of God," and the search for hints of transcendence in the modern world.

Brown, Robert M. *Is Faith Obsolete?* Philadelphia: Westminster Press, 1974. Excellent resource for reflection on the growth of secularism, the so-called decline of faith, and what the word *faith* implies and demands.

   Cox, Harvey. *The Secular City,* 4th ed. Toronto: Macmillan, 1969. An important work on secularity and the secularizing of religious values and symbols.

   Geertz, Clifford. *Islam Observed: Religious Development in Morocco and Indonesia.* New Haven, Conn.: Yale University Press, 1968. A valuable study of the secularization of religious worlds of meaning and different human reactions to modern challenges to traditional beliefs.

   Kaufmann, Walter. *The Faith of a Heretic.* New York: Doubleday, 1963. A critical and honest reflection on faith, agnosticism, atheism, heresy, orthodoxy, and problems of religious belief, from a humanist perspective.

   Marty, Martin E. *Varieties of Unbelief.* New York: Holt, Rinehart and Winston, 1964. Distinguishes between belief and unbelief and various kinds of unbelief, with Christianity as the normative belief system.

   Robinson, Bishop John T. *Honest to God.* Philadelphia: Westminster Press, 1963. A Christian theologian argues that much of the traditional notion of God is no longer defensible and needs to be interred.

   Tillich, Paul. *The Courage to Be.* New Haven, Conn.: Yale University Press, 1952. Relates to the discussion of what is involved in being nonreligious. Tillich argues that the loss of meaning is a more serious spiritual malady than are changes in belief.

Media Guide

Because religious phenomena include things that are performed and observed as well as ideas that are conceived, the subject is admirably suited to audio and visual productions. In fact, it is difficult to discuss sacred rites, speaking in tongues, chants, and other forms of religious expression independent of an opportunity to see and hear them. Films and other media resources can bring such phenomena into an academic context and, in doing so, help bridge the gap between the abstract and theoretical character of an analysis of religious phenomena and the concrete and performative character of religious actions and objects. Since the text is divided into four major parts, I have arranged the guide to media resources on a similar basis. For additional information write directly for catalogues from some of the principal sources of media with religious themes, such as Hartley Productions, Mass Media Ministries, TeleKETICS: The Franciscan Communications Center, and Time-Life Films. There is also an excellent annotated guide to religious films in C. Freeman Sleeper and Robert A. Spivey, eds., *The Study of Religion in Two-Year Colleges* (Missoula, Mont.: Scholars Press, 1975).

Part I: Introducing Religion

   Why Man Creates *(25 minutes, color, Mass Media Ministries).* A film that explores both the creative process and the need to create. It can serve to stimulate discussion about the inventive and meaning-giving character of human existence and the senses in which religion is a human creation.

Man and His Gods *(two 15-minute narrated slide programs, Humanities, Inc.).* Introduces different religious traditions through their distinctive modes of ceremony and worship.

The Dancing Prophet *(15 minutes, color, TeleKETICS).* Raises the question of how one serves God. The film tells the story of Doug Crutchfield, who serves and heals others through dance, and his tension with his father, who understands the Christian ministry more in terms of the preaching of the Gospel. The film can be used to introduce the autobiographical character of religious experience implicit in the questions, Who am I? Why am I here? and Where am I going?

Psychics, Saints, and Scientists *(33 minutes, color, Hartley Productions).* An exploration of some of the research conducted in parapsychology, including psychokinesis, clairvoyance, telepathy, faith healing, auras, out-of-body experiences, and biofeedback. Can be used in conjunction with a discussion of the relationship of magic, science, and religion in chapter three. A discussion of magic usually prompts people to share experiences and ask questions about areas in which magic, religion, and extrasensory perception overlap.

Part II: The Conceptual and Ritual Dimensions of Religion

The Loon's Necklace *(10 minutes, color, Encyclopaedia Britannica Educational Corporation).* A film adaptation of a myth of origin associated with an Indian tribe from British Columbia. In addition to providing an opportunity to illustrate a myth and discuss the distinction between myth and fable, the film introduces a wide range of religious phenomena: a shaman who has magico-religious power; fetishes; ritual masks; and various symbols, including the number four and water, which is a natural and archetypal symbol of purification and rebirth. It also provides a feel for the tribal understanding of the world as filled with sacred power and spirit beings.

The Stray *(14 minutes, color, TeleKETICS).* A visual adaptation of the parable of the lost sheep that can be used in conjunction with the discussion of parable as a type of sacred story. The essential components of the parable are retained in the story of an outing to the San Diego Zoo of a group of children and their bus driver. The joy of the day turns to anxiety and fear when one of the children strays from the group.

To Find Our Life *(90 minutes, color, University of California at Los Angeles).* An excellent introduction to tribal religion and the ritual process. It records a pilgrimage of Huichol Indians (Mexico), who are guided by their shaman-leader to the land of their ancestors. The pilgrimage is an extended ritual involving the preparation and cleansing of the pilgrims before they set foot on sacred ground, offerings and prayers of petition to their Grandfather, the fire, followed by a gathering and eating of their elder brother, peyote, in a ceremonial meal. The film also provides an opportunity to discuss a ritual re-creation of sacred time, the nature of sacred places, and the role of mind-expanding drugs in religious practice.

The Life Cycle in Hinduism *(30 minutes, color, David Knipe of the University of Wisconsin at Madison).* A video-tape of traditional Hindu life-cycle rites, including those associated with birth, initiation, and marriage. Other video-tapes narrated by Dr. Knipe relevant to a discussion of sacred rites are *Death and Rebirth in Hinduism* and *Hindu Temples and the Pilgrimage Tradition.*

Baptism: Sacrament of Belonging *(10 minutes, color, Mass Media Ministries)*. The meaning of baptism is examined through the experience of an orphaned Mexican boy who is accepted by a community of orphans. See also **Resurrection** *(28 minutes, color, Yale University Media Design Studio)*, a celebration of Easter in Los Angeles by a Mexican-American Family.

The Way of the Ancestors *(50 minutes, color, Time-Life Multi-Media)*. One of thirteen films in the BBC television series *The Long Search*, narrated by Ronald Eyre. The film introduces tribal religion through a study of the ritual way of the Torajas of Indonesia.

Christian Symbolism *(80 color slides, narration, Logos Signum Publications)*. A set of slides that can help illustrate the double-intentional and multivalent character of religious symbols. Slides of symbols from non-Christian traditions are available from other sources.

Part III: The Personal and Social Dimensions

Meeting in the Air *(27 minutes, color, Yale University Media Design Studio)*. One of thirteen films in the PBS series *Religious America*. Introduces pentecostalism and a wide range of religious experience, including spirit-possession, spiritual regeneration, speaking in tongues, and faith healing.

Yoga *(14 minutes, black-and-white, David Lawrence, San Bernardino Valley College)*. A nonnarrated introduction to yoga understood as a discipline of the body through exercise and a cultivation of the power to concentrate and relax, which culminates in a unifying and liberating experience. In spite of its lack of narration, the film provides sufficient symbols for its interpretation and can be used for a discussion of meditation and unitive or mystical experience.

Meditation: The Inward Journey *(20 minutes, color, Hartley Productions)*. Discusses meditative techniques, including the importance of posture and breathing and introduces the role of mantras, mandalas, and prayers as instruments of self-awareness.

I Am a Monk *(30 minutes, color, Hartley Productions)*. Introduces the monastic life through the story of an American Buddhist monk in Thailand. It can serve as a springboard for a discussion of religious vocations and roles, including those of monk, priest, prophet, and sage. See also **Vina** *(28 minutes, color, Yale University Media Design Studio)*, which introduces the Christian monastic life through the routines of two Trappist monks.

Lubavitch *(28 minutes, color, Yale University Media Design Studio)*. An introduction to Hasidic Jews who are maintaining their traditional ways in Brooklyn, New York. Discusses Shabat, Torah, and the character of Jewish education. It can also serve to stimulate discussion of different types of religious groups.

New Age Communities: The Search for Utopia *(40 minutes, color, Hartley Productions)*. A look at groups that are seeking alternative patterns of community. See also **Lighthouse in Loleta** *(28 minutes, color, Yale University Media Design Studio)*, the story of a Christian commune in Northern California, and **Kundalini** *(27 minutes, color, Yale University Media Design Studio)*, the story of a Massachusetts ashram or commune that draws on Asian wisdom for its spirituality.

Mother Teresa of Calcutta *(51 minutes, color, Time-Life).* One way of dealing with personal and transformational experiences is to look closely at the lives of people who have been touched by the sacred. Mother Teresa is such a person.

Marjoe *(88 minutes, color, Cinema 5 New York).* The story of a youthful evangelist who travels a revivalist circuit for complex reasons, including a desire for profit. Useful for a discussion of the charismatic personality and the psychopathological implications of religious experience.

Part IV: Belief and Disbelief: The Conceptual Dimension of Religion

Night and Fog *(31 minutes, color, McGraw-Hill Films).* A powerful film of the carnage and brutality of the Holocaust. Introduces the subject of human suffering and can raise the question of the existence of a God who loves humans as parents love their children. Alternate possibilities are **Awareness,** a modern retelling of Buddha's suffering and his pilgrimage to Enlightenment, and **Why** *(25 minutes, color, Mass Media Ministries),* which raises the question of why humans are so often racist, violent, and destructive.

Occurrence at Owl Creek *(17 minutes, color).* A film based on Ambrose Bierce's story of a hanging of a saboteur during the Civil War. It is a statement about the will to live.

Though I Walk through the Shadow *(30 minutes, color, Mass Media Ministries).* A documentary of the last months of a terminal cancer victim.

Life after Death *(35 minutes, color, Hartley Productions).* Introduces different beliefs about life after death.

Hell *(45 minutes, color, Mass Media Ministries).* Discusses hell as a condition of separation or alienation from God, from others, and from the world around us rather than as a place.

Heaven *(45 minutes, color, Mass Media Ministries).* Understands heaven not as something beyond this world but as a touch of eternity in time through which humans grope toward love and wholeness.

Index

Campbellites: 274
Camus, Albert: 304, 313, 319, 343, 350
Capps, Donald: 372
Capps, Walter: 24, 372
Cardenale, Ernesto: 170
Cassirer, Ernst: 189
Castaneda, Carlos: 73, 237
Celibacy: 263
Ceremony: 150, 206
Charisma: 264–267
Chase, Mary: 174
Chastity: 263
Chesterton, G.K.: 32
Cheyenne: 134
Chidika: 154
Chijikijilu: 152
Children of God: 274, 275
Christian Church: 254, 256
Christian humanism: 346
Christianity: 22, 53, 59, 73, 74, 134,
    162, 207, 217, 226, 260, 269, 274,
    285, 321, 330, 331, 332; baptism in,
    93–95; sacrament in, 151; symbols
    in, 88; views of suffering in, 305,
    310–315
Christian Science: 275
Christian signs: 85
Christian theology: 281, 284–285
Christmas: 74, 162
Church: 255, 358
Church-denomination-sect typology:
    270–274
Church of Jesus Christ of Latter-Day
    Saints: 266
Church membership: 270–271
Church of Religious Science: 275
Church-type group: 270–272
Circumcision: 185; rite, 180
Clan: 258, 260
Clark, Walter H.: 372
Cleanthes: 292
Cleaver, Eldridge: 230–231
Coast Salish Indians: 184, 189
Collective rites: 162
Communism: 6, 351
Communitas: 179–182, 358
Comte, Auguste: 47
Confirmation: 187
Conflict and religion: 267–275
Confucianism: 11, 57, 58, 65, 154,

155, 212–214, 254, 260–261, 344,
    345; as historic religion, 54
Confucius: 169, 239, 287, 345–346,
    352
Contagious magic, as low magic: 44
Conversion to the sacred: 232–233; of
    St. Paul, 231–232; of troubled self,
    230–232
Cosmological argument, for God's
    existence: 287–289
Cosmological character of myth: 128
Cosmology: 358
Cox, Harvey: 371, 375
Coyote: 132
Creation of humans: 130–131
Creature-feeling: 208
Creed: 151, 331, 334
Cronus: 130, 138
Crossan, John Dominic: 369
Cult of Reason: 6
Cyclical renewal, myths of: 135

Daedalus: 236
Dali, Salvador: 109–110
Dance: 175
Dante Alighieri: 33, 227, 321, 340, 341
Darwin, Charles: 47, 267
Das Kapital: 47
David, king of Israel: 73, 141
Day of Atonement: 163
Death: 48, 184, 303; acceptance of,
    318–320; as fear of nothingness,
    317–318; fear of, 304, 317–318;
    liberation from, 318–320; life be-
    yond, 320; preparation for, 318;
    resignation in, 318; rites of,
    189–191; survival after, 325–326;
    survival of individuality in,
    321–322; what survives, 282
Death rites: Hindu, 190–191; Jewish,
    190; Mormon, 190
Definitions: functional, 12–13; sub-
    stantive, 12, 13
Deism: 207, 358
Deities: 249
de Jesus, Carolina: 342
Demeter: 135, 136, 137, 191
Denomination: 255, 358
Denominational divisions: 16
Denominationalism: 273–274

Denomination-type groups: 273–274
Descartes, René: 283, 289–290
Deuteronomist: 229
Devil: 45, 333
de Vries, Jan: 367
Dharma: 269
Diamond, Malcolm L.: 373
Dickinson, Emily: 123, 124
Dionysus: 137, 175, 203
Dionysus the Areopagite: 114
Disbelief: 282
Disciples of Christ: 274
Discipline: 215
Disinherited: 336–337
Dispossessed: 337–339
Disquieted self: 225
Divided self: 224–225
Division, causes of, in religious groups: 269–270
Dogen, Eikai: 142
Dogma: 284, 331, 334
Dominic, Saint: 256
Donne, John: 317
Dostoevsky, Fyodor: 314
Double-intentional, religious language: 111–113, 358
Douglas, Mary: 155, 156, 167, 204, 370
Drama: 174–176
Dramatic expression: 174–175
Dreams: 90–91
Dukkha: 305, 307–308
Dunne, John S.: 235, 320, 366
Dupré, Louis: 226
Durandeaux, Jacques: 211
Durkheim, Emile: 159, 248–249, 250, 251, 367
Duty: 240

Early modern religion: 53–54
Easter: 74, 162, 165, 178, 179
Eastern Orthodox: 94, 269, 271
Eastern Orthodox Christianity: as historic religion, 54; icons in, 92
Eckhart, Meister: 218, 297
Ecstacy: 202–206
Effervescence: 202–206
Ekai: 237
Ekido: 141

Eliade, Mircea: 14, 66, 71–73, 137, 157, 217, 229, 367, 371
Elijah Muhammad: 33
Ellwood, Robert S., Jr.: 365
Emotional function of religion: 27
Empathy: 358
Empirical character of science: 103, 358
Empirical evidence: 104
End-of-historical-time myths: 134–135
Enlightenment: 212–214, 216–217, 228–229
Enuma Elish: 192
Episcopal Church, baptism in: 94
Episcopalians: 274
Epistemology: 102, 359
Eschatological myths: 129, 133–134
Eschatology: 134, 359
est: 226
Eternal: 14, 359
Eucharist, mystery of: 152–153
Evaluative religious language: 111, 115–116
Evangelican Christian sects: 272
Evans-Pritchard, E.E.: 52, 248, 258
Evil, origin of: 310–311
Evolution of religion and magic, ideas on: 47
Evon, Vogt: 367
Exegesis: 28, 359
Existentialism: 346, 359
Exodus: 160
Experiences: peak, 7–8; transcendent, 8

Fairy tales: 128
Faith: 199–200, 283, 284, 359; as emotional, 200–201; as passionate, 200–201; emotional depth of, 201
Farb, Peter: 177
Father Divine: 263–265
Feldmann, Susan: 125
Ferré, Frederick: 369
Fetishes: 45, 92, 359
Feuerbach, Ludwig: 15–16
Filial hierarchy: 257
Filial piety: 258–261
Filial relationships: 250–251, 259
Fingarette, Herbert: 154, 169, 370

as quest of, 235-236; experience of, as existential presence, 296-298; pilgrimmage as quest of, 235; quest of, 235-242

Holocaust: 163, 314, 341-342

Holy: 14, 63, 71, 84, 359; approaches to, 241-242; as element of religion, 72; as immanent, 212-217; as non-ordinary, 67-71; as transcendent, 207-208; as ultimate, 66-67; defining, 63-65; human feeling in, 111; in Buddhism, 65; in Confucianism, 65; mystery of, 68; paradox of, 65; paths to, 239-242; power of, 69-71; way of expressing, 72; ways of responding to, 206-218

Holy Being: 35, 66, 202, 206-207

Holy city: 74; Jerusalem as, 74; Mecca as, 74; Rome as, 74

Holy communion: 84, 151-152, 153, 156, 159, 218

Holy communities: 247; change in, 270-271; creation of, 268; discord in, 267-268; division in, 267, 268, 269-270; organization in, 267-275; protest in, 267-270; reform in, 268-269; renewal in, 268-269; secession in, 269-270; symbol system in, 264

Holy dance: 152

Holy dramas, as fantasies: 175

Holy Eucharist: 156, 169

Holy icon: 72

Holy rites: 149, 150; as drama, 173-176; as commemorative, 159-161; as performative, 153-156; as praise, 166-167; as purification, 164-165; as re-creative, 158-159; as reiterative, 157; as repetitive, 156-157; as sacrament, 151-153; as sacrifice, 166-167; as shared experience, 162-164; as social, 161-162; as supplication, 164-165; as thanksgiving, 166-167; in religious experience, 198; participants in, 174; primary features of, 151-164; purposes of, 164-167; qualities of drama in, 174

Holy Spirit: 69, 239, 253; gifts of the, 359

Holy Week: 178, 182

Holy words: 149, 198

Home, loss of: 335-339

Homeopathic magic, as low magic: 43-44

Homolograph: 145

Hopi: 54, 127

Hsuan-chien: 217

Hugh of Saint Victor: 151

Huichol Indians: 74, 159

Hui-neng: 200

Huizinga, Johan: 371

Human-centeredness: 349

Human existence: purpose of, 34; social character of, 248

Humanism: 346-351, 360

Human origin myths: 130

Humans: biological nature of, 9; essential nature of, 8; religiousness of, 7-8; "second nature" of, 9; separation of, from animals, 8-9

Hume, David: 291, 292, 373

Huppah: 188

Hutterite Brethren: 256, 272, 274

Hutter, Jacob: 256

Huxley, Julian: 7, 8, 293

Ibo: 56

Icarus: 236

I Ching: 113-114

Icon: 89, 91, 93, 96, 360

Iconoclasm: 96, 360

Idol, worship of: 17

Idolatry: 17

Iks: 342, 343

Image: 89, 90, 91, 93, 96

Imitative magic, as low magic: 43-44

Immanent: 206-207, 360

Immortality: absence of belief in, 323-324; of the soul, 322, 360; rejection of belief in, 323-324

Incarnation: 93

Incas: 56

Initiation rites: 185-187; bar mitzvah as, 186-187; circumcision as, 186; confirmation as, 187; sexual wounding as, 186

Installation rites: 185

Intellectual function of religion: 27

Interpretation: of religious phe-

nomena, 29; of sacred texts, 28; of
studies of religion, 28
Iroquois: 129
Isaiah: 210
Isis: 59
Islam: 22, 53, 59, 73–74, 93, 157, 207,
209, 285, 321, 332, 344; as historic
religion, 54; as universal religion, 55
Isoma: 91, 179; rite, 150, 152

Jaina: 263
Jainism: 11, 54, 286–287, 352
James, William: 49, 68, 119, 198–199,
224–225, 233, 295–296, 371
Jaspers, Karl: 30, 36
Jehovah's Witnesses: 272, 274, 275
Jen: 65
Jephthah: 166
Jeremias, Joachim: 370
Jesus: 26, 41, 85–86, 111, 113, 134,
140, 197, 201, 224, 252, 263, 265,
296, 298; language of, 113; parables
of, 140–142
Jewish faith: 166
Jewish marriage ceremony: 187–188
Jewish Passover: 160–161
Jewish rites: 150, 178, 189–190
Jewish sacrament: 151
Jewish theology: 284
Jewish worship: 163
Jnana yoga: 239
John of Patmos: 134
Johnson, Dr. Samuel: 14, 35–36
Johnson, James Weldon: 113–114
Jones, Reverend Jim: 265
Joyce, James: 333
Judaism: 22, 54, 60, 73–74, 134, 206,
207, 234, 269, 285, 321, 332, 335,
344, 348–349, 352
Jung, Carl: 137, 177, 228, 368, 372

Ka'ba: 74
Kaddish: 190
Kafu: 179
Kali: 97, 137
Kalki: 135
Kami: 166
Kant, Immanuel: 102
Karma yoga: 239
Karma yogin: 239–240

Katzie Indians: 184, 321
Kaufmann, Walter: 375
Kazantzakis, Nikos: 242, 281
Keen, Sam: 31, 32, 202, 216, 229, 243,
366
Kerenyi, Karl: 174
Kiddish: 161–162
Kiddushin: 188
Kierkegaard, Sören: 200, 205, 209,
225, 282, 296
King, Martin Luther, Jr.: 53
King, Winston L.: 365
Kirk, G.S.: 140, 370
Kisa Gotami: 141–142
Kitagawa, Joseph M.: 373
Khomeini, Ayatollah Ruhollah: 271
Kluckhohn, Clyde: 370
Knowledge: 102, 106, 107
Koan: 118, 126, 360
Konso: 97
Koran: 5, 29, 76, 95, 232, 262, 266,
285
Krishna: 12, 69, 115, 135, 181–182,
208, 240
Krishna Consciousness: 241
Kristensen, W. Brede: 71–73, 365
Kshatriya: 187
Kubler-Ross, Dr. Elisabeth: 317–318,
325, 326
Kumbh Mela: 162
!Kung Bushmen: 204
Kuth: 52
Kwoth: 52, 166–167, 258

LaFontaine, J.S.: 370
Langer, Susanne K.: 96, 125, 174, 368
Latter-Day Saints: 190
Leary, Timothy: 169
Legends: 128–129
Lent: 165
Lenten: 162, 179
Lessa, William: 367
Levi-Strauss, Claude: 139
Lewis, C.S.: 216, 235
Li: 154, 155, 169
Liberation: 216, 323
Lienhardt, Godfrey: 367
Life beyond death: 320–325
Life-crisis rites: 184
Life cycle rites: 184–191; birth rites as,

185; initiation rites as, 185–187; marriage rites as, 187–189; rites of mourning as, 189–190

Lifton, Robert Jay: 344

Liminal: 360

Liminality: 179–181

Liminal period: 177

Lindsey, Hal: 86

Local religion: 55, 56–57; as primitive, 56–57; as tribal, 56–57

Long, Charles H.: 370

Lord's Prayer: 151

Loss: of belief, 330–335; of home, 335–339; of meaning: 339–343; of paradise myths: 130–133

Low magic: 42–43; contagious magic as, 44; fetishes used in, 45; homeopathic magic as, 43–44; imitative magic as, 43–44; purposes of, 43

Loyola: 256

Luiseño: 177

Luther, Martin: 256, 285

Lutheran Church: 94, 271, 273, 274

MacLeish, Archibald: 306, 312

Macquarrie, John: 99, 299, 309–310, 368

Magic: 27, 40–52, 360; as a belief system, 40–42; as expression of confidence, 51; beneficial, 45; evolution of, 47, 48; high, 42–44; imitations in, 42; in tribal cultures, 51; in twentieth century, 45–46; knowledge of, 42; "laws" of, 41–42; low, 42–43; malevolent, 45; manipulation of objects in, 42; power in, 40–41; of primitives, 51; origin of, 47, 48; religion in, 40–41; science in, 40–41; sign reading in, 42; spoken formulas in, 42; types of, 42–45

Magical belief system: 41

Magicoreligious concepts: 40

Mahamantra: 89–90, 92

Mahayana: 270

Mahayana Buddhism: 11

Mahler, Gustav: 109

Maitreya Buddha: 135

Malcolm X: 32–33

Malevolent magic: 45

Malinowski, Bronislaw: 46, 48, 50–51, 138, 370

Mana: 50, 52, 360

Mandalas: 92, 360

"Mandate of Heaven": 59

Mani: 263

Manifesto II: 347–348

Mantras: 90, 91, 360

Mantrayana: 270

Maoists: 345

Mao Tse-tung: 14, 227, 240

Marduk: 192

Maritain, Jacques: 239, 241, 372

Marriage, as life cycle rite: 184

Marriage ceremony, Jewish: 188

Marriage rites: 187–189

Marty, Martin E.: 345, 375

Marx, Karl: 13, 47, 144, 226–227, 267, 350, 351, 353

Marxism: 6, 10, 13, 227, 346, 350, 351, 360

Maslow, Abraham H.: 7–8, 372

Mass, mystery of: 152–153

Matrilineal descent groups: 257–258

May, Rollo: 90, 368

Maya: 239

Mbiti, John: 258–259

Meaning, loss of: 339–343

Mecca: 157, 253

Meditation: 205, 215, 241, 360

Mennonite: 272

Merton, Thomas: 91

Messiah: 134–135

Metaphysics: 47, 102, 361

Methodism: 273

Middle creature: 113–114

Middleton, John: 367

Millay, Edna St. Vincent: 340

Miller, William: 135

Minos, king of Crete: 236

Miracles: 85, 361

Missionaries of Charity: 269

Modern religion: 53–54

Monasticism: 361

Monastic order: 268

Mondo: 118, 124–125, 361

Monism: 52, 361

Monotheism: 48, 51, 52, 58, 251, 268, 298, 361

Moody, Dr. Raymond A.: 325, 326
Moore, Albert C.: 368
Mormonism: 197, 207, 269, 285
Mormons: 116; death rites of, 190;
  marriage of, 188
Moroni: 197
Mortification, of the flesh: 241
Moses: 32, 64, 73, 86, 137, 144, 201,
  210
Mother Earth: 130
Mother Teresa: 269
Mudras: 92, 361
Muhammad: 26, 29, 60, 74, 157, 197,
  201, 210, 252, 263–264, 270, 285,
  298, 325
Muslims: 60, 76, 106, 157, 217, 232,
  253, 331–332
Muslim Ummah: 254, 270, 274
Mystical experience: 217–218
Mysticism: 206, 217–218, 361
Myths: 124, 125, 126–140, 298, 361;
  as cosmological, 128; as creative fantasies, 129; as disclosure of ultimate
  existence: 136–137; as mediation of
  conflicts and contradictions,
  139–140; as nonhistorical, 129; as
  ontological, 128; as projection of the
  unconscious, 137–138; as spiritual
  disclosures, 129; as validation of
  social order, 138; as visions, 129;
  cyclical motif in, 135–136; defined,
  126–127; end-of-historical-time,
  134–135; eschatological, 129,
  133–134; fantasy quality of, 128;
  focus of, 128; function of, 127–128;
  future-time, 129; human origin, 130;
  interpretation of, 136–140; of cyclical renewal, 135; of loss of paradise,
  130–133; of origin of alienation,
  130–133; of origin,
  128–130;phenomena in, 127;
  sacred, 128–129; sexual alienation
  in, 132–133; subject matter of,
  127–128; tellers of, 129; time of
  origin in, 127; truth of, 128; value
  of, 127–128

Nagendra, S.P.: 370
Nanak: 263

Nan-in: 22
Nataraja: 175
Nation of Islam: 33
National religion: 55, 57–59; Confu-
  cianism as, 57–58; Hinduism as,
  57–58; pharaoh in, 59; polytheism
  in, 59; Shinto as, 55, 57, 58
Natural religious groups: 255,
  257–261; ancestral spirits in,
  258–261; filial piety in, 258–261;
  tribal societies as, 257–258
Natural scientists: 105
Navaho: 57, 126, 127, 132
Ndembu: 91, 93, 150, 152, 154,
  179–181
Necromancy, as high magic: 43
Needham, Joseph: 212
Neti, neti: 299
Neusner, Jacob: 284
Newman, Francis W.: 234–235
Nichiren Shōshū: 5, 11, 59, 155, 264
Niebuhr, Reinhold: 143
Niebuhr, Richard R.: 200–201, 371
Nietzsche, Friedrich: 144, 175,
  224–225, 227, 282, 317, 340, 349
Nirvana: 16, 23, 65, 71, 114, 213, 287,
  297, 298, 308, 324, 361
Noah: 137
Noble Eightfold Path: 114, 308
Noetic: 107, 361
Nonordinary: as holy, 67; sacred as, 72
Nothingness: 343
Novak, Michael: 10, 11, 237, 366
Nuer: 166, 258
Numerology, as high magic: 43
Numinous: 68, 361

Occult learning: 42
O'Dea, Thomas F.: 303–304, 373
Oedipus: 138
Old Order Amish: 272, 274
Ol-orun: 74, 129, 130
Ontological character of myths: 128
Ontological argument, for God's exis-
  tence: 289–291
Ontology: 361
Onyankopon: 130–131, 132
Ordinary, profane as: 72
Original sin: 311

224–233; untroubled self as, 233–234

"Religious" question: 24–25, 30

Religious rites: baptism as, 93–95; symbolism of, 92–96

Religious signs: 85–86, 87–88; as ambiguous, 86; types of, 86

Religious symbols: 87–88, 249–250

Religious ways: of seeing, 111–119; of speaking, 111–119

Remotion: 299, 362

Renewal, in holy communities: 268–269

Representational symbol: 87–89, 92; baptism as, 93–85; in Buddhism, 88–89; meaning of, 87; tabernacle as, 88

Reps, Paul: 370

Resignation: 318

Resurrection of the body: 322, 362

Revelation: as discovery, 117–118; as invitation, 117–118; as sacred disclosure, 116–117

Revelatory religious language: 111, 116–119

Revivalism: 203

Revival meeting: 202

Rhea: 130, 138

Ricoeur, Paul: 144, 145, 370

Rigveda: 65, 321

Rissho Koseikai: 344

Rites: as efficacious: 156; as purification, 164–165; as social, 161–162; as supplication, 164–165; as collective, 162; as seasonal, 191–192; of status elevation, 181; of status reversal, 181; pain in, 180; power in, 156

Rites, holy. See Holy rites; Ritual

Rites, life cycle. See Life cycle rites

Rites of mourning, as life cycle rites: 189–190

Rites of passage: 184, 362. See also Life cycle rites

Ritual: 149, 167–170, 205, 362; as performative, 153–156; as repetitive, 156–158; as sacrament, 151–153; as shared experience, 162–164; derivation of, 174; handshake as, 155; in childbirth, 178–179; in pregnancy, 178–179; obligatory quality of, 154; pain in,

180; presidential oath as, 153, 154–155; psychology of, 155–156; triadic structure of, 177–178; wounding in, 181

Ritual drama, pattern of: 177

Ritual pattern: 177–179, 180

Ritual process: liminal phase of, 179–181; stages in, 176–177; transition phase of, 179–181

Robinson, Bishop John T.: 375

Roman Catholic Church: 218, 252, 262, 263, 268, 269, 271–272, 273, 284, 336–337, 345; historic religion of, 54; sacraments of, 151; saints in, 256

Roman Catholic rites of passage: 184

Roman Catholic tabernacle: 88

Rosenzweig, Franz: 206

Ross, Ralph: 368

Rta: 154

Rubin, Jerry: 168

Rudner, Richard: 369

Russell, Bertrand: 351

Russell, Jeffrey B.: 367

Russian Orthodox Church: 344

Sabbath: 73–74, 114, 115, 163, 206

Sacrament: 89, 92, 93, 96, 362; as act of God, 156; as contact, 151; as ritual, 151–153; as tangible, 151–152

Sacred: as element of religion, 72; as nonordinary, 72; Catholic Church as, 73; understanding of, 72

Sacred disclosure: discovery as, 117–118; invitation as, 117–!18; revelation as, 116–117

Sacred dramas: 174

Sacred myths: 128–129

Sacred rites: 150, 206

Sacred story: 123, 149, 206; as imaginative, 124–125; as polysemous, 143; forms of, 125–126; mondo as, 124, 125; myth as, 124, 125, 126–140; parable as, 124, 125, 140–143; prophecy as, 125; revelatory, 125–126; theology as, 125; truth of, 143–145

Sacred time: 73–74

Sacrifice, rites as: 166–167

Sadducees: 321

Suffering: 303; as feature of existence, 304; Buddhist view of, 306–310; Christian view of, 310–315; in Christian theology, 311–313; meaning of, 311–313; reasons for, 304–315
Sunnis: 266, 271
Superstition: 47
Supplication, rites as: 164–165
Suso, Heinrich: 241
Suttles, Wayne: 325
Suzuki, D.T.: 116, 372
Symbol: as bridge, 87; as presentational, 89–93; as representational, 87–89; as sign, 85–86; character of, 96; cup as, 84; dreams as, 90–91; Holy Communion as, 84; natural, 90; rainbow as, 89; rhinoceros as, 197; relationship of, to things, 85; word as, 87, 96–97
Symbolic death: 229
Symbolic process: described, 84–85; in religious expression, 83
Systems of significance: 9, 18–19

Tabernacle: 88
Taboo: 73, 363
Ta Kese: 165
Tallensi: 259
Talmud: 188, 284
Tantric: 203
Tanzan: 141
Tao: 64, 68–69, 71, 108, 213, 287, 298
Taoism: 11, 182–183, 212
Taos Indians: 74
Tart, Charles: 372
Tawa: 127
Tefillah: 163
Teleological argument, for God's existence: 291–293
Teleology: 363
Templars: 263
Temple of Jerusalem: 74
Ten Commandments: 115
Thalawalla: 159
Thanksgiving, rites as: 166–167
Theism: 11, 363
Theocracy: 59
Theodicy: 286, 310, 313–315, 363
Theological breaking point: 313–315

Theological questions: 29–36
Theological study, of religion: 22
Theology: 22, 23, 125, 363; as critical, 284; as form of discourse, 298–299; as paradoxical, 300; as rational, 284; as story, 298–300; Catholic, 284; Christian, 284; Jewish, 284; Protestant, 284; starting point of, 285; understanding of, 282, 283–285
Theravada Buddhism: 270, 324
This-worldliness: 349–351
Tiamat: 192
T'ien: 260
Tillich, Paul: 13–14, 19, 65, 66, 71, 72, 199–200, 201, 218–219, 294–295, 334, 368, 372, 375
Time: as hierophany, 73–74; sacred, 73–74
Titans: 130
Tolstoy, Leo: 316, 319
Toltecs: 128
Torah: 22, 94, 134, 150, 163, 188, 189, 270
Totemism: 52, 363
Tower of Babel: 27
Transcendence: being sought by, 210–212; hints of, 32; seeking by, 210–212
Transcendent: 206–207, 363. *See also* Transempirical
Transcendental Meditation: 107, 155, 241, 344
Transcendent experiences: 8
Transempirical: 102, 363. *See also* Transcendent
Transformation: 228–229, 232–233
Transformed existence: 210
Tribal life: 336
Tribal peoples: religious life of, 257–258; social life of, 257–258
Tribal religion: 58
Tribal societies: 257–258
Trobiand: 138, 139
Troubled self: 224–233; afflicted self as: 225; disquieted self as, 225; divided self as, 224–225; origin of, 226; reasons for, 226–228; spiritual birth of, 228–230; spiritual odyssey of, 224; sudden conversions of the, 230–232